Winston Mano is Director of the Africa Media Centre, University of Westminster. He is also Principal Editor of the *Journal of African Media Studies*, and the author of *African National Radio and Everyday Life: The Impact of Radio in the Digital Age* (I.B.Tauris, forthcoming 2016). His research interests include audiences, broadcasting and media's role in development.

RACISM,
ETHNICITY AND
THE MEDIA IN
AFRICA

MEDIATING CONFLICT IN THE
TWENTY-FIRST
CENTURY

EDITED BY
WINSTON MANO

I.B. TAURIS

LONDON · NEW YORK

First published in 2015 by
I.B.Tauris & Co. Ltd
London • New York
www.ibtauris.com

ISBN: 978 1 78076 705 5 (HB)
           978 1 78076 706 2 (PB)
eISBN: 978 0 85773 565 2

A full CIP record for this book is available from the British Library
A full CIP record is available from the Library of Congress

Library of Congress Catalog Card Number: available

CONTENTS

ILLUSTRATIONS

Figures

Tables

CONTRIBUTORS

Oluyinka Esan brings non-Western perspectives to conceptualisations in media and film studies, giving insight into production practices, audience pleasures and the making of meanings. Author of *Nigerian Television, Fifty Years of Television in Africa*, she is Reader in School of Film and Media, University of Winchester, UK.

Elisabet Helander is a doctoral student funded by a research scholarship at Hong Kong Baptist University, China. She has a Global Media and Post-National Communication MA from SOAS, School of Oriental and African Studies, UK. Her research area is mass media in newly-democratized states with a focus on African media.

Hayes Mawindi Mabweazara is Senior Lecturer in Journalism at Falmouth University, UK. As well as serving on the editorial boards of *Digital Journalism* and the *Journal of Alternative and Community Media*, he is Associate Editor for *African Journalism Studies*. He edited *Digital Technologies and the Evolving African Newsroom* and co-edited *Online Journalism in Africa*. Mabweazara is currently working on a monograph titled *Africa's Mainstream Press in the Digital Era*.

Martin Nkosi Ndlela is Associate Professor at Hedmark University College, Norway. He is currently Head of the Department of Organization and Management Studies and holds a PhD in Media and Communication from the University of Oslo, Norway. Martin has researched on various issues in media and communication.

Francis B. Nyamnjoh is Professor of Social Anthropology at the University of Cape Town, South Africa. He has published widely on mobility and citizenship in Africa. His books include *Africa's Media, Democracy and the Politics of Belonging* and *Insiders and Outsiders: Citizenship and Xenophobia in Contemporary.*

Kristin Skare Orgeret is Professor at the Department of Journalism and Media Studies, Oslo University College, Norway. Her research focuses mainly on the role of media and journalism in (post-)conflict and democratisation processes in Africa, Asia and Europe.

Daniela Ricci teaches cinema at La Sorbonne Nouvelle and Paris X University. She received her PhD from Lyon 3 and Howard University. She has been President of the InterCultural Organization Melisandra since 2006 and organizes the Festival Uno sguardo all'Africa in Savona, Italy. She directed and produced the documentary, *Creation in Exile: Five Filmmakers in Conversation* (2012).

Nkereuwem Udoakah is Associate Professor of Political Communication and Media Studies at the University of Uyo, Nigeria. He is the author of *Development Communication, Special Topics in Public Relations, The Nigerian Press and Political Communication, Issues in Media Practices* and several journal articles and book chapters.

Jacob Udo-Udo Jacob is Assistant Professor of Multimedia/Digital Journalism at American University of Nigeria (AUN), Nigeria. His research interest is located at the intersection between communications and socio-cultural change in Africa. Prior to AUN, he was a PhD Teaching Fellow at the Institute of Communications Studies, University of Leeds, UK.

Herman Wasserman is Professor and Director of the Centre for Film and Media Studies at the University of Cape Town, South Africa. He has published extensively on media in post-apartheid South Africa, including the monograph *Tabloid Journalism in South Africa: True Story!* and the edited collections *Popular Media, Democracy and Development in Africa* and *Press Freedom in Africa: Comparative Perspectives.* He edits the journal *African Journalism Studies* and sits on the editorial board of several other international journals.

Wendy Willems is Assistant Professor in the Department of Media and Communications at the London School of Economics and Political Science, UK. Her research interests include media culture, neo-liberalism and social change, and performance, popular culture and politics. She is co-editor of *Civic Agency in Africa: Arts of Resistance in the 21st Century*.

Muhammad Jameel Yusha'u is a researcher, journalist and public relations practitioner. He was Senior Lecturer in Media and Politics at Northumbria University, UK, and has taught at the University of Sheffield and Bayero University, Nigeria. A former staff member of the BBC World Service, he holds a PhD in Journalism from the University of Sheffield, UK.

ACKNOWLEDGEMENTS

I would like to thank all the contributors, my past and present colleagues at the University of Westminster, in particular Pete Goodwin, Colin Sparks, Paddy Scannell, Daya Thussu, Jean Seaton, Jeanette Steemers, Geoffrey Davies, Kirstin Mey, David Gauntlett and Tarik Sabry. It was Tarik who introduced me to Philippa Brewster at I.B.Tauris. She in turn introduced me to Joanna Godfrey and Cecile Rault, both very helpful in the production of the book. I also wish to thank Maria Way, Shina Babasola, Pedzi Ruhanya, Abram Magowe, David Mwenga and Anuli Agina who helped me organise the conference and also review the papers at the initial stages. The book is dedicated to my family and dedicated to the memory of my late father, Victor Mano Sigobodhla, uncles and aunts who endured and fought against racism to make life better for us. It is also for my late brother, Nicholas Mano, who encouraged me to 'love everyone equally'. I see the book as a collective project for all those who continue to fight against absolute ethnicity and other forms of racism.

FOREWORD

By Fackson Banda

Racism, Ethnicity and the Media in Africa brings conceptual and empirical depth to our understanding of how the media are imbricated in
the layering of racism and ethnicity in Africa. It opens up crucial questions about how the colonial past continues to hold sway in media
constructions of the *fact* of individualised, institutionalised and cultur-
alised racism, along with the ethnic depictions that often underpin
such forms of racism.

As a reminder of their influential role, Branston and Stafford poign-
antly remind us that the media 'give us ways of imagining particular
situations, identities and groups. These imaginings exist materially,
as industries which employ people and can also have material effects
on how people experience the world, and how they in turn get understood, or legislated for, or perhaps beaten up in the street by others'
(Branston and Stafford 2003: 90).

Furthermore, where they occur with a greater degree of regularity, such media representations do not often reflect effective and
meaningful participation by minorities, leading to what a UNESCO
report refers to as a 'false diversity', masking the fact that a significant majority of people are still interested in communicating
only with those who share the same cultural references (UNESCO
2009: 18–19). Moreover, the limited range of representations in
the larger national media and communication networks tends to
promote the creation of stereotypes through what is often called
the process of 'othering', whereby the media fix, reduce or simplify
according to the dictates of standardized programmes and formats.

Such media representations may serve to reinforce the power of vested interests and exacerbate social exclusion by excluding critical or marginalized voices, which usually belong to the category of 'others' (see Van den Bulck and Van Poecke 1996: 159; Branston and Stafford 2003).

The previous observation leads me to conclude that, if this book has a specific political aim, it is to raise *awareness* and institute *action*. That action, apart from the national and transnational analyses presented by the various authors in this book, has solid support from a whole regimen of international treaties and agreements. These include:

- The 2001 Durban Declaration and Programme of Action which, adopted by consensus at the 2001 World Conference against Racism (WCAR) in Durban, South Africa, assigns the primary responsibility of combating racism, racial discrimination, xenophobia and related intolerance to States, while calling for the active involvement of international and non-governmental organisations, political parties, national human rights institutions, the private sector, the media and civil society at large.
- The 2001 UNESCO Declaration on Cultural Diversity which encourages the production, safeguarding and dissemination of diversified contents in the media and global information networks, including promoting the role of public radio and television services in the development of audiovisual productions of good quality.
- The International Covenant on Economic, Social and Cultural Rights, which enjoins upon States Parties to guarantee that the rights enunciated therein will be exercised without discrimination of any kind as to race, colour, sex, language, religion, political or other opinion, national or social origin, property, birth or other status.
- The 2005 UNESCO Convention on the Protection and Promotion of the Diversity of Cultural Expressions, which emphasizes the importance of the recognition of equal dignity and respect for all cultures, including that of persons belonging to minorities, and of the freedom to create, produce, disseminate, distribute and have access to traditional cultural expressions (United Nations 2010: 14–18).

Against this backdrop, I would suggest that this book's political aim very easily lends itself to the notion of intercultural dialogue. In this regard, the UNESCO world report is instructive. It argues that:

> Intercultural dialogue is largely dependent on intercultural competencies, defined as the complex of abilities needed to interact appropriately with those who are different from oneself. These abilities are essentially communicative in nature, but they also involve reconfiguring our perspectives and understandings of the world; for it is not so much cultures as people – individuals and groups, with their complexities and multiple allegiances – who are engaged in the process of dialogue. (UNESCO 2009: 9)

As communicative ability, dialogue has its problems. As Cees Hamelink suggests, dialogue requires the capacity to listen and to be silent. Learning the language of listening is, however, very hard in societies that are increasingly influenced by visual cultures, filled with 'talk shows' and no 'listen shows'. Hamelink concludes that the essence of dialogue could and should be taught in the early stages of people's lives in school, at home and through the media (Hamelink 2004: 29).

Therefore, it would be remiss of me to conclude my foreword without specific mention of the normative role that the media can play in undermining racial and ethnic prejudice. I think it is reasonable to ascribe a tripartite role to the media, namely: (i) facilitating cultural interactions, (ii) unmasking cultural stereotypes and intolerance, and (iii) forging a common narrative.

In terms of facilitating cultural interactions, I see journalism and journalism education as critical to this process of cultural interactivity. Racially and ethnically sensitive editorial policy guidelines and journalism curricula could incorporate the fact that the 'intermingling' of dominant and minority 'cultures throughout history has found expression in a variety of cultural forms and practices, from cultural borrowings and exchanges to cultural impositions through war, conquest and colonialism' (UNESCO 2009: 9–10). Critically important is the fact that 'even in the extreme circumstance of slavery, exchanges take place whereby certain discreet processes of reverse enculturation come to be assimilated by the dominating culture – a form of cultural 'counter flow' (UNESCO 2009: 9–10). Recognition of the universality of human rights, along with respect for cultural diversity, has made it possible today to think in terms of genuine exchanges on the basis of equality between all the world's cultures.

Racially and ethnically sensitive editorial guidelines could help break down the barriers that often discourage and/or distort intercultural conversations. Through such conversations, the dominant-cultural inhibitions that often define the operations of mainstream news media institutions could weaken, facilitating the emergence of a responsive and interactive professional culture that can accommodate racial and ethnic diversity. Journalism education, for its part, can set in motion a long-term process of educational conscientisation that could lead to critically minded graduates, able to interrogate the stereotypical assumptions of dominant cultures in the newsroom.

As for unmasking cultural stereotypes and intolerance, I believe a more racially and ethnically inclusive media discourse can help to unmask cultural stereotypes which serve to 'demarcate one group from the alien "other"'. As the UNESCO world report observes, most 'intercultural tensions are often bound up with conflicts of memory, competing interpretations of past events, and conflicts of values [...]. Where it has not been excluded by the will to power and domination, dialogue remains the key to unlocking these deep-rooted antagonisms and to pre-empting their often violent political expressions' (UNESCO 2009: 9–10). Here, the news media, using their investigative capacities, are better placed to play a key role in unmasking any stereotypical hindrances to meaningful and effective dialogue. A particularly important role for journalists and journalism educators is to work towards reconciling 'the recognition of, protection of and respect for cultural particularities with the affirmation and promotion of universally shared values emerging from the interplay of these cultural specificities' (see UNESCO 2009: 9–10).

A related capacity-building strategy to eliminate stereotypes could include media and information literacy. As the UNESCO world report advises us, such an initiative can help audiences to become more critical when consuming media and also help to combat unilateral perspectives. It is 'an important aspect of media access and a crucial dimension of non-formal education; it is imperative that it be promoted among civil society and media professionals as part of the effort to further mutual understanding and facilitate intercultural dialogue' (UNESCO 2009: 9–10).

And lastly, in terms of forging a common narrative of cultural pluralism, the UNESCO world report observes that divergent memories have been the source of many conflicts throughout history. It goes on to argue that, although intercultural dialogue cannot hope to settle on its own all the conflicts in the political, economic and social spheres, a key element in its success is the building of a shared memory base through the acknowledgement of faults and open debate on competing memories. The framing of a common historical narrative, the report claims, can be crucial in conflict prevention and post-conflict strategies, in assuaging 'a past that is still present'. The report then cites South Africa's Truth and Reconciliation Commission and the national reconciliation process in Rwanda as recent examples of the political application of such a healing strategy. The showcasing of 'places of memory' – such as the Robben Island Prison in South Africa – is key to this process (UNESCO 2009: 9–10).

In the end, this present book affirms my own personal conviction that individuals must not take racism (or ethnic prejudice) lying down. To paraphrase my assertion elsewhere: we should view our action as a key weapon in our arsenal of struggle politics. Achieving a racially and ethnically diverse and respectful Africa consists in a series of often isolated personal struggles. Ours is one such struggle, started by our founding fathers and mothers who fought for emancipation from colonial oppression, which we must continually knead into the dough of our daily politics about human identity, dignity, democracy and all those other values that underpin genuine human civilisation (see Banda 2009: 5).

References

Banda, F. (2009) 'Confronting Racism at Rhodes University: A Personal Story', *RHODOS: The Rhodes University Community Newsletter,* 21/6, p. 5.

Branston, G and Stafford, R. (2003) *The Media Student's Book* (3rd edn), London and New York: Routledge.

Hamelink, C. (2004) 'Grounding the Human Right to Communicate', in Philip Lee (ed.), *Many Voices, One Vision: The Right to Communicate in Practice,* pp. 21–31, Penang: World Association for Christian Communication.

Nordberg, C. (2006) 'Beyond Representation: Newspapers and Citizenship Participation in the Case of a Minority Ethnic Group', *Nordicom Review*, 27/2, pp. 87–104.

UNESCO (2009) *UNESCO World Report: Investing in Cultural Diversity and Intercultural Dialogue,* Paris: UNESCO.

United Nations (2010) *Minority Rights: International Standards and Guidance for Implementation,* New York: United Nations.

Van den Bulck, H., and Van Poecke, L. (1996) 'National Language, Identity Formation, and Broadcasting: The Flemish and German-Swiss Communities', in S. Braman and A. Sreberny-Mohammadi (eds), *Globalization, Communication and Transnational Civil Society,* pp. 157–77. Cresskill, NJ: Hampton.

1

RACISM, ETHNICITY AND
THE MEDIA IN AFRICA

Winston Mano

The book deals with racism, ethnicity and the media in Africa within
the context of increasing local and global transformations. It is published
at a time when political and media discussions on the outbreak of Ebola
focused primarily on the risk it poses to developed countries and the
efforts to contain it by strictly monitoring and isolating 'Africans' at their
boarders. The 'Western' response also fitted in with the growing anti-
immigrant narrative response. It can be observed that responses to crises,
conflicts and other events in Africa seem to add to centuries of racial
profiling and 'othering' (Said, 1978; Mudimbe 1988). Representations
matter because they can influence perceptions, investment decisions or
policy directions. However, it is beyond the scope of this book to discuss
all the crises facing Africa, to map out all the injustices facing its inhabitants, to deal with conspiracy theories on African crises or to attempt to
develop detailed responses to all of them.

Racism and ethnic absolutism are recurrent issues that need to be
taken seriously by all, especially citizens, students, journalists, activists,
politicians, researchers and policymakers. So far, the existence of high
moral grandstanding, forward-facing sentiments and progressive laws
has not stopped totemic or colour-of-skin discriminations, xenophobia,
unwarranted attacks on women and many other sickening racial tragedies. 'Arguments over racial division, over who is human enough to

qualify for rights and recognition, have impinged upon the formation of epistemological and ethical as well as historical and political categories' (Gilroy 2004: 10). There is an urgent need to firmly restate Fanon's (1963: 314) call for mankind to "reconsider the question of cerebral reality and of the cerebral mass of all humanity, whose connections must be increased, whose channels must be diversified and whose messages must be re-humanized'. Racism has had a long history driven by interwoven social, economic and political factors even though it is science that is often brought in to mask it. Critical analysis of racism needs to be updated so that humankind can 'go forward all the time, night and day, in the company of Man, in the company of all men [and women]' (ibid, 315) (My emphasis). This book is an attempt to put racism and ethnicity firmly back on the policy and academic agenda with the aim of generating new knowledge and encouraging more balanced approach to the key issues.

By combining racism, ethnicity and the media, the book attempts to introduce new empirical and theoretical dimensions to the debate. In a way it responds to Gilroy's (2004: 31) critique of work on ethnicity and racism when he notes that: 'Few new ways of thinking "race" and its relationship to economics, politics and power have emerged since the era of national liberation struggles to guide the continuing pursuit of a world free of racial hierarchies.' This book also deals with racism, ethnicity and the media from an interdisciplinary approach, using fresh and unique case studies from Africa and beyond.

At the start of this millennium, people who live in Africa have already witnessed growing uncertainties, anxieties and deepening crises. These include debilitating ethnic conflicts, discriminations and prejudices against minorities, deadly armed insurrections and full-scale wars, recurrent racism, deadly xenophobic attacks, to cite but a few examples. Saying this does not imply a rosy past in contrast to frantic models of the present and future. Rather it is a poignant reflection of a more connected Africa, both internally as well as with other parts of the world. The rapid developments in Africa are giving rise to new cultural questions and possibilities some of which this book attempts to deal with.

Africans have generally refused to be bystanders or victims of the transformations in spite of their impoverishment and weak observance of their basic human rights. As Nyamnjoh (2009: 71) usefully reminds us, 'political, cultural, historical and above all, economic realities, determine what form of meaning and discussion and articulation of citizenship and rights assume in any given context'. The transitional character of nations on the continent has meant that racism, ethnicity and an obsession with belonging are a permanently active part in many African contexts. Individuals and collectives in Africa, in line with others in the Global South, have had to be creative, innovative and convivial in their response to relentless forces of change, despite their often perceived passivity. This book arises out of debates on the interplay between racism, ethnicity and the media, all of which are important cultural questions in Africa at the start of this millennium. The intention is not to discuss Africans as victims or even to simply celebrate African agency. It is also not only to reject deeply held pejorative perceptions of Africa as an 'other', that is, a world 'apart from the world, or as a failed and incomplete example of something else' (Mbembe and Nuttall 2004: 348). Rather the book attempts to also tackle issues to do with racism and ethnicity as part of lived experiences of people in Africa today, both in an historicised sense and as part of an increasingly interconnected society.

In much of contemporary Africa, contestations of ethnicity, citizenship and belonging have failed to disappear as there has been a 'resurgence of identity politics and overt tensions over belonging' (Nyamnjoh 2005: 19). The resultant struggles are behind some of the most protracted conflicts, without clear starting and terminating points, involving communities deprived of their basic needs such as 'security, recognition and accept-ance, fair access to political institutions and economic participation' (Azar 1990: 8). Mobile elites, in these situations, 'can physically leave the squalor while those who cannot afford to move are stuck in' (Morley 2000: 202). It is increasingly the case that politically powerful elites are monopolising and manipulating the allocation of resources in ways that deny the needs of others, including on the basis of their communal belonging. This has arguably fuelled problems associated with identity politics in Africa.

The resurgence of identity politics in Africa also comes at a time when the continent is facing huge development challenges, not least to do with economic growth, poverty reduction, human development and governance (Devarajan and Fengler 2013). The widespread infrastruc-tural deficiencies are evidence that Africa's poor have not fully benefited from national development initiatives. Unstable prices for extractive economies, unequal global trade terms and local corruption have also worked to prevent the benefits from accruing to the intended recipients. An everyday issue such as the provision of basic infrastructure, including water and electricity, is linked to political problems, with priority given to regions or neighbourhoods politicians favour. Such immense problems call into question the meaning of national independence, and when coupled with recurrent tensions, war and conflicts could easily erode the sovereignty that has been so far achieved. Arguably, the challenges have exacerbated religious, ethnic and political instability, contributing to the politics of belonging in contemporary Africa.

It is recognised, in the interdisciplinary contributions in this book, that countries in Africa are 'post-colonies', that is, societies recently emerging from the experience of colonisation and the violence which the colonial relationship, *par excellence*, involves (Mbembe 1992: 3). Gilroy (2004: 31) notes that 'our post-colonial environment reverberates with the catastrophes that resulted from militarized agency and unprecedented victimization of racial and ethnic groups'. It is within such transitional post-colonial frameworks that reported and unreported racial conflicts, xenophobic attacks, acts of terrorism and ethnic bigotry seem to be rising (see Hawkins 2008; Mamdani 2009; Franks and Shaw 2012). Racialism in Africa has become a persistent problem, in some cases requiring contemporary local, national and global responses to historical issues.[1] As is discussed by Banda (2015), in the Foreword to this book, the resurgence of politics of belonging is rife regardless of United Nations' high-level international meetings against racism, including the World Conference on Racism (WCAR) in 1978, 1983, 2001 and also in 2009. International efforts to tackle racialism have helped manage the problem but in reality ethnic biases, racial segregation and discriminations continue in many spheres of life. It is fair to say that the problems are exacerbated by political oppression, human rights abuse, cultural injustice, poverty, rampant global capitalism and uneven globalisation. Some of these issues are discussed by the contributors to the book.

While the book is aware of economic problems, it is more focused on socio-cultural factors and the role played by media in representing, undermining or reinforcing past and contemporary racial and ethnic conflicts in Africa. It is aware that the questions of race and racism have a long history in Cultural Studies, which, for example, involved moments of undermining normative assumptions and original concerns with class and cultural privileges to now include aspects such as gender and ethnicity (Scannell 2007: 215). The book also recognizes the utility of 'intersectionality theory' (Yuval-Davis 2011: 4), which in expanding Stuart Hall's work on identity, 'analyses social stratification as a whole' and as 'mutually constitutive', instead of 'prioritising one facet or category of social difference'. As will be discussed, Yuval-Davis (2011: 4) also makes an important distinction between 'belonging' and 'the politics of belonging', which is useful in understanding the approach taken by contributors to this book. For her, belonging is about emotional attachment, about 'feeling at home' which allows safety and at times anger and other sentiments. Belonging is natural and part of the everyday but can become 'articulated, formally structured and politicised only when threatened in some way' (ibid.). Individuals can '"belong" in many different ways and to many different objects of attachment. These can vary from a particular person to the whole community, in a concrete or abstract way, by self or other identification, in a stable or contested way' (Yuval-Davis 2011: 5). Morley (2000: 209) similarly argues that the 'creation of a more internally integrated and coherent community often goes alongside the creation of even more excusive policies along the border of that community'. For Yuval-Davis (2011: 4–5), 'the politics of belonging comprise of specific political projects aimed at constructing belonging to particular collectivity/ties which are themselves being constructed in these projects in very specific ways and in very specific boundaries'. She adds that not all belonging are important and that only in extreme cases are people willing to 'sacrifice their lives – and the lives of others – in order for their narrative of their identities and objects of their identifications and attachments to continue to exist' (ibid.). Interestingly, Morley (2000: 223) also points out that 'it is not the presence of others *per se* which is problematic, but only that of undomesticated otherness', demonstrating how non-threatening roles and identities appear acceptable in xenophobic situations. The constructivist approach to race and ethnic identity taken here is also cognizant of 'shifting, situational, subjective identifications of self and others, which are rooted in ongoing daily practice and historical experience, but also subject to transformation and discontinuity' (Jones 2003: 13). This will be discussed in more detail below. The contributors are passionate and vigorous in their discussion of the interplay between racism, ethnicity and the media in Africa and on Africans in Europe.

The role of the mass media in reinforcing or undermining ethnicity and racism is also considered to be central. The media are an important but understudied institution in this debate. Today's struggles against racism are a continuation of social justice undertakings in which the 'media have a critical task in human rights education as they should contribute to the teaching and respect of human rights' (Hamelink 2001: 4). The media select what to represent and shape attitudes to existing realities. So, for example, one could question why some major conflicts have either been unreported or underreported. Of note were underreported highly ethnicised killings of close to 300,000 people in Burundi in 1993 and the belatedly publicised Rwandan killings in 1994 which left 800,000 dead. In the Democratic Republic of Congo, an estimated 8 million people have perished in recurrent civil wars since the 1990s (Franks and Shaw 2012; Hawkins 2008; Frere 2007) but this has been largely underreported. The gruesome xenophobic attacks on 'black foreigners' in South Africa and the slaughter of 'Muslim-Christians' by Boko Haram in Nigeria are examples of complex cases of belonging (Abubakar 2012; Musa 2012). Part of the problem has been interpretation of these 'racialised and ethnicised identities' in the media. The new struggles of belonging, citizenship, entitlement, distribution and ownership of resources are largely driven by racism and ethnicity (Ndlovu-Gatsheni 2012). As will be discussed, mass media can help expose violations resulting from racism and ethnic bigotry. Far from being observers, the media have been reflecting and affecting some of the struggles.

The book debates insights and perspectives from local and international journalists and editors as well as academics, human rights activists, researchers and regulators. The contributors are equally from diverse backgrounds and are most knowledgeable about past and current 'racial and ethnic' upheavals in Africa and within evolving socio-economic and political historical frameworks.

The key questions addressed in the book include the following: How are the post-colonial mass media implicated in the growing ethnic and racial conflicts and violence in Africa? In what ways are the media challenging, undermining or reinforcing issues relating to racism and ethnicity in Africa? How have African media and journalists covered racial and ethnic topics? Both old and new media have opened new spaces for debates that were formerly suppressed, but have they not also encouraged extremism?

The next section attempts to conceptualize the terms of reference for the book, particularly African identity, racism and ethnicity. The approach is sympathetic to intersectionality theory which cautions against treating categories of cultural identity as separate and independent of each other. The terms are analysed as part of social stratification as a whole and taken to be connected at different levels.

African Identity

Situated within the constructivist approach to identity, this book proceeds from the perception that identities are contingent, in flux and also subject to change. Identities can be several and contested. People in Africa have known histories, geographies, ethnic groups, languages, genders, skin colours and continental identities. However, such belonging is not unified or homogeneous for as Hall reminds us, 'the one thing we are not is one, only one thing' (1997: 12). The diversity of Africa's peoples and its cultures is remarkable: 'Whatever Africans share, we do not have common traditional culture, common languages, a common religious or conceptual vocabulary [...] we do not even belong to a common race' (Appiah 1992: 15). Achebe also points out that 'African identity is still in the making. There is no final identity that is African. But, at the same time, there is identity coming into existence. And it has a certain context and meaning' (in Appiah 1992: 173).

Contemporary African identity can be seen as plural, evolving and dynamic and as one that 'keeps redefining itself with new experiences and contacts with other people and cultures' (Nyamnjoh 2005: 91). When it comes to the term 'African' and its meaning, 'African is [...] to be a social actor/actress enmeshed in a particular context that has been and continues to be shaped by a unique history that, among others, is marked by unequal encounters and misrepresentations often informed by arrogance and ignorance of the economically and politically powerful who take the liberty to abrogate a cultural superiority to themselves' (Nyamnjoh 2008: 101). Africanity and African citizenship ought to go beyond labels of 'citizens' and 'subjects' (Mamdani 1996) to include essentials of lived experience shaped by daily struggles. Any definition of African identity must include 'the sum of ways in which we've been willing to be recognised. We are the sum of claims we've been willing to make. We are the sum of where we hope we are going' (Hall 1997: 13). While not refuting historical and geographical specificities, this socio-cultural approach firmly challenges racist biological identifications. It means how one who is, for example, a Yoruba, Afrikaner, white, black, Ndebele, Kikuyu, Ashante, Zulu or Shona must also be unpacked in terms of rooted but shifting processes of identification. It must also be based on respect for African humanity, creativity and realities which in themselves are neither in 'question nor a question' (Nyamnjoh 2008: 101). In line with the previously mentioned intersectional approach, 'Africa' is perceived as a space with multi-layered and multiple belongings, and this more applicable to diasporas (Sabry 2005; Tsagarousianou 2007; Pasura 2013).

This book leans towards the anti-essentialist conception of identities as discursive constructs. As is noted by Barker (2012: 249–250) the anti-essentialist approach is dominant in contemporary Cultural Studies but has been challenged by scholars who seek to modify its 'conceptions of identity'. Barker (2012) cites three main criticisms: first, critics argue that the anti-essentialist perspective on identity reduces the social into language, pointing out that when everything becomes discourse then 'there is no material reality' (p. 249). Social constructivists accept that a material world exist but emphasise that knowledge of it is only possible through language and discourse. They see discourse and materiality as inseparable. The second criticism of discourse-based theories of identity is how they downplay 'human agency' and reduce human beings to mere 'effects' of discourse' (p. 250). The anti-essentialist camp responds by robustly delineating agency as the 'socially constructed capacity to act'. They add that: 'Discourse enables action by providing subject positions of agency' (p. 250). The third, and perhaps most interesting, criticism of anti-essentialist arguments about identity is that they are of no practical value: 'We require, it is said, a more constructive and positive account of the politics of identity based on strategic essentialism – that is, the recognition that we act as if identities were stable entities for specific political and practical purposes' (Barker 2012: 250). This third criticism is particularly important in Africa given how identity has been mobilised for political action (Ndlovu-Gatsheni and Mhlanga 2013). Appiah (1992: 15) also argues that Africans share too many problems and projects to be distracted by a bogus basis for solidarity. The categories used by strategic essentialist might appear to have merit for practical purposes but in reality they also 'lead to obscuring of difference and exclusion of certain voices' (Barker 2012: 250). Africa is home to individuals with multiple belongings and many identities, living within countries that have changing cultures which can never be captured by the essentialist approach. The book's aim, drawing on Downing and Husband (2005), is to frame research on race, ethnicity and the media in ways that could meaningfully contribute to a just, peaceful and stimulating African society. By critiquing limitations with essentialist projects, media failures and outrages it could help reframe media knowledge and practice.

Racism

It could be observed that race and ethnicity have overlaps and that both are implicated in politics of belonging and projects of social exclusion, including racism. Racism, as is observed by White (2009: 471), has a wide reference:

> Racism is any activity by individuals, groups, institutions, or cultures that treats human beings unjustly because of colour, physical features, and ethnicity and rationalises that treatment by attributing to them undesirable biological, psychological, social, or cultural characteristic. (White 2009: 471)

The preceding definition clearly shows that racism covers many areas, including ethnicity. 'Race' is a descriptive and explanatory concept whereby human variation can be reduced to one supposedly stable property: 'race' (Downing and Husband 2005: 1). It works by creating classifications, categories that enable people to 'racialise', and the media can be prominent in this role: 'Employing "race" as real, whether in news media or entertainment, is to participate in racialization: it is a reproduction of "race" thinking' (ibid.: p. 15).

According to Dovido and Gaertner (1986: 3), racism has three main meanings. First, it refers to *individual racism* which is similar 'to race prejudice, but places more emphasis on biological considerations and also encompasses discriminatory acts'. The second is *institutional racism*, which refers 'to the intentional and unintentional manipulation or toleration of institutional policies' (for example, poll taxes, admissions criteria) that unfairly restrict the opportunities of particular groups of people. This tends to be more widespread in transitional societies. The third use of racism concerns *cultural racism* as an expression of superiority of one cultural heritage over another. This is also common. In Africa, racism has colonial roots because economic and cultural subjugation went hand in hand. There is a case that the three forms of racism are still present in contemporary Africa, though not practiced as openly as they did in the colonial era. One could therefore very well ask, to what extent have African societies changed? In this regard, wa Thiong'o (1993: 27) insightfully remarks that 'within a given community any change in any major aspects of their lives, how they manage their wealth for instance, or their power, may well bring about changes at other levels and these in turn will bring about mutual action and reaction on all other aspects'. Colonial imperialist traditions 'undermined African people's belief in themselves and made them look up to European cultures, languages and the arts, for measurement of themselves and their abilities' (wa Thiong'o 1993: 43–4). It is the argument here that race and economics were and still are not divorced. Racism is a system of classification of identities. For Hall (1997: 222), ' "Identity" itself is not as transparent or unproblematic as we think. Perhaps instead of thinking of identity as an already accomplished fact, which the new cultural practices then represent, we should think, instead, of identity as a "production", which is never complete, always in process, and always constituted within, not outside, representation'. Identification is an act of power that enables us to classify ourselves in relation to what we are not and 'those are the moments over which politics struggle. Political struggles can make those identifications' (Hall 1997: 12). Racialism is about power because every identity is an exclusion and to leave something out is an act of power (Hall 1997: 14). As is also noted by Gilroy (2014: 9), 'the "race" idea is powerful precisely because it supplies a foundational understanding of natural hierarchy on which a host of other supplementary social and political conflicts have come to rely'. In this millennium, Africans seem to continue with narrow politics of excluding others on the basis of race and absolute ethnicity. In most cases, the excluded return to haunt the supposedly settled.

Ethnicity

The term *ethnicity* overlaps with race, but specifically describes the state of belonging to a social group which has common cultural traditions, which according to Smith (1986: 15), include 'myths, memories, values and symbols'. It is not unusual for the terms race and ethnicity to be used as if they are synonyms. Mamdani (2009: 169) points out that anthropologists have used the word 'ethnic' and 'tribe' synonymously, in both cases to denote groups that are culturally identifiable, such as through language. *Tribe* is an administrative political entity which often carries pejorative meanings and has been used to describe Africans more than say Europeans. In terms of *ethnicity* in Africa, Vail (1997: 52) has observed how political authorities in Africa see ethnicity as an impediment to national unity while those

> Commentators on the Left, recognising it as a block to the growth of appropriate class consciousness, inveigh against it as a case of 'false consciousness.' Apologists for South African apartheid, welcoming it as an ally of continued white dominance, encouraged it. Development theorists, perceiving it as a check on economic growth, then deplored it. Journalists, judging it as an adequate explanation for a myriad of otherwise puzzling events, deploy it mercilessly. Political scientists, intrigued by its continuing power, probe at it endlessly. If one disapproves of the phenomenon, 'it' is 'tribalism;' if one is less judgemental 'it' is 'ethnicity.' (Vail 1997: 52)

As with racism, the definition of ethnicity should also be placed in the context of socio-economic and political dynamics in Africa. Much of Africa is to an extent still under the influence of ethnic and racial typologies, most developed during the colonisation of Africa. In today's Africa, ethnicity and belonging have been blamed for the failure by Africans to institutionalise liberal democracy largely because elites, at times with help of international actors, mobilise ethnic ideology to defend or seek power (Nyamnjoh 2005: 34). As previously discussed, intersectional theory helps bring together ethnicity and race as linked categories. Race and ethnicity make more sense when considered in a relationship. It matters most how they are operationalized into workable categories and policies.

Operationalising Difference

The categorisation of Africans according to skin colour was part of racial ideologies developed by white colonial settlers to give greater legitimacy to economic exploitation of different groups. Ibbo Mandaza (1997), for example, discusses how black Africans, or natives as they were initially called, were placed right at the bottom of the colonial racial pecking order, and no matter how civilised they became, they still remained native and only in rare cases were they referred to as 'civilised native'. Mandaza (1997) also observes how the racial term 'coloured' has its basis in the colonial racial ideology of white supremacy which characterised colonial society in terms of the race-caste-class hierarchy, in which the person of mixed race occupied the position of the socio-racial ladder between whites at the top and blacks at the bottom. Although the races would perform the same type of work and functions, the levels of remuneration followed the pecking order, with the philosophy that the black Africans should receive the least pay and comparably bad conditions of service. However, such frozen racial ideologies were non-exact, problematic and difficult to contain or operationalize, hence fissures were inevitable. When tested against the background of politically and socially dynamic circum-stances the racial typologies produced contestations and demands for equality which eventually led to African independence.

Similar racist and discriminatory laws in the United States of America were informed by an ideology that sought to downgrade the status of descendants of slaves, today's African American. From being asked to give up seats for whites to being asked to eat at different restaurants, among other things, a set of cultures were developed to operationalise difference. Dovido and Gaertner (1986: 1) remind us that 'it was not until Civil Rights Laws were passed in the early 1960s, over 175 years after human rights were proclaimed in the Declaration of Independence and guaran-teed by the Constitution, that the United States formally recognised that black and white people were equal before the state'. In Africa majority rights and equality came after wars and other forms of struggle against colonial forces, since the formal establishment of colonial rule in Africa in 1884. Most African countries achieved independence in the 1960s and immediately sought to reverse the effects of racial rule. Just like in the case of the United States, new legislation and affirmative action policies could not readily correct hundreds of years of racial injustice. 'The process of abandoning racist traditions and prejudiced beliefs may be especially difficult because of their deep-seated nature in American culture' (ibid). Similarly, in independent Africa, new governments have attempted to deal with the colonial legacies but serious challenges remain.

Debates about racism and ethnicity should be linked to the broader context and to the growing poverty in Africa and the evident lack of basic human needs faced by many people on the continent. Some of the world's poorest people are Africans, despite a wealth of nat-ural resources. Rising levels of poverty among the poorer groups have sharpened struggles between and among different groups over resources in Africa. It has become more common that

> the construction of race as identity may be linked with ethnicity, especially when variations in physical characteristics coincide with assumed cultural, linguistic and religious differences. [...] In Burundi and Rwanda, despite the fact that the two groups share skin colour, language, religion and names, variations in height, body structure and nose shape are used to establish difference. [...] In some contexts, a group may identify itself as a separate race even if there are no clear physical differences between it and the groups it seeks to categorize as the 'other'. (Bangura and Stavenhagen 2005: 4)

As seen with the xenophobic attacks in South Africa, black-on-black violence was based on slight differences in physical characteristics, for example, those who had darker skin were regarded as outsiders. The cultural boundary was least secure because of similarity between symbolic forms. Such 'othering' is ultimately linked to the distribution of resources, in this case: jobs and housing. It can also be argued that domestic workers and security guards were accepted while white-collar workers were seen as 'foreign' and as a threat to South Africans. In this regard Morley (2000: 223) has indicated, 'Homebuilding (at both micro and macro levels), we might argue, is to be seen as much as a process of domestication as of the exclusion of otherness. Alterity, on this model, is non-threatening as long as it is "in its place", homebuilding does not require its absolute displacement but, rather, only its domestication'. It is also the case that some of the media referred to the others as 'aliens' or foreigners, thereby inviting action against them. The use of social categories of difference for strategic reasons could be seen as behind the resurgence of identity politics in Africa. Self-serving projects of strategic essentialism leave out others with the result that those left outside will return to trouble the status quo. The media are crucial when it comes to operationalizing difference in daily life.

Mediating Race and Ethnicity in Africa

Having located racism and ethnicity, the next task is to define and contextualise the role of *media*. The mass media in Africa were mainly introduced in the colonial era. Levi Obonyo (2011: 18) summarised the emergence of new media networks in independent Africa and how they have evolved into diverse institutions with local, national and international dimensions. Funding and ownership aspects are mixed, from community, state to private enterprise: 'Their reach is equally mixed, from ethnically oriented community media, to national and even regional ones' (Obonyo 2011: 18). Although communication media have expanded rapidly at the start of this millennium, their penetration is still poor. 'They remain unstable, unequal and uneven in their development within and among countries' (Zeleza 2009: 19). In many countries the radio tends to be more important given its wide reach and its proximity to indigenous communication. Nyamnjoh (2005: 4) notes that, although in developed countries 'there is already talk of new media taking over from old media, in Africa the so-called old media are yet to take over from indigenous forms of communication'. The institutions of media are still 'infrastructurally weak' compared to what exists in other countries. There are huge differences between and within media in African countries. The extent to which African media influence audiences is also debatable as people get different messages from the same source and media influence is dependent on other factors. Nonetheless, mass media in Africa have a small but growing following. In the multimedia age, racial and ethnic language groups are now able to set up their own media and this increases their sense of belonging. However, Nyamnjoh (2005) emphasises that media objectivity under liberal democracy contradicts other forms of media behaviour in popular democracies in Africa:

> [African] journalists and the media are under constant internal and external pressure to promote the interests of the various groups competing for recognition and representation. (Nyamnjoh 2005: 38–9)

Media reflect, represent and shape realities in Africa and to some extent they match individual readers in how they are creatively 'merging their traditions with exogenous influences to create realities that are not reducible to either but enriched by both' (ibid.). Zeleza (2009: 19) argues that 'the media have been crucial to the development of African socialities, and in the construction and articulation of collective identities at various social and spatial scales from gender to generation, and from the local to the global'. Wasserman (2011) investigates the linkages between popular media, democracy and development in Africa. Obadare and Willems (2014) deal with alternative media and popular protests to challenge limited

Western notions of understanding how power and resistance operate in the African society. Ronning and Kasoma (2004) discuss relevant ethical and legal frames of reference for African media, and their cultural implications. Similarly in her analysis of media and conflict in Central Africa Marie-Soleli Frere (2007) observes that the mass media constitute a two-edged sword: 'They can be the instrument of both destructive and constructive strategies, especially in societies undergoing change, destabilised by conflicts, or in the throes of political liberalisation' (p. 1). The questionable broadcasts from Radio Télévision Libres des Mille Colines (RTL) in Rwanda in 1994 represents how media can be a tool for ethnicised war. RTL remains a troubling case about the role of radio during conflicts. However, not only are journalists capable of inciting hatred, provoking mass violent movements and manipulating information, they can also help communicate peace: 'It is undeniable that the media have the capacity to both increase and decrease tensions within countries in crisis' (Frere 2007: 1). It is in this regard that journalists and media commentators should assist in the mediation of conflict by informing public opinion and increasing public pressure. Traber provides a good example:

> The British media, for example, portrayed Nelson Mandela as an outstanding public figure at a time when Prime Minister Margaret Thatcher still vowed she would never meet with this 'terrorist'. The media thus helped to change the attitude of the British public towards the African National Congress (ANC) which, in the end, became the main peace-maker in South Africa. (Traber 2008: 239)

The need to decrease ethnic and racial tensions is also linked to observance of human rights. In Africa many are unaware of their rights. As is noted by Hamelink (2001: 3),

> too many people do not know they are entitled to the protection of fundamental rights. Particularly, in the world's rural areas there is widespread ignorance about human rights legislation and jurisprudence. As a consequence, since rural people lack knowledge whether an illegality occurs, they will often not seek legal redress. Knowledge and awareness of human rights are so essential, because though the awareness that one possess fundamental rights, the development of self-confidence is encouraged.

The media have a duty to educate citizens and expose perpetrators of human rights. Hamelink (2001: 4–5) is concerned that in their daily practices media pay limited attention to human rights issues. The media should instead be helping to eliminate beliefs that motivate people to kill each other as these are social constructs, which rely on social institutions for their dissemination in society.

The problem at the moment is also that media reports on racism and ethnicity often lack context, something which leads to misinformation on causes of the conflicts in Africa. In his analyses of conflicts in Darfur and Rwanda, Mamdani (2009: 7) has, for example, strongly argued that researchers need to consider racial and ethnic clashes 'in a national and global context, which over the past century has been one of colonialism, the Cold War, the War on Terror'. Karikari (2007: 12) similarly argues that 'quite often, and well into the 1980s, the continent's problems became fodder for big power contestations in the so-called "Cold War", a political-ideological conflict disguising a fierce combat for the control of Africa's very same natural wealth that had brought in colonialism to begin with. Angola and the Congo (Zaire) epitomised this scramble for control and influence'. The increased quest for resources by China, especially from 2006, has reignited a new political-ideological eco-nomic war between China and the West (the US, Australia, Canada and European countries) over Africa, with Beijing acting as the new Moscow and Africa as the main battleground. As is noted by Virgil Hawkins (2008: 3), Africa is a 'veritable storehouse of minerals and other nat-ural resources, including large quantities of oil, upon which the outside world is increasingly coming to rely'. The selective attention given by the media to African conflicts is linked to the interests of big powers:

> Why, for example, was the humanitarian tragedy caused by conflict and famine in Somalia chosen for intervention in the early 1990s when a similar situation in Southern Sudan was not? Why did large-scale massa-cres in Rwanda attract some measure (albeit belated) of outside attention, indignation and a great deal of guilt in 1994 and beyond, whereas similar massacres in neighbouring Burundi in 1993, leaving 200,000 dead, had failed to attract outside attention or residual guilt? Why, after eight years of relative silence on the problems of violence in Africa, did the outside world suddenly begin to collectively suffer the pangs of moral outrage over the conflict in Darfur, at a time when death toll estimates from con-flict in the DRC were almost 80 times greater? (Hawkins 2008: 3)

The media from developed countries have selectively focused on low-level conflict in countries such as Zimbabwe in March 2007 at the expense of worse conflict at the same time in Guinea which left 130 people dead (Hawkins 2008). The media routinely ignored some violence and have often portrayed some conflicts as more prominent than others owing to their preconceived agendas and vested interests.

At the beginning of the twenty-first century, African conflicts must also be understood within the global context of increasing competition over resources and from the perspective of the deepening global recession, especially in Europe and North America. The need for new markets has seen new global initiatives that at a local level involve arming and promoting groups over one another. Groups enjoying privileges, ethnic or otherwise, seek to keep others out and wars are inevitable. In most African countries the conflicts and power play between different groups and individuals can be explained by such politics of belonging and in terms of race and ethnicity. As Hall reminds us, 'when we constitute an identity which leaves some voices more marginal and leaves some voices out; that which is excluded almost always picks itself off the floor, gets itself together, walks around to the back door, breaks a window and comes back in. It comes back to trouble the fixed, settled, well-ordered structure of who-is-in and who-is-out' (1997: 14). The issues raised in this book will illustrate this in more detail.

Media reporting of the conflict and the resulting violence can exaggerate and misrepresent reality. The biased coverage often worsens the situation. The framing of violence in Africa, as Mamdani also argues, continues the error that came out of the colonial tradition of racialising Africa, in some cases with the result of 'conferring an ethic of impunity on those who resist genocide. Such impunity led to the killing of some of the millions who died in Congo between 1998 and 2002' (2009: 7). He advocates the model of *victor's justice*, given how 'a relentless pursuit of justice in the post-independence period in Africa had all too often turned into vengeance'. This should give way to a more relevant paradigm of *survivors' justice* based on South Africa's transition to a post-apartheid society. Its primary function would be 'to reconcile rather than to punish, to look forward rather than backward' (Mamdani 2009: 7). This book represents such new thinking on racism, ethnicity and the media in Africa and in a broader context.

In fact, as struggles over resources intensify in new African democracies, other new and fierce struggles have ensued, most of which are characterised by racial and ethnic strife. Racism and ethnicity have been implicated in the politically destabilising, divisive and often cyclical conflicts in many regions and countries. As previously stated, in the Congo there have been massive deaths since the 1990s with up to 1,000 people killed a day, with minimal media coverage and scarce attention from the outside world (Franks and Shaw 2012: 9). In 2011, in Libya, Morocco, Algeria, Egypt, Tunisia and other Maghreb countries there were increased reports of racism against dark-skinned people in the wake of mercenaries hired by Gaddafi from Sub-Saharan African countries. In 2012, President Jacob Zuma alleged racism when his manhood was repeatedly caricatured by cartoonists in South African newspapers. Academic research and media coverage have not yet fully engaged with frequent racist attacks on white farmers and black workers in South Africa or with reasons for recurrent violence at Kenyan elections where many are killed and displaced. Other alleged racial ethnic and racial killings happened in Darfur (Mamdani 2007) and in Tanzania albinos were reportedly murdered for ritual purposes. The 2008 xenophobic attacks in South Africa, the anti-gay demonstrations in many African countries from 2009 to 2012 and the routine killings of white farmers in Zimbabwe and South Africa (from 1994 to 2001 about 1,200 white farmers were killed on South African farms) and the continued enslavement and discrimination against women and black workers (Gazi 2004) are indicative of the wide scope of the problem. The state-sponsored killing of Ndebeles in south-western Zimbabwe in the 1980s and other reported/unreported conflicts in Africa have continued to raise many questions, not only about ethnicity, but also about the ability of Africa to fully democratise. Karikari (2007: 12) argues that such conflicts are 'primarily born out of political and socio-economic contradictions internal to the countries, including problems arising from relations among ethnic communities in the new states. But in the most critical cases, those which had sub-regional or continental ramifications, external interests encouraged, supported, or fanned them.' This book revisits the issues about racism and ethnicity in contemporary Africa and discusses how communication media are implicated in what has so far happened.

The power play in identifications in racism and ethnicity is linked to economic and political power. Unsurprisingly post-colonial African states have attempted to reverse the historical marginalisation of particular races in resource distribution. In Zimbabwe, the new government from 1980 adopted a land redistribution programme and from 1997 a fast-track land reform process to give the previously marginalised black race access to land (Gazi 2004; Scones et al. 2010). In 2012, the Zimbabwe government also introduced measures to give 51 per cent economic ownership to locals located where global businesses operate in the country, potentially giving previously disadvantaged black groups more opportunities to participate in the economy. In South Africa, after 1994 the post-apartheid majority-rule government similarly introduced the Black Economic Empowerment (BEE) (later Broad-Based Black Economic Empowerment (BBEE)) regulation as a way to correct the racialised economic inequalities under apartheid. Previously disadvantaged groups, including Indians and some Chinese groups, are now defined as blacks and have been beneficiaries of economic privileges such as employment preference, skills development, ownership, management, socio-economic development and preferential procurement, all of which were previously not distributed to them in a fair manner. That this is important is beyond debate even though the main criticism has been that most of the benefits are going to elites aligned to the ruling parties or that such programmes will threaten investment from abroad. The chapters in this book contribute new thinking on such racial and ethnic issues in Africa, and also in relation to the role of media and communication in perpetuating, reinforcing and undermining racism, ethnicity and other discriminations across Africa.

Globalisation, migration, power and resource struggles in today's Africa are connected to existing racial conflicts. Increased racial and ethnic strife across the continent can be linked to adverse economics and impoverishment as well as increasing social intolerance fuelled by the mass media. Scapegoating becomes a widespread problem. Authorities failing to provide for their citizens use the media to blame others, especially foreigners for taking jobs or putting a strain on available resources. A good example was in Morocco in November 2012 when the Employment and Vocational Training minister, Abdelouahed Souhail, was quoted as partly blaming 'the country's employment crisis' on 'black' immigrants from Sub-Saharan Africa. A northern regional Moroccan magazine had earlier on courted controversy by devoting an issue to 10,000–15,000 'black immigrants' whom it referred to as 'the black crickets invading Morocco's north'. The November 2012 edition of *Maroc Hebdo* magazine also sought to ignite a national debate on the struggles faced by 'black' Africans living in Morocco. Among the many responses to the reports of racism in Morocco, one reader wrote: 'Racism in Morocco is a real problem, and Moroccan people need to get off their high horse and realize that sub-Sahara Africans [sic] are their brothers. This racism is especially disturbing in light of the fact that most Moroccans profess Islam as their religion, and Islam completely and categorically rejects racism as a construct of the devil' (submitted by unregistered user on 9 November 2012, 10:07). Other responses saw language as a problem since the Arabic for 'black person' is the same as 'slave'. Some readers accused journalists and Moroccan media of bias, particularly failing to note how 'many illegal-immigrants have not only flooded to Morocco as a gateway to Europe, but as an alternative to Europe, thus burdening both the state and native population which are both still considerably poor' (submitted by unregistered user on 9 November 2012, 00:48).[2] Racism was promoted under colonialism and has continued into this millennium. Below are the main themes and cases discussed in the following chapters of the book.

Contested Racialised and Ethnicised Mediated Identities

The 15 contributors tackle debates about racism and ethnicity and the media in various African countries, including how African issues and diasporas are represented in French film, and British and Norwegian news media. In Chapter 2, Francis Nyamnjoh deals with the growing and often complex linkages between the media and belonging in Africa. He uses interesting case studies of xenophobia in Cameroon and South Africa, and discusses the evidence in relation to identity and social justice issues in a globalising context. More importantly, Nyamnjoh argues that under liberal democracy, the media ought to promote more inclusive national citizenship rather than narrow interests.

In Chapter 3, Herman Wasserman analyses the attempts at repositioning of the Afrikaans press after majority rule in 1994. Its challenge was to embrace a human rights culture and to denounce racism in line with the norms of the post-apartheid Constitution, but still trade in Afrikaans cultural goods for an Afrikaans audience which had itself been marked by conflicting negotiations of its cultural identities and, at the same time, to survive economically in an increasingly competitive local-global media market. This complex relationship between a changing press and an audience which had become difficult to define, against the backdrop of a changing local and global media marketplace, gave rise to often contradictory discourses of race and ethnicity in the Afrikaans press. This chapter seeks to highlight one such case, to illustrate how the changing local socio-political environment, linked to global shifts in media markets, impacted on discourses of 'race' and racism in the Afrikaans press (see also Tomaselli and Teer-Tomaselli 2008). By showing the strategy it adopted in dealing with a crisis of normativity, namely that of denial, it is hoped that this case study can provide an insight into how press discourses reflect the contradictions between cultural identities, liberal-democratic normative frameworks and neo-liberal market demands.

In newly established democracies in Africa decolonisation involved replacing European names with 'authentic' African names. Soon after majority rule was achieved, part of the reclaiming of identities by previously marginalised Africans involved replacing colonial names with those of new role models from among those who inspired the fight against apartheid in South Africa. In Chapter 4, Kristin Skare Orgeret discusses this Africanisation process and the contestations that it is raising in South Africa. She focuses on how *The Mercury* covered the renaming action. *The Mercury* was selected for this in-depth study both due to its accessibility and because it covered the process quite substantially in terms of space.

Although the indigenous-language press is increasingly becoming recognised as an important area of study, very few researchers have attempted to theorise and engage with its reception, in particular the connections between its consumption and the immediate conditions of everyday life, as well as the broader social structures that collectively shape media reception practices. Drawing on data from in-depth interviews with readers of one of Zimbabwe's leading indigenous language newspapers, *Umthunywa*, Hayes Mabweazara in Chapter 5 suggests that local-language media can serve an important socio-political and cultural role. The study contends more specifically that indigenous language media, such as *Umthunywa*, can provide historically marginalised readers with an alternative public space in which they articulate issues pertinent to their collective identities which are burdened by feelings of disillusionment, ethnic victimisation and exclusion by hegemonic power structures. In Chapter 6, Nkereuwem Udoakah similarly discusses the conflict in the Niger Delta region of Nigeria, as one of the minority regions. The national media seem to be dominated by the majority ethnic groups. He analyses how much environmental issues about the region are reported in the media, the type of issues raised, together with the prominence attached to them. The chapter points to the press's commitment to the principle of social responsibility, and its contribution to conflict resolution and peace building in society.

The post-colonial conflict and tensions between ethnic groups is clearly noticeable in the Nigerian context. In Chapter 7, also on Nigeria, Muhammad Jameel Yusha'u analyses the media coverage of the Boko Haram uprising, led by a group claiming to be against 'Western education'. The two newspapers studied are the *Daily Trust* from northern Nigeria and the *Guardian* from the south. Although both newspapers carry national news, their reporting cannot be divorced from the influence of their region and ethnic loyalty, as will be discussed later. The chapter contributes original insights on a unique post-colonial problem with many implications for identity.

Sex, Race and Ethnicity within National and Multinational Media

National media cultures in Africa have not been sufficiently inclusive. In Chapter 8, Oluyinka Esan analyses the structures of Nigerian television in attempts to create national culture in a country with over 250 languages and many ethnic loyalties. Expectations that accompany this notion, such as the facilitation of national unity, are lofty. Yet, in the final analysis, the media's ability to realise them is severely limited. Intended meanings often differ from meanings received from media messages. As the chapter acknowledges, audiences adopt reading positions that are autonomous from those suggested by the media. Consequently, the media may be culpable of fanning the embers of resentment, thus stoking the very flames they seek to quell. In this lies the paradox this chapter highlights.

Narrow nationalism has led to absolute ethnicity and both have been detrimental to many societies in Africa. The killings in Rwanda of the 1990s, persuaded the United Nations to set up media for the purpose of preventing genocide which can result from hate speech, ethno-nationalist propaganda and information deprivation in conflict areas. In Chapter 9, Jacob Udo-Udo Jacob examines the nature and impact of such Information Intervention Operations of the UN Mission in the Democratic Republic of Congo.

The book shows that the efforts to curb ethnic conflicts have managed them but not eliminated them. In Chapter 10, Dan Omanga investigates how the media in Kenya helped to resurrect and circulate an ancient 'Bukusu' prophecy whose revival played a critical role in ethnic politics in the run-up to the 2007 presidential elections. Using frames, the study shows how this ancient prophecy was covered, contested and deployed through the print media, and how this nexus may have paved the way for complicated and deep-seated historical differences among ethnic groups to be momentarily forgotten.

The two chapters that follow similarly deal with media performance under difficult circumstances. In Chapter 11, Elizabeth Helander focuses on how political reporting is perceived by Kenyan media practitioners. Using thematical analysis of 15 individual semi-structured interviews, conducted with a broad spectrum of journalists and editors in Nairobi, she uncovers the difficulties they face and how they relate to the media system's structure. In Chapter 12, Cecilia Strand discusses Ugandan newspaper coverage of the Anti-homosexuality Bill in an attempt to understand what created a situation where the initially reluctant journalists revised their position, at least in the privately owned media, and began to award the proposed Bill both salience and prominence, i.e., a higher frequency, as well as front-page coverage. The resultant debate on sexual minorities in the media was influenced by party politics and the legal environment among other things.

Representations in Film and Diasporic Media

In addition to the fascinating cases already introduced, the book offers an interesting discussion of the circular transformation of film mythology into communal knowledge in Ghana. In Chapter 13, Felix Riedel discusses the formation of a Ghanaian rumour complex. The content analysis of a film genre about cyberfraud and occult economies is situated within the ethnographic realities. Films can then be interpreted as reflections of society's faultlines. At the same time they were found to act like affirmative costumes in the prevalent ideological settings.

Filmmakers of African origin also grapple with themes and issues that speak to racism and identity politics in a changing context. In Chapter 14, Daniela Ricci analyses how key exiled black African filmmakers deal with identity and racial issues as witnesses to the existential quest in today's post-post-colonial hybrid world. She questions how their life experiences, in terms of migration and, especially, of their confrontation with 'otherness', even after colonialism, influence their work and 'film objects'. She argues for the need to consider identity's importance on a personal and social scale in today's increasingly complex and interconnected world.

Racialised Coverage of Africa(ns) in European media

The book also includes cases that worryingly reveal continued 'othering' in 'Western' media in spite of official attempts to undo institutional racism. In Chapter 15, Wendy Willems offers a post-colonial reading of constructions of race in British newspaper reporting on Zimbabwe, focusing particularly on the *Daily Telegraph* newspaper. While many analyses in the field of Media Studies consider media representations as the product of a set of professional routines that are inherently part of media institutions, she interprets these texts primarily through a post-colonial lens, thereby tracing the remnants of earlier colonial constructions of race, and thus contributing to emerging post-colonial approaches to media. The evidence supports Gilroy's (2004: 13) point that in Britain, a 'refusal to think about racism as something that structures the life of the post imperial polity is associated with what has become a morbid fixation with the fluctuating substance of national culture and identity'.

National cultures can shape the way media represent racial minorities. In Chapter 16, Martin Nkosi Ndlela discusses the connection between immigrants and crime within Norwegian media discourses. Focusing on visible immigrants, especially of African origin, Ndlela examines the relationship between the media and perceptions of crime as represented in the main discourses. It looks at the mainstream media's role in mediating differences, focusing mainly on the issue of security, crime control and discrimination.

Altogether, the chapters contribute new evidence, critical and fresh thinking about racism, ethnicity and the media in contemporary Africa. In terms of strategies for communicating peace there is need to introduce new ethics and laws that genuinely promote intercultural communication.

Notes

1 Some victims of colonial prejudices, discrimination and torture in Africa are seeking redress in British courts. On 6 June 2013, the British government accepted and regretted the abuses. They agreed to compensate Kenyans tortured by British colonial forces during the Mau Mau uprising with a payout totalling £20 million (http://www.bbc.co.uk/news/uk-22790037, accessed 6 June 2013). The Mau Mau, was a liberation war group against white settler rule in Kenya. The country became independent in 1963.

2 'Being black in Morocco: 'I get called a slave'', France24, 8 November 2012 http://observers.france24.com/content/20121108-being-black-morocco-slave-insult-sub-saharan-african-physical-assault-casablanca-immigration-guinea?page=1 (accessed January 2013).

References

Abubakar A. T. (2009) 'The Media, Politics and Boko Blitz', *Journal of African Media Studies*, 4/1, pp. 97–110.

Appiah, K. A. (1992) *In My Fathers' House: Africa in the Philosophy of Culture*, Oxford: Oxford University Press.

Azar, E.E. (1990) *The Management of Protracted Social Conflict. Theory and Cases*, Aldershot: Dartmouth.

Bangura, Y., and Stavenhagen, R. (2005) *Racism and Public Policy*, London: Palgrave.

Barker C. (2012) *Cultural Studies: Theory and Practice*, London: Sage.

Devarajan, S., and Fengler, W. (2013) 'Africa's economic boom: why the pessimists and the optmists are both right', *Foreign Affairs*, May/June, pp. 68–81.

Dovido, J. F., and Gaertner, S. L., eds (1986) *Prejudice, Discrimination and Racism*, San Diego, CA: Academic Press.

Downing, J., and Husband C. (2005) *Representing 'Race': Racisms, Ethnicities and Media*, London: Sage.

Esman, M.J., and Herring, R.J., eds (2001) *Carrots, Sticks, and Ethnic Conflict; Rethinking Development Assistance*, Ann Arbor, MI: University of Michigan Press.

Fanon F. (1963) *The Wretched of the Earth*, New York: The Grove Press.

Franks, S., and Shaw I. S., eds (2012) 'Introduction/global media and the war on terror: why some wars matter', *Journal of African Media Studies*, 4/1, pp. 5–11.

Frere, M. S., ed. (2007) *The Media and Conflicts in Central Africa*, Boulder, CO, and London: Lynne Rienner Publisher.

Gazi, D. (2004) *Zimbabwe: Racism and the Land Question*, London: Tiger Publishing.

Gilroy, P. (2004) *After Empire: Melancholia or Convivial Culture*, Abingdon: Routledge

Giorgis H. (2014) 'The problem with the west's Ebola response is still fear of a black patient', 16 October, 2014, http://www.theguardian.com/commentisfree/2014/oct/16/west-ebola-response-black-patient (accessed: 16 October 2014).

Hall, S. (1997) 'Random thoughts provoked by the conference: identities, democracy, culture and communication in Southern Africa', *Critical Arts: Identity and Popular Culture*, ed. R. T. Tomaselli and D. Roome, 1/1–2, pp. 1–16.

—— (2006) 'Cultural identity and diaspora', in Jana Evans Braziel and Anita Mannur (eds), *Theorizing Diaspora*, pp. 233–46, Malden, MA: Blackwell.

Hamelink, C. J. (2001) 'Introduction: human rights and the media', *Critical Arts: A Journal of North-South Cultural and Media Studies*, 15/1–2, pp. 3–11.

Hammar, A., Raftpolous, B., and Jensen S., eds (2003) *Zimbabwe's Unfinished Business: Rethinking Land, State and nation in the Context of Crisis*, Harare: Weaver Press.

Hawkins, V. (2008) *Stealth Conflicts: How the World's Worst Violence is Ignored*, Aldershot and Burlington, VT: Ashgate.

Jones, S. (2003) *The Archaeology of Ethnicity: Constructing Identities in the Past and Present*: Taylor & Francis e-Library: http://www.karant.pilsnerpubs.net/files/Jones.pdf (accessed May 2013).

Karikari K. (2007), "Overview" in G. Berger and E. Barratt eds, *50 Years of Journalism: African media since Ghana's independence*. Johannesburg: The African Editors' Forum, Highway Africa and Media Foundation for West Africa, pp. 9–20 (available at: http://guyberger.ru.ac.za/fulltext/50years.pdf) (accessed 21 November 2015)

Mamdani, M. (1996) *Citizen and Subject: Contemporary Africa and the Legacy of Late Colonialism*, Princeton, NJ: Princeton University.

—— (2009) *Saviours and Survivors: Darfur, Politics and the War on Terror*, London: Verso.

Mandaza, I. (1997), *Race, Colour and Class in Southern Africa*, Harare: Sapes.

Mbeki, T. (1996) 'I am African', speech delivered on the occasion of the adoption of Constitutional Assembly of the Republic of South Africa Constitutional Bill, Cape Town. New York: Palgrave Macmillan.

Mbembe, A. (1992) 'Provisional notes on the post-colony', *Africa: Journal of the International African Institute*, 62/1, pp. 3–37.

Mbembe A and S. Nuttall (2004) 'Writing the World from an African Metropolis' in *Public Culture* 16/3, pp. 347–372.

Morley D. (2000) *Home Territories: Media, Mobility and Identity*, London: Routledge.

—— (2007) *Media, Modernity and Technology*, London: Routledge.

Mudhai, O.F. (2013) *Civic Engagement, Digital Networks and Political Reform in Africa*.

Mudimbe V.Y. (1988) *The Invention of Africa: Gnosis, Philosophy and the Order of Knowledge*, Bloomington, IN: Indiana University Press

Musa A.O. (2012) 'Socio-economic incentives, new media and the Boko Haram Campaign of Violence in Northern Nigeria', *Journal of African Media Studies*, 4/1, pp. 111–124.

Ndlovu-Gatsheni, S. J. (2012) 'Racialised ethnicities and ethnicised races: reflections on the making of South Africanism', *African Identities*, pp. 1-16.

Ndlovu-Gatsheni, S. J. and Mhlanga B. eds. (2013), *Bondage of Boundaries and Identity Politics in Post-colonial Africa*, Africa Institute of South Africa: Pretoria

Nwosu, I.E., (1990) 'Mass Media and Development: An Analysis of Some Basic Cases, Theories and Strategies', in Nwosu, I., (ed.) *Mass Communication and National Development*. Aba: Frontier Publications, pp. 65–78.

Nyamnjoh, F. B. (2005), *Africa's Media: Democracy and the Politics of Belonging*, London: UNISA Press.

—— (2008) 'Journalism in Africa: modernity versus Africanity', in P. Lee (ed.), *Communicating Peace*, pp. 97-114, Penang: WACC/Southbound.

—— (2008) 'Africa's Media: Democracy and Belonging' in K. Njogu and J. Middleton eds. *Media and Identity in Africa*, Edinburgh University Press, pp. 62–75.

Obadare E. and Willems W. eds. (2014) *Civic Agency in Africa: Arts of Resistance in the 21st Century.* Woodbridge: James Currey.

Obonyo L. (2011), 'Towards a theory of communication for Africa: The challenges for emerging democracies', *Communicatio: South African Journal for Communication Theory and Research*, 37/1, pp. 1–20.

Pasura D. (2013), *African Transnational Diasporas Fractured Communities and Plural Identities of Zimbabweans in Britain,* Basingstoke/New York: Palgrave Macmillan.

Ronning H. and Kasoma F.P. (2004) *Media Ethics: An Introduction and Overview,* Kenwyn: Juta & Company.

Sabry, T. (2005) 'Emigration as popular culture: the case of Morocco'. *European Journal of Cultural Studies*, 8/1, pp. 5–22.

SAHRC (2000), *Faultlines: Inquiry into Racism in the Media*, Johannesburg: South African Human Rights Commission.

Said E.W. (1978), Orientalism, Pantheon Books: New York

Scanell P. (2007) *Media and Communication.* Los Angeles/London: Sage

Scoones I., Marongwe N., Mavedzenge B., Murimbarimba F., Mahenehene J. and Sukume C. (2009), *Zimbabwe's Land Reform: Myths and Realities*, James Currey/Weaver Press: Woodbridge/Harare.

Smith, A. D. (1986). *The Ethnic Origins of Nations,* Oxford: Blackwell.

Tomaselli K and Teer-Tomaselli R. (2008) 'Exogenous and endogenous democracy: South African politics and media'. *The International Journal of Press/ Politics*, 13(2). Pp. 171–180.

Traber, M. (2008) 'Communicating conflict (1998)', in P. Lee (ed.), *Communicating Peace*, pp. 231–41, Penang: South Bound/World Association for Christian Communication (WACC).

Tsagarousianou, R. (2007) *Diasporic Cultures and Globalisation.* Maastricht: Shaker Publishing.

Vail, L. (1997). 'Ethnicity in Southern African history', in R. R. Grinker and B. S. Christopher (eds), *Perspectives on Africa: A Reader in Culture, History and Representation,* pp. 52–68, Oxford: Blackwell Publishing.

wa Thiong'o, Ngugi (1993) *Moving the Centre: The Struggle for Cultural Freedoms*, London: James Careys.

Wasserman H. ed. (2011) *Popular Media, Democracy and Development in Africa*, Abingdon: Routledge.

White K.R. (2009) 'Scourge of Racism Genocide in Rwanda', *Journal of Black Studies*, 39/3, January 2009, pp. 471–81.

Yuval-Davis (2011) *Power, Intersectionality and the Politics of Belonging*, Working Paper No. 75, Published by FREIA & Department of Culture and Global Studies, Aalborg University, Denmark, FREIA Working Paper Series, available at http://www.freia.cgs.aau.dk/publikationer+og+skiftserie/Skriftserie/ pp. 1–16.

Zeleza P. (2009) 'The Media in Social Development in Contemporary Africa' in K. Njogu and J. Middleton eds. *Media and Identity in Africa*, Edinburgh University Press, pp. 19–35.

2

MEDIA AND BELONGING IN AFRICA: REFLECTIONS ON EXCLUSIONARY ARTICULATION OF RACIAL AND ETHNIC IDENTITIES IN CAMEROON AND SOUTH AFRICA

Francis B. Nyamnjoh

Introduction

This chapter demonstrates the extent to which the media and belonging in Africa are torn between competing and often conflicting claims of bounded and flexible ideas of culture and identity.[1] It draws on studies of xenophobia in Cameroon and South Africa, inspired by the resilience of the politicization of culture and identity, to discuss the hierarchies and inequalities that underpin political, economic and social citizenship in Africa and the world over, and the role of the media in the production, enforcement and contestation of these hierarchies and inequalities. In any country with liberal democratic aspirations or pretensions, the media are expected to promote national citizenship and its emphasis on large-scale, assimilationist and territorially bounded belonging, while turning a blind eye to those who fall through the cracks as a result of racism and/or ethnicity. Little wonder that such an exclusionary articulation of citizenship is facing formidable challenges from its inherent contradictions and closures, and from an upsurge in the politics of recognition and representation

by small-scale communities claiming autochthony at a historical junc-
ture where the rhetoric espouses flexible mobility, postmodern flux
and discontinuity.

Racism and ethnicity become issues of concern for media when tracing belonging and identity through exclusion becomes *obsessive* and
problematic – forcing upon others exclusion when they expect inclusion,
and seeking to justify such exclusion with porous arguments, stereotypes, stigmatisation and scapegoating. Xenophobia (whether racially
or ethnically inspired) is indicative of such problematic and obsessive
tendencies to define and confine belonging and identity in terms of
cultural differences, with little regard to the reality of interconnections
and ongoing relationships forged across communities by individuals as
navigators and negotiators of various identity margins. Racism and
ethnicity in obsession link culture and place in very essentialist and
politicised terms. This makes it difficult to account for cultural differences and similarities within individuals and communities in a world
where particular cultures are mapped onto or confined to particular
spaces, places and races. Belonging and identity based on the logic of
exclusion are informed by the erroneous assumption that there is such
a thing as the ultimate insider, found through a process of selective
elimination and ever diminishing circles of inclusion. The politics of
nativity, authenticity, autochthony, indigeneity or citizenship, prem-
ised narrowly around cultural difference and the centrality of culture,
are pursued with this illusion of the ultimate insider in mind. Yet,
even the most cursory of looks into the lives of Africans and the daily
relationships they forge with difference would suggest that such frozen
representations of cultures and identities are in no way a reflection of
real life. Is there anything in real terms to the frozen claims of authenticity, autochthony, indigeneity or citizenship on which cultural
difference is predicated? To define indigenous peoples simply as those
who 'were there first and are still there, and so have rights to their
lands' (Maybury Lewis 2005), or even as those 'particular groups who
have been left on the margins of development', 'are perceived negatively by dominating mainstream development paradigms', 'whose
cultures and ways of life are subject to discrimination and contempt' and
'whose very existence is under threat of extinction' – a definition adopted
by the African Commission's Working Group of Experts on Indigenous
Populations/Communities (ACHPR and IWGIA 2005: 87–97) – is to

incite inquiry about the reality of internal and external migration and the political, cultural, economic and historical factors that have configured competing articulations of being indigenous. Although such strategic essentialism may be understandable and indeed useful in the pursuit of common ambitions of dominance, or in redressing injustices collectively experienced as a colonised or subjected people, it hardly provides for theorising pre- and post-colonial identities as complex, negotiated, relational and dynamic experiences that respond to and feed from local and global interconnected hierarchies. Qualifying to be considered 'authentic', 'autochthonous', 'indigenous' or *'bona fide'* is a function of the way race, geography, culture, class, gender and generation define and prescribe, include and exclude. These hierarchies of humanity assume different forms depending on encounters, power relations and prevalent notions of personhood, agency and community. Africa offers fascinating examples of how the terms *indigenous* and *native* were employed in the service of colonising forces, of how colonially created or deformed ethnicities have had recourse to indigeneity in their struggles against colonialism and of how groups vying for resources and power among themselves have deployed competing claims to indigeneity in relation to one another (Vail 1989; Nnoli 1998; Salih and Markakis 1998). In Africa, the meaning of 'indigenous' has varied tremendously. Communities large and small have both accepted and contested arbitrary colonial and post-colonial administrative boundaries and the dynamics of dispossession. Failing to achieve the idealised 'nation-state', relatively weak *vis-à-vis* global forces, governments and cultural communities have often sought to capitalise on the contradictory and complementary dimensions of civic, ethnic and cultural citizenships. In this context, being indigenous socioanthropologically is much more than merely claiming to be or being regarded as the first. Colonial and apartheid regimes of divide and rule created and imposed a proliferation of 'native identities' circumscribed by arbitrary physical and cultural geographies. They made distinctions between colonised 'natives' and colonising Europeans but also between 'native citizens' and 'native settlers' among ethnic communities within the same colony. In this context, to be called 'indigenous' meant to be *primitive*, which became a perfect justification for the colonial *mission civilisatrice* and for dispossession and confinement to officially designated tribal territories, homelands or Bantustans, usually with callous disregard for the histories of relationships and interconnections forged with excluded others, and the differences and tensions even among the included. In all, being indigenous was, for the majority colonised 'native' population, to be shunted to the margins in socio-economic and juridico-political terms. These dynamics of classification and rule conceived of the 'natives' through frozen ideas of culture and imagined traditions applied under 'decentralised despotisms' in rural areas, while the town and city were reserved for the minority colonial settler population and their purportedly 'modernising', 'cultured' and 'detribalised' African servants and support staff (Mamdani 1996, 1998). Even then, the colonial and apartheid authorities made it extremely difficult for their African servants and support staff to feel at home away from home, thus driving even the most enthusiastic of them to look back to their home villages for solidarity and sustenance, when they would have preferred permanent integration as bona-fide townsmen and townswomen (Mayer 1971). This meant that effective assimilation or integration into the so-called universal 'modern' culture or civilisation was impossible for the modernising native, however hard he tried, and whatever the rhetoric encompassed in various variants of modernisation theory. African townsmen and townswomen were thus compelled in reality to bond with the place where their umbilical cords were supposedly buried, and to celebrate primordial solidarities with their imposed ethnic kin, while dramatizing differences with purported ethnic strangers. This effectively discouraged or disciplined mobility among Africans, as it confined them to home lands of labour reserves for the colonial economy. If this negative history still shapes the highly critical stance of African intellectuals and nationalists toward nebulous claims of autochthony today (Mbembe 2006; Ndlovu Gatsheni 2009), it has also, quite paradoxically, tended to render invisible the everyday reality of post-colonial Africans (including those same intellectuals and nationalists) as straddlers of civic, ethnic and cultural citizenships and of multiple global and local cosmopolitan identities. Yet terms such as 'multiculturalism', 'racial minorities', 'ethnic minorities', 'subcultures', 'multiple identities', 'hybridity', and 'cosmopolitanism' are explicit or tacit admissions that cultures and individuals as embodiments of cultural influences do defy their mappings or spaces and that spatial purity in cultural terms is more assumed than real (Gupta and

Ferguson 1992: 14), just as, in some cases, multiculturalism is also more assumed than real. It is thus a dangerous illusion to seek to naturalise obviously socially constructed (racial, ethnic, national) cultural identities (Jenkins 1996: 819). In the light of the global obsession with exclusionary ideas and practices of belonging, this chapter uses the examples of Cameroon and South Africa to argue that xenophobia arises from the failure by politicians, policy makers, media, intellectuals and other key social actors in public life to problematize both taken-for-granted assumptions of similarity (belonging together) and difference (not belonging together) and preconceptions of peoples and cultures as tied to particular places and spaces. Local and global hierarchies in Africa, just like similar hierarchies in Europe, North America and elsewhere, are, often with the assistance of global consumer media, actively producing inequalities based on bounded notions of race, place, culture, nationality, citizenship, class, gender and age, and the prejudices that derive from this process in turn produce xenophobia, especially in a world of rapidly globalising uncertainties and insecurities (Nyamnjoh 2005a, 2006, 2007a, 2007b). The obsessive investment in exclusionary claims to cultural belonging and identity in Africa is part of an intensifying global trend (Geschiere 2009; Comaroff and Comaroff 2009). In Europe, the political right has – especially since the late 1970s and early 1980s and since accelerated mobility became possible for people from the underdeveloped worlds of former colonies, facilitated by information and communications technologies (ICTs) – developed a political rhetoric of exclusion through cultural fundamentalism in which cultural difference is seen and treated as a threat to the assumed congruence between polity and culture in the 'host' countries with the power to define and confine belonging (Stolcke 1995; Wright 1998; Geschiere 2009). As Jean and John Comaroff observe, although anthropologists, sociologists and political scientists have largely moved away from 'primordialism, pure and simple', 'ethno nationalists around the world continue to kill for it' (2009: 39). Similarly, while modernisation theory and its teleological assumptions of progress and development are largely *passé* in serious scholarly circles, 'some organic intellectuals persist in protecting "ancestral customs" from historical deconstruction' (2009: 39). It is for these reasons that any primordial or exclusionary claims of cultural difference based on assumed purity of racial or ethnic belonging are inherently problematic, even when understandable. As Verena Stolcke argues, 'making sense of cultural diversity without losing sight of shared humanity' is fraught with 'formidable difficulties' (1995: 1), which the media might collude with, contest or mediate. For a closer look at the relationship between problematic articulations of belonging and identity in Africa, I have chosen studies of Cameroon and South Africa as cases in point.

On Media and the Politics of Belonging in Africa

Cameroon as a Case Study

In 2005, I published *Africa's Media: Democracy and the Politics of Belonging*. One of the main findings of that study was that the media had assumed a partisan, highly politicised, militant role in Africa. They had done so by dividing citizens into the righteous and the wicked, depending on their political party, ideological, regional, cultural or ethnic belonging. By considering the Cameroonian experience, the book sought to understand how scapegoatism, partisanship and regional and ethnic tendencies in the media have affected their liberal democratic responsibility to act as honest, fair and neutral mediators – accessible to all and sundry. The study did this by looking at polarisation in the press and at how the media have shaped and been shaped by the politics of belonging. Characterised by the politicisation of culture and ethnicity, this politics of belonging privileges an obsession with differentiating nationals into 'ethnic/regional citizens' and 'ethnic/regional strangers' – likened to 'camnogos', a stubborn skin rash that itches terribly – and feeds on and into stereotypes, stigma and xenophobia. Neither the state, nor intellectuals, nor the media, nor even religious institutions seem in a hurry to challenge these exclusionary articulations that make it possible for Cameroonians to be simultaneously insiders and outsiders in their national territory (Nyamnjoh 2005a).

The following excerpt from *Married But Available* (Nyamnjoh 2009: 53–4), gives an idea of the sort of struggles over belonging that go on even at a university purportedly modelled on an overarching 'Anglo-Saxon' colonial cultural heritage. The Vice Chancellor and Registrar – daughter and son of the native soil where the university is located – would go to all lengths, including mobilising ethnic kin and kith outside of the university, to fight

off perceived ambitions by ethnic others to take over the leadership
of *their* university:

> The elephant men reassured the VC and the Reg that what they had
> buried 'will numb every student and member of staff who thinks evil
> of you.' Before leaving the scene, the elephant men promised to inten-
> sify their magical powers to ensure that 'our daughter and our son, and
> all those who mean them well, are protected by our native soil from
> all camnogos.'
>   'What are camnogos?' Lilly Loveless asked.
>   'These are a skin rash that itches like mad,' Bobinga Iroko laughed.
> 'You scratch and scratch and scratch, but the itches go nowhere.'
>   'So the VC and Reg have been attacked by this skin rash?' Lilly
> Loveless was baffled.
>   'Yes, and it disturbs them like hell,' he continued to laugh.
>   'Really?' Now Lilly Loveless knew that Bobinga Iroko was in his
> joking mode.
>   'Yes, and embarrassing too. At parties and official functions the
> camnogos do not allow the VC and Reg to do their jobs. They attack,
> and the VC and Reg would scratch and scratch to no avail. They can't
> even take their fingers from their skins to take a drink or something
> to eat. It is terrible, because the camnogos make them feel like going
> naked, and grating themselves against a rough surface till they find
> satisfaction.'
>   Lilly Loveless finally understood the metaphor. 'So people have
> borrowed from this skin rash to refer to others they don't like?' she
> asked.
>   'That's right. Camnogos are people whom the sons and daughters of
> the native soil consider a pain in the arse.'
>   'You mean ethnic others?'
>   'Yes, ethnic, regional, and whatever others ... Anyone not perceived
> to belong really.'
>   'Isn't that rather parochial and dangerous?'
>   'That is the way those who run this country have fought to ensure that
> we remain forever divided. They're out to mar, not to make.'
>   'It's like racing where angels fear to tread.'

Belonging in Cameroon goes beyond protecting control of university
spaces from invading camnogos. Almost everywhere in Cameroon,
citizens expect the urban elite – including journalists and media
proprietors – to make inroads into the modern centres of accumulation.

The state, a major source of patronage and resources, together with other economic institutions, must be manipulated to divert the flow of finance, jobs and so forth to the home regions from which the heterogeneous urban originally derive. Elites are under pressure to act as facilitators and manipulators with respect to the state. Through elite development associations, they lobby foreign agencies and NGOs to provide their home villages or regions with new sources of wealth and livelihood. In return, they may be rewarded with neo-traditional titles in their home villages. These honours confer on them symbolic or cultural capital, not expressed in material wealth but sustained by what Fisiy and Goheen (1998: 388) have termed 'the conspicuous display of decorum and accompanied by public respect', that in turn can always be exploited for political ends at regional and national levels where elites are expected to serve as vote banks for a regime that has little legitimacy in liberal democratic terms. In certain cases, investing in the village is a way of consolidating success in the city, especially in the politics of ethno regionalism (Nyamnjoh and Rowlands 1998; Konings and Nyamnjoh 2003). Modern big men and women thus live with one foot in the city and the other in the village. They take advantage of the economic and political opportunities of the city while redistributing wealth back to the home village. They play an active role in the cultural affairs, government and development of their home areas, which they define, confine and seek to represent in often essentialist and instrumentalist terms. Their survival within the politics of belonging of the failing modern state often depends on doing just that. At the same time, their rural ties lead them to consider customary law and local opinion when making national decisions. They thus become, in the words of Mitzi Goheen (1992), mediators between local and national arenas, interpreters as well as architects of the intersections between national law and customary law, which they often treat as unproblematic and consensual.

For this project, the elite recruit journalists and the media (preferably from their home areas) for communication and public relations within and between communities and also with the state and the outside world. In Cameroon, almost every appointment and promotion into high office is the prerogative of the head of state, and most appointed ministers and director generals of state corporations return to their home villages to celebrate with kin and kith and express gratitude to the president.

This would seem to suggest that they are appointed primarily to cater to the interests of their home villages or regions and are only marginally at the service of all and sundry (Nyamnjoh 1999). The stereotyping and xenophobic violence they encourage or condone towards ethnic or cultural others in their home villages and regions is indicative of how far they are ready to carry their politicisation of belonging in the name of democracy (Geschiere and Nyamnjoh 2000).

The practice of patriotism to the home village does not escape media professionals. The study of Cameroon reveals a tension between dominant normative media theories that demand of media practitioners' professional independence and detachment from conflicting loyalties to cultural and ethnic communities. The country case study points to the interconnectedness and interpenetration between citizenship and subjection, the cosmopolitan and the local, the individual and the collective, the insider and the outsider, tolerance and xenophobia. These tensions make understanding democracy in Africa far more complex than simplistic liberal notions would suggest. In discussions of the media, democracy and rights, a heightened sense of cultural identity cannot simply be dismissed as 'tribalism' or 'politicisation of ethnicity' and consigned to the past or to the primitive mind sets of its advocates. The Cameroonian experience offers interesting empirical material to inform discussions of how to marry liberal democracy with African historical, cultural and indigenous political and economic realities, however contested. While the study clearly highlights the shortcomings of ethnicised and politicised media in liberal democratic terms, it also shows the limitations of liberal democracy in a context where people are obliged or ready and willing to be *both* citizens and subjects, *both* inclusive and exclusive. They identify with their ethnic group or cultural community on the one hand (*ethnic* or *cultural citizenship*) and with the nation state on the other (*civic citizenship*). The argument for democracy both as an individual and as a community or cultural right cannot simply be dismissed when there are individuals who, for multiple reasons, straddle realms of individual rights (liberal democracy) and of group rights. As the book maintains, major characteristics of Africa's second liberation struggles since the 1980s have been a growing obsession with belonging and the questioning of traditional assumptions about nationality and citizenship. Identity politics are central to the political process. Exclusionary conceptions of nationality and citizenship have increased. Group claims for greater cultural recognition are countered by efforts to maintain the status quo of an inherited colonial hierarchy of racial and ethnic groupings. As ethnic groups, either local majorities or minorities, clamour for status, they are countered by an often aggressive reaffirmation of age-old exclusions informed by colonial registers of inequalities among the subjected. This development is paralleled by an increased distinction between 'locals' and 'foreigners' and between 'indigenes' and 'settlers' within and between countries, with the emphasis on opportunities and economic entitlements. It is the latter preoccupation with distinction that is the subject matter of my second case study, South Africa.

South Africa as a Case Study

My second case study, South Africa, was part of a study that resulted in my 2006 book *Insiders and Outsiders: Citizenship and Xenophobia in Contemporary Southern Africa*. In pockets of economic prosperity in South Africa, Namibia and Botswana, where hierarchies of humanity informed by race, place and culture (among other things) are at play, xenophobia is rife against migrants from other African countries. Referred to derogatorily as *Makwerekwere* (meaning those incapable of articulating local languages that epitomise economic success and power), some of these migrants come from countries that were instrumental in the struggle against apartheid. The rhetoric of government authorities, immigration officials, the media and the general public suggests that black migrants and immigrants are collectively unwelcome. The construction of the *Makwerekwere* and of boundaries between South Africans as 'deserving citizens' and *Makwerekwere* as 'undeserving outsiders' has been skilfully recounted by Phaswane Mpe (2001) in a novel titled *Welcome to Our Hillbrow*. The novel is written in two voices. The first celebrates official rhetoric internalised by ordinary black South Africans of having graduated into citizenship, only for this to be endangered by the influx of *Makwerekwere* with little but trouble to offer. The second voice is more measured and tries to mitigate the tendency to scapegoat and stereotype *Makwerekwere*, who most of the time are not as guilty as painted. This well-informed novel is more subtle and nuanced than some of the surveys which have sought to capture the relationship between South Africans and *Makwerekwere*. We gather from it that negative attitudes are not towards foreigners as a homogeneous entity but rather towards black African migrants in general and those from certain countries in particular. The hierarchy of humanity inherited from apartheid South Africa is replayed, with white South Africans at the helm as superiors, black South Africans in the middle as superior inferiors, and *Makwerekwere* as the inferior scum of humanity. Coloureds and Indians are not part of the picture in a big way. There is a clash between those who have learnt to stutter no more (blacks) and those still embedded in stuttering (coloureds and Indians), and the stutterers are a challenge to blacks' ability to harness modernity. Black South Africans come across as having basically two attitudes towards foreigners: they either look up to them as articulate and accomplished or look down on them as stuttering and depleting. The articulate and accomplished white migrants are presumed to bring opportunities; the stuttering and depleting *Makwerekwere* compound the insecurities and uncertainties in South African lives. There are black South Africans who feel strongly that *Makwerekwere* 'should remain in their own countries and try to sort out the problems of these respective countries, rather than fleeing them', because South Africa has 'too many problems of its own', and in any case 'cannot be expected to solve all the problems of Africa'. Others would agree but argue that this is 'no excuse for ostracising the innocent'. Negative views about African migrants are particularly dangerous when held by the police. In the novel, we see how policemen arrest *Makwerekwere* and '[d]rive them around Hillbrow for infinite periods of time', saying: 'See it for the last time, bastards'. As we learn from the novel, it is outright dishonest to blame the woes of post-apartheid South Africa on *Makwerekwere*. Novelists like Phaswane Mpe and social scientists alike find South Africa's public culture has become increasingly xenophobic (Landau 2004a, 2004b, 2006; Mattes et al. 1999; Morris and Bouillon 2001; Sharp 2008; Sichone 2008a, 2008b; Hadland 2008). Politicians often make unsubstantiated and inflammatory statements that the 'deluge' of *Makwerekwere* is responsible for the current crime wave, rising unemployment or even the spread of diseases (Crush 1997; Morris 2001b). Seen as hailing from 'an impoverished and unhealthy wasteland where health measures have ceased to be operative', *Makwerekwere* are considered a threat to the physical and moral health of the nation and 'should therefore be kept out of South Africa' (Peberdy 2002: 24; 2009). As the unfounded perception that migrants are responsible for a variety of social ills grows, *Makwerekwere* have increasingly become the target of abuse by South African citizens, the police, the army, the Department of Home Affairs and even the media. Dark-skinned refugees and asylum seekers with distinctive features from 'far away' countries are especially targeted for abuse (Bouillon 2001a, 2001b; Landau 2004b; Morris 2001b; Sichone 2001). According to Sichone (2001: 1), migrants are subject to more state regulation and open to victimisation by 'owners of the means of violence'. Xenophobia is not just an attitude of dislike but, as in May 1998, is often accompanied by violence and is racist and ethnic in its application. Victims are predominantly black and are targeted for their very blackness by a society where skin colour has always served as an excuse for whole catalogues of discriminatory policies and practices. You are repeatedly made to 'mind your colour' (February 1991) until you are entirely minded by colour. Individuals are often assumed to be *Makwerekwere* on the basis that they 'look foreign' or are 'too dark' to be entitled to South Africa, and '[p]olice are supposedly able to identify foreign Africans by their accents, hairstyles or dressing styles, or, in the case of Mozambicans, vaccination scars on the left front arm' (Bouillon 2001a: 38). In the frenzy to root out foreigners, they also victimise and arrest their own citizens. Since the beginnings of the Portuguese, Dutch and English transatlantic slave trade in the fifteenth and sixteenth centuries, blackness has been a curse (Bernal 1995: 999). In *Heart of Darkness*, the darker character is less qualified for citizenship (Mamdani 1996; Elbourne 2003). This tendency continues. '[T]he best qualified black' is seen 'as worse than the worst white', thereby justifying black dehumanisation and inhumane treatment (Bernal 1995: 999–1000). Even in post-apartheid South Africa, salvation for blacks seems linked to how successfully they 'try for white', 'play white' or 'pass for white', in the manner of the coloureds under apartheid. Lightening one's darkness with chemicals and philosophical enrichment might help in aspirations for 'honorary whiteness' (Fanon 1967a: 166–99; 1967b; Fonlon 1967: 20), but it cannot guarantee against mistakes by fussy policemen and authorities with a nose for appearances. Black South African citizens are sometimes mistaken for the dark invading barbarians or stutterers who must be confined to the fringes. To the police and authorities, South African modernity, like its identities, is all about appearances. Being unable to belong as an

'insider' makes *Makwerekwere* all too vulnerable to 'excessive criminalisation' and 'primitivisation'. They cannot vote or benefit from social
services, and *Makwerekwere* are especially vulnerable to mistreatment
by the police, who know that non-citizens 'are less likely to lay a complaint and, if they do, they are not likely to be given a fair hearing'
(Landau 2004a: 10–13; Morris 2001b: 86), especially if they are black.
Black *Makwerekwere* are largely seen as deportable criminals even by
the Minister of Home Affairs and the forces of law and order (Landau
2004a: 13–14).

South African Media and
the Narrow Focus on *Makwerekwere*

In South Africa, the conventional media were until the end of apartheid in the early 1990s in the service of white racism aimed at black
disempowerment and dehumanisation. The media were preponder-
antly white-controlled businesses and, although the end of apartheid
has led to some degree of black ownership and partnership, this has
not necessarily 'made the newspapers more representative of South
African society' (Van Kessel 1998: 4–10; see also Tomaselli 2002).
There continue to be claims and counterclaims of 'racism in the media'
and the 'racialized and stereotypical portrayal of blacks' (Berger 2001;
Glaser 2000; Pityana 2000; Neocosmos 2006, 2008), which is indicative of how much bridge building remains to be done. The rise of
mass circulating tabloids such as the *Daily Sun* and the *Daily Voice* and
their popularity with the poor and working class, black majority, for
most of whom broadsheets are irrelevant, elusive and oppressive, is
indicative of a post-apartheid South Africa determined to renegotiate
skewed professional assumptions and practices in the interest of an
ethic of effective inclusion and of common humanity in journalism
(Wasserman 2010). Typically, however, the logic of bounded citizenship means that, even as they make a case for inclusion of the poor
and the sidestepped working-class South African black majority of the
townships, the tabloids are all too ready to caricature and misrepresent
Makwerekwere as the greatest obstacle to the fulfilment of their dreams
of material abundance and comfort. It is hardly surprising, therefore,
that following the May 2008 violent uprisings against *Makwerekwere*,
the *Daily Sun*, one of the leading tabloids and the most widely circulated

in areas affected, not only failed to condemn the violence forthrightly but was also found guilty of employing inappropriate and discriminatory terminology to describe black African immigrants.[2] There is still little real investment in geographical and cultural knowledge of Africa, despite much political rhetoric to the contrary, and in spite of the aggressive expansion of South African businesses into Africa north of the Limpopo (Miller 2006; Adebajo 2007).[3] Much has changed within an extremely short space of time in South African media and society, while much seems to have stayed the same. The rhetoric of transformation does not match realities and expectations, as the media continue to 'talk left, act right' (Duncan 2000). Whites in South Africa may not be a unified bloc, but the edification of biological and cultural racism under apartheid made it possible for their collective interests to be privileged, regardless of class, gender, status or the resistance of some against the structures in place (Steyn 2008; Posel 2010). This makes it extremely difficult for non-white South Africans not to equate whiteness with power and privilege, as they seek to situate themselves in the racialised hierarchy of humanity imposed upon them since the days of the Cape 'Hottentots' in the 1640s (Johnson 2007). That the media in post-apartheid South Africa are still dominated by white interests in ownership, control and content is a good case in point that talking or scripting change is different from living change. If the media in general and the print media in particular still mainly serve elite white interests and the economy is largely still under elite white control, it means that how the media cover immigration and migration is likely to be indicative of dominant elite white views and interests on these issues. And if in the face of negative coverage, black South Africans were to reinforce their hostility towards *Makwerekwere*, they would be acting in tune with dominant elite white interests, even as they may claim to be defending their own interests as emerging citizens. The media thus play a critical role in the production, circulation and reproduction of prevalent attitudes and perceptions of foreigners by South Africans, who are reified as a homogeneous entity with common interests to be collectively defended against undeserving 'others'. In other words, the media are part of a national obsession with the production of a fixed, essential, stable, unified and exclusive South Africa where the subjected of the apartheid era are included only to the extent they are able to uncritically internalise, reproduce and aggressively defend the apartheid rhetoric of biological and cultural purity. The media offer a platform for the South African public to comment on 'foreigners' through letters to the editor, talk shows and television debates. While *Makwerekwere* are absent from public discussions about them and their purported ills, Indians were very present in the debate around Mbongeni Ngema's controversial song *AmaNdiya*, accusing South African Indians of exploitation and resisting change. *Makwerekwere* are an absent presence, to be acted upon but not expected to act or react. Perceived essentially as a negation to civilisation, they can be talked at, talked about and sometimes talked to or for, but rarely talked with.

As a collective menace to citizenship and opportunity, *Makwerekwere* are denied the legitimacy of a voice by the media as the voice of civilisation and legitimacy. In this way, the media do not simply carry information to the public as a neutral vehicle reflecting the workings of society. They reproduce certain ideologies and discourses that support specific relations of power in accordance with hierarchies of race, nationality, culture, class, and gender (Nyamnjoh 2006). Racism – both in its biological and cultural forms (Mac an Ghaill 1999: 61–80; Stolcke 1995; Wright 1998) – is constantly produced and reproduced in South African print media (Glaser 2000; Pityana 2000), thereby making what is reported and how it is reported essential for a fair appreciation of the place of the media in creating or reinforcing perceptions of *Makwerekwere* as the constructed 'Other' (Danso and McDonald 2001; Harris 2001; Fine and Bird 2006; Sichone 2008a, 2008b). Representations of *Makwerekwere* by the print media in South Africa are largely negative and 'extremely unanalytical in nature', as the majority of the press has tended to reproduce 'problematic research and anti-immigrant terminology uncritically' (Danso and McDonald 2001: 115–17; Fine and Bird 2006: 18–62). The mainly white-controlled media have thus been instrumental in the creation, reproduction and circulation of the frozen imagery of black immigrants as a threat to an equally frozen or homogeneous South African society. In both cases, the media have failed to accommodate the overwhelming diversity of cultural identities, social experiences and subjective realities of individuals and communities, preferring instead to caricature. *Makwerekwere* are regularly connected with crime, poverty, unemployment, disease and significant social costs in the media and by authorities whose declarations the media reproduce uncritically (Danso and McDonald 2001; Harris 2001; Landau 2004a, 2004b, 2005; Morris 2001b: 77–8; Shindondola 2002). *Makwerekwere* are uncritically portrayed by the bulk of the print media as constituting a social problem and a threat to the locals, first through their coming to the country and then through their illegalities (Danso and McDonald 2001; Fine and Bird 2006; Neocosmos 2006, 2008).

Such 'harsh treatment' has in turn pushed *Makwerekwere* to view South Africans and their obsession with autochthony and rootedness negatively (Landau 2005, 2006). Nigerians and Congolese, for example, perceive black South African men as 'extremely violent', 'brutal', 'lazy', 'adulterous and not nurturing of their partners', 'shackled by colonial attitudes and [...] feelings of inferiority [to whites]' and South Africans in general as 'poorly educated and ignorant', 'narrow minded', 'hostile', 'indifferent', 'unpredictable' and 'unenterprising and wasteful' (Bouillon 2001b: 122–40; Morris 2001b: 78–80). But these counter perceptions and stereotypes by *Makwerekwere* seldom make their way into the dominant media, or into the conventional research sponsored by and conducted in the interest of the status quo. By replying with stereotypes of their own, *Makwerekwere* only attract further hatred from black South African men in particular, who are incensed by their perceived popularity with local women (Morris 2001b: 74–80), and by their success in the informal sector (Morris 2001b; Simone 2001, 2004). The media, in conjunction with other institutions of social control, succeed (with or without conspiring) in diverting the attention of blacks seeking meaningful integration into the South African economy. The ANC black majority authorities, by opting for neo-liberalism without justice or restitution, are thus co-opted by a white-dominated economic system that can then conveniently deny accusations of racism, while the racial outcome of its policies and practices persists (Glaser 2000; Hendricks 2004; Pityana 2000; Fine and Bird 2006; Crush 2008; Sichone 2008a, 2008b; Sharp 2008; Steyn 2008; Posel 2010).

For over two decades following independence in 1980, Zimbabwe experienced serious outflows of its white and black populations to South Africa and Botswana, among other destinations (Tevera and Crush 2003). While black Zimbabweans are castigated and stereotyped for transgressing South African borders (Mate 2005), curiously, white Zimbabweans fleeing into South Africa because of Mugabe's land redistribution policies are uncritically welcome. Any noise by the local media is rather to criticise the ANC government for its 'quiet diplomacy' towards Mugabe's 'diabolical' land redistribution policies while whites suffered the loss of 'legitimately' acquired land.

The coverage of crimes by black migrants from African countries is common, even as criminal activities by other nationalities are rarely reported. Little is said about Thai, Romanian and Bulgarian women involved in prostitution, or Taiwanese and Chinese 'illegals' responsible for the smuggling of poached contraband. There is also almost a complete blackout of 'references to crime and illegality on the part of Western Europeans and North Americans in South Africa, despite the fact that nationals from these regions also commit crimes and many are in the country "illegally"'. The hierarchy of races and cultures dictates a sense of newsworthiness, which is ill informed by the real impact of different categories of immigrants on the South African economy (Danso and McDonald 2000: 127; see also Fine and Bird 2006). Babacar, a francophone *Makwerekwere* and street vendor, cannot understand the double standards:

> Why don't they talk about the Chinese or the Yugoslavs? There are so many foreigners, other nationalities in South Africa. The Chinese are here. They sell in the streets! I know Yugoslavs. They sell. But they are not mentioned. They use South Africans to sell in the streets. There are other nationalities which sell here, but they don't have black skins like us. (Bouillon 2001b: 132)

Crime has been racialised, and the print media have also tended to stereotype crime attributed to *Makwerekwere*. Criminal syndicates, smuggling and drug trafficking are usually associated with particular groups of foreign nationals, with black *Makwerekwere* being portrayed either as perpetual criminals or more prone to commit serious crime than non-black immigrants from Africa or elsewhere. Nigerians are associated with controlling the drug trade (cocaine) and, as depicted in the film *District 9*, represented as dangerous extra-terrestrial refugees to be watched at close range. The Congolese are identified with passport racketeering and diamond smuggling; Lesotho nationals with the smuggling of gold dust and copper wire; and Mozambican and Zimbabwean women as indulging in prostitution (Danso and

McDonald 2001: 126–7; Mate 2005). The media have also sensationalised immigration, with screaming and alarmist headlines such as: 'Illegals in SA add to decay of cities', '6 million migrants headed our way', 'Africa floods into Cape Town' and 'Francophone invasion'. Aquatic or mob metaphors such as 'hordes', 'floods', 'flocking' and 'streaming' are quite common. Also frequent are derogatory and unsubstantiated references to the rest of Africa (e.g., 'Strife torn Central Africa', 'Africa's flood of misery') and comments that portray persons from those areas essentially as real or potential economic refugees (e.g., 'as long as South Africa remains the wealthiest and strongest country on a continent littered with economically unstable and dysfunctional nations, it will continue to attract large numbers [of mi grants]'). The tendency is to report on black *Makwerekwere* in South African cities as turning the clock of civilisation back to the primitive realities of their home cities (e.g., 'Johannesburg's inner city is now assuming the appearance of a typical sub-Saharan African city'), which predicts doom for South African urbanites if not contained. The presumed primitivity of *Makwerekwere* is meant to presuppose an inability to articulate life in a modern 'world class city' like Johannesburg (Gotz and Landau 2004; Landau 2004a, 2004b, 2005, 2006), where only whites or those for long directly subjected by settler whites can cope (Steyn 2008; Posel 2010). This criminalisation of migration by black Africans is 'just as true of black oriented newspapers as it is of white' (Danso and McDonald 2001: 127–9; Fine and Bird 2006). In view of such sensational and uncritical reporting, hostile attitudes towards black *Makwerekwere* could be described as partly driven not by experience but by mass-mediated stereotypes and myths of the dangerous, depleting and encroaching 'Other' from the 'Heart of Darkness' north of South Africa (Crush 2001: 28; Morris and Bouillon 2001; Sichone 2008a, 2008b). The South African media and nationals thus give the impression that black African migration is The Problem, not migration as a whole (Landau 2004a: 6). Flexible mobility is for those at the top of the hierarchy of humanity (determined by race, place, class, gender, age, etc.), not those at the bottom. Thus, whites from everywhere are free to come and go, and are hardly represented as a burden to the economy or society. Negative attitudes and hostility towards black *Makwerekwere* are actively promoted and sustained by the draconian immigration policy of detection, detention and deportation

(Landau 2004a, 2004b). As Morris (1998) argues, 'even though progressive legislation and positive reporting can alter perceptions over time', 'there has been little endeavour by the authorities or the media to construct narratives that would counter xenophobia' targeted at black African immigrants. It is hardly surprising that public opinion towards *Makwerekwere* 'is shaped by the attitude of the media and the authorities' (Morris 1998: 1126), and that, in turn, the media and authorities are influenced by the interests of the elite whites and blacks who, in partnership with multinationals, control the South African economy. It is neither in the interest of the elite whites (Steyn 2008; Posel 2010) nor in the interest of the crystallising, young and old, upwardly mobile, black elite in power and business to encourage balanced media reporting (Fine and Bird 2006), when stereotyping and scapegoating black African migrants can serve a useful diversionary purpose in the face of the rising expectations of ordinary black and white citizenship. In South Africa we see how race, culture, class and citizenship intersect in the interest of global consumer capitalism, to the detriment of those with the wrong race, the wrong culture, the wrong class, the wrong gender, the wrong nationality or the wrong citizenship.

More importantly, we see the extent to which investing obsessively in regressive indicators of belonging is an unending endeavour. There will always be someone to exclude if the policy and practice is to dramatize difference rather than celebrate commonalities in humanity. There is thus little to suggest current obsessions with belonging and South Africa's problems would disappear once the obvious outsiders or demons – the *Makwerewere* in this instance – have been exorcised (Landau 2011). We have already referred to the instance in 2002 when Indian South Africans were perceived and presented as enemies within, by Mbongeni Ngema, who claimed his critical *AmaNdiya* song was merely a translation of popular sentiments shared by black South Africans, especially in KwaZulu Natal. In the song, he criticized Indians for not wanting to change, and for being worse than whites (Nyamnjoh 2006: 56–63).

Until his expulsion from the African National Congress (ANC) at the end of February 2012, Julius Sello Malema provided another example of a public figure in the new South Africa privileging the rhetoric of exclusion over actively exploring cohesion among all and sundry in the 'rainbow nation'. In 2010 Malema, then leader of the

Youth League of the ANC (ANCYL), identified white South Africans as the enemy within, and nationalization and land restitution as his favourite themes While he invited his mostly unemployed supporters among black South Africans to aspire to be like the whites in comfort and consumption, he particularly targeted Afrikaners in his choice of the song he sang in public. On 3 March 2010, for example, at his birthday party in Pholokwane, Malema sang *Ayesab' Amagwala* – a popular Zulu anti-apartheid liberation struggle song that contains the words 'dubul'ibhunu', which translate into English as 'Shoot the *Boer*'. *Boer*, 'farmer' in Dutch, refers to white South Africans from Dutch, German or Huguenot descent who speak Afrikaans, and are also known as Afrikaners. Malema sang the song repeatedly – including in April 2010 during a visit to Zimbabwe where he openly supported Robert Mugabe's land restitution programme – causing much uproar in the media and the wider South African society. A debate ensued as politicians and others discussed whether the song should be allowed as part of South Africa's heritage and history, or prohibited as hate speech. The choice was between prioritizing heritage to the detriment of harmony; or harmony to the detriment of memory, in a context where equality and redress was much more a constitutional provision than a real-life experience for the bulk of those dispossessed and dehumanized by apartheid. The situation was only further enflamed by the death of Eugene Terre'Blanche – founder and leader of the Afrikaner Weerstandsbeweging (AWB, Afrikaner Resistance Movement), an organization formed in 1973 by right-wing extremist Afrikaners to resist what they saw as the weakening of apartheid regulations at the time – allegedly killed on 3 April 2010 by two of his black workers in his farm in Ventersdorp over unpaid wages. Tensions rose as some sought to link Malema's singing of 'Shoot the *Boer*' and Terre'Blanche's murder. Right-wing extremist groups such as the AWB and the Suidlanders, for long quiescent, conducted protest marches in Ventersdorp, and threatened to avenge the murder. Other groups became involved, including AFRIFORUM and TAUSA, who lodged a complaint with the Equality Court against Malema, accusing him of hate speech. On 18 March, a 'Prosecute Malema' online campaign was launched to gather signatures for a letter directed to President Zuma; by 25 March the South African Human Rights Commission had received 109 complaints against Malema for singing the song;

and on 26 March and 1 April, the song had been ruled unlawful and unconstitutional by the North and South Gauteng High Courts, respectively, much to the dissatisfaction of many an ANC member (Rodrigues 2011: 1–4). Malema may live in Sandton, Johannesburg, and cherish flashy designer clothes and shoes, big Breitling watches and gold, diamond-studded rings, the choicest wines and sushi off the belly buttons and nipples of naked beautiful girls (Forde 2011; Shapiro 2011) – indeed, he may share the same appetites and material comforts of the richest of those who systematically and actively excluded him and those he claims to represent from the old South Africa – but somehow he feels more legitimately entitled to the new South Africa. Belonging is an unending cycle of ever diminishing circles.

Conclusion

In this chapter I have sought to demonstrate the extent to which the media and belonging in Africa are torn between competing and often conflicting claims of bounded and flexible ideas of culture and identity. I have drawn on my study of xenophobia in Cameroon and South Africa, inspired by the resilience of the politicisation of culture and identity, to discuss the hierarchies and inequalities that underpin political, economic and social citizenship in Africa and the world over, and the role of the media in the production, enforcement and contestation of these hierarchies and inequalities.

In Cameroon and South Africa, as elsewhere in Africa and the world, accelerated mobility and increased uncertainty are generating mounting tensions fuelled by autonomy seeking difference. Such ever decreasing circles of inclusion demonstrate that no amount of questioning by immigrants immersed in the reality of flexible mobility seems adequate to de-essentialise the growing global fixation with an 'authentic' place called home. Trapped in cosmopolitan spaces where states and their hierarchy of 'privileged' citizens try to enforce the illusion of fixed and bounded locations, immigrants, diasporas, ethnic minorities and others who straddle borders are bound to feel like travellers in permanent transit. This calls for scholarship, politics and policies informed by historical immigration patterns and their benefits for recipient communities. Such scholarship and political attention should focus on the success stories of forging new relationships of understanding between citizens and subjects. Understanding these relationships will point to new, more flexible, negotiated, cosmopolitan and popular forms of citizenship, with the emphasis on inclusion, conviviality and the celebration of difference. Flexible and negotiated belonging, while a popular reflection of how ordinary people live their lives, is clearly not compatible with the prevalent illusion that the nation state is the only political unit permitted to confer citizenship in the modern world. Nor is it compatible with a regime of rights and entitlements narrowly focused on yet another illusion,' the autonomous individual' (Comaroff and Comaroff 1999). The price of perpetuating these illusions has been the proliferation of ultra-nationalism, chauvinism, racism and xenophobia that has consciously denied the fragmented, heterogeneous, and multinational cultural realities of most so called 'nation states'. The challenge for Africa's media, in a context of racism and ethnicity, is to seek to capture and promote that flexibility in navigating and negotiating democracy and articulating belonging.

Notes

1 A version of this chapter was previously published as Francis B. Nyamnjoh, 'Racism, ethnicity and the media in Africa: reflections inspired by studies of xenophobia in Cameroon and South Africa', *Africa Spectrum*, 45/1 (2010), pp. 57–93. The online version of this and the other articles can be found at: <www.africaspectrum.org>.
2 The Media Monitoring Project (MMP) and the Consortium for Refugees and Migrants in South Africa (CoRMSA) submitted a complaint against the *Daily Sun*'s reporting on the xenophobic attacks to the Press Ombudsman and the South African Human Rights Commission <http://www.iol.co.za/index.php?art_id=nw20080529190816434C483974&set_id=1&click_id=13&sf=#more>.
3 See Louise Haigh, 'What fuels the hatred', *Cape Argus*, 19 May 2008.

References

ACHPR and IWGIA (2005) *Report of the African Commission's Working Group of Experts on Indigenous Populations/Communities*, Copenhagen: Transaction Publishers.
Adebajo, Adekeye (2007) 'South Africa in Africa: messiah or mercantilist?', *South African Journal of International Affairs*, 14/1, pp. 29–47.

Berger, Guy (2001) 'Deracialisation, Democracy and Development: Transform-ation of the South African Media, 1994–2000', in Keyan Tomaselli and Hopeton Dunn (eds), *Media, Democracy and Renewal in Southern Africa*, Denver, CO: International Academic Publishers.

Bernal, Martin (1995) 'Race, class, and gender in the formation of the Aryan model of Greek origins', *South Atlantic Quarterly*, Special Issue, Nations, Identities, Cultures, 94/4, pp. 987–1008.

Comaroff, John L., and Comaroff, Jean (1999) 'Introduction', in John L. Comaroff and Jean Comaroff (eds), *Civil Society and the Political Imagination in Africa: Critical Perspectives*, pp. 1–43, Chicago: University of Chicago Press.

——— (2009) *Ethnicity, Inc.*, Scottsville: University of KwaZulu Natal Press.

Crush, Jonathan, ed. (1997). "Exaggerated figures are creating a xenophobic at-mosphere", *Business Day*, 30 June 1997 (www.queensu.ca/samp/).

——— (2001). "The Dark Side of Democracy: Migration, Xenophobia and Human Rights in South Africa", *International Migration*, 38(6), 103–133. http://dx.doi.org/ 10.1111/1468-2435.00145

——— (2008) *The Perfect Storm: The Realities of Xenophobia in Contemporary South Africa*, Southern African Migration Project, Migration Policy Series, 50, <www.queensu.ca/samp/sampresources/ samppublications/policyseries/ Acrobat50.pdf> (accessed Feb. 2010).

Crush, Jonathan and Pendleton, Wade (2004) *Regionalizing Xenophobia? Citizen Attitudes to Immigration and Refugee Policy in Southern Africa*, Southern African Migration Project, Migration Policy Series, 30, <www.queensu.ca/samp/ sampresources/samppublications/policyseries/Acrobat30.pdf> (accessed June 2005).

Crush, Jonathan, Williams, Vincent, and Peberdy, Sally (2005) *Migration in Southern Africa*, Global Commission on International Migration, <www.gcim.org/attachements/RS7.pdf> (accessed Jan. 2006).

Danso, Ransford, and McDonald, David E. (2001) 'Writing Xenophobia: Immigration and the print media in post-Apartheid South Africa', *Africa Today*, 48/3, pp. 115–37.

Duncan, Jane (2000) 'Talk left, act right. what constitutes transformation in Southern African media?', *Communications Law in Transition Newsletter*, 10 June, pp. 1, 6.

Elbourne, Elizabeth (2003) ' "The Fact so often Disputed by the Black Man": Khoekhoe Citizenship at the Cape in the Early to mid-Nineteenth Century'. *Citizenship Studies*, 7/4, pp. 379–400.

Fanon, Frantz (1967a) *The Wretched of the Earth*, Harmondsworth: PenguinBooks.

——— (1967b) *Black Skin, White Masks*, New York: Grove Press.

February, Vernon (1991) *Mind Your Colour: The Coloured Stereotype in South African Literature*, London: Kegan Paul.

Fine, Jack, and Bird, William (2006) *Shades of Prejudice: An Investigation into the South Africa's Media's Coverage of Racial Violence and Xenophobia*, Braamfontein: Centre for the Study of Violence and Reconciliation (Race and Citizenship in Transition Series), <www.csvr.org. za/docs/foreigners/ shades.pdf> (accessed Feb. 2010).

Fisiy, Cyprian, and Goheen, Mitzi (1998) 'Power and the quest for recognition: neo-traditional titles among the new elite in Nso', Cameroon', *Africa*, 68/3, pp. 383–402.

Fonlon, Bernard (1967) 'Idea of Culture (II)', *ABBIA: Cameroon Cultural Review*, 16 (Mar.), 5–24.

Forde, Fiona (2011) *An Inconvenient Youth: Julius Malema and the 'New' ANC*, Johannesburg: Picador Africa.

Geschiere, Peter (2009) *The Perils of Belonging: Autochthony, Citizenship, and Exclusion in Africa and Europe*, Chicago: Chicago University Press.

Geschiere, Peter and Nyamnjoh, Francis B. (2000) 'Capitalism and Autochthony: The Seesaw of Mobility and Belonging', in Jean Comaroff and John L. Comaroff (eds), *Millennial Capitalism and the Culture of Neoliberalism* (Public Culture, 12/2), pp. 423–52, Durham, NC: Duke University Press.

Glaser, Daryl (2000) 'The Media Inquiry Reports of the South African Human Rights Commission: A Critique', *African Affairs*, 99/396, pp. 373–93.

Goheen, Mitzi (1992) 'Chiefs, subchiefs and local control: negotiations over land, struggles over meaning', *Africa*, 62/3, 389–412.

Gotz, Graeme, and Landau, Loren B. (2004) 'Introduction', in Loren B. Landau (ed.), *Forced Migrants in the New Johannesburg: Towards a Local Government Response*, pp. 13–23, Johannesburg: Witwatersrand University Press.

Gupta, Akhil, and Ferguson, James (1992) 'Beyond "Culture": Space, Identity, and the Politics of Difference', *Cultural Anthropology*, 7/1, pp. 6–23.

Hadland, Adrian (2008) *Citizenship, Violence and Xenophobia: Perceptions from South African Communities*, Human Sciences Research Council paper presented to the Department of Home Affairs Imbizo on Xenophobia, <www.hsrc.ac.za/Research_Publication20862.phtml> (accessed Feb. 2010).

Harris, Bronwyn (2001) *A Foreign Experience: Violence, Crime and Xenophobia during South Africa's Transition*, Johannesburg: Centre for the Study of Violence and Reconciliation (Violence and Transition Series, 5), <www.csvr.org.za/wits/papers/papvtp5.htm> (accessed June 2004).

Jenkins, Richard (1996) 'Ethnicity etcetera: social anthropological points of view', *Ethnic and Racial Studies*, 19/4, 807–22.

Johnson, David (2007) *Representing the Cape 'Hottentots', from the French Enlightenment to Post-Apartheid South Africa* (Eighteenth-Century Studies, 40/4), pp. 525–52, Baltimore, MD: Johns Hopkins University Press.

Konings, Piet, and Nyamnjoh, Francis B. (2003) *Negotiating an Anglophone Identity: A Study of the Politics of Recognition and Representation in Cameroon*, Leiden: Brill.

Landau, Loren B. (2004a) *The Laws of (In)hospitality: Black Africans in South Africa* (Forced Migration Working Paper Series, 7), Johannesburg: University of the Witwatersrand.

—— ed. (2004b) *Forced Migrants in the New Johannesburg: Towards a Local Government Response*, Johannesburg: University of the Witwatersrand.

—— (2005) 'Urbanisation, Nativism, and the Rule of Law in South Africa's "Forbidden" Cities', *Third World Quarterly*, 26/7, pp. 1115–34.

—— (2006) 'Transplants and transients: idioms of belonging and dislocation in inner-city Johannesburg', *African Studies Review*, 49/2, pp. 125–45.

—— (2011) *Exorcising the Demons Within: Xenophobia, Violence and Statecraft in Contemporary South Africa*, Johannesburg: Wits University Press.

Lucas, Robert E. B. (1987) 'Emigration to South Africa's Mines', *American Economic Review*, 77/3, pp. 313–30.

Mac an Ghaill, Martin (1999) *Contemporary Racisms and Ethnicities: Social and Cultural Transformations*, Buckingham: Open University Press.

Mahmud, Tayyab (1997) 'Migration, identity and the colonial encounter', *Oregon Law Review*, 76, pp. 633–90.

Mamdani, Mahmood (1973) *The Myth of Population Control: Family, Caste and Class in an Indian Village*, New York: Monthly Review Press.

—— (1996) *Citizen and Subject: Contemporary Africa and the Legacy of Late Capitalism*, Cape Town: David Philip.

—— (1998) *When Does a Settler Become a Native? Reflections of the Colonial Roots of Citizenship in Equatorial and South Africa*, Text of Inaugural Paper as A. C. Jordon Professor of African Studies, University of Cape Town, 13 May (New Series, 208).

—— ed. (2000), *Beyond Rights Talk and Culture Talk. Comparative Essays on the Politics of Rights and Culture*, Cape Town: David Philip.

Mate, Rekopantswe (2005) *Making Ends Meet at the Margins? Grappling with Identity, Poverty, Marginality and Economic Crisis in Beitbridge Town, Zimbabwe*, Dakar: CODESRIA.

Mattes, R., Taylor, D. M., McDonald, D. A., Poore, A., and Richmond, W. (1999) *Still Waiting for the Barbarians: SA Attitudes to Immigrants and Immigration* (Migration Policy Series, 14), Cape Town: Southern African Migration Project.

Maybury Lewis, David (2005) 'Defining indigenous', *Cultural Survival Quarterly*, 29/1, http://www.culturalsurvival.org/publications/cultural-survival-quarterly/none/defining-indigenous (accessed 9 April 2014).

Mayer, Philip (1971) *Townsmen or Tribesmen: Conservatism and the Process of Urbanization in a South African City*, Cape Town: Oxford University Press.

Mbembe, Achille (2006) 'South Africa's second coming: the Nongqawuse syndrome', *Open Democracy*, 15 June, <www.opendemocracy.net/content/articles/PDF/3649.pdf> (accessed Feb. 2010).

Mercer, Claire, Page, Ben, and Evans, Martin (2009) *Development and the African Diaspora: Place and the Politics of Home*, London: Zed Books.

Miller, Darlene (2006) 'Spaces of resistance: African workers at Shoprite in Maputo and Lusaka', *Africa Development*, 31/1, pp. 27–49.

Morris, Alan (2001a) 'Introduction', in Alan Morris and Antoine Bouillon (eds), *African Immigration to South Africa: Francophone Migration of the 1990s*, pp. 9–18, Pretoria: Protea and IFAS.

—— (2001b) ' "Our fellow Africans make our lives hell": the lives of Congolese and Nigerians living in Johannesburg', in Alan Morris and Antoine Bouillon (eds), *African Immigration to South Africa: Francophone Migration of the 1990s*, pp. 68–89, Pretoria: Protea and IFAS.

Morris, Alan and Bouillon, Antoine, eds (2001) *African Immigration to South Africa: Francophone Migration of the 1990s,* Pretoria: Protea and IFAS.

Moser, Caroline (1999) *Violence and Poverty in South Africa: Their Impact on Household Relations and Social Capital*, South Africa: Poverty and Inequality Informal Discussion Paper Series, World Bank.

Mpe, Phaswane (2001) *Welcome to Our Hillbrow*, Pietermaritzburg: University of Natal Press.

Ndlovu Gatsheni, Sabelo J. (2009) 'Africa for Africans or Africa for "Natives" only? "New nationalism" and nativism in Zimbabwe and South Africa', *Africa Spectrum*, 44/1, pp. 61–78, <http://hup.sub.uni hamburg.de/giga/afsp/article/view/29/29> (accessed March 2010).

Neocosmos, Michael (2006) *From 'Foreign Natives' to 'Native Foreigners': Explaining Xenophobia in Post-Apartheid South Africa*, Dakar: CODESRIA.

—— (2008) 'The politics of fear and the fear of politics: reflections on xenophobic violence in South Africa', *Journal of Asian and African Studies*, 43/6, pp. 586–94.

Nnoli, Okwudiba, ed. (1998) *Ethnic Conflicts in Africa*, Dakar: CODESRIA.

Nyamnjoh, Francis B. (1999) 'Cameroon: a country united by ethnic ambition and difference', *African Affairs*, 98/390, pp. 101–18.

—— (2005a) *Africa's Media, Democracy and the Politics of Belonging*, London: Zed Books.

—— (2005b) 'Images of Nyongo amongst Bamenda Grass fielders in Whiteman Kontri', *Citizenship Studies*, 9/3, pp. 241–69.

—— (2006) *Insiders and Outsiders: Citizenship and Xenophobia in Contemporary South Africa*, Dakar and London: CODESRIA/Zed Books.

—— (2007a) 'Ever diminishing circles: the paradoxes of belonging in Botswana', in Orin Starn and Marisol de la Cadena (eds), *Indigenous Experience Today*, pp. 305–31, Oxford: Berg.

—— (2007b) 'From bounded to flexible citizenship: les sons from Africa', *Citizenship Studies*, 11/1, pp. 73–82.

—— (2009) *Married But Available*, Bamenda: Langaa.

Nyamnjoh, Francis B. and Rowlands, M. (1998) 'Elite associations and the politics of belonging in Cameroon', *Africa*, 68/3, pp. 320–37.

Oucho, John O. (2002) 'The relationship between poverty and migration in Southern Africa', paper presented at *SAMP/LHR/HSRC workshop on Regional Integration, Poverty and South Africa's Proposed Migration Policy,* Pretoria, <www.sarpn.org.za/documents/d0001212/oucho/oucho.pdf> (accessed July 2004).

—— (2007) *Migration in Southern Africa: Migration Management Initiatives for SADC Member States*, Institute for Security Studies, Occasional Paper, 157, <www.iss.co.za/pgcontent.php?UID= 3044> (accessed Feb. 2010).

Oucho, John O. and Crush, Jonathan (2001) 'Contra free movement: South Africa and the SADC migration protocols', *Africa Today*, 48/3, pp. 139–58.

Peberdy, Sally (2002) 'Hurdles to trade? South Africa's immigration policy and informal sector cross border traders in the SADC', presented to a *workshop of the Southern African Poverty Network (HSRC) Lawyers for Human Rights and the Southern African Migration Project 'Regional Integration, Migration and Poverty',* Pretoria, April.

—— (2009) *Selecting Immigrants: National Identity and South Africa's Immigration Policies 1910–2008*, Johannesburg: Wits University Press.

Pityana, N. Barney (2000) 'South Africa's inquiry into racism in the media: the role of national institutions in the promotion and protection of human rights', *African Affairs*, 99/397, pp. 525–32.

Posel, Deborah (2010) 'Races to consume: revisiting South Africa's history of race, consumption and the struggle for freedom', *Ethnic and Racial Studies*, 33/2, pp. 157–75.

Rodrigues, Erika (2011) '(Un)papering the cracks in South Africa: the role of "traditional" and "new" media in nation-negotiation around Julius Malema on the eve of the 2010 FIFA World Cup™', MA thesis, University of Cape Town, South Africa.

Salih, M. A. Mohamed, and Markakis, John, eds (1998) *Ethnicity and the State in Eastern Africa*, Uppsala: Nordiska Afrikainstitutet.

Shapiro, Jonathan (2011) *Zapiro: The Last Sushi: Cartoons from Mail & Guardian, Sunday Times and The Times*, Johannesburg: Jacana.

Sharp, John (2008) 'Fortress SA: xenophobic violence in South Africa', *Anthropology Today*, 24/4, pp. 1–3.

Shindondola, H. (2002) 'Xenophobia in South Africa: the experiences of students from Africa. A case study of RAU', paper presented at *South African Sociological Association 2002 Congress*, 30 June–3 July, East London, South Africa.

Sichone, Owen (2001) 'The making of Makwerekwere; East Africans in Cape Town', paper for the workshop *Interrogating the New Political Culture in Southern Africa; Ideas and Institutions*, Harare, 13–15 June.

—— (2008a) 'Xenophobia and xenophilia in South Africa: African migrants in Cape Town', in Pnina Werbner (ed.), *Anthropology and the New Cosmopolitanism: Rooted, Feminist and Vernacular Perspectives*, pp. 309–32, Oxford: Berg.

—— (2008b) 'Xenophobia', in Nick Shepherd and Stephen L. Robins (eds), *New South African Keywords*, pp. 255–63, Johannesburg: Jacana.

Steyn, Melissa (2008) 'Repertoires for talking white: resistant whiteness in post-Apartheid South Africa', *Ethnic and Racial Studies*, 31/1, pp. 25–51.

Stolcke, Verena (1995) 'Talking culture: new boundaries, new rhetorics of exclusion in Europe', *Current Anthropology*, 36/1, pp. 1–24.

Tevera, Daniel S., and Crush, Jonathan (2003) *The New Brain Drain from Zimbabwe*, Southern African Migration Project (Migration Policy Series, 29), <www.queensu.ca/samp/sampresources/samppublications/policyseries/Acrobat29.pdf> (accessed June 2004).

Tomaselli, Keyan (2002) 'Media ownership and democratization', in Goran Hyden, Michael Leslie, and Folu Ogundimu (eds), *Media and Democracy in Africa*, pp. 129–55, Uppsala: Nordiska Afrikainstitutet.

Vail, Leroy, ed. (1989) *The Creation of Tribalism in Southern Africa*, Berkeley, CA: University of California Press.

Van Kessel, I. (1998) 'Mass Media in South Africa: From Liberation to Black Empowerment', paper presented at *African Studies Centre seminar on The Role of Media in Africa*, Leiden, The Netherlands, Oct.

Vigneswaran, Darshan (2007) *Free Movement and the Movement's Forgotten Freedoms: South African Representation of Undocumented Migrants*, Oxford: Refugee Studies Centre (RSC Working Paper, 41), <www.rsc.o x.ac.uk/PDFs/ RSCworkingpaper41.pdf> (accessed Feb. 2010).

Wasserman, Herman (2009) 'Extending the theoretical cloth to make room for African experience: an interview with Francis Nyamnjoh', *Journalism Studies*, 10/2, pp. 281–93.

—— (2010) *Tabloid Journalism in South Africa: True Story!* (African Expressive Cultures), Bloomington, IN: Indiana University Press.

Wright, Susan (1998) 'The politicization of culture', *Anthropology Today*, 14/1, pp. 7–15.

Zeleza, Paul Tiyambe (2003) *Rethinking Africa's Globalization*, vol. 1, *The Intellectual Challenges*, Trenton, NJ: Africa World Press.

3

DISCOURSES OF RACE
IN THE AFRIKAANS PRESS
IN SOUTH AFRICA[1]

Herman Wasserman

The arrival of majority democracy in South Africa in 1994 has brought unprecedented freedoms for that country's media. However, in 2010–12 there were worrying attempts to narrow down the space for freedom of expression and information dissemination in the public sphere. These attempts included a proposed Media Appeals Tribunal, as an alternative to the current self-regulatory appeals system, and the passing by Parliament of a Protection of State Information Bill (POSIB) that has the potential to prevent journalists, citizens and civil society from accessing important information that could keep the security apparatuses of government accountable (see Wasserman, 2012; Wasserman and Jacobs, 2012). These latest tensions between the media and the African National Congress (ANC)-led government (for earlier examples see Berger 2009; Chotia and Jacobs 2002: 157; SANEF 2007, 2008a; Wasserman and De Beer 2005) can be at least partly explained by the adversarial – and at times rather antagonistic – definition that the South African media have given to their role in the new democracy.

The dominant normative role that the South African media have adopted has been that of a watchdog over the democratic state, based on the notion that 'the freedom of the press is indivisible from and subject to the same rights and duties as that of the individual and rests on the public's fundamental right to be informed and freely to receive and to disseminate opinions' (SANEF 2008b; see also BCCSA 2008). Such an individualised view of the media's duties and responsibilities is in line with the broad liberal consensus interpretation of the constitution (Johnson and Jacobs 2004).

Although, in an African context, this normative positioning can be critiqued (see Nyamnyoh 2005: 25; Wasserman 2006), this chapter's concern is not so much with the suitability of this framework for post-apartheid South Africa, as with how its underpinning of liberal individualism informs the discourse on race and racism in the media.

Here, the focus will be on the Afrikaans-language printed press, as their transition from the apartheid to the post-apartheid environment has arguably required a more complex repositioning than their English-language counterparts. For the Afrikaans press, whose development was closely linked to the ideology of Afrikaner nationalism and which provided support for the white minority regime during its reign, the shift to a democratic, liberal-individualist, human rights culture required a dramatic change of stance. Most mainstream Afrikaans newspaper titles, with the exception of the few Afrikaans-language 'alternative' press titles such as *Saamstaan, Namaqua Nuus, Vrye Weekblad* and *Die Suid-Afrikaan*, lent support to the apartheid regime (albeit in varying degrees, and with some dissident *verligte* (enlightened) voices appearing from time to time: see Claassen 2000 for a discussion of this). Owned by mining capital, the English-language press under apartheid provided a limited critique on human rights infringements, without questioning the capitalist underpinnings of the system (Tomaselli et al. 1989). Although having to restructure on a political-economic level (Tomaselli 2000a), the advent of democracy in the country did not necessitate as radical an ideological shift for the English-language press as it did for their Afrikaans counterparts.

The repositioning of the Afrikaans press meant that it now had to embrace a human rights culture and denounce racism in line with the norms of the post-apartheid Constitution, but still trade in Afrikaans cultural goods for an Afrikaans audience which had itself been marked by conflicting negotiations of its cultural identities and, at the same time, to survive economically in an increasingly competitive local-global media market. This complex relationship between a changing press and an audience which had become difficult to define, against the backdrop of a changing local and global media marketplace, gave rise to often contradictory discourses of race and ethnicity in the Afrikaans press.

This chapter seeks to highlight one such case, to illustrate how the changing local socio-political environment, linked to global shifts in media markets, impacted on discourses of 'race' and racism in the Afrikaans press. By showing the strategy it adopted in dealing with a crisis of normativity, namely that of denial, it is hoped that this case study can provide an insight into how press discourses reflect the contradictions between cultural identities, liberal-democratic normative frameworks and neo-liberal market demands.

Repositioning the Afrikaans Media[2]

In the early 2000s, marketing brochures for the media conglomerate Naspers, the home of the majority of Afrikaans publications, celebrated the continued economic power of Afrikaans audiences and portrayed their language as that of 'thousands of consumers' (Ads 24 2000: 2). In these marketing strategies, Afrikaans was marketed to media buyers as a language that had adapted to changing circumstances and had left behind the baggage of apartheid. Its speakers were portrayed as successful consumers who still ranked among the top household consumer spend (Media 24 n.d.). The assumption seemed to be that, by positioning the Afrikaans media as commodities within the discourse of consumerism, the historical links between Afrikaans media and Afrikaner nationalist ideology would be erased or obscured (without critical questions being asked about the historical origins of the wealth of Afrikaans audiences). By using the typical postmodern metaphors of consumption and mobility, which diminish relations with and responsibilities towards local Others (Featherstone 2007: xx), the positioning of the Afrikaans media within a seemingly ideology-free discourse of individualist consumption may have been an attempt to provide Afrikaans audiences with the social capital (Bourdieu 1979) to solidify their class position in a transitional society marked by alliances between new elites (see Bond 2000) and to free them from their historical heritage of 'race'.

Yet the repositioning of Afrikaans media was not simply a shift from the ideology of Afrikaner nationalism to the 'ideology-free ideology' of consumerism. Simultaneously with attempts to redefine Afrikaans language and culture as saleable commodities, rather than as markers of 'race' or ethnicity, Afrikaans media also engaged in new Afrikaans identity politics. In the late 1990s and early 2000s, when debates about the perceived erosion of the language's official status were at their most heated, the economic status of Afrikaans speakers was often mentioned as a reason to take this group seriously. Conversely, their language's commercial value was seen as something to be flaunted in order to ensure its continued recognition. This commodification of the language was expressed as follows by the then editor of the Afrikaans daily newspaper, *Die Burger*, once the National Party's mouthpiece:

> As newspaper editor and businessman, this is how I like to see Afrikaans: What role does it play in the world of buying and sell-ing? What does Afrikaans offer its speakers where products and money change hands? Of what benefit is Afrikaans to those doing business? [...] Someone once said that if you want to save the black rhino from extinction, you have to try turning them into dairy cat-tle. Livestock do not stand the danger of extinction. Serve an eco-nomic purpose and people will be interested in you. Be marketable and it will be difficult to become extinct. Afrikaans is marketable. (Rossouw 2001)[3]

Rossouw's argument for an economically driven promotion of Afrikaans during his tenure as *Die Burger's* editor was meant to signal a radical departure from the paper's historical background as the 'mother of Afrikaner Nationalism' (Tomaselli 2000b: 287). It also marked a move away from the paper's stubborn reactionary stance during the 1990s transitional period under the previous editor, Ebbe Domisse, when it criticised the Truth and Reconciliation Commission (TRC), took up arms in the *taalstryd* (language battle) against the public broadcaster and civil service, for scaling down language use (see Louw 2004, for an account of this process), emphasised the ruling ANC's alliance with the South African Communist Party and the Confederation of South African Trade Unions (Cosatu) in an attempt to activate its reader-ship's historical fear of communism, and represented the ruling party as hostile to Afrikaners and Afrikaans. When the TRC held hear-ings into the role of the media under apartheid, Naspers, home to *Die Burger* and other papers, refused to testify. Rossouw's emphasis on Afrikaans as an economic commodity should therefore be read as a disavowal of the paper's inherited ideological position which it had until then occupied – by turning to an economic discourse, Rossouw tried to underplay the political. However, the link between the economic and the political could not be denied – the continued attention to language issues could be seen as directed especially to the more affluent white section of the Afrikaans market, where the fear that the language might become extinct was higher than among black, including those referred to in apartheid nomenclature as 'coloured', speakers (Schlemmer 2001: 95). The latter group outnumbered the white speakers of the language (Giliomee 2003: 658), but the former still held more economic power. To retain the economically powerful, yet politically more conservative section of its readership, without alienating its black readership, and to embrace the country's new democratic culture, a fine balance had to be struck between commodifying the language in the private sphere (e.g., by sponsoring Afrikaans arts festivals) and using it to engage in minority politics in its newspapers' pages (Botma 2006). It remains important to bear in mind that this minority politics was dependent on an acceptance (celebration, even) by the Afrikaans press of the new, post-apartheid constitution, in which minority rights and the official status of Afrikaans (together with ten other languages) were guaranteed. The Afrikaans press was, therefore, repositioned within the discourse of liberal democracy, especially in relation to the interpretation of this democracy as a system that guarantees the rights of individuals and minorities, proscribes hate speech and racism, and protects freedom of speech.[4]

What are the implications of this balance between an individualistic, free-market approach to democracy on the one hand, and support for minority group rights, when it comes to news coverage of 'race' and racism? The answer may be illustrated by the example of a crisis that presented itself in Afrikaans society, that threatened to fracture the dominant narratives of transformation and reconciliation in this community.

'We're Not All Like That'[5]: Strategic Denial of Racism

The emphasis on individuality in the liberal-democratic framework within which the Afrikaans press positioned itself in the transitional period, linked to the commodification and privatisation of cultural identity, had implications for the discursive construction of racism in the Afrikaans press. Within this discourse it became possible and even imperative for racism to be seen as an individual's transgressions rather than as a phenomenon rooted in history and within which a younger generation might continue to be socialised through what Jansen (2009: 171) referred to as 'knowledge in the blood': 'knowledge embedded in the emotional, psychic, spiritual, social, economic, political and psychological lives of a community'. However, by repositioning Afrikaans identity in a discourse of progress and consumption, the Afrikaans press was able to obscure links between contemporary incidents of racism and the persistence of racist attitudes carried over from the apartheid past (in which it had been complicit). After all, the free-market philosophy presents itself as colour blind (Durrheim et al. 2005: 168).

An example of the discursive response to racism (as previously described) manifested in the Afrikaans press, was seen in the case of the so-called 'Reitz Four', a group of students whose racist video capturing the degrading mock initiation of black staff at one of the country's historically Afrikaans universities, surfaced in 2008.

The delicate balance that the Afrikaans media had to strike to reject the students' behaviour, yet at the same time continue to be seen as an 'explainer' and 'protector' of (a reimagined) Afrikaans cultural identity and group interests, may be seen in a series of discursive strategies that the Afrikaans press used to deny complicity in persistent racist attitudes. These strategies will be illustrated by an analysis of media commentary following the emergence of the student video, applying the discursive strategies of denial of racism identified by Durrheim et al. (2005). This current chapter's aim is not to provide an exhaustive analysis of all media commentary around the incident, but to demonstrate how these discursive strategies function in relation to the repositioning of the Afrikaans media in post-apartheid society.

In March 2008, it came to light that a group of white students at the historically white, Afrikaans University of the Free State (UFS) had filmed black university employees while forcing them to enact humiliating initiation rituals (including eating a meat concoction into which one of the students appeared to have urinated) in order to be 'inducted into' the Reitz university residence where they were working as cleaning staff. In the video, explicit and derogatory mention was made of attempts by university administrators to integrate black and white students in university residences (see *Mail & Guardian*, 2008, for a summary). The video sparked a national and international outcry after it became publicly available on the video-sharing site YouTube. The university expressed regret over the incident (*UV Digest* 2008) and called it an 'isolated manifestation of resistance against the impact of continued transformation initiatives by the University'. It was also announced that the residence would be closed down and turned into an Institute for Diversity (ibid). The four students faced criminal charges (Van Rooyen 2008).[6]

While the Afrikaans media reported and commented on the incident widely, this chapter will focus on comments in the daily newspaper press, because this sector of the Afrikaans media has histor- ically played a central role in discourses of Afrikaner nationalism and the 'imagined community' (see Anderson 1983) of Afrikaners. Despite dwindling circulation figures, the Afrikaans press remains a central platform for debates around cultural politics.

Discursive Strategies

Durrheim et al. (2005) refer to the discursive strategy of 'denial of racism' in the South African media's response to an investigation into racism in the media, conducted by the country's Human Rights Commission (see Tomaselli 2000a) in 1999. According to this study, the media reacted scathingly to allegations that they continued to display racist attitudes well into the post-apartheid dispensation. The authors list a number of interlocking discursive strategies through which the South African media attempted to 'remodel the field of racist practices and representations into a terrain suited to preserving white privilege', namely: 'strategies of splitting, (dis)locating, relativising, trivialising, de-racialising and, ultimately, reversing racism' (Durrheim et al. 2005: 167).

In order to analyse responses in the Afrikaans press to the emer- gence of the racist video by the UFS students, the categories identified by Durrheim et al. (2005) will be used deductively to establish whether similar strategies were used by the Afrikaans press to deny any association with the students' racist attitudes. Texts chosen for analysis appeared in the mainstream Afrikaans newspapers *Die Burger*, *Beeld*, *Volksblad* and *Rapport*. Analysis was limited to opinion pieces and commentaries, as these texts were considered to most clearly convey the respective newspapers' positions although, of course, news reports could also be critically read to establish assumptions informing their reporting on 'race'. The majority of these comment articles were written by editorial staff, although some were contributed by freelance writers or contributors. In addition to applying Durrheim et al.'s (2005) categories to the selected texts, texts were also read inductively to establish additional or alternative discursive strategies. What follows is a summary of the ways in which discursive categories of racism denial were found to apply to texts that responded to the racist video incident.

Splitting

Splitting, as displayed by the South African media in response to the 1999 Human Rights Commission's Report, refers to the strategy of distinguishing between different 'types' of racism, e.g., forms that are considered acceptable or innocuous, versus unacceptable, harmful racism.

Although some commentators reacted to the UFS incident as harmless student fun rather than as crude racism, the form such responses took would more accurately correspond to the strategy of 'de-racialising' (discussed below) than to a strategy that sought to construct the events as a harmless type of racism. Racism as such was unequivocally condemned by most Afrikaans newspapers, although some leeway was created by questioning whether the UFS video was indeed a case of racism or, instead, a misguided student prank.

(Dis)locating Racism

After racism has been spliced into acceptable and unacceptable forms, the latter is displaced so that it now falls beyond the speaker's sphere of responsibility. Tactics used as part of this strategy during the HRC investigation, according to Durrheim et al.'s study, included the use of the passive form for statements by which media commentators wanted to distance themselves, the media-as-mirror metaphor, according to which the media are seen as merely passively reflecting social reality rather than as contributing to its construction, and taking a historical view of racism in an attempt to relativise contemporary incidents of racism. To this may be added the individualisation of racism, rather than its viewing as a systemic problem to which media discourses might have contributed. Racism is, therefore, displaced to a point outside the community or group.

In his comment on the UFS video incident, the black academic and Director of the Afrikaans Culture and Language Association, Danny Titus, called this type of dislocation the 'yes, but-excuses' used by (white) Afrikaners (cited in Scholtz 2008a). The dislocation strategy is often also linked with those that relativise, trivialise or reverse racism, which will be discussed below.

Several examples of this type of 'yes, but' dislocation of racism were found in media commentary on the UFS incident. One came from a *Die Burger* correspondent, the historian Hermann Giliomee (2008). Giliomee pointed out that the incident confirmed stereotypes about Afrikaners and displaced the event's cause (which he does reject as 'unmentionably stupid and totally deplorable') from racism to other causes, such as initiation practices and poor integration management in university residences. For Giliomee, reaction to the video was an attempt to find a scapegoat for problems experienced by the ANC government. Giliomee thus deflects the public anger unleashed by the video's emergence, by explaining the outcry as a way for the ANC government to blame whites. Through this rhetorical shift, Giliomee equated Afrikaners' perceived victimisation (they are blamed for racism to hide the ANC government's sins) to the persecution of Jews in twentieth-century Europe:

> In a sober assessment, reaction to the Reitz incident also serves as a symbol of something else: a badly torn, leaderless nation uncertain about its future prospects. For ANC leaders the previous four months were a nightmare – the succession [to the presidency of the ANC – HW] question was handled extremely badly, and the Eskom [power supplier responsible for widespread blackouts – HW] debacle confirmed the worst white suspicions about transformation. For the first time there was a huge man-made disaster for which whites could not be blamed. Then the Reitz-atrocity came, like manna from heaven. Suddenly the whole of Afrikanerdom and the whole University of the Free State were guilty. This is how anti-Semitism in Europe worked in the interwar years.

The dislocation of racism in media commentaries also served a political goal. *Volksblad* provided column space for the Leader of the Opposition

Democratic Alliance in the Free State, Roy Jankielsohn, who held the ANC responsible for the 'deterioration of relations and trust between race groups in South Africa' (Jankielsohn 2008). He also made use of the strategies of relativising and reversal, by accusing the ANC of using its 'racial obsessions' to deflect attention from failures at municipal level and party infighting. By using a reversal of racism strategy, Jankielsohn (2008) laid the blame for the students' behaviour at the door of the government:

> The government cannot call for non-racialism while legislation [affirmative action and 'black economic empowerment' policies – HW] specifies racial categories. Furthermore discriminatory affirmative action has driven many young white South Africans overseas to seek employment. It embitters parents and families against the governing party and the state. Within such an environment, loyal citizens cannot but look at events in the country through racialised lenses. [...] While politicians play the race card at every corner, four students [...] cannot get all the blame for South Africa's race problems.

Jankielsohn (2008) also used the 'looking back at history' strategy identified by Durrheim et al. (2005) in their study of responses to the HRC enquiry as a way to displace racism to beyond the current sphere of influence by equating the ANC's affirmative action policies to apartheid: 'Just like the old National Party used the Communist (Red) Danger to achieve its apartheid goals, the ANC is now using 'White Danger' to achieve its transformation goals'.

Deracialisation

'Deracialisation' is the strategy of stripping potentially racist statements of racial meaning, by finding causes for the state of affairs elsewhere. According to Durrheim et al.'s study, the media used this strategy during the HRC investigation to explain that preference had been given to white crime victims on the basis of 'news value' rather than of racism. Press responses to the UFS video, in which the incident was described as student fun, can be placed in this category. These reactions focused on questions such as whether students really urinated on black workers' food or faked it, or considered the incident an error of judgement rather than a manifestation of racism. Theron's (2008) nostalgic romanticisation of the Reitz residence's macho culture and 'tradition spelt with a capital T' is an example. The enthusiastic support by 'guys from other cultures and racial groups' who participated in the residence's rugby games prove to this commentator that the incident was 'very distasteful' rather than downright racist.

Die Burger's decision to post a poll on its website, in which readers were asked to vote whether the video should be seen as racism or innocent student fun, provided further credibility to this discursive strategy.

Relativising, Trivialising and Reversing Racism

By relativising or trivialising racism, the moral and political sting is taken out of accusations of racism. Through these strategies a reversal of racism is also made possible – a process through which the perpetrator of racism is instead represented as its victim. Relativising is achieved by individualising events (e.g., in Van Staden's 2008 comment), by attributing racism to a small group of Afrikaners (e.g., in *Die Burger* 2008), by suggesting that black people can also be racists or 'bullies' (e.g., *Beeld* 2008) or even that misconduct at the ANC Youth League's conference 'cancelled out' human rights violations by the Reitz students (*Rapport* 2008a).

Reversal takes place by attributing racist attitudes to the victimisation of Afrikaners (i.e., 'black-on-white racism'), as *Die Burger's* (2008) editorial comment on the Reitz residence's closure did. The paper supported this closure as being an 'important symbolic gesture':

> But it is not going to be so easy to achieve the essential mindshift among the makers of the video and those defending them. The feeling exists among a significant group of Afrikaners that transformation programmes on campuses are aimed at assimilating minorities or destroying them.

In several comments in the Afrikaans press, the UFS incident was related to other recent cases of white racism, but also to intolerance in all racial groups. An example was *Volksblad's* (2008b, 2008d) juxtapositioning of other incidents of racist or ethnic violence with that of the UFS incident, as it called for greater introspection among South Africans of all racial groups. This juxtaposition clearly did not attempt to justify or excuse the UFS students' behaviour, yet it managed to relativise the racist video as a symptom of a disease from which all South Africans suffer:

> To merely blame whites for racism would be misleading and will not bring us any closer to a solution or healing. The same goes for blaming blacks or Coloureds. Over the centuries of human history stronger tribes dominated, displaced or murdered weaker ones. [...] The colonial era brought big offences [...] but black Africans simply have to look deeper than that in the search for what went wrong. Not all misery can be laid at the door of the colonial era – and therefore whites. In the scope of the whole of history, colonialism was a relatively short period.

A few months later, when widespread xenophobic attacks on foreign nationals rocked the country, *Volksblad* (2008d) referred back to the UFS incident to call for greater tolerance among South Africans. Without justifying the student video, it was relativised by explaining racism as endemic to South African society and as 'not only a white disease', even pointing out such occurences in the 'human and animal kingdom'.

While a broader perspective on an individual incident of racism may be instructive, choosing centuries of history as the context in which to explain the UFS students' behaviour seems to indicate a discursive strategy on *Volksblad*'s part to widen the focus so much that it diverted attention from the specific transgression, explaining its causes as biological or psychological rather than as being systemic or political; rooted in individual psychology rather than in the continuation of the country's highly unequal social and economic power.

Denying collective guilt or responsibility for the UFS incident occasionally crossed over into being a trivialisation of the event. A UFS professor, Hennie van Coller (2008), bemoaned the stain the incident left on his reputation as a university staff member, by sarcastically equating his lack of responsibility (for an incident reflecting student culture on the campus where he teaches) to that of a spectator at a sports event:

> My long face is therefore the result of all the collective guilt crippling me. As resident of Bloemfontein and the Free State and supporter of the Cheetahs [rugby team – HW] I am complicit to each of the seven

> hundred and thirteen tackles that they missed to date in their Super 14
> [rugby tournament – HW] games. As a UFS member of staff, I am
> being put in the dock for the Reitz video. So now I am also guilty of
> all the other mistakes ever made on campus: making out in cars, theft,
> damage to property, poor management and truancy.

Van Coller concludes that the outcry over the UFS incident is
misplaced, in light of the '2000 murdered and tortured farmers' about
whom 'no soul ever has something to say' *('vermoorde en gemartelde boere'
waaroor 'geen siel iets sê' het nie)*. Apart from Van Coller's inaccuracy
regarding the lack of reporting on crime,[7] shifting the focus to farm
murders serves the function of relativising and trivialising the UFS
video incident.

The simultaneous deployment of rejection, relativisation, dislocation and reversal of racism is probably best illustrated by the editorial
comment in the conservative Sunday paper *Rapport* (2008b), in which
the UFS incident was 'unconditionally' rejected, yet it was argued that
it would be unfair to 'taint the whole Afrikaans community with the
behaviour of a handful of students'. However, a reversal of racism took
place when it was argued that racism against whites was still obscured:

> What bubbled to the surface, amongst other things, is the pent-up
> anger among white South Africans that a big brouhaha occurs when-
> ever whites are handing out racism, but that racism is airbrushed out
> when blacks are the perpetrators and whites the victims.

This statement provoked an indignant reaction from Danny Titus, in
his column in *Volksblad* (2008):

> This (*Rapport*'s complaint about black-on-white racism) misses the
> point. Keep to the disgust for the time being, because such statements
> detract from the honesty with which racism is rejected.

Karriem (2008) also criticised *Rapport* for its editorial comment, and
Esterhuysen (2008) asked the pertinent question (which also informs
this chapter's focus): do Afrikaans newspapers not indirectly contribute to a climate in which racism can flourish? *Rapport*'s then
editor, Tim du Plessis (2008b), responded to Titus' attack by accusing
him of bad faith, insisting that he never meant to use anger in the
Afrikaans community to justify the video incident. Yet Du Plessis

goes further, seeing the video incident as a 'symptom of a systemic disease' affecting whites as well as blacks, by equating the UFS video to other incidents of racism, including a pop song that expressed anti-white sentiments.

Collective Acceptance of Racism and Self-Criticism

While studying the selected newspaper texts to establish whether Durrheim et al's (2005) categorisation of media discourses still held true for Afrikaans press reporting on race, an additional category was identified that emerged from reading newspaper opinion columns. This category describes the group of texts that offered critical introspection on the event from commentators who either accepted collective guilt or responsibility for the event, or who insisted on a broader investigation into racism in the country, without using such a call as a strategy for denying or relativising racism. This form of self-criticism included a critical perspective on the media, which sometimes meant pointing out strategies of denial, discussed above.

Although several commentators (e.g., Scholtz 2008b; *Volksblad* 2008e) were very critical of UFS's attempts to defuse the crisis and avoid repetition of the incident, such criticism was often directed at the university and student culture, rather than at Afrikaner culture and Afrikaner institutions (which would include the Afrikaans press). Several commentators also called on Afrikaners to use the incident as an opportunity for introspection and self-criticism.

A subtle and nuanced version of such self-criticism may be found in Etienne van Heerden's contributon to the debate (Van Heerden 2008). He pointed to the polysemic nature of video-as-text and the possibility for multiple interpretations. Instead of positioning the video simplis-tically within a cause-and-effect chain, Van Heerden saw the event as a text in itself, inviting a reading within the broader context of the country's power relations, demanding a critical attitude from both white and black South Africans:

> The text does much more than just tell a little old story. And it plays out its story within a context. This is why the film from Bloemfontein looks to me more like a trailer for something that has already occurred. A type of trailer for the past, which we had thought was already over. The video clip from Bloemfontein as a construction has symbolic

meaning that broadcasts far beyond the walls of the Republic of Reitz.
It reflects deep into the past and throws a shadow far into the future,
and draws in, by implication, all Afrikaners and all black people.

The clearest warnings that responsibility for the UFS incident should
not be individualised, came from Painter (2008) and Du Preez (2008).
Painter pointed to the rhetorical functions of the denial of racism and
the various strategies deployed. He called for a collective acceptance of
shame for the incident, through which the complicity of various institutions and persons might be acknowledged. Du Preez, in turn, connected
the incident to other recent cases of violent behaviour aimed at black
people by Afrikaner youths, notably the killing of a homeless person by
schoolboys (the so-called Waterkloof Four[8]) and the shooting of black
shack dwellers by 18-year-old Johann Nel, dubbed the 'Skierlik Shooter'
after the informal settlement where he shot four people, including a
baby and a child. Du Preez argued that the causes of all these incidents
should be sought in the Afrikaner community as such (within which Du
Preez positioned himself), rather than in the psyches of individuals:

> These thugs did not come from Mars. They all came from one com-
> munity. The white Afrikaner community. My community. It is only
> logical to accept that there are probably thousands of others who also
> think and feel like they do and will do the same when confronted by
> the same circumstances. This thought gives me cold shivers. These
> young people were not brainwashed by the Afrikaner politicians of the
> Total Onslaught years, or during military service. They were in pri-
> mary school when South Africa became a democracy in 1994. Nelson
> Mandela was the first black leader they came to know as they were
> growing up. No, these guys learnt from their fathers and mothers and
> uncles and aunts to despise and fear black people.

In addition to Afrikaner politicians, educators and community as well
as cultural leaders, who were blamed by Du Preez for not providing
an antidote to 'this poison they were fed with their mother's milk',
he pointed a finger at the Afrikaans media who were, he believed,
guilty of creating the victim mentality which underpins intolerance
and racism: 'All these people should carry part of the guilt for so many
Afrikaners today feeling deeply troubled, unloved and marginalised,
believing they are hated by the government and black people. And this
is why our Afrikaner youth are bringing such shame over us today'.

Similarly critical questions regarding collective guilt and responsibility were asked by other columnists, such as Du Toit (2008), who cited the sociologist Andries Bezuidenhout's critique of Afrikaans media coverage of violent crimes, which created the impression of an onslaught against whites. Such introspection also took the form of calls for the Afrikaner community to work towards reconciliation and to root out racist attitudes in their midst (Cornelissen 2008; Smith 2008a, 2008b), and a refusal to associate an Afrikaner cultural identity with racism (Van Staden 2008) or to accept feelings of marginalisation in the white community as a justification for racist behaviour (Taljaard 2008).

Some commentators (Esterhuyse 2008; Kombuis 2008) chose to view widespread condemnation of the UFS video by Afrikaans organisations, and the public debate that followed the incident, as a hopeful sign of progress on the road to tolerance. The majority of writers who commented on the UFS video in the Afrikaans press were white. This may be taken to suggest that language in itself was not a strong enough identity marker to cause 'coloured' Afrikaans speakers to associate with the identity crisis experienced by white Afrikaners. 'Race' therefore seems to remain a strong marker of identity and difference. The few black commentators who did venture into the debate, pointed at exactly these divisions between white and black speakers of the language, as symptomatic of the perpetuation of racism of the former against the latter (Karriem 2008; Van der Berg 2008). Some commentators were willing to accept that the incident did not point to widespread racism in the white Afrikaner community (Karriem 2008), but others (Mda 2008) saw the UFS video as just another item on an ongoing list of racist incidents reported in the media:

Oh, you can't call it racism, some say.

The rest of us drop our jaws and wonder: have we not heard this before? Yes, we did.

When a white farmer dragged a black worker behind his pickup-truck until he was dead.

When a white farmer shot a worker because he thought he was a baboon.

When a white farmer helped to feed his black worker to lions.

When a white teenager drove some kilometers from his community to an informal settlement and shot and killed four black people, among them a three-month-old baby.

Conclusion

In various respects discursive strategies deployed by the Afrikaans press in reaction to the racist initiation video shot by the four UFS students (and in their reaction to the outcry that followed) correspond with those strategies used roughly a decade earlier in the media's reaction to the Human Rights Commission's investigation into racism in the media. Several examples could be found where press reports attempted to dislocate racism from the students' group or from Afrikaners as a group, by blaming it on some other group or political party, or found causes in the perceived victimisation and marginalisation of Afrikaners. The media consistently, and with only a few exceptions, denied, suppressed or ignored its own complicity in, or contribution to, a climate in which racism could flourish. Perhaps the most important symbolic moment of the controversy was the release of a joint declaration by Afrikaans cultural organisations in which the video was condemned. Through this act a normative beacon was established to reconfirm racism as deplorable. The irony of this declaration and its support in the Afrikaans press was that it made it possible for racism to be seen as something found *outside* the moral universe of the majority of Afrikaners, rather than turning the gaze inward to search for racism's roots *within* the Afrikaner community.

Racism was associated with the Other instead of the Self, and was largely viewed in individual rather than collective terms. This individualisation of racism can be linked to the repositioning undergone by the Afrikaans media with the transition from apartheid to democracy, as described in this chapter's introduction. The Afrikaans press was able to deny any complicity in racist attitudes because it had been repositioned within a discourse of liberal individualism, where behaviour is explained not through structures and power relations, but through individual choice. By conveying the message that 'we are not like that', it became possible for Afrikaans commentators to engage in an Othering of racism, which in turn prepared the moral ground on which to reinscribe issues of importance to the Afrikaner community – feelings of marginalisation, victimisation, minority rights, etc. – onto the public agenda.

Despite the dominant discursive strategy of racism denial, some examples were found of Afrikaans commentators engaging in self-criticism and introspection, and refusing to individualise the racist attitudes manifested in the UFS student video. In these cases, the role that Afrikaner culture, the Afrikaans media and Afrikaans families played to create fertile soil for racism, was investigated. This uncompromising attitude to the UFS incident, albeit present in only the minority of responses, could be seen to be a positive development. An optimist might take this as the seeds being sown for a new attitude that is beginning to emerge in the Afrikaans press.

Notes

1 This chapter draws on the article Herman Wasserman, ' " 'We're not like that'": denial of racism in the Afrikaans Press', *Communicatio*, 36/1, pp. 20–36, copyright © Unisa Press reprinted by permission of (Taylor & Francis Ltd, http://www.tandfonline.com) on behalf of Unisa Press.
2 The argument in this section is developed more fully in Wasserman 2008, and Wasserman and Botma 2008.
3 All citations taken from Afrikaans sources have been translated by the author. For reasons of space, the original texts have not been reproduced here.
4 *Die Burger*'s editorial policy states the values it supports as a 'multiparty democracy', a 'free-market economy', 'personal freedom', 'press freedom' and 'full and equal status for Afrikaans' (http://www.media24.com/en/newspapers/dailies/die-burger.html).
5 This phrase, origninally coined by the Afrikaans novelist Jeanne Goosen (1990) as the title of a book that became something of a cult classic, was used by at least three columnists in the Afrikaans media (Kay Karriem, Desmond Painter and Rene-Jean van der Berg) in reaction to the racist video episode. The joint declaration by 11 organisations from the Afrikaans community also included the words: 'These students' values are not typical of the broad Afrikaner community. It simply isn't us' (*Rapport* 2008a).
6 In October 2009, the new Rector and Vice-Chancellor of UFS, Prof. Jonathan Jansen, announced that he would reverse the university's prior decision to expel the students accused of racism to allow them to continue their studies. A 'cleansing ceremony' was held in which the students publicly admitted guilt and asked for forgiveness. The legal case against them went ahead and they were found guilty of *crimen injuria* and fined R20, 000 or 12 months in jail – a sentence later reduced on appeal. Jansen explained that his decision was based on the acknowledgement that the racism of which the four students stood accused related to structural and cultural factors and would be best remedied by institutional reform rather than individual prosecution. While this decision led to an outcry by some commentators, led by the ANC (with particularly vicious comments against Jansen made by members of its Youth

League), that Jansen was undermining the rule of law and the fight against racism, the Afrikaans press by and large supported Jansen's decision. This signalled an about-turn by the Afrikaans press, who now seemed to agree with Jansen's acknowledgement of structural and cultural factors underpinning individual acts of racism while, little more than a year before, they had ostracised the accused students for individually being 'bad apples'. It is, however, likely that the Afrikaans media's new support for Jansen's viewpoint has more to do with the popular figure of Jansen as a dynamic, forward-thinking leader brave enough to take on the ruling ANC, than with a fundamental shift in orientation on the structural causes of racism. This favoured narrative of an individual taking on the ANC would also be in line with the mainstream press's more general normative view of acting as an informal opposition to the ruling party. For a discussion (in Afrikaans) of the Afrikaans media's response to Jansen's pardoning of the Reitz Four, see Wasserman and Jacobs (2009).

7   According to research by Media Tenor (personal communication, Wadim Schreiner, CEO), crime is still high on the agenda of all South African newspapers. Murder and other violent crime consistently top the list of crime reports. In the first six months of 2008, 52 news reports were devoted to farm murders, 70 per cent of these in papers with a traditionally black readership (e.g. *City Press* and *Sowetan*).

8   In 2011, when two of the 'Waterkloof Four' were released on bail, the Afrikaans press painted a sympathetic picture of the perpetrators as belonging to 'us', through a detailed exposition of their family life, their return to their homes and the suffering they endured in jail (for a critique, in Afrikaans, see Wasserman 2011).

References

Ads 24 (2000) 'Afrikaans market survey', Marketing brochure, Naspers.

African National Congress (ANC) (2008) 'The voice of the ANC must be heard', *ANC Today*, 18–24 Jan. <http://www.anc.org.za/ancdocs/anctoday/2008/at02.htm> (accessed July 2008).

Anderson, B. (1983) *Imagined Communities: Reflections on the Origin and Spread of Nationalism*, London: Verso.

Beeld (2008) 'Reitz-sluiting', 30 May <http://152.111.1.251/argief/berigte/beeld/2008/05/30/B1/20/pkreitsubart.htm> (accessed Aug. 2008).

Berger, G. (2009) 'For media, SABC is the frontline for preventing political creep', *Mail & Guardian Online* <http://www.mg.co.za/article/2009-05-14-for-media-sabc-is-the-frontline-preventing-politicalcreep> (accessed May 2009).

Bond, P. (2000) *Elite Transition: From Apartheid to Neoliberalism in South Africa*, Durban and London: University of KwaZulu-Natal Press and Pluto Press.

Botma, G. (2006) 'Sinergie as politiek-ekonomiese strategie by *Die Burger*, 2004–2005', *Ecquid Novi*, 27/2, pp. 137–58.

Bourdieu, P. (1979) *Distinction: A Social Critique of the Judgement of Taste,* London: Routledge & Kegan Paul.

Broadcasting Complaints Commission of South Africa (BCCSA) (2008) 'Code of the BCCSA' <http://www.bccsa.co.za> (accessed July 2008).

Chotia, F., and Jacobs, S. (2002) 'Remaking the presidency', in S. Jacobs and R. Calland (eds), *Thabo Mbeki's World*, pp. 145–61, Scottsville: University of Natal Press.

Claassen, G. (2000) 'Breaking the mold of political subservience: *Vrye Weekblad* and the Afrikaans alternative press', in L. Switzer and M. Adhikari (eds), *South Africa's Resistance Press: Alternative Voices in the Last Generation under Apartheid*, pp. 404–57, Athens, OH: Ohio University Center for International Studies.

Cornelissen, A. (2008) 'Wat doen ons as ouers om nog Reitz-voorvalle te keer?', *Beeld*, 8 March <http://152.111.1.251/argief/berigte/beeld/2008/03/08/B1/8/doenandries.html> (accessed Aug. 2008).

Dawie (2000) 'Uit my politieke pen', *Die Burger*, 26 Feb. <http://152.111.1.251/argief/berigte/dieburger/2000/02/26/14/2.html> (accessed Aug. 2008).

Die Burger (2008) 'Reitz-sluiting', 29 May <http://152.111.1.251/argief/berigte/dieburger/2008/05/29/SK/20/2sub29Mei08.html> (accessed Aug. 2008).

Du Plessis, T. (2008a) 'Die brugbouers het ophou bou', *Rapport*, 17 March <http://152.111.1.251/argief/berigte/rapport/2008/03/17/RH/20/raak-punt16-3.html> (accessed Aug. 2008).

—— (2008b) 'Hoe gemaak na die Reitz-skande? Kollektiewe skuld sal nie deug nie', *Rapport*, 12 March <http://152.111.1.251/argief/berigte/rapport/2008/03/12/RH/16/raakpunt9-3.html> (accessed Aug. 2008).

Du Preez, M. (2008) 'Sê maar dit was jou ma?', *Die Burger*, 8 March <http://152.111.1.251/argief/berigte/dieburger/2008/03/08/BY/4/MaxReitz-500.html> (accessed Aug. 2008).

Durrheim, K., Quayle, M., Whitehead, K., and Kriel, A. (2005) 'Denying Racism: Discursive Strategies Used by the South African Media', *Critical Arts*, 19/1–2, pp. 167–86.

Du Toit, P. (2008) 'Reitz-video "gaan lei tot stereotipering, spanning" ', *Volksblad*, 3 March <http://152.111.1.251/argief/berigte/volksblad/2008/03/03/VB/11/pdtreitz4_1547.html> (accessed Aug. 2008).

Esterhuysen, W. (2008) 'Die olifant in ons sitkamer', *Rapport*, 12 March <http://152.111.1.251/argief/berigte/rapport/2008/03/12/RH/17/RHNews014-001-StoryA.html> (accessed Aug. 2008).

Featherstone, M. (2007) *Consumer Culture and Postmodernism*, London: Sage.

Giliomee, H. (2003) *The Afrikaners: Biography of a People*, Cape Town: Tafelberg.

—— (2008) 'Die uitdaging vir beter menseverhoudinge', *Die Burger*, 20 Mar. <http://152.111.1.251/argief/berigte/dieburger/2008/03/20/SK/21/hab20-Mrt.html> (accessed Aug. 2008).

Goosen, J. (1990) *Ons is nie almal so nie*, Pretoria: Haum-Literêr.

Hall, S. ([1973] 1980) 'Encoding/decoding', in Centre for Contemporary Cultural Studies (ed.), *Culture, Media, Language: Working Papers in Cultural Studies, 1972–1979*, pp. 128–38, London: Hutchinson.

Jankielsohn, R. (2008) 'Partye moet nou aandag skenk aan toenemende polarisasie', *Volksblad*, 20 March <http://152.111.1.251/argief/berigte/volksblad/2008/03/25/VB/11/jankielart.html> (accessed Aug. 2008).

Jansen, J. D. (2009) *Knowledge in the Blood: Confronting Race and the Apartheid Past*, Cape Town: University of Cape Town Press.

Johnson, K., and Jacobs, S. (2004) 'Democratization and the rhetoric of rights: contradictions and debate in post-apartheid South Africa', in F. Nyamnjoh and H. Englund (eds), *Rights and Politics of Recognition in Africa*, pp. 84–102, London: Zed Books.

Jordaan, W. (2008a) 'Die boosheid van die groep', *Rapport*, 18 April <http://152.111.1.251/argief/berigte/rapport/2008/04/18/RU/2/wilhelom.html> (accessed Aug. 2008).

Karriem, K. (2008) 'Waarheid lê in dade, nie woorde nie', *Die Burger*, 4 March <http://152.111.1.251/argief/berigte/dieburger/2008/03/04/SK/12/hab4-MRT.html> (accessed Aug. 2008).

Kombuis, K. (2008) 'Pas op, die duif in die Afrikaner is wakker!', *Rapport*, 7 March <http://152.111.1.251/argief/berigte/rapport/2008/03/07/RU/8/kombuis.html> (accessed Aug. 2008).

Kriel, M. (2006) 'Fools, philologists and philosophers: Afrikaans and the politics of cultural nationalism', *Politikon*, 33/1, pp. 45–70.

Louw, P. E. (2004) 'Anglicising post-apartheid South Africa', *Journal of Multilingual and Multicultural Development*, 25/4, pp. 318–32.

Mail & Guardian (2008) 'Racist video surfaces at the University of the Free State', 26 Feb. <http://www.mg.co.za/article/2008-02-26-racist-video-surfaces-at-the-university-of-free-state> (accessed Aug. 2009).

Mda, L. (2008) 'Van erg na veel erger met rassisme', *Rapport*, 3 March <http://152.111.1.251/argief/berigte/rapport/2008/03/03/RH/16/stoep.html> (accessed Aug. 2008).

Media 24 (n.d.) 'Why the Afrikaans market?' Marketing submission in the possession of the author.

Nyamnjoh, F. B. (2005) *Africa's Media: Democracy and the Politics of Belonging*, Pretoria, London and New York: Unisa Press and Zed Books.

Painter, D. (2008) 'Ons behoort ons te skaam', *Die Burger*, 8 March <http://152.111.1.251/argief/berigte/dieburger/2008/03/08/BJ/5/desmond-painter-402-403-503.html> (accessed Aug. 2008).

Rapport (2008a) 'Ons is nie so nie', 3 March. <http://152.111.1.251/argief/berigte/rapport/2008/03/03/RH/1/reitzlead.html> (accessed Aug. 2008).

—— (2008b) 'Dade het gevolge', 17 March <http://152.111.1.251/argief/berigte/rapport/2008/03/17/RH/20/eenarts.html> (accessed Aug. 2008).

—— (2008c) 'Die Reitz-vier', 18 March <http://152.111.1.251/argief/berigte/rapport/2008/03/18/RH/1/reitzhoofart.html> (accessed Aug. 2008).

—— (2008d) 'Pollux', 14 April <http://152.111.1.251/argief/berigte/rapport/2008/04/14/RH/21/pollux13-04.html> (accessed Aug. 2008).

Rossouw, A. (2001) 'Hoe gaan Afrikaans en ander minderheidstale in Suid-Afrika oorleef?' Lesing gelewer by Klein Karoo Nasionale Kunstefees, Oudtshoorn <http://www.oulitnet.co.za/seminaar/06arrie.asp> (accessed Aug. 2008).

Schlemmer, L. (2001) 'Taaloorlewing en die glybaan van goeie gesindhede: n meningsopname en ontleding', in H. Giliomee and L. Schlemmer (eds), *Kruispad: Die toekoms van Afrikaans as openbare taal*, pp. 94–114, Kaapstad: Tafelberg.

Scholtz, H. (2008a) 'Staak "ja-maar-verskonings": Danny Titus', *Volksblad*, 11 July <http://152.111.1.251/argief/berigte/volksblad/2008/07/11/VB/8/streitz.html> (accessed Aug. 2008).

—— (2008b) 'Die wyse magte sal wéér nie n Reitz kan keer', *Die Burger*, 21 June <http://152.111.1.251/argief/berigte/dieburger/2008/06/21/BJ/3/BJNews005-StoryA-486-487.html> (accessed Aug. 2008).

—— (2008c) 'Die struggle vir apartheid in die Kovsie-republiek', *Beeld*, 3 March <http://152.111.1.251/argief/berigte/beeld/2008/03/03/BJ/6/beeld01kovsie.html> (accessed Aug. 2008).

Smith, C. (2008a) 'Regte Afrikaners staan op' <http://152.111.1.251/argief/berigte/volksblad/2008/03/14/VB/8/gutenssss.html> (accessed Aug. 2008).

—— (2008b) 'SA is nie ál wat oor ras versmoor', *Beeld*, 18 March <http://152.111.1.251/argief/berigte/beeld/2008/03/18/B1/10/dlSmith.html> (accessed Aug. 2008).

South African National Editors' Forum (SANEF) (2007) 'Bid for Johncom and other concerns', <http://www.sanef.org.za/press_statements/675906.htm> (accessed July 2008).

—— (2008a) 'Concern at ANC President's attack on print media' <http://www.sanef.org.za/press_statements/815940.htm> (accessed July 2008).

—— (2008b) 'Press Code of Professional Practice' <http://www.sanef.org.za/ethics_codes/press_ombudsman> (accessed July 2008).

Taljaard, R. (2008) 'Vermy nuwe strike: was saam wonde van die verlede', *Volksblad*, 7 March <http://152.111.1.251/argief/berigte/volksblad/2008/03/07/VB/8/ranetee.html> (accessed Aug. 2008).

Theron, B. (2008) 'n Laaste vaarwel aan die "hart en siel" van die UV' <http://152.111.1.251/argief/berigte/volksblad/2008/08/05/VB/7/artikelblouwillem.html> (accessed Aug. 2008).

Titus, D. (2008) 'Dié gesprek bly lank. Burgerlike samelewing sal nou moet help', *Volksblad*, 8 March <http://152.111.1.251/argief/berigte/volksblad/2008/03/08/VB/8/tittusss.html> (accessed Aug. 2008).

Tomaselli, K. G. (2000a) 'Faulting "faultlines": racism in the South African media', *Ecquid Novi,* 21/2, pp. 7–27.

—— (2000b) 'South African media, 1994–1997: globalizing via political economy', in J. Curran and M. Park (eds), *De-Westernizing Media Studies*, pp. 279–92, London: Routledge.

—— Tomaselli, R., and Muller, J. (1989) 'The construction of news in the South African media', in K. G. Tomaselli, R. Tomaselli and J. Muller (eds), *The Press in South Africa*, pp. 22–38, London: James Currey.

UV Digest (2008) 'Die Universiteit van die Vrystaat kondig die sluiting van die Reitz-kamerwoningsendievestigingvanninstituutvirdiversiteitaan' <http://www.ufs.ac.za/faculties/content.php?id=5812&FCode=Z4&NewsID=11> (accessed Aug. 2008).

Van Coller, H. P. (2008) 'Kruppel van al die skuld', *Volksblad*, 2 April <http://152.111.1.251/argief/berigte/volksblad/2008/04/03/VB/6/gm2.html> (accessed Aug. 2008).

Van der Berg, R.-J. (2008) 'Hoe ek op 25 n kleurling geword het', *Rapport*, 21 March <http://152.111.1.251/argief/berigte/rapport/2008/03/21/RU/6/rjintegrasie.html> (accessed Aug. 2008).

Van Heerden, E. (2008) 'Die rituele Reitz', *Die Burger*, 8 March <http://152.111.1.251/argief/berigte/dieburger/2008/03/08/BJ/7/Bysaaketienne-366.html> (accessed Aug. 2008).

Van Rooyen, M. (2008) 'Reitz-video: 4 só aangekla', *Beeld*, 6 Aug. <http://152.111.1.251/argief/berigte/beeld/2008/08/07/B1/2/MIDATUM_1756.html> (accessed Aug. 2008).

Van Staden, C. (2008) 'Brief aan die video-makers', *Volksblad*, 7 March <http://152.111.1.251/argief/berigte/volksblad/2008/03/07/VB/8/cvsmore.html> (accessed Aug. 2008).

Volksblad (2008a) 'UV, DA, Volksblad kop in een mus? – VF+', 20 March <http://152.111.1.251/argief/berigte/volksblad/2008/03/26/VB/2/cdvryheidsfront.html> (accessed Aug. 2008).

—— (2008b) 'Keditlhotse en Anna: wat gaan aan, SA?' 11 March <http://152.111.1.251/argief/berigte/volksblad/2008/03/11/VB/6/art10.html> (accessed Aug. 2008).

—— (2008c) 'VF Plus se leuenagtige ras-verklaring', 26 March <http://152.111.1.251/argief/berigte/volksblad/2008/03/26/VB/8/art24a.html> (accessed Aug. 2008).

—— (2008d) 'Doodsboodskap: wat sou u sê?', 24 May <http://152.111.1.251/argief/berigte/volksblad/2008/05/24/VB/8/artt23.html> (accessed Aug. 2008).

—— (2008e) 'Reitz: Billikheid jeens inwoners ontbreek', 30 May <http://152.111.1.251/argief/berigte/volksblad/2008/05/30/VB/12/artt29.html> (accessed 7 Aug. 2008).

Wasserman, H. (2005) 'Ready to adapt', *The Media*, June, pp. 21–3.

—— (2006) 'Globalized values and post-colonial responses: South African perspectives on normative media ethics', *International Communication Gazette*, 68/1, pp. 71–91.

—— (2009) 'Learning a new language: culture, ideology and economics in Afrikaans media after apartheid', *International Journal of Cultural Studies*, 12/1, pp. 59–78.

—— (2011) 'Onthou: dit was moord' (Remember: it was murder), *Beeld*, 19 Dec. <http://www.beeld.com/In-Diepte/Nuus/Onthou-Dit-was-moord-20111219> (accessed April 2012).

—— ed. (2012) *Press Freedom in Africa: Comparative Perspectives*, London: Routledge.

—— (2012) 'The state of the media', in J. Jansen, U. Pillay and F. Nyamnjoh (eds), *State of the Nation 2011*, Cape Town: HSRC Press.

Wasserman, H. and Beer, A. S. de (2005) 'A fragile affair: the relationship between the mainstream media and government in post-apartheid South Africa', *Journal of Mass Media Ethics*, 20/2–3, pp. 192–208.

Wasserman, H. and Botma, G. (2008) 'Having it both ways: balancing market and political interests at a South African daily newspaper', *Critical Arts*, 22/1, pp. 1–20.

Wasserman, H. and Jacobs, S. (2009) 'Die evangelie van strukturele faktore', *Litnet* <http://www.litnet.co.za/cgibin/giga.cgi?cmd=cause_dir_news_item&cause_id=1270&news_id=77087&cat_id=165>

4

'WHERE THE STREETS HAVE NO NAMES …': MEDIATING NAME CHANGE IN POST-APARTHEID SOUTH AFRICA

Kristin Skare Orgeret

At the beginning of December 2011, 240 'Sutcliffe Drive' stickers, named after the eThekwini (Durban) municipality manager, Mike Sutcliffe, were put up on central Durban street signs by artists who wanted people 'both to laugh and to think about what makes a good leader'.[1] At about the same time, the South African Supreme Court of Appeal ordered the municipality to replace nine of the new street names with the old ones because of their failure to conduct proper consultations in line with legislation. There are few reasons to believe this is the end of Durban's street renaming conflict.

In 2008, Sutcliffe, referred to as 'the dictator' by his enemies, played a central role as 99 name changes were adopted and implemented by the ANC-led eThekwini Council between July and September alone, and another 142 name changes were proposed in the following months. The renaming process in South Africa's third largest city, Durban, received a lot of attention and many people with strong opinions were brought into the public sphere. It resulted in the biggest audience response ever experienced in *The Mercury*.[2]

The Mercury (formerly *Natal Mercury*) was inaugurated in 1852 as Durban's English morning newspaper. It belongs to the Independent Newspaper group. Independent Media, owned by Irish Tycoon Tony

Figure 4.1. Sutcliffe DR, Durban; photo by Kristin Skare Orgeret

O'Reilly first acquired a stake in local South African newspapers in 1995 when it took control of Argus Newspapers and later renamed it Independent Newspapers. Independent Newspapers publishes 14 daily and weekly newspapers in South Africa's three major metropolitan areas. Although isiZulu is the mother tongue of most inhabitants of KwaZulu Natal (KZN), English is most South Africans' second language and is often considered the country's *lingua franca*. Many discussions of local and national importance thus take place in the English media.

This chapter aims to investigate how *The Mercury* covered the renaming action. Through a qualitative discourse analysis of newspaper articles covering the name changes between February 2007 and February 2009 (42 altogether) and some additional articles from December 2011,[3] the chapter seeks to study the renaming process and its coverage from different perspectives. In addition to the news articles, opinion pieces or letters to the editor (51 altogether) are also included in the analysis. *The Mercury* was selected for this in-depth study both due to its accessibility and because it covered the process quite substantially in terms of space. The qualitative content analysis is combined with interviews with three journalists, all white men, who were most central in covering the renaming process at *The Mercury*. These interviews were carried out in Durban in October 2008.

Questions of identity politics, collective memory, the rewriting of history and post-colonial discourses in the era of democracy are issues dealt with in this chapter. It draws inspiration from some of the discussions linked to the concept of 'intersectionality', coined by Kimberlé Crenshaw (1991). Intersectionality may be defined as a theory for the analysis of how social and cultural categories intertwine (Knudsen 2006). The framework suggests that power structures based on gender, race, ethnicity, political orientation, class and the like do not function independently of one another but must be understood together. Such a multifaceted approach seems fruitful when one sets out to study media coverage of the renaming process and the audience perceptions that guided the coverage. The following exploratory analysis will hopefully allow for a more complex understanding of which groups and themes gain attention and representation in the media.

Discussions in this chapter feed into the theme of how post-apartheid transformation may open up ways of belonging to the new nation and the creation of a new, national 'We'. Its findings have a direct bearing on debates about the formation of contemporary identities at a range of different levels.

New Names Nationwide

When erecting the first batch of new street name signs in Durban in July 2008, the municipality kept the old name signs with a thin strip of red tape over them, alongside the new ones, to allow people to adjust. This resulted in powerful visual manifestations of the transformation process.

Many of the new names were rapidly painted black or pulled down as an expression of local residents' dissatisfaction with the renaming process. Naming may tell us a lot about the socio-political biography of a nation. The previous apartheid system in South Africa had been based on spatialised planning:

> The apartheid regime prided itself on its fine roads built with cheap, black labour. These roads were symbols of power. Road signs denoted white towns while black squatter camps were hidden from view, their names excluded from highway exits. (Fox 2000: 449)

Figure 4.2. New street name signs in Durban (July 2008);
photo by Kristin Skare Orgeret

At the end of apartheid no major town or city had an African name,
except in the so-called Bantustans:

> the naming of places, cities, mountains, rivers and other natural phe-
> nomena celebrates the culture and history of the Afrikaner, to the exclu-
> sion of other peoples. [...] the English also have the privilege of having
> their history and culture inscribed on the landscape, with names which
> commemorate their imperial past. Durban, for instance, is named
> after Sir Benjamin D'Urban (1777–1849), Governor of the Cape from
> 1834–38. (Maake 1996: 150)

The break with the apartheid past in 1994 began a process of redefining
national holidays, old memory sites and eventually the renaming of
streets and buildings. Several towns and cities carrying the names of
Afrikaner personalities were renamed during this period and many
areas and cities reverted to their original names from before the apart-
heid/colonial era. For instance, Pietersburg, Pretoria and Warmbaths
got back their original names: Polokwane, Tshwane and Bela-Bela,
respectively. Throughout history renaming has been a central element
of transformation processes worldwide. In South Africa, renaming has
been on the agenda since the very first day of democracy, but three

elements made the changes of Durban street names special. First, the process was carried out in a highly imperative manner. Second, it was executed rapidly, and third, the aim was not to revert to original names. Street naming in the city happened in tandem with urbanisation and thus the creation of the city itself, and many of the names dated back to the 1850s. A central argument for name changing is the need to get rid of colonial geography. A Road Name Change Act was initiated by the South African Government in 2007 in order to rename streets 'which have links to pre-1994 colonialism', as many of the Durban streets had. This leads us directly to the first dimension of the renaming: the post-colonial perspective.

'The Place from which we Call': A Post-Colonial Approach to the Renaming

Several scholars writing in the post-colonial tradition have raised the issue of 'space' and 'place' and their intersections with identity. For example, Carter et al. (1993: xii) argue that:

> It is not spaces which ground identifications but places. How then does space become place? By being named: as the flows of power and negotiation of social relations are rendered in the concrete form of architecture; and also of course, by embodying the symbolic and imaginary investment of a population. Place is space to which meaning has been ascribed.

The significance of names is further developed through the writing of Carrol Clarkson (2008). Clarkson stresses how names refer not to the place named, but *to the namer* who gave the object's name, and to this process of naming. In the context of colonialism, Clarkson reminds us that *the namer* is always a white, Christian European, who assigns names to himself and all others:

> Being in the position of the one who chooses the names is to be in the position of power; but since names speak of the relation between namer and named, the name for the other is also a way of positioning the self. [...] We use names to refer to something, or to call someone at a place in language, but equally, the names we use give an indication of the place from which we call. That name-place is at a complex intersection of social, cultural, and historical routes. (Clarkson 2008: 135)

There are several such interesting name-place aspects to be found in some of the old Durban names in relation to the colonial legacy and the *namers*. Some of the old Durban street names were clear expressions of the sense of displacement and longing for where early immigrants came from. Argyle Road, which was renamed Sandile Tusi, had for instance been named after immigrants from Argyleshire, Scotland.[4] Such names may remind us that the early immigrants to South Africa also had personal histories they had brought with them. As Nuttall and Coetzee (1998: 5) have argued, 'the task of memory is to reconstitute turbulence and fragmentation, including those painful reminders of what we were and what we are'.

The complexity of changing names that carry traces of the early immigrants feeds into what Melissa Steyn (2003: 92) calls one of the 'hotly contested themes' in relation to post-apartheid South Africa, which is 'whether white South Africans can legitimately call them-selves African'. This post-colonial perspective is frequently reflected in the articles analysed: 'In debating the matter, ANC councillor Visvin Reddy lambasted opposition councillors for trivialising the renaming process, saying the people had languished under colonial street names for too long'.[5] The critical approach to colonial memories did not strictly follow racial lines in *The Mercury* readers' letters:

> Although I agree with some objections to the road renaming propos-als, there are two areas that perhaps objectors should think about. The first is the nostalgia for colonial names. English-speakers may forget, or maybe never learnt, just how violent and punitive colonial rule was. [...] Just because we are white and of British descent, is this what we want to claim as our heritage?[6]

An interesting case, which also shows how the name-place is at a complex intersection of social, cultural and historical routes, is the name of the large township outside Durban, KwaMashu. KwaMashu was Durban's first black township. It was established in 1959 under the apartheid regime's Group Areas Act (Act No. 41 of 1950) which assigned racial groups to different areas and resulted in forced remov-als. KwaMashu, meaning 'the place of Marshall', was named after the sugar pioneer, Marshall Campbell (Bunn 1996: 40). Campbell was only 2 years old when he arrived in Durban with his parents from Glasgow, Scotland, in 1850. According to Stayt (1971), the Zulus held Sir Marshall 'in very high regard' as 'friend and protector'. Interestingly and exceptionally, *the namers* here were Zulu people and KwaMashu is hence an expression of both a colonial heritage and a distinctive isiZulu name. Such complexity might be seen in the light of Homi Bhabha's point that the 'colonial presence is always ambivalent, split between its appearance as original and authoritative and its articulation as repetition and difference' (Bhabha 1994: 110). KwaMashu was put up for consideration for a new name in 2008. Here it seemed that the eThekweni political leadership focused more on the colonial heritage aspect of the name than on who Marshall actually had been as a person, or the fact that the namers of Kwa Mashu were Zulu people.

An Apartheid Struggle Approach to the Renaming

Many South Africans of all backgrounds seemed happy to get rid of names that honoured the old colonial and, especially, apartheid leaders. This was also clearly reflected in *The Mercury*, as voices which argued that the apartheid leaders' names could be changed, while other names should be kept unchanged, were often heard in interviews or letters to the editor.

A rather special case that attracted a lot of attention in *The Mercury* was the renaming of Kingsway Road, Amanzimtoti, to Andrew Zondo Road. An anti-apartheid activist and MK[7] member, Zondo was judged and later hanged for the bombing of the Sanlam Centre Shopping Centre in Amanzimtoti on 23 December 1985. Zondo, who was then 19 years old, detonated a bomb in a rubbish bin in an act of anti-apartheid resistance. Two women and three children were killed in the blast and more than 40 injured. The Zondo-renaming provoked some of the angriest reactions in the material analysed:

> Andrew Zondo (the Amanzimtoti bomber) used his skills to shame-lessly kill innocent civilians queuing up to see Father Christmas. He was armed – his targets were unarmed women and children; a really brave hero.[8]

The Mercury mainly covered the case from the viewpoints of those who had suffered the consequences of the attack and interviewed family members who had lost their dear ones. These victims, all women, were described in emotional terms such as 'tearful when she relived the horrible ordeal' or 'infuriated at the name change'.[9]

The pain felt by victims or families who still lived in the area when a street was named after the person responsible for this crime seemed obvious to many Durbanites. A few sources were quoted in *The Mercury* as defending the name choice, arguing that Zondo was fighting for democracy. For instance, eThekwini Mayor Obed Mlaba said it was strange that people praised Mandela for his role in the struggle, but were quick to condemn Zondo's role:

> There is a distortion, which I find completely nauseating. For us, any liberator will always be a hero. Any person who participated in liberating us from apartheid is a hero, even more so if they were incarcerated for their activities.[10]

In general, however, through their selection of angles and sources, *The Mercury* did little to put the story into a broader context, Moreover, the newspaper primarily portrayed Zondo as a criminal and a terrorist, referring to him as 'the Amanzimtoti bomber',[11] 'the shopping centre bomber'[12] or, simply, 'bomber Andrew Zondo'.[13] In the articles analysed there were no attempts to present the violent actions in the light of the then ongoing struggle against apartheid. If we turn to the Truth and Reconciliation Commission (TRC) report (1998: 20), we see that Zondo was reacting in anger to the Maseru Raid by the South African Defence Force (SADF) four days earlier in which nine people were killed. This important contextual information, or the fact that Andrew Zondo apologised to the families of those who died before his death sentence was passed (TRC 1998: 21), was totally ignored in the newspaper coverage analysed. *The Mercury*, however, did report that Zondo's father, Pastor Aiken Zondo, was also opposed to the renaming of Kingsway Road after his son, saying it would 'open old wounds'.[14]

It was also proposed that Lovu Primary School in Amanzimtoti be renamed after Zondo to Andrew Zondo Primary. *The Mercury* reported on how a local production company 'has been enlightening the school community and getting their opinion on the proposed name change through a play about Zondo called 'The Human Being'.[15] In complete contrast to *The Mercury*'s label 'the bomber', the term 'human being' obviously offered Zondo a different identity. The performance was shown to the parents of the school and was succeeded by a question and answer session. After the show, 97 per cent of the crowd favoured the school using Zondo's name in future.[16] This may be taken as an example of the need to prepare people for name changes and to explain the rationale behind them. In what was described as a reconciliation gesture, Lovu School officials proposed that the on-site crèche be named after Willem van Wyk, a two-year-old boy killed in the bombing. Through this process, the people exposed to the new names obtained a broader understanding of their own complex history and felt a greater degree of ownership over the names.

Several of the articles analysed show clear signs of the apartheid struggle.

Linking the colonial approach and the apartheid struggle approach to the racial dimension makes it crystal clear which group of people suffered the most during colonial times, as well as during the apartheid regime. However, what is ignored in many of *The Mercury* articles is that the apartheid struggle division lines were not drawn completely on the basis of racial groups. It is well-known that some white South Africans fought fiercely against the apartheid regime, while some black South Africans would argue that, for instance, renaming Kingsway Road after Zondo would not encourage an increase in understanding and dialogue between different sections of society.[17]

A Racial Approach to the Renaming

Both colonial and anti-apartheid approaches often fed into more racial approaches in *The Mercury*. Another of Steyn's (2003: 92) themes when analysing the whiteness of post-apartheid South Africa is 'whether [whites] owe black South Africans financial restitution'. These are issues seldom expressed openly in the South African media, but the renaming debate brought the discussion to the forefront in *The Mercury* on a number of occasions.[18] As Steyn (2003: 92) reminds us, these issues are hotly contested precisely because they affect the boundaries between two hemispheres: the retention of current alignments and identification, the separation of interests, and the differentiation of realities. Differentiated interests were also seen when many of *The Mercury*'s readers, and according to the journalists interviewed, especially those of Indian origin, were furious about the decision to rename Point Road after Mahatma Gandhi. The Point area is often referred to as Durban's red-light district, notorious for prostitution and drugs, and many opposed the name change because of the negative connotations of the area. Mahatma Gandhi Road was one of the name changes that the

Supreme Court of Appeal finally rejected in December 2011. While such angry Indian voices were not included in the articles analysed, the weekly newspaper *The Post* frequently referred to Gandhi's granddaughter, Ela Gandhi, who lives in Durban, as a source.

The journalists explained that quite a number of the letters to the editor that were not published had racist inclinations or included elements of hate speech (interviews, 2008). One journalist said he felt that race played an important role in the resistance to name changes and that this was never properly discussed in *The Mercury*:

> The fact that a part of the audience just doesn't want black names is perhaps difficult to address when your intended reader is a white person. We could have voiced more people who felt relieved and empowered by the changes. (journalist, *The Mercury*, 2008)

In South Africa it has been, and to a large degree still is, a challenge to break through racially structured markets. Earlier research has shown that, although there was a tendency amongst journalists to strive for non-racial approaches, the markets hindered them (see Orgeret 2006). Some argued this was natural, as it will take a long time before South Africa becomes 'colour-blind', whereas others argued that this segmentation was the ghost of apartheid.

A Party-Political Approach to the Renaming

The conceptual reclaiming of land that happened through the renaming of Durban's streets was highly politicised. Quite early in the process, the ANC was given a major platform in *The Mercury*: 'ANC pushes for city renaming'.[19] According to a journalist who followed the process, the new names originated from ANC Head Office in Johannesburg (interview, 2008). One article stated that one man alone had recommended more than 100 of the 242 name changes.[20] A majority of the new Durban street names honoured ANC heroes,[21] reflecting the political dispositions in the eThekwini Municipality where 125 of 200 seats were taken by ANC.

While ANC personalities' names were promoted, proposed street names referring to Inkatha Freedom Party (IFP) personalities were removed in the renaming process. Before 1994, Zulu culture had no national voice, nor was it reflected in national memory.[22] After apartheid's end, a highway in Umlazi was named after the IFP leader, Mangosuthu Buthelezi, and KwaMashu's stadium was renamed after the Zulu Princess Magogo, a renowned artist and Buthelezi's mother. The exclusion of IFP names must be seen in relation to historical difficulties between the ANC and the IFP, and the fact that more than 20,000 died in the internecine violence between the two parties in the late 1980s and early 1990s. On 25 April 2007, *The Mercury* reported how IFP leader, Thembi Nzuza, called all citizens to join an IFP-led march, protesting against the renaming:

> 'The ANC believes Durban is an ANC-run show,' she said, adding that her party was vexed by proposals to rename KwaMashu's Princess Magogo Stadium in honour of the late ANC MP Dumisani Makhaye.[23]

In April and May, 2007, there were violent demonstrations as people barricaded the Mangosuthu Highway with dustbins and burning tyres against the removal of Mangosuthu Buthelezi's name.[24] The most critical voices saw the changing of the IFP-related names as pertinent examples of what they would call the 'bulldozing tendencies' of the ANC.[25] Both Democratic Alliance (DA) and IFP representatives were given considerable space in *The Mercury*'s coverage of the process. Both political parties accused the municipality of not carrying out the process in a fair and transparent manner and of abusing its majority.[26]

> The arrogance and insensitivity of the ANC, coupled with the fact that 12 000 objections and submissions were simply ignored, exposes for all to see that the process was nothing more than skewed ANC triumphalism.[27]

Such statements can be seen to echo concerns about tendencies within the ANC towards increasing arrogance and intolerance of opposition: exclusivist tendencies that a growing number of scholars link to the specific history of the South African liberation movement (see Gumede 2008; Orgeret 2008).

The selection of sources in the articles analysed on name changes in *The Mercury* followed a rather static model. Often DA representatives would be concerned about the 'anti-white aspect' and the IFP would raise the 'anti-IFP' aspect. Sometimes an ANC spokesperson would be included to represent the official view on name changing. Hence, the categories these sources represented were often presented as static and mutually exclusive and there seemed to be very little room for sources whose identities intertwined in the analysed newspaper articles.

Honouring Chicks: A Gender Approach to the Renaming

Naming geographical areas can be seen as a strategy for embodying knowledge and experience. The negotiation of space under apartheid was defined solely by patriarchal hegemonic power. In Clarkson's words, the *namer* is always the white, male, Christian European who assigns names to *himself* and to all others. Such a patriarchal regime was also in place in this case, as only 15 of the new Durban street names represented women. Yet, these 15 names represented a great increase, as previously only five of Durban's street names carried names representing females – all related to British royalty.[28] Quite strikingly, the gender aspect of the street-renaming process was not mentioned in any of the *The Mercury* articles analysed.

The only time that women as a group are referred to in the analysed articles is in reporter Greg Arde's ironic column 'Dear Obed', referring to Obed Mlaba, the Durban Mayor, jokingly discussing the name of the new soccer stadium: 'I think the Queen Nandi Stadium would be cool. It's not politically partisan, is easy to say and *it honours chicks*'.[29] Women have played a crucial but seldom acknowledged role in the history of South Africa, in its struggle for freedom and equality and against apartheid, oppression and subjugation. Many women suffered restriction, torture and brutal assassination by the apartheid regime, and were subject to what Spivak (1988) has referred to as 'double colonization', by the patriarchy of men and the patriarchy of the colonial power. As early as 1912, in what was probably the first mass passive resistance campaign in South Africa, Indian women encouraged black and Indian miners to strike against starvation wages. In 1913, black and coloured women in the Free State protested against having to carry identity passes, which white women were not required to do.[30] However, when it came to creating an equal society after apartheid, the questions linked to race received much more priority than those linked to gender.

Almost 18 years after democracy, women continue to make up the highest number in the unemployed population, are the most affected by HIV/AIDS, and constitute a majority of people living below the poverty line in South Africa. Women continue to face brutal abuse, with the highest incidence of rape in the world. Their literacy rate remains lower than the South African average and so they have a much lower chance of getting into higher education.

Six of the total of 14 journalists who covered the renaming process in the material discussed here were women. There were, however, no obvious differences in articles written by female and male reporters. This corresponds to the research findings of the non-governmental organization Gender Links (2009: executive summary) which showed that gender sensibility was low both among men and women in South African media. Furthermore, most of the articles analysed here belong to the news story genre and followed a rather standardised structure where a large majority of the sources were men. Guy Berger (2008) shows how in South African media one in five sources are white women, whereas only one in ten sources are black women. A 2006 study found that there were 45 per cent women in South African newsrooms. Black women, however, who constitute 46 per cent of the population, only account for 18 per cent of newsroom staff, compared to 45 per cent of the population and 28 per cent of newsroom staff in the case of black men, and 4 per cent of the population and 28 per cent in newsrooms in the case of white men (Morna 2007). Such numbers show the fruitfulness of gaining inspiration from the intersectionality framework, as combining different categories results in a more nuanced reality description.

Within this framework it is perceived that, if one were truly committed to dismantling racism, one would also have a commitment to dismantling sexism, because these often operate hand in hand.[31] However, sexism has been described as a recurrent practice in post-apartheid South Africa (Naylor 2004). The absence of representation or 'symbolic annihilation' (Tuchman 1978) refers to processes where women are either not covered or are depicted in a highly stereotypical manner. This was to a large extent the case in relation to the renaming coverage in *The Mercury*. Women were used far less frequently as sources in articles than men, and all the specialist sources were male. When women were referred to, they were often portrayed as victims.

Only a few of the published letters to the editor in the issues of *The Mercury* analysed were written by women. None referred to gender issues in relation to the renaming. One letter presented a movement titled 'pink power', which was started by Sonja Davis in order to mobilise women against the renaming of the city's streets.[32] However, the letter and the movement were simply against the renaming as such and did not add any gender perspective to the discussion. It should be mentioned that the different translations of male roles represented through the names were also quite limited. Men whose names were adopted were mainly ANC heroes with 'struggle credentials'. No artists, academics or other individuals who could have contributed to a wider spectrum of possible masculinities were suggested through the male street name choices.

Introducing gender as an alternative angle to cover the renaming process, one could more easily have avoided the static categories described above, both in relation to journalistic angles and the source in the articles.

A Historical Approach to the Renaming

Some of the newspaper articles analysed used local historians as sources and presented both their criticisms and their thoughts about what they valued as positive and fruitful name changes. These articles counteracted the tendency in the articles that did little to give a broader picture of the complex renaming process. Some of the most investigative and informative articles on renaming in *The Mercury* were written by journalists who had been working in close cooperation with local historians. Two long investigative articles presented the old and the new names with historical explanations.[33]

According to the journalists interviewed, local historians felt ignored in the political process leading to the proposed name changes. They felt that they could have made an important contribution and feared the city would lose important aspects of its local history (interviews, 2008). Whereas local historians were excluded from the actual process of changing Durban's street names, they were quite often included in *The Mercury*'s coverage of it. The historian Ken Gillings expressed concerns at some of the 'neutral' names that were being changed: 'An example is Brickfield (Felix Dlamini) Road. This road led to fields where bricks were made early in Durban's development'.[34]

Historians feared that early aspects of Durban's development would be lost because of the name changes. Including the historians' view in newspaper coverage resulted in new suggestions about how some of the cases debated could have been solved, and how the degree of understanding, and possibly also the audience's ownership of the new names could have been increased.

A Personal Belonging Approach to the Renaming

Street names may be seen as cartographies of identity and many felt that something very personal was taken away from them when their old street name was removed. At times, audience reactions were a result of both losing the dear old name and a strong opposition to, or dislike of, the new name. One such case that received much attention in *The Mercury* was the change of Cowey Road, arguably one of Durban's poshest addresses, to Problem Mkhize. As Mkhize was found difficult to pronounce by people with English as their mother tongue (many of the street's inhabitants), what would remain was 'Problem Road'.

Cowey/Problem Mkhize was one of the roads where inhabitants frequently spray-painted over the new name signs. Another name change that received many complaints from its residents was the renaming of Moore Street to Che Guevara. Advocate Pat Jefferys said that Guevara was considered by some to be a 'murderous thug' and a 'racist'.[35] 'ANC

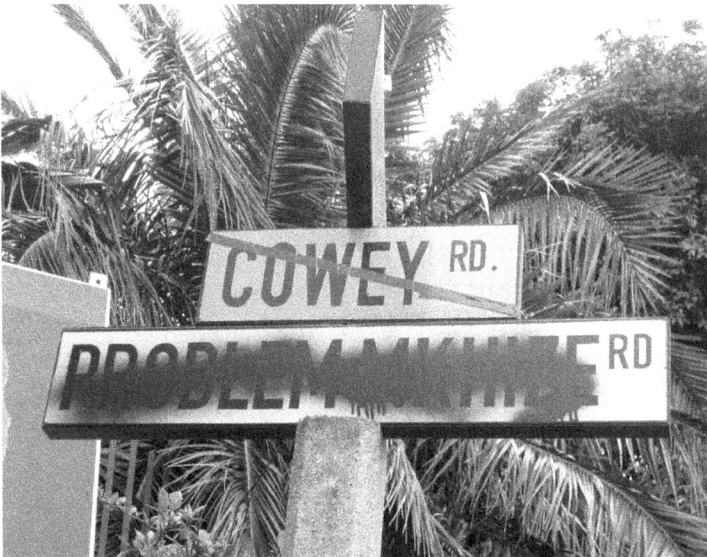

Figure 4.3. Cowey RD/Problem Mkhize RD; photo by Kristin Skare Orgeret

has not grasped the point: people need to make their own choices about the names of streets where they live'.[36] Much of the criticism in letters to the editor in *The Mercury* focused on how badly the Durban renaming process was conducted. Some sources argued that the media could have played a central role in a consultation process to ease the introduction of the new names. In some rare examples, however, *The Mercury* quoted people who were pleased by their new street name. One example was John Patrick Giddy, a lecturer in the School of Philosophy and Ethics at the University of KZN: 'On a personal level I am actually lifted up by the thought that my own street, Nicholson Road, is soon to be known after the educationalist Z K Matthews'.[37]

Some *Mercury* articles also referred to the practical challenges associated with the renaming process for police officers and commercial businesses. The newspaper articles portrayed a strong feeling of ownership of street names on behalf of the people living and working in the areas concerned. These feelings were to a large degree connected to the journalists' typical 'intended reader', as we will see in the next section.

Journalistic Processes and the Intended Reader

The changing nature of journalistic work and organisation and how it affects news content quality has been the concern of several critical writers who stress the continuing pressures on journalists (see Davies 2008). An increasing attenuation of the press, merging of business interests and news has resulted in a higher workload shared by fewer journalists and, as a result, less time spent investigating news stories. Being a journalist working under a lot of pressure obviously does not allow the inclusion of all possible perspectives at all times. In interviews, *The Mercury* journalists mentioned busy days with a stressful schedule where, as a result, one used the phone more than going out to talk to people (interviews, 2008).

The interviewed journalists' intended reader was male, middle-aged, white, upper middle class (interviews, 2008). The street name changes led to the highest ever response level in the history of *The Mercury*, but in the articles the voices of readers with other backgrounds than the typical 'intended reader' were not heard to the same degree. The limited focus was related to pressures on journalists in terms of workload and journalistic routines within the newspaper, but was also partly due to skewed impressions of who the readers really were. In hindsight, some of the journalists said that even with the stressful working conditions they could have been more open to other perspectives on the name change. In October 2008, *The Mercury* received new AMPS[38] statistical data about who their readers were. The typical reader turned out to be very different from the imagined one of the journalist:

> My imagined reader was a white, middle-aged man. I guess I thought some 60 per cent of the readership was white. But only 33 per cent is white and as many as 46 per cent are women! [...] Had I realized this I would have gone out more and talked to people from different back-grounds while covering the [renaming] process. I have become aware of the fact that the views reflected in my articles on this burning issue are way too narrow. (interview, *The Mercury* journalist, 2008)

The journalists still seemed to be more concerned about the race dimension than the class or gender dimensions and showed little interest in how these different aspects might operate together. The intersectionality line of thinking is a useful inspiration to the exercise of opening up to more approaches. What happens, for instance, when the ethnicity, post-colonial, political and gender dimensions are combined? Class, religion and certainly many other perspectives could be included. Especially in South Africa, a country still divided by its historical past as well as present cleavages, as well as having one of the world's largest divides between rich and poor. As Conboy (2004: 224) argues: 'if journalism is to survive, it has to assert a specific location within this media sphere, demonstrate that it can deliver a particular form of service to the public, however fragmented and commoditized that public might become'.

Conclusion

This chapter has explored how the process of covering the renaming jour-nalistically dramatised the tensions involved in the shift to democracy. Renaming is a central feature in many transformation processes, and more comparative research needs to be done in post-independence Africa. The renaming issue illustrates the complexities of contemporary South Africa and the challenges of representing this in the media. Intersections of political power, economic forces, colonisation, history, race, ethnicity and patriarchy create an environment of tensions which the renaming process both partly reflected and partly contributed to the construction thereof. To rest the journalistic coverage on static binary oppositions or scales without trying to catch the dynamic and multiple relationships between socio-cultural categories and identities easily leaves out a lot of understanding, and may make it more difficult for audiences to imagine the complexities of the society in which they live.

To reflect South Africa in a more multifaceted manner, this chapter has stressed the value of reading different aspects as they operate together. The essential point of this exercise is that, although all the approaches do not necessarily add up to one, unified story about South African identity, or a social reality to which journalists or researchers should adhere, it shows a wide range of possible trajectories reflecting the truth.

Notes

1 Lesley Perkes to *Daily News,* 7 Dec. 2011.
2 *The Mercury* is currently owned by Independent News and Media Limited, and covers 99.7 per cent of KwaZulu-Natal Province (KZN) in terms of circulation, with a readership of 219,000 in 2008 according to www.saarf.co.za.
3 After the Supreme Court of Appeal's rejection of changes to nine street names in Durban.
4 Other such examples are Bellair Road, named after the British settler John Hillary's home town; Blair Atholl Road, named after a Scottish town with the same name; Kensington Drive, named after the district in London, while Richmond Road and Warwick Avenue were probably named after English towns with the same names.
5 'ANC pushes for city renaming', letter to the editor from Crispin Hemson, *The Mercury,* 21 Feb. 2007.
6 'Road renaming should be seen as a new start', *The Mercury,* 30 May 2007.
7 MK, or Umkhonto we Sizwe (Spear of the nation), was the armed wing of the ANC.
8 'Chilling memories evoked by Andrew Zondo', letter to the editor from Nicky Armstrong, *The Mercury,* 17 June 2008.
9 'Name change outrage: Amanzimtoti bomber on list of those to be honoured', *The Mercury,* 21 April 2007.
10 'Amanzimtoti primary school to be named after Andrew Zondo', *The Mercury,* 17 July 2008.
11 For instance, 'Durban name changes continue', *The Mercury,* 1 May 2007.
12 For instance, 'Renaming saga turns personal', *The Mercury,* 1 Dec. 2008.
13 For instance, '"No rush" to finish street renaming', *The Mercury,* 11 Aug. 2008.

14 'Name change outrage: Amanzimtoti bomber on list of those to be honoured', *The Mercury*, 21 April 2007.
15 'School cannot be renamed just yet', *The Mercury*, 8 Sept. 2008.
16 Ibid.
17 'Tempers flare over new names', *The Mercury*, 15 May 2008.
18 'Street naming is about restoring dignity; can an African be a foreigner in Africa? Asks Thamsanqa Ngwenya', *The Mercury*, 14 Nov. 2007.
19 *The Mercury*, 21 Feb. 2007.
20 'Secret behind name changes', *The Mercury*, 5 April 2007.
21 ANC/MK leaders or activists among the new street names: Khoto Mkhunya; Sandile Thusi; Charlotte Maxeke; Vusi Mzimela; S'bu Mkhize; Problem Mkhize; Harry Gwala; Dorothy Nyembe; Mary Thipe; Basil February; Jabu Ngcobo; Dr Pixley ka Seme; Andrew Zondo; Steven Dlamini; Sbu Magwanyane; Adelaide Tambo; Mazisi Kunene; Oliver Tambo; Berta Mkhize; Mthoko Mkhize; Gopalal Hurbans; Lillian Ngoyi; Josiah Gumede; Musa Dladla; Griffiths Mxenge; J. B. Marks; Zinto Cele; Henry Pennington; Solomon Mahlangu; Chris Ntuli; Chris Hani; Moses Kotane; Krishna Rabilal; Albert Dlomo; Joseph Nduli; Anton Lembede; R. D. Naidu; Methews Meyiwa; Rodger Sishi; Dumisani Makhaye; Dr Langalibalele Dube and Peter Mokaba.
22 In terms of naming, the names of the rivers in KZN are an exception here. As John M. Murray has pointed out ('Let sense and sensibility prevail', *The Mercury*, 15 May 2007), it is noteworthy that notwithstanding decades of British colonial rule and apartheid oppression, virtually every river in the province is officially known by a mellifluous and descriptive Zulu name.
23 'Secrets behind name changes', *The Mercury*, 25 April 2007.
24 'Durban protesters on rampage against name changes', *The Mercury*, 2 May 2007.
25 For instance, 'Name changes "will be in one go"', *The Mercury*, 1 March 2007.
26 For instance, 'Tempers flare over new names', *The Mercury*, 15 May 2008.
27 'Ndebele's name change comments way of mark', letter to the editor, *The Mercury*, 13 June 2008.
28 Beatrice Street, Queen Mary Avenue, Lorne Street, Queen Street and Victoria Street.
29 *The Mercury*, 30 May 2007.
30 <http://www.sahistory.org.za/pages/governence-projects/womens-struggle/index.htm>.
31 See e.g. <http://princetonprofs.blogspot.com/2009/03/intersectionality.html>.
32 'The power of pink', letter to the editor, *The Mercury*, 9 May 2007.
33 'Who's who of the new street names', *The Mercury*, 2 Sept. 2008, and 'The people behind the old street names', 2 Oct. 2008.
34 'Durban's street names should reflect its history say historians', *The Mercury*, 8 Oct. 2008.

35 'Proper procedure "was applied" over street renaming', *The Mercury*, 19 Jan. 2009.
36 'ANC has taken wrong turn', letter to the editor from Tom Stokes, *The Mercury*, 9 Oct. 2008.
37 'The ethics of naming public roads; names have to reflect the new values of our common society', *The Mercury*, 29 May 2008.
38 AMPS is a demographic, media, and product consumption survey of over 17,000 homes conducted annually by the South African Advertising Research Foundation.

References

Berger, Guy (2008) 'State of South African media', unpublished lecture.

Bhabha, Homi (1994) *The Location of Culture*, London and New York: Routledge.

Bunn, David (1996) 'Comparative barbarism: game reserves, sugar plantations, and the modernization of the South African landscape', in K. Darian-Smith, L. Gunner and S. Nuttall (eds), *Text, Theory, Space: Post-Colonial Representations and Identity*, pp. 37–52, London: Routledge.

Carter, Erica, Donald, James and Squires, Judith (eds) (1993) *Space and Place: Theories of Identities and Location*, London: Lawrence and Wishart.

Clarkson, Carrol (2008) 'Remains of the Name', in Attie de Lange et al. (eds), *Literary Landscapes: From Modernism to Postcolonialism*, pp. 125–142, Basingstoke: Palgrave Macmillan.

Conboy, Martin (2004) *Journalism: A Critical History*, London: Sage.

Crenshaw, Kimberlé (1991) 'Mapping the margins: Intersectionality, identity politics, and violence against women of color', *Stanford Law Review*, 43, pp. 1241–99.

Davies, Nick (2008) *Flat Earth News*, London: Chatto and Windus.

Fox, Justin (2000) 'On the Road' in S. Nuttall and C.-A. Michael (eds), *Senses of Culture: South African Culture Studies*, Cape Town: Oxford University Press.

Gender Links (2009) *Glass Ceilings: Women and Men in Southern Africa Media*, Johannesburg: GL.

Gumede, William M. (2008) 'Mbeki, Zuma: a political earthquake', *Pambazuka News*, 401, Oct. <www.pambazuka.org/en/category/features/51032>.

Knudsen, S. (2006) 'Intersectionality: A theoretical inspiration in the analysis of minority cultures and identities in textbooks', *Caught in the web or lost in the textbook*, pp. 61–76. www.caen.iufm.fr/colloque_iartem/pdf/knudsen.pdf (accessed Dec. 2011)

Maake, Nhlanhla (1996) 'Inscribing identity on the landscape: national symbols in South Africa', in K. Darian-Smith, L. Gunner, and S. Nuttall (eds), *Text, Theory, Space: Post-Colonial Representations and Identity*, pp. 145–56, London: Routledge.

Maleka, Malesela (2007) 'Forward to a truly non-sexist society', <http://groups-beta.google.com/group/COSATU-Daily-News/web/forward-to-a-truly-non-sexist-society-sacp-9-august-2007>.

Morna, Colleen Lowe (2007) 'In South Africa, women still are underdogs in the media' <www.afrol.com/articles/25318> (accessed Dec. 2011).

Naylor, Nikki (2004) 'A women's issue?', *Rhodes Journalism Review*, 24, Sept., pp. 56–57.

Nuttall, Sarah, and Coetzee, Carli (1998) *Negotiating the Past: The Making of Memory in South Africa*, Cape Town: Oxford University Press Southern Africa.

Orgeret, Kristin Skare (2006) *Moments of Nationhood: The SABC News in English – The First Decade of Democracy,* doctoral thesis, Oslo University, Unipub.

—— (2008) 'From his master's voice and back again? Presidential inaugurations and South African television – the post-apartheid experience', *African Affairs*, 107/429, pp. 611–29.

Spivak, Gayatri (1988) *In Other Worlds: Essays in Cultural Politics,* London: Routledge.

Stayt, D. (1971) *Where on Earth? A Guide to the Place Names of Natal and Zululand*, Durban: Argus Group.

Steyn, Melissa (2001) *Whiteness Just Isn't What it Used to Be: White Identity in a Changing South Africa*, Albany, NY: State University of New York.

TRC (*Truth and Reconciliation* Commission) (1998). *Truth and Reconciliation Commission of South Africa Report*, Cape Town: Truth and Reconciliation Commission.

Tuchman, Gaye (1978) *Making News: A Study in the Construction of Reality,* New York: Free Press.

5

'IT'S OUR PAPER!' ETHNIC IDENTITY POLITICS AND INDIGENOUS LANGUAGE NEWSPAPER READERS IN ZIMBABWE: THE CASE OF *UMTHUNYWA*

Hayes Mawindi Mabweazara

Introduction

> Can you please speak in a language that I can understand [...], what
> makes you assume that every Jack and Jill in the streets of Bulawayo
> can make sense of the language you're using?

These ostensibly harsh words were uttered by an infuriated middle-aged woman at an automated teller machine one busy public holiday in Bulawayo, Zimbabwe's second largest city, in reaction to a young man who had naively voiced his complaint to her about the perennial tradition of long and winding queues in Zimbabwe, apparently using the 'wrong' language, Shona,[1] which the woman could hardly understand. From my experiences of growing up in Bulawayo, the woman's outburst was certainly not unique nor was it an isolated incident. On many occasions, I have witnessed acrimonious public altercations. Quite often, the encounters trigger serious thoughts about language and ethnic identity politics in Zimbabwe.

While the woman in the example may have expressed a legitimate concern related to the young man's naïve assumption that Shona was a language bound to be understood by all and sundry in the streets of Bulawayo, her fiery response pointed to covert but pervasive counter-hegemonic sentiments of ethnic victimisation among Ndebele-speaking people in Zimbabwe. These feelings are anchored in the perceived exclusion of 'minority' languages (and their speakers) from the mainstream domains of everyday social life in Zimbabwe. The encounter further highlights subtle feelings of cultural oppression and a desire for linguistic recognition as a reaction to the dominant Shona linguistic, cultural and political hegemony.

These ethno-linguistic tensions have preoccupied the work of a number of media and cultural studies scholars. Writing from a Kenyan context, Ogechi (2008: 75) observes that: 'Of all cultural elements, language is a powerful instrument of marking identity (and belonging)'. Similarly, wa Thiong'o contends: 'The choice of language and the use to which language is put is central to a people's definition of themselves in relation to their natural and social environment, indeed in relation to the entire universe' (1981: 4). Focusing on Zimbabwe, Ndhlovu (2009) contends that language is a major factor contributing to the social exclusion of 'minority' ethnic groups. Ndhlovu further submits that various forms of perceived language-based exclusion exercised by the predominantly Shona 'power bloc'[2] over minority groups constitute a form of 'linguistic imperialism' (Ndhlovu 2009) that resonates with endemic feelings of disillusionment and exclusion from 'mainstream' society. These feeling are largely a result of the socio-political history of Southern Zimbabwe – Bulawayo in particular and Matabeleland at large – a region characterised by enduring material deprivation and political marginalisation (I discuss this in detail shortly).

Writing about the centrality of language in identity formation, particularly among 'situated ethnic groups' who locate themselves at the fringes of mainstream society, Haarmann notes that language is 'a major marker for many local groups around the world, and there have been historical periods when language was assigned an ideological role as the marker par excellence of ethnic identity' (1999: 64). Taking this argument further, Hanusch (2008: 51) argues that language 'cannot be separated from culture and it is through language that we construct and deconstruct our culture, learning who "we" are and who "they" are'. For Clement et al. (2005: 401): 'language is of central importance to identity [formation] because through language we negotiate and share our identity with others'.

Against this background, this chapter investigates the reception of the Zimbabwean indigenous language (isiNdebele) newspaper, *uMthunywa*, amongst its Bulawayo readers, who account for about three-quarters of its total circulation. Although distributed nationally, *uMthunywa*, by virtue of it being an isiNdebele paper, has wide readership in the Ndebele-speaking provinces of Zimbabwe, especially in Bulawayo Metropolitan Province (where it is printed).[3] The chapter draws on wide-ranging discourses on language and ethnic identity in the media as well as Habermas' concept of the public sphere[4] to explore the meanings readers take from the paper's content and how such meanings resonate with their everyday lives. Particular attention is given to the impact of the newspaper's use of a local indigenous language and the extent to which the paper provides an alternative arena for public discourse.

While the chapter is specifically focused on the politics of language and identity in the readership of *uMthunywa*, the case study also gives an insight into the complexities underlying the reception of indigenous language media in Africa. The chapter submits that local language media can serve an important socio-political and cultural role by providing historically marginalised readers with an alternative public space in which to articulate issues pertinent to their collective identities as a people burdened by feelings of disillusionment, ethnic victimisation and exclusion by hegemonic power structures. The chapter concludes that there are points of intersection between the consumption of indigenous language media and the information that their consumers desire 'in order to extend their control over the conditions of their lives within that macro-political order' (Fiske 1992: 61).

To generate empirical data, this study followed a qualitative research design (rooted in reception theory[5]) that placed emphasis on the comparative empirical analysis of 'media discourses' with 'audience discourses' to closely examine the processes of reception which have a bearing on the appropriation of *uMthunywa*'s content. A cursory qualitative content analysis was thus undertaken on every issue of the paper between August 2004 and May 2005 (inclusive). This was followed by in-depth interviews (both group and individual) with readers purposively selected using convenience and snowball sampling in Bulawayo.

Indigenous Language Press in Zimbabwe: Locating *uMthunywa*

Unlike other African countries, such as Kenya and Nigeria, where political developments have, over the years, spurred the development of the indigenous language press (Olukotun 2006; Ugandu 2006), in Zimbabwe indigenous language media have largely remained underdeveloped. Both electronic and print media are characterised by widespread use of the English language. As Mano observes: 'little more than two decades after Zimbabwe gained full independence, Shona and Ndebele languages were hardly ever used in the mass media' (2006: 276–7). Zimbabwe television carried relatively few programmes in local languages and only two of four Zimbabwe Broadcasting Corporation (ZBC) radio stations broadcast in local languages (Mano 2006).

Although all top-selling dailies and weeklies publish in English, it is the Zimbabwean print media sector that has made noteworthy milestones in embracing indigenous languages, particularly the state-controlled establishments – the Community Newspaper Group (CNG) and the Zimbabwe Newspapers Group (Zimpapers). While the former's main editorial agenda was to foster links between the state and the masses through regional English and indigenous language newspapers, such as *Indonsakusa/Ilanga* (Matebeleland North province), the papers never made any significant impact, either in terms of circulation or editorial visibility. The prime reason for their poor performance was the CNG's weak capital base and managerial incompetence (Mandava 2006). In general, however, this appears to have been a culmination of the absence of a codified policy on the use of language in the media, thus relegating the broader language mandate to the state-controlled media rather than the private media.

It is not surprising, therefore, that leading indigenous language newspapers have emerged from Zimpapers, which is by far the most well resourced and thus dominant print media company in the country (Mabweazara 2011). In particular, two weeklies, *Kwayedza* and *uMthunywa*, which publish in Shona and isiNdebele respectively, have emerged as the most significant. Over the years, these newspapers have gained popularity by giving priority to the immediate issues of everyday life over those traditionally ascribed to the public sphere, through printing gossip and human-interest stories in typical tabloid fashion (Mabweazara 2005).

UMthunywa, however, presents an interesting dynamic to the politics of language, identity and indigenous language media reception in Zimbabwe. The paper was conceived in 1985, ostensibly to cater for Ndebele readers who hitherto had no vernacular newspaper covering Bulawayo and the Matabeleland region. While the creation of the paper (alongside the Harare-based *Kwayedza*) is broadly seen as a response to the post-independence reality of black majority rule, and the urgent need to mediate national development and reconciliation in local languages (Matenda 2001), the paper's origins were also enmeshed in politics. It was in many ways a well-calculated political gesture in the face of the post-independence political tension that engulfed Matabeleland. The circumstances of its birth 'mirrored material deprivation and the political marginalization of Bulawayo by the "power bloc" over the years' (Mabweazara 2009: 455). The early version of *uMthunywa*, however, succumbed to political interference and viability problems in 1993.

On 4 July 2004, *uMthunywa* re-emerged as a new brand, with a populist editorial thrust anchored in the 'values of tabloid journalism, gaining popularity as a paper that prints gossip and human-interest stories that the "man" in the street can relate to and identify with' (Mabweazara 2005: 32). Its circulation rose sharply beyond that of its Bulawayo-based English language sister weekly, the *Sunday News*, from 2,500 in its first week of publication to about 30,000 at its peak (see Mabweazara 2009; Mabweazara and Strelitz 2009). Strikingly, the paper's resurgence came at the height of political tension in the country, which preceded national elections the following year. In many ways, therefore, the paper was a political project.

As previously noted, *uMthunywa*'s content prioritises social issues related to ordinary people; this is evident in the pictorial content and the fact that most of its news sources are ordinary people. Stories are mostly about rural people or other disadvantaged members of urban communities who reside mainly in the townships. Coverage hinges on township gossip, rumour-mongering and other unconventional stories, peppered with idiomatic and slang expressions usually reserved for spoken rather than written communication. The paper's use of an

indigenous language (isiNdebele) is central to its sensationalist character – Ndebele tends to be more brazen and sensational than English.
The paper appears to reinvent expressions and words that resonate
with colloquial street talk – the language of its readers, which is conversational in nature (Mabweazara 2005, 2009).[6]

In its new editorial thrust, the newspaper became very popular for
breaking ranks with its sister papers by criticising government policies.
It disguised sensitive political messages by presenting them in the
form of sensational and humorous headlines or even in metaphorical
form. For example, during the controversial March 2008 presidential
election campaign, the paper published a story headlined: 'Ngiza gida
isitshikitsha mhlaka 29' (I will take to the dance floor on 29 March),
based on a statement uttered by President Robert Mugabe at a campaign rally in Matabeleland south, clearly parodying the prospect of an
unpopular 84-year-old president dancing to an unlikely electoral victory. After the same general election results were announced (showing
the opposition winning control of parliament) *uMthunywa* splashed the
headline: 'Sebekhulumile abantu' (The people have spoken). Further
bold reporting followed during Independence celebrations; the paper
ran a story under the headline 'Kuyini uzibuse?' (What is the meaning of independence?), and detailed how people were suffering due to
inflation and political violence in independent Zimbabwe. The paper
further riled the authorities when it ran another headline story: 'Kuyini
iBACCOSI?', an acronym for a much-hyped government-sponsored
Basic Commodities Supply Side Intervention scheme in which people
received food hampers at ridiculously low prices which encouraged
corruption among politicians. These headlines carried loaded sub-texts
that ridiculed as well as challenged authority in humorous ways – they
worked as a strategy for discussing political issues in the context of the
risks associated with direct government criticism. It is not surprising
therefore that the editor of the 'new' *uMthunywa* did not last and was
dismissed for running stories that ridiculed government policies.

A Socio-Political History of Bulawayo and Ethnic Identity Politics in Zimbabwe

Any understanding (and interpretation) of the reception of media texts
must be situated within historical traditions because a people's history

plays an important role in the way they consume texts. The reception of media texts, after all, is a process situated in a definite socio-historical context. This section thus discusses the socio-political history of Bulawayo – the context of *uMthunywa*'s consumption in this study.

Located in the Matabeleland region, Bulawayo Metropolitan Province is the second largest urban province after the Harare Metropolitan Province. As noted earlier, Matabeleland is home to the Ndebele ethnic group, whose main language is isiNdebele. The Ndebele ethnic group constitute about 15 per cent of Zimbabwe's population of about 14 million[7] and is the second largest in Zimbabwe after the Shona ethnic group, which comprises about 70 per cent of the country's total population (Zaaijer 1998: 30).

The predominance of isiNdebele, as the main language, has shaped the socio-cultural and political identities of the people of Matabeleland. Kramsch (1998) observes that for people to identify themselves as members of a community they have to define themselves jointly as insiders against others they define as outsiders; language (as an embodiment of common attitudes, beliefs and values) plays a critical role in cementing this identity. Samovar and Porter similarly aver that: '[s]o related are language and culture that language holds the power to maintain [...] cultural identity' (2001: 139). For the people of Matabeleland, language (isiNdebele) is, therefore, an integral component of their regional identity and is indispensable to cultural integration.

While feelings of exclusion from mainstream socio-political life characterise the people of Bulawayo (and Matabeleland), much of contemporary life is largely defined by the immediate post-independence disturbances that took place in the region. The ruling Zimbabwe African National Union: Patriotic Front (ZANU PF) clamped down on alleged dissidents thought to be loyal to Joshua Nkomo, leader of the Patriotic Front: Zimbabwe African People's Union (PF ZAPU) in Matabeleland, and sought to eliminate what they saw as the potential for a (PF) ZAPU *coup d'état* (Kaarsholm 1995: 242). The government deployed a special army unit (the Fifth Brigade) that oversaw the massacre, rape and detention of more than 20,000 civilians in Matabeleland (CCJPZ and LRF 1999). The disturbances left a lasting impression in the region, creating a climate of fear that has seen many of those that remain afraid of officials and of being victimized for voicing their opinions at public gatherings. As Ndlovu-Gatsheni

(2008: 167) argues, the episode reconstructed and reinforced Ndebele identity, resulting in the deep polarization of the Zimbabwean nation. It heightened the victims' awareness of being Ndebele at the expense of their being Zimbabwean.

However, identity construction among the Ndebele and the Shona is a highly contested subject inextricably connected to historical struggles over socio-political power, cultural domination and control. According to Ndlovu-Gatsheni, identity politics in Zimbabwe should be understood, in part, as a historical issue related to colonial processes that 'contributed to the construction of Ndebele and Shona identities by creating a bi-modal ethnic problem' (2008: 167). For him, the Ndebele identity is a particularly heavily contested terrain, often reduced to an 'ethnic problem', although it is clearly a 'power problem related to the representation of the Ndebele in the political power hierarchy in Zimbabwe' (Ndlovu-Gatsheni 2008: 167). This has given rise to a 'common imagined identity of belonging' (Mazarire 2003) among the people of Matabeleland which has taken the form of a 'coalescence of grievances and resentment of Shona triumphalism, including threats of Ndebele secession from a Shona-dominated Zimbabwe' (Ndlovu-Gatsheni 2008: 167). It is no wonder, then, that Matabeleland has been a stronghold of the opposition for a long time. With (PF) ZAPU incorporated into the government, the Movement for Democratic Change (MDC) emerged as a potential 'saviour' of the people of the region, who complained of years of marginalisation and underdevelopment. High-density suburbs continue to be characterised by poverty and deprivation; unemployment, crime, homelessness and destitution persist as everyday problems (Kaarsholm 1995).

It is important, however, to mention that the key dynamics and fundamental contours of Ndebele ethnic identity, particularly how it continues to be recreated and reconstructed through the media, remain highly contested. One may thus suggest, as Ndlovu-Gatsheni does, that Ndebele ethnic identity is best understood 'as a socially constructed phenomenon rather than as a fixed primordial identity. It must be understood as a protean outcome of the continuous and generally conflict-ridden interaction of political, economic and cultural forces' (2008: 181). The following sections discuss the study's findings.

The 'Political' and 'Cultural' Readings of *uMthunywa*

Although *uMthunywa* readers indicate profound distrust and alienation from traditional politics, the newspaper clearly serves a significant political need and purpose in their lives if 'politics' is defined as more than political party manoeuvrings and governmental action. This political attitude is deeply rooted in the readers' relationship to the broader political formation, previously discussed. Many comments from respondents reflected feelings of alienation from mainstream politics, and the sense that the government was conspiring against the people of Matabeleland. Some even expressed surprise that the government had decided to resuscitate *uMthunywa* after a long period of dormancy. As one respondent put it: 'everyone knows the government has long neglected this side of the country. In fact, it's shocking that the government has finally decided to revive *uMthunywa*'.

Given the express feeling of discontentment and the general lack of confidence in the 'power bloc', it is arguable that *uMthunywa* offers 'ammunition' against what is seen as a biased establishment that denigrates the Ndebele people. Their position in some kind of underclass, unable to do anything significant about events in the mainstream, is the key source of their frustrations and underpins outbursts like the one cited at the beginning of this chapter. As Fiske observes: if the social distance between the 'power bloc' and the people is wide then we should 'not be surprised if the political energies of the people are directed more towards the micro-politics of everyday life than to the macro-politics of socio-economic structures, for it is in these micro-politics that popular control is most effectively exercised' (1992: 60).

Sparks argues that 'while popular journalism would speak in an idiom recognisable by the masses as more or less related to their own, it would only speak of their concerns, joys and discontents *within the limits set for it by existing structures of society*' (1992: 28, emphasis added). This, however, is not to cast away the interpretive autonomy of *uMthunywa*'s readers. In fact, it emerged from participants' views that there is need to broaden our notion of what 'politics' means, to include participation outside the *existing structures* of 'traditional' politics. In this way, more contemporary models of counter-hegemonic public spheres (composed of small interest groups) are accommodated. The need to broaden the scope of our notion of 'politics' was implied in one reader's response: 'The paper deals with everyday experiences that occur in the townships [...]. These issues are very important. It's important, for instance, for me to know if my neighbour is a witch [...]. These things are real to us!'

The potential for *uMthunywa* to liberate its readers from the strictures of 'everyday life' was seen by readers as being rooted in the paper's focus on issues previously not open to public debate and discussion, such as witchcraft and other paranormal phenomena. Most readers expressed hardly any disbelief or shock at the paranormal occurrences covered in the paper – instead they described them as constituting real experiences in their lives. *UMthunywa* thus mediates an everyday life that is culturally relevant to its readers and shows the 'political' potential of identity construction taking place in indigenous language media. As one reader explained:

> When I visit my rural home in Lupane, I even collect old copies of the paper for them. I know what they want. I know fully well what they identify with [...] These are my people we are talking about. *This would explain why, for example, non-Ndebeles would see as bizarre a story about a man who grows tomatoes on his backside after stealing from a neighbour's garden. This to us is a traditionally held belief which doubles as a form of social control. It has a deeper meaning which any other reader would not understand.* (Emphasis added.)

From the preceding, one can suggest that belief in the paranormal and witchcraft among *uMthunywa*'s readers is not a simple cultural phenomenon but rather provides an existential explanatory framework relating to the readers' precarious and unpredictable living conditions. As Shoko (2007: 46) observes: 'witchcraft thrives in the contexts of quarrels, jealousies and accusations in the community'. In this sense, *uMthunywa,* as an indigenous language newspaper, challenges the structural elitism of the mainstream public sphere by providing representations that resonate with the readers' lived experiences. It is thus important to heed Fraser's assertion that 'public spheres are not only arenas for discursive opinion; in addition, they are arenas for the formation and enactment of social identities' (1992: 124). *UMthunywa* helps produce the fabric of its readers' everyday life by providing materials from which they 'forge their very identities' (Kellner 1995: 1). The readers 'actively and creatively sample [...] cultural symbols, myths, and rituals as they produce their identities' (Brown et al. 1994: 813). Machin and Papatheoderu (2002: 47) similarly posit that texts dealing with personal problems can create among readers a sense of proximity to their own lives and experiences. They are, in theory, important forms of knowledge, engaging audiences who might feel alienated by the broader political formation. These assertions found support in the following interview extract:

> The most important aspect about *uMthunywa* compared to the stories we read in other newspapers is that we can easily locate its stories in our daily lives. The places where they would have occurred are, in some cases, familiar to us. For example, a lot has been published in *uMthunywa* about Nkayi my rural home. I remember one story, last year or early this year, about a scotch cart accident that claimed a boy's life at Sikobokobo [...] a very familiar territory to me.

> Some of the stories have even circulated as rumours before they appear in the paper. For example, the story about the family that went to collect the body of their deceased relative in Nkayi on a scotch cart [...] There are also other negative stories about woman killing their infants [...] All these are stories taken from places I know and identify with in one way or another.

This extract shows that *uMthunywa* transposes the daily experiences of its readers from the private sphere into the public arena. To use Nyamnjoh's words 'what [*uMthunywa*] in general has done is transpose the debate from the streets and neighbourhoods to the public sphere, while staying faithfully ethnic and partisan' (Nyamnjoh 2005: 244–5). It appeals to the readers' sense of proximity to their own lives and experiences. This is particularly important in light of the reader's general feeling of alienation from the broader political formation.

Language and *uMthunywa's* Entrenchment in Local Culture

The use of isiNdebele in the editorial content of *uMthunywa* also emerged as central to the paper's reception among Ndebele speakers. Given that language is 'central to a people's definition of themselves in relation to their [...] social environment' (wa Thiong'o 1981: 4), most interviewees saw the paper as playing a key role in 'fostering cultural convergence' (Mazrui 2009: 43) among the Ndebele. As one reader explained: 'This paper is written in our own local language which is understood by all and used in our daily conversation [...] but you need to understand the fact that the language is linked to our history and culture, so the paper reminds us of who we are'. This finds support in Kramsch's (1998) view that for people to identify themselves as members of a community they have to define themselves jointly as insiders against others they define as *outsiders*, and language, the embodiment of common attitudes, beliefs and values, plays a critical role in cementing this identity. Similarly, Mwaura observes that 'Speakers of different languages and cultures see the universe differently, evaluate it differently, and behave towards its reality differently' (cited in Mazrui 2009: 36). From this membership, they draw personal strength and pride, as well as a sense of social importance and historical continuity (wa Thiong'o 1981). For the people of Matabeleland, then, isiNdebele is central to their regional identity; it underpins their feeling of belonging and shapes their socio-cultural and political identity. *UMthunywa* reinforces that sense, as one of the readers explained:

> You see what, my brother, *uMthunywa* is in our mother language and traditionally; language is the carrier of culture. We, therefore, see the paper as reviving our cultural values through its use of pure isiNdebele and proverbs which explore issues that we, the poor of Matabeleland, experience [...] *It's our paper and we pray that it doesn't disappear again.* (Emphasis added.)

The feelings of social and political marginalisation discussed earlier also appear to have a strong bearing in the fostering of a cohesive sense of cultural convergence among *uMthunywa*'s readers who, as the extract above shows, 'pray that [the paper] doesn't disappear again'. Language is a key factor in fostering these sentiments. As Kramsch observes: 'Members of a group who feel that their cultural and political identity is threatened are likely to attach particular importance to the maintenance or resurrection of their language' (1998: 75).

The study's participants also highlighted that *uMthunywa*'s departure from 'official', correct language use in preference for colloquial street talk adds to its overall conversational tone, which connects with readers still deeply rooted in oral culture. IsiNdebele thus allows its readers to understand their world more easily. As Matenda (2001: 35–6) rightly observes, people can speak confidently and express themselves clearly if they speak in their own languages. Language is only one aspect of *uMthunywa* that gives readers the sense that it belongs to them and their culture. Most interviewees pointed out that *uMthunywa*'s stories follow the narrative conventions and formulae of their cultural repertoires. As one reader explained: 'I really enjoy reading stories in *uMthunywa*; they make me feel as though my grandmother is telling me a story. The stories are written in a different way, it's as though you are going through a folk narrative'.

The brazen and graphic nature of isiNdebele also emerged as central in attracting readers to *uMthunywa*. As discussed earlier, the paper achieves this largely through departure from 'official', correct language and reinvents expressions and words that resonate with its readers' language. One reader observed that the paper reinvents phrases and comes up with catchy and interesting ones like 'Idlalichatsha' (used as a euphemistic title for mischievous women who prey on married men). The extract below explains the foregoing view on *uMthunywa*'s language use.

> IsiNdebele has a certain way of portraying issues in a very brazen manner which English can hardly match. Take for instance, a headline like 'Umhlolo batayi!' (What a disaster!). I can't think of a more graphic and striking way of putting it across in any different language. The other thing is that isiNdebele is my first language; I can easily understand it much better than any other language.

Thus, *uMthunywa*, as a vernacular tabloid, is a rare treasure among the Ndebele-speaking readers – it gives them an identity and consequently a particular citizenship. It is arguable; therefore, that language is instrumental in popularising *uMthunywa*. Even more apparent is the fact that the language has enabled more people, including those not so comfortable when reading English, to take part in the paper's discourses. As one reader explained:

> It's not everyone who can read English, isiNdebele caters for everyone, young and the old. My grandmother can read *uMthunywa*, and if any other old people are not literate enough to read, they can always ask their grandchildren to read for them and they will understand.

By bringing on board a wider readership inclusive of those not able to read English, *uMthunywa* allows its readers to actively engage with its discourses. In this sense, the paper sets up a more egalitarian relationship with its readers. This, in part, points to the fact that people understand their world better if they use their own languages. As Chibita contends: 'Giving people a voice in their own languages brings [them] into the arena of public discourse [...] once in this arena, people are better placed to have a say [...] on issues that touch on their governance and their general well-being' (2006: 239). Similarly, Mazrui (2009: 43) avers that: 'It is only by providing access to information in the languages that the people understand that will allow them to participate in political reconstruction towards a healthier future'.

Conclusion

The findings presented in this chapter point to the fact that the reading of *uMthunywa* is symptomatic of a deeper social malaise in Bulawayo and Matabeleland at large – precisely the political alienation experienced by the readers. As an indigenous language newspaper, *uMthunywa* offers the people of Bulawayo something they do not find in other Zimbabwean print media. It deals with issues experienced by readers in their everyday experiences, which encompass the socio-political conditions that have alienated them from the nation's macro-political life. The indigenous language used by the paper not only influences the readers' attraction to it, but also sharpens their understanding of the meanings of the content as well as appealing to their cultural identity as Ndebele people.

The paper thus constitutes a valuable alternative mediated public sphere that appeals to readers who feel alienated from the 'power bloc'. It is ironic that *uMthunywa,* as a state-controlled newspaper, provides a space which serves an anti-hegemonic function. By helping to reinforce and solidify the Ndebele community it creates a striking paradox of a state-owned newspaper that provides space for readers who traditionally avoid the public spheres dominated by the state. The paper's ostensible desire to offer its pages as a platform for the exchange of local (regional) information has turned it into a political instrument that is appropriated by citizens for the realisation of their own interests. The newspaper is therefore an excellent platform for the inscription of alternative and independent ideas and discourses outside the confines of the epistemological repertoires imposed by the state. Its popularity says more about the relationship of its readers to the social and political processes that govern their lives – it speaks in 'an idiom recognisable by the masses as more or less related to their own' (Sparks 1992: 28).

Notes

1 Shona is a language spoken by the dominant ethnic group in Zimbabwe, which comprises about 70 per cent of the country's total population (Zaaijer 1998: 30).
2 'Power bloc', in this case, refers to an alliance of forces of domination exerting social power along a number of relatively congruent lines of force, expressed in institutions such as government, politics and the media (see Fiske 1992: 45).
3 In recent years, the circulation of the paper has plummeted as a result of changes to its editorial content, as well as the difficult economic conditions that continue to bedevil the country.
4 Since Habermas' conception of the public sphere concept, it has been developed and updated (not least by himself) to take into account a number of different aspects – one of the more important ones being the changing nature of the media landscape (Habermas 1996: 360). In its revised form, it aptly illustrates how journalism can be viewed as being at the forefront of forms of public discourse.
5 Reception theory is concerned with how people interpret and make sense of media texts within their socio-cultural and historical circumstances: i.e. meanings that are culturally shared by 'interpretive communities' or 'subcultures' (Ang 1990: 160).
6 One notes the following examples: 'Ijazi lika mkwenyana' (lit. 'son in law's jacket', 4–11 June 2004), used as a euphemism for a condom; 'Z'khuphani ngempelaviki' (What's happening over the weekend); and some expressions used for emphasis or to express surprise, e.g., 'Umhlolo batayi!' (What an awfully strange incident) (3–10 Dec. 2004).
7 That the Ndebele constitute 15 per cent of Zimbabwe's population is a highly contested and politicised issue. In fact, the 2002 census figures were heavily disputed.

References

Ang, Ien (1990) 'The nature of the audience', in J. Downing, A. Mohammadi and A. Sreberny-Mohammadi (eds), *Questioning The Media: A Critical Introduction*, pp. 155–65. London: Sage.
Brown, Jane, Dykers, Carol, Steele, Jeanne, and White, Anne (1994) 'Teenage room culture: where media and identities intersect', *Communication Research*, 21/6, pp. 813–27.

CCJPZ (Catholic Commission for Justice and Peace in Zimbabwe) and LRF (Legal Resources Foundation) (1999) *Breaking the Silence: Building True Peace*, Harare: CCJPZ.

Chibita, Monica (2006) 'Our tongues count: a Ugandan perspective on indigenous language, local content and democracy', in A. Salawu (ed.), *Indigenous Language Media in Africa*, pp. 238–70. Lagos: Centre for Black African Arts and Civilisation.

Clement, Richard, Baker, Susan C., Josephson, Gordon, and Noels, Kimberly A. (2005) 'Media effects on ethnic identity among linguistic majorities and minorities: a longitudinal study of a bilingual setting', *Human Communication Research*, 31/3, pp. 399–422.

Fiske, John (1992) 'Journalism in popular culture', in P. Dahlgren and C. Sparks (eds), *Journalism and Popular Culture*, pp. 45–63. Thousand Oaks, CA: Sage.

Fraser, Nancy (1992) 'Rethinking the public sphere: a contribution to the critique of actually existing democracy', in C. Calhoun (ed.), *Habermas and the Public Sphere*, pp. 109–42. Cambridge, MA: MIT Press.

Habermas, Jürgen (1996) *Between Facts and Norms: Contributions to a Discourse Theory of Law and Democracy*, Cambridge, MA: MIT Press.

Haarmann, Harald (1999) 'History', in J. A. Fishman (ed.), *Handbook of Language and Ethnic Identity*, pp. 60–76. New York: Oxford University Press.

Hanusch, Folker (2008) 'The impact of cultural dimensions on language use in quality newspapers', *Estudos em Comminicao*, 3, pp. 51–78.

Kaarsholm, Preben (1995) 'Si ye pambili – which way forward? Urban development, culture and politics in Bulawayo', *Journal of Southern African Studies*, 21/2, pp. 225–46.

Kellner, Douglas (1995) *Media Culture: Cultural Studies, Identity Politics between the Modern and the Postmodern*, London: Routledge.

Kramsch, Claire (1998) *Language and Culture*, Oxford: Oxford University Press.

Mabweazara, Hayes M. (2005) 'Taking the gap: the tabloid press in Zimbabwe', *Rhodes Journalism Review*, 25, p. 32.

Mabweazara, Hayes M. (2009) 'Regional identity and the politics of belonging in the consumption of Zimbabwe's vernacular tabloid newspaper, *uMthunywa* in Bulawayo', *Journal of African Media Studies*, 1/3, pp. 449–60.

—— (2011) 'Newsmaking practices and professionalism in the Zimbabwean press', *Journalism Practice*, 5/1, pp. 100–17.

—— and Strelitz, Larry N. (2009) 'Investigating the popularity of the Zimbabwean tabloid newspaper, *uMthunywa*: a reception study of Bulawayo readers', *Ecquid Novi: African Journalism Studies*, 30/2, pp. 113–33.

Machin, David, and Papatheoderou, Fotini (2002) 'Commercialisation and tabloid television in southern Europe: disintegration or democratisation of the public sphere?', *Journal of European Area Studies*, 10/1, pp. 31–48.

Mandava, Peter (2006) 'Commercial imperatives and their implications on the community newspaper group: the case of *The Times* and *Masvingo Star*', *The Dyke: Journal of the Midlands State University*, 2/1 <http://www.msu.ac.zw/research/THE%20DYKE%202_1%20Abstracts.pdf> (accessed Nov. 2011).

Mano, Winston (2006) 'African public service radio versus national languages: mixed responses to Radio Zimbabwes bilingual service', in A. Salawu (ed.), *Indigenous Language Media in Africa*, pp. 271–306, Lagos: Centre for Black African Arts and Civilisation.

Matenda, Stanford (2001) 'Problems and prospects of Shona newspapers in Zimbabwe: a case study of *Kwayedza*', unpublished MA thesis. University of Zimbabwe.

Mazarire, Gerald C. (2003) 'Who are the Ndebele and the Kalanga in Zimbabwe?' paper prepared for Konrad Adenauer Foundation Project on Ethnicity in Zimbabwe, Nov.

Mazrui, Alamin (2009) 'Language and the media in Africa: between the old empire and the new', in K. Njogu and J. Middleton (eds), *Media and Identity in Africa*, pp. 36–48, Edinburgh: Edinburgh University Press.

Ndhlovu, Finex (2009) *The Politics of Language and Nation Building in Zimbabwe*, Oxford: Peter Lang.

Ndlovu-Gatsheni, Sabelo J. (2008) '"For the nation to live, the tribe must die": the politics of Ndebele identity and belonging in Zimbabwe', in B. Zewde (ed.), *Society, State and Identity in African History*, pp. 167–200, Ethiopia: Forum for Social Studies.

Njogu, Kimani (2008) 'Introduction', in K. Njogu (ed.), *Culture, Performance and Identity: Paths of Communication in Kenya*, pp. ix–xviii, Nairobi: Twaweza Communications.

Nyamnjoh, Francis (2005) *Africa's Media: Democracy and the Politics of Belonging*, London: Zed Books.

Ogechi, Nathan O. (2008) 'Sheng as a youth identity marker: reality or misconception?', in K. Njogu (ed.), *Culture, Performance and Identity: Paths of Communication in Kenya*, pp. 75–92. Nairobi: Twaweza Communications.

Olukotun, Ayo (2006) 'The indigenous language press and democratic mobilisation in Nigeria: a historical structural overview', in A. Salawu (ed.), *Indigenous Language Media in Africa*, pp. 126–40, Lagos: Centre for Black African Arts and Civilisation.

Samovar, Larry A., and Porter, Richard E. (2001) *Communication between Cultures*, Belmont, CA: Wadsworth.

Shoko, Tabona (2007) *Karanga Indigenous Religion in Zimbabwe: Health and Well-Being*, Aldershot: Ashgate Publishing.

Sparks, Colin (1992) 'Journalism in popular culture', in P. Dahlgren and C. Sparks (eds), *Journalism and Popular Culture*, pp. 24–44, Thousand Oaks, CA: Sage.

Ugandu, Wilson (2006) 'The development and political mobilisation role of Kenyan indigenous language press', in A. Salawu (ed.), *Indigenous Language Media in Africa*, pp. 86–94, Lagos: Centre for Black African Arts and Civilisation.

wa Thiong'o Ngugi (1981) *Decolonising the Mind: The Politics of Language in African Literature*, Harare: Zimbabwe Publishing House.

Zaaijer, Mirjam (1998) *Urban Economic Restructuring and Local Institutional Response: the case of Bulawayo, Zimbabwe*, PLACE: Institute for Housing and Urban Developments Studies (HIS) Project Paper Series, Project paper no. UM1, Rotterdam (The Netherlands).

6

REPORTING ETHNIC MINORITY ISSUES IN AFRICA: A STUDY OF NIGERIAN NEWSPAPERS

Nkereuwem Udoakah

Introduction

Communication is a very important part of human life and existence, and contemporary society has been moulded and controlled through the use of media such as radio, television, magazines, billboards, the internet, newspapers, books, telephone or through face-to-face meetings. These media are commonly acknowledged as features of modern societies, their development being accompanied by an increase in the scale and complexity of societal activities and arrangements, rapid social change, technological innovation, rising personal income and standard of life, and the decline of some traditional forms of control and authority (Ekanem 2003). Nonetheless, communication powered by media channels has proved to be the pivot on which society develops and rests, and Nigeria is not an exception in this regard. In all of Africa, the Nigerian media have been known to be very vocal, unrelenting and dogged in their pursuit of the ideals of social justice and political equality (Ekanem 2003). In addition, Olutokun and Seteolu (2001) further observed that Nigeria has the biggest and most virile African press community, followed by South Africa. The number of publications (weeklies, dailies and magazines) has been conservatively put at 116, although many of these are at the margin of survival.

Although the Nigerian media have faced several obstacles with courage and fortitude, they have been viewed as a formidable partner in progress by many corporate entities, as a pillar of strength by the government and as a watchdog by society. For an industry that draws its strength from the noble cannons of educating, informing, mobilising and entertaining the public, as well as influencing public opinion along the narrow track of the public good, the Nigerian media cannot afford to be static. On one hand, it is evident that Nigerian media have helped change the fortunes of Nigerian polity over time, especially as they were at the forefront of the struggle to change the population's docility towards colonial rule, and then led the crusade against military dictatorship in the 1980s and 1990s. Furthermore, under the current civilian dispensation, the media have clamoured for a more humane social order (Ekanem 2003), and Nigerian journalists have contributed in no small measure to moving the country forward and to sustainable development and environmental management.

On the other hand, it is clear that public concern for the environment is not a new phenomenon, as many people have been concerned about their closest surroundings in one way or another for quite a while. As Gooch (1995) observed, what is relatively new is the globalisation of environmental problems and the mass media's role in the popularisation of environmental issues. Commemorated each year on 5 June, World Environment Day (WED) is one of the principal vehicles through which the United Nations (UN) stimulates worldwide awareness of the environment and enhances political attention and action. The WED was established in 1972 by the UN General Assembly to mark the opening of the Stockholm Conference on the Human Environment. The main agenda of WED is to give a human face to environmental issues; to empower people to become active agents of sustainable and equitable development; promote an understanding that communities are pivotal to changing attitudes towards environmental issues; and to advocate partnership which will ensure that all nations and peoples enjoy a safer and more prosperous future. WED is generally a people's event with colourful activities such as street rallies, bicycle parades, green concerts, school essay and poster competitions, tree planting, as well as recycling and clean-up campaigns. In many countries, this annual event is used to enhance political attention and action on environmental issues. It is common practice for heads of state, prime ministers and ministers of the environment to deliver statements and commit themselves and their people to caring for the environment. More serious pledges are also made which lead to the establishment of permanent governmental structures dealing with environmental management and economic planning. This observance also provides an opportunity to sign or ratify international environmental conventions.

In Nigeria, cases of industrial pollution (air and water), especially in the Niger Delta region, are well documented (see, e.g., Moffat and Linden 1995), as well as problems of solid waste disposal, floods, erosion and deforestation in other parts of the country. Regrettably, although environmental journalism has gained increased importance in many countries since the 1990s, from the amount of airtime and pages given by the media to environmental issues, it is evident that the Nigerian press has not given high priority to the coverage and reporting of environmental issues affecting the country. Several questions must thus be asked, including:

- How much information is available in the Nigerian press to people who are affected in one way or another by adverse environmental conditions?
- Considering the multifaceted nature of environmental subjects, what types of environmental issues and problems does the Nigerian press report?

Ironically, environmental problems in Nigeria, particularly in the Niger Delta region, seem to receive considerable media attention only when there is an oil spill, an environmental conference or a seminar in the region. This situation makes the question of press coverage and the reporting of environmental problems a matter of utmost concern. The notion of mass media agenda-setting suggests that public salience of an environmental issue will rise and fall with the salience of the issue in the mass media (see Chan 1999; Soroka 2002; McCombs 2004). The influence mass media can exert on the public therefore differs according to spatial aspects of the environmental problem, and the effects of the mass media on public salience of environmental problems differ according to the alternative sources of information available to the public (Gooch 1996).

Against this background, this chapter's objective is to examine the extent to which the Nigerian press is socially responsive to the need to provide sufficient information on environmental issues to the Nigerian public, as well as the types of environmental issues reported and the prominence given to them. The working hypothesis is that the Nigerian press would give more coverage to environmental issues than to non-environmental issues, particularly during the celebration of the World Environment Day in June 2004 and 2005.

Nigerian Media Structure

The media structure and political tradition in Nigeria are rooted in ethnic prejudice. Before independence, Nigeria had a national press which fought a national cause. History points to the Nigerian press as having been the catalyst in the fight for Nigeria's independence (Udoakah 1988). As Golding and Elliot (1979) note, the steady advancement of nationalist ideas found expression in the pages of the embryo press. Since independence, the Nigerian media have been structured along ethnic lines to fight the causes of ethnic groups (Udoakah 1988). This followed the creation of states which apparently coincided with ethnic divisions and the founding of their media outlets.

According to Udoakah (1998), the Nigerian media are now no more than multiple pressure groups seeking things that are not of general benefit to all. He observes that, although these media may occasionally speak in the national interest, issues likely to bring about such a position were few and far between, and even federal government-funded media are managed in the interest of those who control them. Indeed, what is known as the Nigerian press today is an amalgam of the Hausa, Igbo, Yoruba and minority presses. Obviously, the minority press seems to exist in name, but it is managed by editors of majority ethnic group extraction. For instance, *This Day*, the *Guardian*, *Vanguard* and *Independent* newspapers are owned by Niger Delta businessmen, but their editors in 2009, except for the *Independent*, were of Yoruba extraction! Apart from this, schism in some media houses still raises concern for the coverage of minority issues. Femi Kusa, a Yoruba and one-time editor-in-chief on the *Guardian*, in his reply to criticisms of his write-up on the demise of Alex Ibru (*The Nation*, 27 Nov. 2011), revealed the ethnic polarity that played out in the company. He says that the situation only developed when the publisher, the late Mr Ibru, brought Mr Andy Akporugo, an Igbo, to the company and later made him an executive consultant in his office. Soon, Kusa recalled, there were talks of Yoruba dominance in the newspaper, which led about three times to Mr Ibru calling for a staff audit. Each time, the Igbos accounted for more than half of the newsroom, while Yorubas, Urhobos (from the publisher's state of origin) and others accounted for the other half.

Furthermore, as the editor-in-chief of the *Daily Independent* said in an interview with the author in 2011, media establishments cannot afford to play Father Christmas in the face of their huge operational costs as a result of decrepit infrastructure in the country, e.g., roads, electricity and other public utilities. According to him, the media would naturally focus more on matters that would help cushion their financial burden rather than on issues with no pecuniary benefits to them. These situations obviously raise concern about the type of attention that will be given to events affecting minority ethnic groups.

Conceptual Framework

In many ways, the news media influence their audiences' perception of the world around them. Information about non-experienced environmental conditions often comes from the mass media, and access to information is usually considered an important factor in most models that attempt to explain the formation of environmental perceptions. Many environmental problems cannot be personally experienced as they are either too distant, or cannot be directly seen, tasted or smelled. In the case of environmental hazards that are not personally experienced, and of places outside the public's closest experienced environment, the mass media, as communicators of public information, play a significant role in knowledge distribution.

Studies have shown that the most important effect of mass media is their ability to structure and organise people's perception about what is happening around them (McCombs and Shaw 1972). The agenda-setting hypothesis, which has received increasing attention in mass communication literature, posits a relationship between the relative emphasis given by the media to various topics and the degree of salience these topics have for the general public (Chan 1999). An important question is whether the mass media focus attention on some issues to the neglect of others, or whether they report attention rather than create it (see Driedger and Eyles 2003). Similarly, Zhu et al. (1993) and Soroka (2002) observe that the mass media were most likely to influence public salience when issues were international and unobtrusive.

There are conflicting theories about how the media may influence the public. Several authors suggest that, while the media can rarely persuade people to change a well-established opinion, they are able to set an agenda by aiming the public's focus at certain issues of the media outlet's choosing. Others have suggested a more overt media role in terms of their ability to directly influence public opinion. In either case, one of the important implications of the relationship between the media, the process of agenda-setting and public opinion is that, if the audience deems media sources credible, media coverage is able to create a feedback loop to enable the codifying of issues. This is because issues often become legitimised when they receive media coverage (Arvai and Mascarenhas 2001).

Agenda-setting has been defined as a process through which the mass media communicate the relative importance of various issues and effects to the public. Put simply, agenda-setting theory maintains that the public will attach more importance to an issue or event on the basis of the importance the media give such issues or events. McCombs and Shaw (1972) first tested agenda-setting theory in their study of the 1968 US presidential elections. They found a nearly perfect rank-order correlation between the issues considered most important by voters and coverage of these issues in the print news media used by voters.

Several studies have provided further empirical support for the agenda-setting theory and many studies have applied agenda-setting theory to the study of environmental issues (see e.g., Hansen 1993; Chapman et al. 1997). Atwater et al. (1985) studied six environmental sub-issues, including disposal and quality of water, hazardous substances, quality of land, air and wildlife conservation. They found moderate correlation between article frequency on sub-issues and their perceived salience among the public. Research has also shown that, by simply keeping an issue alive through reporting on it for some time, the media may transmit to the public not just the information, but also a subtle message concerning the legitimacy of an issue. In addition, research by Ader (1995) indicated that there was a positive correlation between the amount of media attention devoted to pollution and the degree of public salience on the issue. The negative correlation between the media agenda and the total pollution index of air and water pollution indicated that, despite an overall reduction in pollution, there was an increase in media coverage.

Research Method

For this study, media coverage of environmental issues in Nigeria was measured through a content analysis of four leading national Nigerian newspapers (i.e., *Guardian*, *This Day*, *Punch* and *Vanguard*) during a four-week period (i.e., 1–14 June 2004 and 1–14 June 2005). The four newspapers were chosen because of their regularity of production and availability on newsstands; circulation in all the states of the Nigerian federation; the wide scope of editorial interest; and the high level of their editorial credibility. The *Punch* and *Vanguard* have an average print run of 70,000 copies per day, while the *Guardian* and *Vanguard* both have a print run of over 100,000 copies per day (see Olutokun and Seteolu 2001). However, these figures are controversial since there are no audited circulation statistics in Nigeria and newspapers just give their own figures. The *Guardian* is a favourite of intellectuals and is respected for its independent and sober views, while *This Day* is widely known for its in-depth coverage of economic issues. The weeks were chosen because the WED is normally celebrated worldwide on 5 June each year. It was thus expected that there would be a lot of environmental reports in the Nigerian print media, given the global significance of the WED, discussed earlier. Unfortunately, the June 2005 edition of *This Day* was not available. Ten issues from each newspaper were used, with a total of 70 issues from the chosen period. Only the weekday (Monday to Friday) issues of newspapers were used since the weekend editions tend to provide more coverage of social and cultural issues and rarely give attention to environmental issues. All 70 issues were studied using content analysis.

Content analysis is a research technique used for empirically analysing articles by systematically identifying specified characteristics, words or themes (see Chapman et al. 1997; Brewer 2003). The assumption underlying the content analysis approach to enquiry is that what is learnt about the materials under study will reflect the values and attitudes of those who created the materials (see e.g., Berger 1993). Moreover, content analysis avoids the problem of the presence of the researcher affecting or influencing subjects and the subjects of the study. It involves the description and analysis of text in order to represent its content. This takes the form of enumeration, e.g., counting word frequency and numbers of column inches, and more qualitative assessment of words and terms used, as undertaken in certain forms of discourse analysis (Brewer 2003). Content analysis can be undertaken quantitatively and qualitatively, or both. The text can be from written forms, such as newspaper articles, official and personal documents, books, pamphlets, tracts, etc., or from accounts people proffer in interview, later transcribed in written form. Used quantitatively, the frequency of particular words can be counted, as well as the number of times one descriptive term is used rather than another, the column inches devoted to one topic over another, variants of particular words and the conceptual categories used in the text. Content analysis can become a stage in data analysis itself, rather than solely a data collection technique (Brewer 2003). As Arvai and Mascarenhas (2001) observed, content analysis has been widely used in environmental research, including the analyses of public attitudes to wildlife, forest planning, media characterisations of nuclear waste disposal and environmental messages from the forest industry.

In the research for this chapter, the units of analysis were all editorial matter on the environment in the four newspapers. Environmental content was defined as dealing with human interaction with the environment, positive or negative. As a result, the content analysed included all news items, editorials, opinions, letters to the editor, pullouts, features, cartoons, pictures, supplements and interviews on environmental issues within and outside Nigeria. The environmental issues reported by the newspapers were grouped into six main categories (see Table 6.1).

To deal with the problem of coding reliability (i.e. whether everyone studying these papers and counting the quantity and types of environmental issues would arrive at the same figures), the services of research assistants (i.e. two graduate students in the Department of Communication Arts, University of Uyo) were employed. The assistants' role was to count all the editorial content in the four newspapers during the study period and to provide an independent set of results to the author.

Table 6.1 Categories of environmental issues

- Atmospheric environment – air pollution, gas emission ozone, depletion, green house and acid rain, gas flaring and gas leaks
- Environmental accidents – oil spills, pipeline explosion
- Environmental management – solutions to all kinds of environmental degradation
- Marine environment – water pollution, rising sea levels
- Natural environmental incidents – erosion, floods, landslides, windstorms, bush fires
- Terrestrial environment – land degradation, desertification, deforestation, solid waste

Results and Hypothesis Testing

Results

Results from the two research assistants confirmed that there were a total of 8,152 editorial items in the 70 newspaper issues used in the study. Of this total, 240 items (2.94 per cent) focused on environmental issues, while the non-environmental items amounted to 7,912 (97.172 per cent). Data presented in Tables 6.2 and 6.3 provide striking information about the state of environmental reporting in the Nigerian press during the research period.

It is evident that, when the world was celebrating Environment Day, the Nigerian press published only 240 items focusing on the environment in four weeks (Table 6.2), compared with 7,912 non-environmental items in the same period. The *Vanguard* led in the reporting of non-environmental items (Table 6.3), with 2,460 items (31.09 per cent), followed by *The Punch* with 2,284 items (28.86 per cent), the *Guardian* (1,815 items, or 29.93 per cent) and *This Day* (1,353 items, or 17.10 per cent). It is clear from Table 6.2 that the top three environmental content types in the four newspapers consisted of the news (50.44 per cent), pictures (25.21 per cent) and feature articles (20.86 per cent). There were two editorial pieces (0.9 per cent) focusing on environmental issues in the newspapers during the study period and no interviews focusing on environmental issues within the study period. However, limited efforts were made to report on environmental issues

Table 6.2   Reporting of environmental items

Newspaper/ Editorial Contents	*Guardian*	*This Day*	*Punch*	*Vanguard*	Total
News	31	4	55	26	116 (50.44%)
Editorial	1	0	0	1	2 (0.9%)
Opinions	4	0	2	1	7 (3%)
Letters	1	0	0	1	2 (0.9%)
Pullouts	0	0	2	0	2 (0.9%)
Features	22	9	4	13	48 (20.86%)
Cartoons	1	0	0	1	2 (0.9%)
Pictures	25	2	15	16	58 (25.21%)
Supplements	1	0	2	0	3 (1.3%)
Interviews	0	0	0	0	0 (0%)
Total	86 (37.39%)	15 (6.5%)	80 (34.78%)	59 (25.6%)	240 (100%)

through letters to the editor (0.9 per cent), pullouts (0.9 per cent), opinion (3 per cent) and supplements (1.3 per cent).

Further analysis of data in Table 6.2 indicates that, of the 240 editorial contents, the *Guardian* took the lead with 37.39 per cent, followed by the *Punch* (34.78 per cent), *Vanguard* (25.06 per cent) and *This Day* (6.05 per cent). Data presented in Table 6.4 show the distribution of the environmental items across the different categories created for the study (see Table 6.1). From Table 6.4, it is evident that environmental management (i.e., possible solutions to all kinds of environmental degradation) and marine environmental issues were given more emphasis

Table 6.3   Frequency of coverage of non-environmental issues by the four Nigerian newspapers

Newspaper/ Editorial Contents	Guardian	This Day	Punch	Vanguard	Total
News	707	720	1,376	1,275	4,078 (51.54%)
Editorial	17	11	17	17	62 (0.78%)
Opinions	66	25	77	84	252 (3.18%)
Letters	51	36	126	41	254 (3.21%)
Pullouts	15	8	6	15	44 (0.55%)
Features	168	67	133	145	513 (6.48%)
Cartoons	18	3	82	112	215 (2.71%)
Pictures	755	476	448	754	2,433 (30.61%)
Supplements	4	2	4	4	14 (0.17%)
Interviews	14	5	15	13	47 (0.59%)
Total	1,815 (22.9%)	1,353 (17.1%)	2,284 (28.9%)	2,460 (31.1%)	7,912 (100%)

(49.32 per cent and 18.38 per cent, respectively), by the four newspapers. Matters relating to the terrestrial environment accounted for 10.76 per cent, followed by natural environmental incidents (10.31 per cent) and the atmospheric environment (4.48 per cent). On the basis of these categories, data presented in Table 6.4 show that the *Guardian* took the lead in the reporting on issues relating to environmental management and marine environment, followed by *Punch* and *Vanguard*.

For this study's purposes, the prominence of an issue was measured in terms of space allocated to the issue, either in the front,

Table 6.4   Reporting of categories of environmental issues

Newspapers/ Categories of Issues	Guardian	This Day	Punch	Vanguard	Total
Terrestrial environment	6	2	12	4	24 (10.76%)
Marine environment	14	4	15	8	41 (18.38%)
Atmospheric environment	6	1	3	0	10 (4.48%)
Environmental management	42	5	31	32	110 (49.32%)
Natural environmental incidents	4	3	8	8	23 (10.31%)
Environmental accidents	4	0	6	5	15 (6.72%)
Total	76 (34.08%)	15 (6.72%)	75 (33.63%)	57 (25.56%)	223 (100%)

back or inside pages of the papers. The front page was considered 'high', the back page 'medium' and the inside pages 'low'. The data collected and analysed show that none of the environmental issues covered by the four Nigerian newspapers in 1–14 June, 2004, and 1–14 June, 2005, were on the front page. In fact, 60 per cent of environmental content was published in the inside pages of the newspapers, while 40 per cent was found on the back pages. From this, it can be concluded that the Nigerian press did not give prominence to environmental issues.

Hypotheses Testing

Tables 6.2 and 6.3 provide the data for testing the hypotheses. They record the frequency of environmental and non-environmental items in the Nigerian press during the period under study. For the purposes of this study, the chi-square (X^2) was used. This is a non-parametric test, and does not require the sample data to be more or less normally distributed, which parametric tests like t-tests would require. However, it is important to acknowledge here that chi-square relies on the assumption that the variable is normally distributed in the population from which the sample is drawn. A non-parametric test, like chi-square, is a rough estimate of confidence; it accepts weaker, less accurate data as input than parametric tests (e.g., t-tests and analysis of variance) and therefore has less status in the pantheon of statistical tests.

Based on data collected and analysed, the calculated value for X^2 was 617.31 at 62 degrees of freedom and a confidence level of 0.05, while the table value was 40.11. Since the calculated value is greater than the table value, the study's working hypothesis was rejected, while the alternative hypothesis (i.e., that the Nigerian press would give more coverage to non-environmental issues) was therefore accepted. This implies that the Nigerian press did not give significant coverage and reporting to environmental issues during the celebration of the WED in June 2004, despite its global importance, local and national relevance and the implications of the celebration period.

Discussion and Conclusion

Data presented in Tables 6.2 and 6.3 reveal an abysmal level of under-reporting on the environment in Nigeria. It is startling to observe that, despite the grave implications of environmental problems in Nigeria, especially in the Niger Delta region, the Nigerian press gave only 2.94 per cent of its editorial content to environmental issues in the two-week period. Even this paltry percentage was mostly tucked away in the inside pages of the papers. If this happened in the month of June, when the WED was celebrated globally, then the Nigerian press's attention to the environment at any other time of the year is best imagined, rather than described. Yet the news media are the primary source from which people obtain knowledge of local, national and global events and issues.

There is no doubt that news is the public's primary source of information on environmental issues and problems. News disseminates information that people want, need and should know, and news organisations (such as newspaper publishing houses) both circulate and shape knowledge. As such, the news media play a critical role in legitimising and shaping the definitions of environmental issues over time. As the news media confer legitimacy on problems as they emerge in the public agenda, most news reported is assumed to be problem-focused as a result of values used by editors and reporters to determine what news is. This study has shown that the Nigerian mass media do not often carry sufficient information about the environment, if compared with other issues (e.g., political, social, and economic) ones. Several factors may be responsible for this development.

First, it is very likely that the Nigerian press (as elsewhere) is influenced by agenda-setting theory. By focusing more on non-environmental issues during WED celebrations, the Nigerian media not only serve as an agenda-setter, but also as a determinant of merit with regards to individual stories. In the process, the media impress upon people which news is 'important' and which 'unimportant', therefore inadvertently making decisions for the public. They owe society an obligation to meet its information, moral and social needs. As Cohen (1963: 13) noted, the press 'may not be successful much of the time in telling people what to think, but it is stunningly successful in telling its readers what to think about'.

It was sad to note that the Nigerian press, the watchdog of society, did not hold an opinion on the state of the environment, as was evident from the lack of an editorial on the environment during the WED celebrations in June 2004. Of concern also was the dearth of public opinion and of letters to the editor on environmental issues. This may be the outcome of cumulative under-reporting on the environment in previous years. If members of the public are not sufficiently informed about environmental issues they are unlikely to be aware of them, or to express any views and participate in decision-making to solve environmental problems. Although many subjects were reflected in the few reports on the environment, environmental management issues topped the table (see Table 6.4); with terrestrial and atmospheric environmental issues drawing a dismal number of reports. However, it is pertinent to observe here that reports on solutions to environmental problems would not make a lot of sense to a population that is not already familiar with the problems. The public needs to be made aware of the broad spectrum of environmental problems (e.g., marine, terrestrial, atmospheric), their causes and consequences, before they can appreciate any information on solutions to these problems.

Secondly, the under-reporting of environmental issues observed in the course of this research could also reflect the attitude of editors to environmental reporting and concern for the environment in Nigeria. It could be argued that the Nigerian press is not committed to regular coverage and reporting of environmental issues, unless such issues are sufficiently linked to the political and economic headline stories which usually dominate the newspapers' front pages. This is also logically expressed in the fact that none of the environmental issues reported was given a front-page treatment by the newspapers. To extend the argument further, it is not very surprising that few reporters are assigned to the environment beat by newspapers. Yet the media have a social responsibility to inform the public about environmental matters and questions to ensure true public participation in environmental decision-making. Journalists should see the moral principle of the right to life as being threatened not only by environmental degradation, but also by their negligence in effectively reporting the situation to the general public. They should see the job of reporting incidents of environmental degradation as a significant contribution to social and environmental sustainability in Nigeria.

Cosell (1985) reported George Bernard Shaw as saying that the worst sin against our fellow creatures is not to hate them, but to be indifferent to their needs, an action which Shaw is said to have noted was the essence of inhumanity. Over time, the media in every society have presented themselves as stewards or trustees that act in the people's interest. For this reason, the notion of the press as the watchdog of society has emerged. They owe society an obligation to meet its information, moral and social needs. For them to be seen as not being alive to this obligation could be interpreted as their being indifferent to society's needs, therefore showing inhumanity.

If journalism's principal mission is to inform, then the public should be interested in the amount and quality of information available in the media about the environment. In the context of Nigeria, the environment reporter should inform the public about the positive and negative developments affecting the Nigerian environment. Journalists should report not only on oil spills, gas flares and their accompanying water and air pollution, but also on estate management, town planning, construction company activities, housing conditions, public health, urban management and rural conditions, conservation and overcrowding.

This requires a particular knowledge and considerable expertise, energetic digging and a sensitive interpretative touch (see e.g., MacDougall 1977). The cornerstone of the 'environment beat' is questioning and testing so-called conventional wisdom, exploring the national policies that put economic values above human ones. According to Friedman (1990), environmental reporting should provide background information that empowers readers and viewers, giving them information with which to make decisions. Furthermore, he says:

> Control over environmental risks and hazards are a major factor for citizens, who are more apt to accept risk if they feel they have some degree of control over it. But people seeing only facts without context in hazardous situations may decide that they are helpless to intervene or change a situation, and therefore do not participate in the debate. (Friedman, 1990: 19)

Thirdly, these newspapers' performance in respect of their coverage and reporting of environmental issues might be influenced to some extent by their editorial policy, mission and focus, as well as financial considerations. For example, the *Guardian* is well known and liked for its coverage of environmental issues, while *This Day* is known for its significant interest in covering business and economic issues. It is thus not very surprising that *This Day* contributed a paltry 15.30 per cent of the total coverage and publication on environmental issues during the reviewed period. The volume of each paper (i.e., the number of pages per issue) might also determine space allocated to social, economic, political and environmental issues. Of the four newspapers, the *Guardian* is the most voluminous and *Punch* the least. The *Guardian* can afford to allocate more space to environmental issues in the light of competition for space from other issues, e.g. politics, economy, sports. On the other hand, from a financial perspective, the four newspapers are privately owned and managed. The need to generate sufficient revenue might influence what is eventually printed. According to Ekanem (2003: 207):

> Experience has shown that in most cases economic considerations usually override editorial judgment in Nigeria. In several cases, it has been revealed that editors authorized the replacement of a science page with an advertisement paid for at the closing hours of production. This is very frustrating to the media personnel on the science and technology

desk and to the devoted readers and stakeholders. The industry has been treated with levity and contempt primarily because the financial resources required to assert its rightful position as the engine of growth in the society are lacking.

To conclude, this chapter maintains that the Nigerian press is out of line with the mission of the communication enterprise advocated by Horace Greeley, an editor of the *New York Tribune*, in 1841. According to Johnson (1997: 104), Greeley declared that his paper would not merely record congregational, domestic and foreign news, but also whatever appeared calculated to promote morality, maintain social order, extend the blessings of education, or in any way subserve the great cause of human progress in ultimate virtue, liberty and happiness.

In support of this point of view, Johnson (1997: 102) sees the media in the last instance as: 'Potentially, a great secular church, a system of evangelism for dispersing the darkness of ignorance, expelling error and establishing truth'. This is a great responsibility for the media in any age. By focusing on non-environmental issues during the WED celebrations, the findings confirm that the Nigerian media are now driven less by social responsibility and more by the market. Unless citizens have adequate and accurate information on all issues and the problems confronting them, they will be unable to take informed decisions on how to tackle the problems and resolve conflicts. Without such information, they will be unable to comprehend the government's day-to-day working or to participate. Such information is also useful in holding those in authority accountable and responsible for their acts of omission and commission. The media therefore have a social responsibility to act on such information in ways that are good for society in general and not only in the interest of certain persons or organisations. It is the media's role to keep the citizenry well informed in a democratic setting like Nigeria (Ojo 2003).

Table 6.5 Page placement of all environmental issues in the selected newspapers

Front Pages	Inside Pages	Back Pages	Total
0	184	39	223
(0%)	(82.51%)	(17.49%)	(100%)

Table 6.6 Chi-square within bivariate table showing the frequency of environmental and non-environmental issues covered by the four newspapers in the period

Newspaper/ Editorial Contents	Environmental Issues				Non Environmental Issues				Grand Total
	Guardian	This Day	Punch	Vanguard	Guardian	This Day	Punch	Vanguard	
News	31	4	55	26	707	720	1,376	1,275	4,194
Editorial	1	0	0	1	17	11	17	17	64
Opinions	4	0	2	1	66	25	77	84	259
Letters	1	0	0	1	51	36	126	41	256
Pullouts	0	0	2	0	15	8	6	15	46
Features	22	9	4	13	168	67	133	145	561
Cartoons	1	0	0	1	18	3	82	112	217
Pictures	25	2	15	16	755	476	448	754	2,491
Supplements	1	0	2	0	4	2	4	4	17
Interviews	0	0	0	0	14	5	15	13	47
Total	86	15	80	59	1,815	1,353	2,284	2,460	8,152

References

Ader, C. R. (1995) 'A longitudinal study of agenda setting for the issue of environmental pollution', *Journalism and Mass Communication Quarterly*, 72, pp. 300–11.

Arvai, J. L., and Mascarenhas, M. J. (2001) 'Print media framing of the environmental movement in a Canadian forestry debate', *Environmental Management*, 27/5, pp. 705–14.

Atwater, T. M., Salwen, B., and Anderson, R. B. (1985) 'Media agenda setting with environmental issues', *Journalism Quarterly*, 62, pp. 393–7.

Berger, Arthur A. (1993) *Media Research Techniques*, London: Sage Publications.

Brewer, J. (2003) 'Content analysis', in Robert L. Miller and John D. Brewer (eds), *A to Z of Social Research*, pp. 43–5, London: Sage Publications.

Chan, K. (1999) 'The media and environmental issues in Hong Kong', *International Journal of Public Opinion Research*, 11/2, pp. 135–51.

Chapman, G., Kumar, K., Fraser, C., and Gaber, I. (1997) *Environmentalism and the Mass Media*, London: Routledge.

Cohen, B. C. (1963) *The Press, the Public and Foreign Policy*, Princeton, NJ: Princeton University Press.

Cosell, H (1985) *I Never Played the Game*, New York: Avon Books.

Defleur, M. L., and Ball-Rokeach, S. J. (1982) *Theories of Mass Communication*, New York: Longman.

Driedger, S. M., and Eyles, J. (2003) 'Different frames, different fears: communicating about chlorinated water and cancer in the Canadian media', *Social Science and Medicine*, 56, pp. 1279–93.

Ekanem, I. A. (2003) 'Communicating science information in a science-unfriendly environment: the experience of Nigeria', *Public Understanding of Science*, 12, pp. 203–9.

Friedman, Sharon M. (1990) 'Two decades of the environmental beat', *Gannett Center Journal*, 4/3, Summer, pp. 13–23.

Golding, P. and Elliot, P. (1979), *Making the News*, London, Longman.

Gooch, G. D. (1996) 'The Baltic press and environment: a study of the coverage of environmental problems in Estonian and Latvian newspapers 1992–1993', *Geoforum*, 26/4, pp. 429–43.

Hansen, A., ed. (1993) *The Mass Media and Environmental Issues*, Leicester: Leicester University Press.

Johnson, Paul (1997) 'The media and truth: is there a moral duty?', in *Annual Editions: Mass Media*, pp. 102–5, Guildford: McGraw-Hill.

Kodilinye, G. (1990) *Nigeria Law of Torts*, Ibadan: Spectrum Law Publishers.

McCombs, M. (2004) *Setting the Agenda: The Mass Media and Public Opinion*, Cambridge: Polity Press.

McCombs, M. and Shaw, D. L. (1972) 'The agenda-setting function of mass media', *Public Opinion Quarterly*, 36/2, pp. 176–85.

MacDougall, Curtis D. (1977) *Interpretative Reporting*, New York: Macmillan.

MacDougall, Curtis D. and R. D. Raid (1987) *Interpretative Reporting*, New York: Macmillan.

Moffat, D., and Linden, O. (1995) 'Perception and reality: assessing priorities for sustainable development in the Niger River Delta', *Ambio: Journal of Human Environment*, 24, pp. 527–38.

Odu, M. A. C. (1992) *Introduction to Estate Management in Nigeria: The Handbook on Land Policy, Private and Public Wealth*, Lagos: Ultraspec Ltd.

Ojo, E. O. (2003) 'The mass media and the challenges of sustainable democratic values in Nigeria: possibilities and limitations', *Media, Culture and Society*, 25/6, pp. 821–40.

Olutokun, A., and Seteolu, D. (2001) 'The media and democratic rule in Nigeria', *Development Policy Management Network Bulletin*, 13/3, pp. 30–4.

Osibanjo, Oladele (1998) 'Environmental pollution and dispute resolution in industrial communities', a paper at the international workshop on industrial pollution management for sustainable community development, Uyo.

Soroka, S. N. (2002) 'Issue attributes and agenda-setting by media, the public, policymakers in Canada', *International Journal of Public Opinion Research*, 14/3, pp. 264–85.

—— (1988) *Government and the Media in Nigeria*, Calabar: Centaur Publishers.

Udoakah, Nkereuwem (1998) *Development Communication*, Ibadan: Stirling-Horden Publishers.

Zhu, J., Watt, J. H., Snyder, L. B., Yan, J. and Jiang, Y. (1993) 'Public issue priority formation: media agenda-setting and social interaction', *Journal of Communication*, 43, pp. 8–29.

7

REGIONALISM AND ETHNICITY IN THE NIGERIAN PRESS: AN ANALYSIS OF THE COVERAGE OF BOKO HARAM AND THE NIGER DELTA CONFLICTS IN THE *GUARDIAN* AND *DAILY TRUST*

Muḥammad Jameel Yusha'u

Introduction

Since the amalgamation of Northern and Southern Nigeria in 1914, there has always been a struggle for self-assertion between various regions and ethnic groups. Nigeria had to undergo a bloody civil war in 1967–70 before the country was kept together. Different ethnic militias, like the Odua People's Congress (OPC), Arewa People's Congress (APC), Movement for the Survival of Sovereign State of Biafra (MASSOB) (Badmus 2006) and Movement for the Emancipation of the Niger Delta (MEND) have emerged, each claiming to protect the interest of its people. These ethnic militia organisations have an elite wing, like the Afenifere, who claim to represent the interest of the Yoruba, Ohaneze Ndigbo which claims to protect the interest of the Igbo, the Arewa Consultative Forum which claims to represent the interest of the North, and the Middle-belt Forum, claiming that it champions the interests of the middle-belt, especially the Christian-dominated states in northern Nigeria. This chapter

studies the coverage of the Boko Haram uprising, a group claiming
to be against 'Western education', which took place in some northern Nigerian states and the confrontation between the military and
Niger Delta militants seeking control over the region's oil fields. The
two newspapers studied are the *Daily Trust* from northern Nigeria
and the *Guardian* from the south. Although both newspapers carry
national news, their reporting cannot be divorced from the influence of their region and ethnic loyalty, as will be discussed in later
sections of this chapter.

The news media, the press in particular, are owned by members of
elite organisations. In times of crisis, therefore, the newspapers that
should serve as watchdogs, and lead the way in exposing the truth,
also become ethno-regional champions, promoting regional or ethnic
interests. Nyamnjoh (2005) discussed how the press in Africa is
obsessed with the politics of belonging, looking at issues from ethnic
and regional perspectives. This, according to Nyamnjoh, has affected
the ability of the media in Africa to serve as impartial and honest arbi-
ters. Instead, the media have succeeded in dividing society. Nowhere
is this description more apt than in Nigeria, where the press, which is
predominantly located in one section of the country, the south-west,
frames stories from the north *vs.* south, Muslims *vs.* Christians perspectives, with Northerners and Muslims more likely to be portrayed in a
negative light.

This is one reason why studies like this have become relevant,
since it involves coverage of stories about the Niger Delta, which is
predominantly Christian from the south, and Boko Haram, which
is predominantly Muslim from the north. In both cases there was
an encounter with Nigerian security forces in which lives were lost,
including those of innocent civilians. The newspapers to be studied are
the *Daily Trust*, a northern newspaper with a predominantly Muslim
ownership, and the *Guardian,* a southern newspaper with a predominantly Christian ownership. The dates for the study are 25 July to 7
August 2009, for the Boko Haram uprising, which runs from the date
when the event was first reported by the newspapers to the following two weeks when the reporting of the crisis was at its peak. For
the Niger Delta conflict, the time period is 16–29 May 2009, which
is the period when the federal government's Joint Task Force (JTF)
descended on the militants who carried out attacks on oil installations

and other areas of interest to the federal government and foreign oil companies. The study was conducted qualitatively by means of critical discourse analysis (CDA).

Critical discourse analysis, or what was previously known as critical linguistics, is a study method that focuses on the use of language as a social practice. It is a method of study that is interested in discovering the structures used in communicating messages whether verbal, textual or conversational (Van Dijk 1993). In his discussion on the principles of critical discourse analysis, citing Norman Fairclough, Van Dijk suggested that critical discourse analysis is 'a true multidisciplinary, and an account of intricate relationships between text, talk, social cognition, power, society and culture' (Van Dijk 1993: 253). It is an analysis methodology that looks at the intertextual nature of a text. 'The methodological advantage' of critical discourse analysis, according to Chouliaraki, is the ability to bring together 'the discursive with the textual, through a conjunction of analysis of both text and its intertextual context'. Chouliaraki's view is that critical discourse analysis 'not only views the text as intertextual but maintains that linguistic processes in a text encode multiple social functions' (Chouliarki 2000: 297).

Another interesting study using critical discourse analysis is Fairclough's study on the use of language by New Labour,[1] which explains how different linguistic tools can be used to transmit a message by emphasising or de-emphasising certain issues through the manipulation of sentence and vocabularies, or by using metaphors that can create a meaning, consciously or unconsciously, in the readers' minds. His work also shows how the order of discourse, genres, styles and discourses were used to communicate the stand of New Labour. Vagueness was created through nominalisation by using sentences without an agent or actor while, in some instances, metaphors are used to create an impression that will leave a strong mark on the mind of the reader (Fairclough 2000).

This is particularly interesting for this chapter because of the ethno-regional divide in the stories on Boko Haram and the Niger Delta militants. This chapter will therefore study the headlines of the stories for the period under study by specifically paying attention to nominalisation, and the use of simple sentence structure involving

Subject-Verb-Object (SVO), and identify the possible reasons why newspapers frame stories in a particular way. Previous studies have focused only on headlines, such as Chiluwa (2007). He conducted a study of how the press in Nigeria frame the discourses of political scandals in their headlines.

Brief History of Boko Haram and the Niger Delta Conflicts

Boko in Hausa means Western education, while *haram* is an Arabic word, adopted in Hausa, meaning forbidden or prohibited. So the simple translation of *Boko Haram* is 'Western education is forbidden'. However, the word *boko* has a loaded meaning in the Hausa language. A Western-educated person is called '*Dan Boko*' (the son of Boko) or '*Yar Boko*' (the daughter of Boko). Among Hausa people, to be associated with *Boko* means a person has strange behaviour compared to other community members. This could be associated with different dressing, eating habits, socialising with people, etc. Tilde (2009) discussed the origin of the word *boko*:

> On the authority of Professor Mahdi Adamu Ngaski, a celebrated historian, author of *The Hausa Factor in the History of West Africa,* '*boko*' simply means 'fake'. Before it was largely consigned to Western education, *boko* was often used to connote the 'fake bride', *amaryar boko*, who rode the horse in place of the real bride as the convoy of celebrants escorted her to her new home. The real bride would secretly be carried earlier by two or three women to her home. So when Western education came to Hausaland, the learned rejected it and gave it a derogatory connotation, *ilimin boko*, 'fake education.' Sadly, this name has remained the standard translation of 'Western education' among all the Hausa speaking people of West Africa and I have never heard of any effort to change it, except the *ilimin zamani* that is sparsely applied. To date, there is no alternative nomenclature for *makarantar boko*, 'fake school' that connotes modern schools for Western education.

This is not the only view on the meaning and origin of *boko*. Ibrahim (2009) suggests that the word *boko* originates from the English word 'book', so *boko* is a corrupted version of the word 'book' in Hausa-speaking areas. The reason for this, according to Ibrahim, is that when the colonialists came to the Hausa city states, they came up with an educational system that is different from the traditional one, where people learn by using a wooden slate. So people who learn from a book are referred to as *yan boko* (people learning from a book).

Here, it is important to make some clarifications. If we accept the version that sees the origin of *boko* as coming from the English word 'book', it doesn't mean that there were no books in Hausaland. On the contrary, there was abundant literature on Islam, theology and even science education taught at *Makarantun ilmi* (traditionally, post-primary and tertiary schools). Perhaps the reason for seeing it that way was because pupils were taught by using the wooden slate *allo*, until they matured, and joined *makarantun ilmi*, so it looked unusual for pupils at an early stage to be using books in place of the wooden slate.

Another important thing to note in Ibrahim's contribution (2009) is that *boko* is not restricted to Western education. Any form of knowledge that is taught in a modern setting using classrooms and an organised school structure, including Islamic education, is also part of *boko*. From this viewpoint, all the Islamic scholars in Nigeria, such as Sheikh Abubakar Mahmoud Gumi, or Sheikh Adam Ilori, who attended the School of Arabic Studies in Kano and then studied in other universities around the world, are *yan boko*. This could explain why it is difficult for the Muslim community to accept the view of the group that *boko* is bad. So the *Boko Haram* group have simply taken a one-sided view of knowledge, due either to ignorance or for selfish motives, or both.

Despite this, it is still important to note that resentment against Western education is not a new phenomenon. It is a historical issue which can be traced back to the arrival of Christian missionaries and British colonial administrators. Muslims, especially those from northern Nigeria who were under the auspices of the Sokoto Caliphate and the Borno Empire, saw Western aspects of education or *ilmin boko* as a means to dilute their cultural and religious values with foreign ones. Another factor that contributed to the continuation of resentment against Western education was British colonial policy which denied Muslims access to Western education. This created an imbalance between Muslims and Christians throughout Nigeria in terms of the acquisition of Western education.

From this background, it is easier to understand the context of the resentment against Western education by the group called Boko Haram. There are different versions giving the exact time that the group was formed. Some say 2002 and others 2004 (Oriyomi 2009; Mahjar-Barducci 2010). However, the group became prominent in July 2009 due to the violent clashes between its members and security forces. The news media reported different stories about the origin of the crisis. Some versions had it that the group was attacked by the police during a funeral procession and group members retaliated afterwards. Other versions had it that the group attacked police stations as part of their mission against anything Western, which they see as being evil and responsible for Nigeria's predicament (Watts 2009). What is interesting, however, is how the news media, both foreign and local, reported the story up to the killing of the group's leader, Muhammad Yusuf.[2]

Today, the group has become more complicated, especially with the attack on the UN building in Abuja, Nigeria's capital, in August 2011. However, other criminal groups and regional militias have also used the group's name to attack individuals and places of worship. This was illustrated by Jane Herskovits, a US Professor of History and a Nigeria expert, in a *New York Times* article on 2 January 2012:

> *Boko Haram* has evolved into a franchise that includes criminal groups claiming its identity. Revealingly, Nigeria's State Security Services issued a statement on Nov. 30, identifying members of four 'criminal syndicates' that send threatening text messages in the name of *Boko Haram*. Southern Nigerians – not Northern Muslims – ran three of these four syndicates, including the one that led the American Embassy and other foreign missions to issue warnings that emptied Abuja's high-end hotels. And last week, the security services arrested a Christian Southerner wearing Northern Muslim garb as he set fire to a church in the Niger Delta. In Nigeria, religious terrorism is not always what it seems. None of these excuses *Boko Haram's* killing of innocents. But it does raise questions about a rush to judgment that obscures Nigeria's complex reality.

As for the crisis in the Niger Delta, it is a story that can be traced to colonial times before Nigeria became independent. In a study on the Niger Delta conflict, Obijiofor (2009) states that the history of the crisis in the Niger Delta is related to British colonial administration, particularly on the issue of oil exploration. At the time, ethnic minority groups, especially the Ijaws, objected to the amalgamation of the northern and southern protectorates. This led the British government to establish a commission under the leadership of Sir Henrey Willink to investigate the needs of ethnic minority groups. The increase in oil production escalated the tensions in the region in the 1950s. By 1966 there was a clamour by some local activists under the leadership of Isaac Boro who was fighting for an independent Niger Delta Republic. However, he was overpowered by the federal government between February and March 1966. Since then the struggle calmed down until the emergence of Ken Saro Wiwa, another activist who wanted the independence of Niger Delta. He was killed in 1995 by the federal military government of the late General Sani Abacha (Obijiorfor 2009: 176–7), after his militia was accused of killing some Ogoni people who are among the ethnic groups in the Niger Delta region. Since then, the Niger Delta region has known little peace. Media stories are always of kidnapping and confrontation between the federal government and various regional militia groups.

> On May 13th 2009 federal troops launched a full scale military offensive against what the government sees as violent organised criminals who have crippled the oil and gas industry. Thousands of dirt-poor villagers in the region around Gbaramatu, SouthWest of the oil city of Warri in Delta State – an area known to harbour a number of militant encampments including the notorious Camp 5 – have been displaced and hundreds of innocent civilians killed. (Watts 2009: 1)

Here, it is important to compare the Boko Haram uprising and the Niger Delta militants. According to the preceding information, the resistance to Western education which Boko Haram champions, as well as the resistance to the Nigerian State by Niger Deltans, started in the colonial period. In a way, therefore, these crises are continuations from and remnants of Nigeria's colonial and post-colonial heritage. In both cases there is confrontation between the state using its security forces and activists who have certain grievances against the state. In both cases the Nigerian security forces used force that resulted in the killing of innocent civilians. The two groups belong to different religious, ethnic and regional sections of Nigeria. As the press is regionally and ethnically divided, it is interesting to see how the two newspapers, the *Daily Trust* and the *Guardian* frame the two stories.

Ethnicity, Regionalism and the Nigerian Press

It is common for individuals and groups in different societies to have a way of defining themselves through the creation of an identity that makes them distinct from other members of their society. In his discussion on the concept of identity, Parekh (2008) identified three different kinds of identities. Through *personal identity* an individual distinguishes himself through his features, biographical achievement and his/her sense of self consciousness. By *social identity* group members define themselves in terms of belonging to a particular ethnic, religious or cultural group. Finally, there is the *individual or overall identity* in which the two are combined together as a means of self-differentiation (Parekh 2008: 9).

In Nigeria, people are conscious of both individual and group identity. This was further promoted by the colonial and post-colonial arrangement of the country, in which access to state resources and even individual achievement related to one's social group, ethnically or regionally. The formation of political parties from independence to date, appointment into federal positions, and even the distribution of the resources reflect this sense of identity.

According to Osaghae and Suberu (2005: 9–10), 'ethnic identities in Nigeria have been summarised into two broad categories of majority and minority groups'. This is one of the reasons why Nnoli states that 'ethnicity is the fundamental basis for identity and political cleavages in Nigeria' (Kalu 2004: 15).[3]

At the beginning of 1999 when Nigeria once again came under civilian administration, the speaker of the House of Representatives, Alhaji Ibrahim Salisu Buhari, was a focus of attention. Investigations by *The News*, a southern magazine, confirmed that he had neither attended the University of Toronto as he claimed, nor was he honest about his age. The entire southern press followed the story aggressively.

Alhaji Salisu Buhari had to resign. Another scandal followed: the governor of Lagos state, Bola Tinubu, was accused of falsifying his certificate by claiming to have attended the University of Chicago in the United States. Investigations by *Today* newspaper revealed that he had not. Yet the Nigerian press, which is predominantly located in the South, remained silent, and Bola Tinubu continued to serve in office for two terms (Olukoyun 2004; Jibo and Okoosi-Simbine 2003). Two comments made by various stakeholders on the differences in reporting the Buhari and Tinubu stories deserve attention. The first was made by one of the editors of *This Day* newspaper Waziri Adio. According to him:

> Buhari (the former Speaker) is from the North. That section of the country has always claimed that the press has a sectional agenda. It is now turning out that the region of origin decided Buhari's fate. Tinubu, however, comes from the haven of the 'Ngbati press'. Some of us have fooled ourselves that this is a fair independent press. Now we know better. (*Media Review*, Oct./. 1999, in Olukoyun 2004: 83)

The second remark was made by the then Chairman of the Senate Committee on Special Duties, Senator Bala Adamu:

> It is very clear from what has happened in the past few months, beginning from the Bola Tinibu saga to the current attempts from the outside to unseat the Senate president, that the media, except for a few ones, has clearly shown that it is biased, sectional and tribalistic, and it has been disappointing – Had Mr Okadigbo been a Yoruba man the bashing, the negative publicity and campaign of calumny that has been waged assiduously against him would not have taken place. (*Media Rights Agenda* (2000), 118, in Olukoyun 2004: 84)

While the media in the south-west of Nigeria remained silent about the Bola Tinubu story, one exception from the region was the late Alhaji Abdulganiyu Fawahenmi, popularly called Gani, who took the matter to court in order to challenge Bola Tinubu to produce his certificate. Gani Fawahenmi was one of the few Nigerians who could live above ethnicity and look at issues dispassionately. Despite his effort, the media remained silent and Bola Tinubu finished his tenure in office.

With this background in mind, this chapter will analyse the coverage of the Boko Haram uprising in northern Nigeria in comparison with the coverage of Niger Delta conflict in the *Daily Trust* and the *Guardian* newspapers.

Findings and Discussion

The two newspapers framed the stories of Boko Haram and the Niger Delta conflict in different ways. The sentences used to frame the headlines in both newspapers reveal the position of those papers in terms of the sympathy, or otherwise, that each exhibits towards either Boko Haram or the Niger Delta crisis. Let us start by analysing the discourses of the Niger Delta conflict.

Starting with the *Guardian*, this newspaper ensures that the reader is left in no doubt as to who is speaking and with what tone. In most of the headlines in Table 7.1, the subject is very clear, so also is the object on whom the action falls. Consider these two headlines in Table 7.1,

Clark wants Yar'adua to stop military action
Rights group condemns govt's refusal to halt Niger Delta action

The newspaper quotes Edwin Clark, an elder in the Niger Delta region and one of the supporters of the struggle over control of oil resources in the region, calling on President Yaradua to stop bombarding the militants. The second headline quoted human rights groups who condemned the military action. If you follow all the headlines in the *Guardian*, it mainly quoted voices that condemned action taken by the military or framed its headlines around the need for amnesty for the militants. The voices being quoted are those of Anthony Enahoro, a leading political figure in the country since colonial times, or of Wole Soyinka. These are voices sympathetic to the Niger Delta cause. From this, it is easy to discern the newspaper's position, i.e., sympathy for Niger Delta militants, since the paper's ownership is also from the Niger Delta region.

However, there are other headlines which expose the ethno-regional divide in Nigerian journalism. Consider the following:

Arewa backs action in Delta, S'South alleges genocide
Northern elders okay military action in Delta

Table 7.1 Sentence structure in the coverage of the Niger Delta conflict, based on nominalisation and subject-verb-object (SVO)

Nominalisation	SVO	Newspaper	Date
	Clark wants Yaraduwa to stop military action	*Guardian*	24 May 2009
	Rights group condemns govt's refusal to halt Niger Delta action	*Guardian*	23 May 2009
	Yaraduwa reaffirms amnesty for Niger Delta militants	*Guardian*	23 May 2009
	Senate probes military action in Delta	*Guardian*	21 May 2009
	MEND, INC decry Arewa's nod for military action	*Guardian*	29 May 2009
	Delta Gov, leaders meet over JTF attacks	*Guardian*	18 May 2009
	Enahoro, Soyinka, others want halt to military action in Niger Delta	*Guardian*	22 May 2009
The Niger Delta	Ibru urges end to military operation in Delta State	*Guardian*	22 May 2009
Genocide (opinion)		*Guardian*	25 May 2009
	Arewa backs action in Delta, South-South alleges genocide	*Guardian*	28 May 2009
	Northern elders okay military action in Delta	*Guardian*	28 May 2009
	MEND warns oil coys, seize worker	*Daily Trust*	14 May 2009
	100,000 bpd lost to MEND attack	*Daily Trust*	26 May 2009
	Niger Delta crisis: NEMA calls for cease fire	*Daily Trust*	26 May 2009
	JTF recovers arms in N/Delta	*Daily Trust*	22 May 2009
	JTF over runs Iroko militants' camp	*Daily Trust*	19 May 2009
	JTF suspends air raid, frees 14	*Daily Trust*	25 May 2009
	Senator flees military action in N/Delta	*Daily Trust*	20 May 2009

Arewa is a Hausa word which means 'North', so while the elders of the South were calling for restraint and an end to military action against militants, those from the North wanted the action to continue and it is this message the paper conveys to the ordinary reader. This is how newspaper editors frame stories that directly or indirectly shape our perception of events. The point that should be understood here is that although language is used to communicate a message, it is in itself powerless about how discourses are assembled, rather, it is the people behind the language who make it sound as it does. According to Wodak, 'for CDA language is not powerful on its own – it gains power by the use powerful people make of it' (2001: 10).

While *Guardian* headlines gave more attention to bringing an end to the military offensive on the militants in the Niger Delta, the *Daily Trust* concentrated on the economic angle, trying to expose what Nigeria was losing in terms of oil revenue, as well as the activities of the militants that caused the military action. It also quoted the Joint Task Force (JTF), to which the government had given responsibility for fighting the militants. The following headlines from Table 7.1 serve as examples:

100,000 bpd lost to MEND attack
JTF recovers arms in N/Delta
JTF over runs Iroko militants' camp

When these headlines from the *Daily Trust* are compared those of the *Guardian*, it becomes clear that regionalism is at play in framing the Niger Delta story. The reader who restricts himself to only one section of the press, therefore, is more likely to receive a more partisan view of the crisis. There is also no ambiguity in the way the stories have been framed; the subject, verb and object are very clear. This is one of the reasons why critical discourse analysis is interested in the social effect of the text. Here is an example: if you elevate the discourse levels of the two newspapers' headlines into our day-to-day interactions, there is a possibility that the *Guardian* reader will view military action in the Niger Delta as an attempt by the Nigerian government, which at the time of the crisis was headed by a Northerner, as a regional attempt to deny the Niger Delta people control over their land and resources, while the *Daily Trust* reader can view the conflict from the effect of the militants' activities in disrupting oil production, which has serious consequences for the country since the entire Nigerian economy depends on oil exports. This is why Fairclough (2003: 8) states that 'texts can also start wars, or contribute to changes in education, or to changes in industrial relations, and so forth'.

Coverage of the Boko Haram crisis in the two newspapers demonstrated that the *Daily Trust* had more sympathetic headlines, while the *Guardian* employed other discourses to try and link the crisis with the wider coverage of issues about Islam and Muslims globally. A point of interest in the way the headlines are constructed by the two newspapers is the use of nominalisation in various *Daily Trust* headlines. 'Nominalisation involves abstraction from the diversity of processes going on, no specification of who or what is changing, a background of the processes of change themselves, and a foregrounding of their effect' (Fairclough 2000: 26); 'one common consequence of nominalisation is that the agents of processes, people who initiate processes or act upon other people or objects, are absent from texts' (ibid., p. 13). In nominalised sentences, therefore, the subject is removed from the text and in some cases attention is concentrated on the object rather than on the subject who committed the act. Here are a few examples of nominalised *Daily Trust* headlines reporting on Boko Haram.

> 33 Boko Haram followers killed
> Concern over killing of civilians
> Boko Haram school closed in Jalingo

In all three headlines, the newspaper did not mention the main perpetrator of the act. The first headline claims that 33 members of Boko Haram were killed, but who killed them? The subject is missing. It is common knowledge that the clash was between the security forces and members of the Boko Haram group, so the headline could easily be written as 'Police Killed 33 Boko Haram Followers', or 'Soldiers Killed 33 Boko Haram Followers' – in that case we would know who the subject was who had committed the act. The same applies to the remaining two headlines. The question to be asked, for instance, in the case of the second headline is: who expresses concern over the killing of civilians, and in the case of the third headline: who closed the Boko Haram school in Jalingo?

To be noted here are the similarities between the *Guardian* news-paper's reports on the Niger Delta conflict and *Daily Trust*'s reports on the Boko Haram uprising. In both cases the newspapers used head-lines to draw attention to the plight of those involved in the conflict with security forces, i.e., Niger Delta militants for the *Guardian* and Boko Haram for the *Daily Trust.*

So how does the *Guardian* frame the story of the Boko Haram uprising? Here are some examples:

Police, Islamic Sect Clash in Bauchi
Soldiers Attack Islamic Sect's Base
Boko Haram's Suspected Financier Executed

Apart from two headlines at the beginning of the crisis that have an element of nominalisation in the coverage of Boko Haram, the *Guardian* remained consistent in using Subject-Verb-Object (SVO) in its headlines. The key difference between the *Guardian* and the *Daily Trust* is in making reference to the faith of members of Boko Haram in the headlines. This was not the case in its coverage of the Niger Delta conflict, as exemplified by the three headlines from Table 7.2. The first two headlines, above, have confirmed the encounter between members of Boko Haram and the security forces. What the *Guardian* did is not new, it is a global trend, particularly in Western news media, to include the faith of a Muslim if involved in conflict. Edward Said gave a detailed explanation of this in his book *Covering Islam* (1997), noting how the news media are more likely to include the faith of a Muslim in news reporting than those of other faiths.

What the coverage of both Boko Haram and the Niger Delta con-flict tells us is the division in Nigerian newspapers in terms of ethnicity and regionalism. As discussed earlier, little has changed from colo-nial and post-colonial times in the way Nigerian newspapers report issues. From a critical discourse analysis perspective, this could signify a number of things. It could signify how language is used by the elite to retain a line of thinking that could help them to maintain political

Table 7.2   Headlines on Boko Haram uprising in the Guardian and *Daily Trust* based on nominalisation and subject-verb-object (SVO)

Nominalisation	SVO	Newspaper	Date
	Police, Islamic sect clash in Bauchi	*Guardian*	27 July 2009
Sectarian violence spreads, (157 feared dead in Borno, Kano)		*Guardian*	28 July 2009
Fighting rages, death toll hits 300 in Borno		*Guardian*	30 July 2009
	Rep blames crisis on poverty, illiteracy	*Guardian*	31 July 2009
	Catholics, Kumuyi condemn crisis, urge respect for human lives	*Guardian*	31 July 2009
	Soldiers attack Islamic sect's base	*Guardian*	29 July 2009
	Yaradua says violence under control...	*Guardian*	29 July 2009
	Boko Haram's suspected financier executed	*Guardian*	1 August 2009
	Northern govs move to stem religious crisis	*Guardian*	4 August 2009
	Yaraduwa orders probe of Boko Haram crisis, Yusuf's death	*Guardian*	5 August 2009
The Boko Haram crisis (editorial)		*Guardian*	5 August 2009
Sect leader at large		*Daily Trust*	30 July 2009
33 Boko Haram followers killed		*Daily Trust*	30 July 2009
	Kano demolishes sect leader's mosque, house	*Daily Trust*	30 July 2009
	Sultan warns against inciting comments	*Daily Trust*	30 July 2009
Boko Haram school closed in Jalingo		*Daily Trust*	30 July 2009
Boko Haram leader killed		*Daily Trust*	31 July 2009
	Ulama wants govs, JNI to meet on Boko Haram	*Daily Trust*	31 July 2009

Table 7.2   Continued

Nominalisation	SVO	Newspaper	Date
Police parade 18 members of sect		*Daily Trust*	31 July 2009
Sect members desert mosque		*Daily Trust*	31 July 2009
	PDP govs back FG action to tame sect violence	*Daily Trust*	31 July 2009
	OIC slams Nigeria radicals	*Daily Trust*	31 July 2009
Concern over killing of civilians		*Daily Trust*	31 July 2007
As police, sect clash ... Dozens killed in Bauchi		*Daily Trust*	27 July 2009
Sect leader vows revenge		*Daily Trust*	27 July 2009
	Sheriff assures of security in Maiduguri	*Daily Trust*	27 July 2009
Sect violence spreads in the North		*Daily Trust*	28 July 2009
Sectarian violence in the North:		*Daily Trust*	28 July 2009
Why they attack police-AIG			
	ACF condemns sect crisis	*Daily Trust*	28 July 2009
	CAN blames security agencies	*Daily Trust*	28 July 2009
	Yar'dua order security to route Boko Haram	*Daily Trust*	28 July 2009
	Boko Haram hostages; Yuguda releases 120 women, children	*Daily Trust*	4 August 2009
	Boko Haram: wives, mothers lament loss of bread winners	*Daily Trust*	4 August 2009
	Video shows ex-commissioners execution	*Daily Trust*	4 August 2009
	Police rescued abducted students	*Daily Trust*	4 August 2009
	Yaradua orders probe of sect leader's death	*Daily Trust*	5 August 2009
Boko Haram leader's in law killed		*Daily Trust*	6 August 2009

power. It could also suggest how newspapers promote a particular ideological position through language manipulation.

It is important to note the choice of vocabulary in both the *Guardian* and *Daily Trust*, what Fairclough (1995) calls 'choices in the processes of categorisation'. In reporting the Niger Delta conflict, the *Guardian* persistently used the phrase 'military action' to draw attention to the role of the security forces in dealing with the militants, including the occasional use of the word 'genocide' in its headlines. *The Daily Trust*, on the other hand, made reference to the 'recovery of arms' from the militants by JTF, or the 'loss of oil barrels' as a result of the conflict, thereby drawing attention to the role of organisations like MEND in the crisis. Even in the stories' texts, *Daily Trust* refers to Boko Haram as a 'radical group', the *Guardian* as 'Islamic fundamentalists', sometimes even linking them to Taliban and Al-Qaeda. What this tells us is that the news we consume is not a neutral product, rather it is a partisan and ideological construct communicated to the reader through careful selection of words that will express an intended meaning.

Conclusion

This chapter has discussed coverage of the *Boko Haram* and Niger Delta conflicts in two leading Nigerian newspapers, the *Guardian* and *Daily Trust*. It is fair to state that both papers carried headlines that signified the security forces' excesses and gave prominence to civilian casualties, as can be seen in some of the headlines in Tables 7.1 and 7.2 but, in general terms, the two newspapers exhibited signs of ethnicity and regionalism in framing the stories of the conflicts studied. Presentation of the stories confirmed the categorisation of Nigerian newspapers that Nigerians commonly call the 'Lagos-Ibadan' and 'Kaduna-Abuja' axis. There is an imbalance in Nigerian newspaper ownership, with the south far ahead of the north due to the advantages of history and economy. Coverage of issues in Nigeria still reflects this regional and sectional divide.

Recent examples on ethnicity and regionalism which are also related to the issues under discussion can be seen from the criticisms against the Nigerian president when he exonerated the MEND from the Independence Day bombings in October 2010 after MEND had claimed responsibility (*Africa Review* 2010). Similar criticism also trailed the decision of the Central Bank of Nigeria Governor Sanusi Lamido Sanusi for donating 100 million naira to the victims of the January 2012 alleged Boko Haram bombings in Kano, when there were similar bombings in Madalla near the capital Abuja. After the criticisms in the Nigerian press, the Governor also donated 25 million naira to the victims of Madalla bombings (Haruna 2012). Ethnicity and regionalism are so deep in the Nigerian psyche that public officials make appointments or suggest the retirement of individuals in order to replace them with people from their region or ethnic groups.

Notes

1   New Labour refers to the Labour Party in Britain after its rebranding by Tony Blair when he became the party's leader.
2   In February 2010, Al-Jazeera television transmitted footage which showed how security forces extra-judicially killed unarmed civilians in the name of searching for Boko Haram members. The footage is available on <http://english.aljazeera.net/news/africa/2010/02/20102102505798741.html>.
3   In their work on the *Misrepresentation of Nigeria*, the late historian, Usman Abba (2000) debunked the notion of Hausa-Fulani as a single ethnic group, and provided examples which show that other ethnic identities, such as Yoruba or Igbo, were colonial constructs.
4   Is an ethnic group in Nigeria.

References

Africa Review (2010) 'Nigeria's political intrigues get messier after bomb blasts' <http://www.africareview.com/News/-/979180/1029194/-/view/printVersion/-/otbg6u/-/login> (accessed 22 Feb. 2012).
Aljazeera (2010) 'Nigeria killings caught on video', <http://english.aljazeera.net/news/africa/2010/02/20102102505798741.html (accessed 18 Feb. 2010).
Badmus, Isiaka Alani (2006) 'Ethnic militia movements and the crises of political order in post-military Nigeria', *Journal of Social Science*, 13/3, pp. 191–8.
Chiluwa, Innocent (2007) 'News headlines as pragmatic strategy in Nigerian press discourse', *International Journal of Language Society and Culture*, 27, pp. 63–71.
Chouliarki, Lilie (2000) 'Political discourse in the news: democratising responsibility or aestheticizing politics?', *Discourse and Society*, 11/3, pp. 293–314.
Fairclough, Norman (1995) *Media Discourse,* London: Arnold.
—— (2000) *New Labour New Language?*, London and New York: Routledge.

—— (2003) *Analysing Discourse: Textual Analysis for Social Research*, London and New York: Routledge.

Haruna, Mohammed (2012) 'Sanusi, Boko Haram and his "Marshal Plan" for the North', <http://dailytrust.com.ng/index.php?option=com_content&view=article&id=155249:sanusi-boko-haram-and-his-marshal-plan-for-the-north&catid=6:daily-columns&Itemid=6> (accessed Feb. 2012).

Herskovits, Jane (2012) 'In Nigeria, Boko Haram is not the problem', <http://www.nytimes.com/2012/01/02/opinion/in-nigeria-boko-haram-is-not-the-problem.html?pagewanted=all> (accessed Jan. 2012).

Ibrahim, Muhammad Mansur (2009) 'Matsayin Karatun Boko da Aikin Gwamnati a Musulunci' (Islamic position on Western education and working for the government), paper presented at one-day conference organised by Jama'atu Izalatul Bid'a wa Iqamatussunah, Bauchi, Nigeria, 10 May.

Jibo, Mvendaga & Okoosi-Simbine, Antonia T. (2003), 'The Nigerian Media: An Assessment of its Role in Achieving Transparent and Accountable Government in the Fourth Republic', *Nordic Journal of African Studies*, 12/2, pp. 180–195.

Kalu, Kelechi A. (2004) 'Constitutionalism in Nigeria: a conceptual analysis of ethnicity and politics', *West Africa Review*, 6, pp. 1–27.

Mahjar-Barducci, Anna (2010), Al-Qaeda in Nigeria available at http://www.gatestoneinstitute.org/979/al-qaeda-in-nigeria retrieved 10/04/2014

Nyamnjoh, Francis B. (2005) *Africa's Media, Democracy and the Politics of Belonging*, London and New York: Zed Books.

Obijiofor, Levi (2009) 'Journalism in the digital age: the Nigerian press framing of the Niger Delta Conflict', *Ecquid Novi: African Journalism Studies*, 30/2, pp. 175–203.

Olukoyun, Ayo (2004) 'Media accountability and democracy in Nigeria, 1999–2003', *African Studies Review*, 47/3, pp. 69–90.

Oriyomi, Rafiu (2009): *Nigeria's Boko Haram* available at http://www.onislam.net/english/news/3337/432136.html retrieved 10/04/2014

Osaghae, Eghosa E., and Suberu, Rotimi (2005) *A History of Identities, Violence, and Stability in Nigeria*, Centre for Research on Inequality, Human Security and Ethnicity (CRISE) working paper, 6, Oxford: Queen Elizabeth House, University of Oxford.

Parekh, Bhikhu (2008) *A New Politics of Identity: Political Principles for an Independent World*, New York: Palgrave Macmillan.

Said, Edward W. (1997) *Covering Islam: How the Media and the Experts Determined How We See the Rest of the World*, London: Vintage.

Tilde, Aliyu (2009) 'We are Boko Haram' <http://www.gamji.com/tilde/tilde99.htm> (accessed Feb. 2010).

Usman, Yusufu Bala, and Abba, Alkassum (2000) *The Misrepresentation of Nigeria: The Facts and Figures,* Centre for Democratic Research, Development and Training, Nigeria, <http://www.ceddert.com/publications/ceddert009.pdf> (accessed March 2010).

Van Dijk, Teun A (1993) 'Principles of critical discourse analysis', *Discourse and Society*, 4/2, pp. 249–83.

Watts, Michael (2009) *Crude Oil Politics: Life and Death on the Nigerian Oil Fields*, Berkeley, CA: University of California, Institute of International Studies, Working Paper, 25.

Wodak, Ruth (2001) 'What CDA is about: a summary of its history, important concepts and its developments', in Ruth Wodak and Michael Meyer (eds), *Methods of Critical Discourse Analysis*, pp. 1–13, London. Sage Publications.

8

PROGRAMMING FOR NATIONAL UNITY: THE PARADOX OF TELEVISION IN NIGERIA

Oluyinka Esan

Introduction

This chapter focuses on television, which must be regarded as the true novelty of the twentieth century. In spite of the increasing dominance of new social media and the pressure to which the mass media have been subjected, television continues to hold its ground as a popular medium. It is still relevant, in spite of the increased number of channels in the digital age, and with its messages rebroadcast in new media spaces. Although in African contexts, television is regarded as a more exclusive medium of broadcasting (radio being more universal), it still occupies a prominent position in homes across the social spectrum. In Nigeria, television is popular amongst both the affluent and the poor. It can be found both in urban and rural areas, is enjoyed by the young and old. The Nigerian television industry serves the most populous and most diverse African nation, as discussed in this chapter. Its television is the oldest and most prolific in Africa and it is therefore an appropriate example for this discussion of the medium's role in fostering national unity.

This chapter seeks to appraise the performance of television because of its peculiar socio-technical characteristics. The fact that it simulates reality, capturing sound, moving images and actions, that it transports people to distant lands and beckons them to witness events for themselves, endears television to both the educated and the unschooled who form the majority in African populations. It can be argued that television is better able than other mass media to simulate the oral culture that is the prevalent mode of communication known to the diverse traditional societies and practices which reverberate in modern African states. These are practices which are central in the construction of ethnicity. Television is thus an appropriate medium with which to bridge gaps in information and to harness different parts of society, as is its remit at its inception. Principally, it has served to link those in government with the governed. What is the paradox in its service; and what accounts for this? In this chapter, I argue that in its representations and its other routine operational practices, especially its attempts to foster social cohesion amongst a culturally diverse people, it inadvertently breeds division in the social fabric. The argument stems from a focus on institutional practices, and audience engagement with them in Nigeria. It demonstrates how the medium's technical capacities are deployed. This chapter's premise is that the media structure the formation, maintenance and transformation of identity and social relations.

As Anderson (1991: 6) argues, nations are imagined political communities. Even when contact among its members remains limited, there is recognition of the essence of their shared identity, the imagining of their communion, their shared experiences, values and aspirations. Whereas these imaginings may build on knowledge of historical antecedents transmitted to different generations through families, religious, political and educational institutions, one can argue that the mass media are today more crucial to the social construction of personal and group identities. With particular reference to soap operas, Gillespie's work (1995) demonstrates how viewers of Southeast Asian origins use television to construct and transform their identities. Esan (1993, 2008) found that Nigerian audiences' consumption of media texts, including news and Nollywood films, acted similarly: the texts were instructive to the viewers' ethnic or national consciousness. In many instances, viewers engaged with texts with the clear intention of using them to shape their view of self and others.

National unity requires social cohesion, since national administrative structures consist of disparate communities that are thrown together; attention to identity is essential in forging this. In constructing one's identity, emphasis may shift from irrational, primordial ethnic allegiances (shared ancestry or birth ties and religion can be added to this) to the logical, reification of civic rights (legal entitlements to share resources within stated geographical boundaries). Far from being essentialised, identity is dynamic, fluid and complex. It is informed by a range of positions in which individuals and groups have been situated. Consequently, narratives or myths drawn to feed the imaginings vary; what is preferred at particular points reflects which layer of identity is being 'performed' (Butler 1990). Patriotism and parochialism thus coexist and the media are critical in fuelling both, through the stories told of self and others. Citing Goffman's sociological idea of performance, Lewis and Phoenix (2004: 119) show that through performance established associations about groups may be reclaimed. This confirms the dynamic nature of identity. Such identity politics are played out through the media – to clamour for due recognition or equitable distribution of resources. As Cottle (2006) suggests, in such mediatisation, television offers vivid examples where the politics of recognition are deliberated on or displayed. There are aspects of performance, read by others, which were not intentionally disseminated. The assumed primacy of television in this process is consistent with Curran's observation (2000), albeit of the UK, that 'television has eclipsed parliament as the central forum of national debate', hence the need to address any inherent paradox.

Bairner (2001) discusses different forms of national identity: ethnic, civic or social nationalism. One of these tends to be vilified while another is reified, but Bairner warns against the tendency to oversimplify the distinctions between these. We should not attach negative connotations of irrationality to ethnic nationalism simply because it draws on primordial instincts; neither should we assume that civic nationalism is less malevolent because of its apparent transparency, based on the clearly established membership criteria for civic citizenship. Both forms have the capacity to promote or undermine national unity, as is often demonstrated in Nigeria. Whether used alongside or against each other, civic and ethnic identities may be summoned in acts that promote divisive sentiments. For instance, tax-paying citizens assert membership of states in which they have long been resident, yet for failing to be 'sons of the soils' – a term arrogated to invoke primordial affiliations in order to mark boundaries of exclusion – citizens may be spurned in their states of residence. Social nationalism can be more inclusive. It is often invoked (around sporting or social events), when outsiders to a nation can choose to identify with it. This is most remarkably demonstrated in the wholesale adoption of football teams. All types of nationalism rely on media narratives to circulate and entrench the frames for shaping self/group imaginations.

Narratives are shaped by the salient characteristics of each medium. Television appears to be iconic, implying that it is a neutral conduit for recreating narratives, but the logic of semiotics shows how culturally rooted its messages are. Television positions viewers and semiotics exposes the cultural anchors of language by calling attention to the manner in which thoughts and concepts (the signified) are linked to images, sounds (signifiers) to convey meaning (signs). Icons are merely the first of three orders of signification identified by Barthes. They appear to be self-referential; the signifier bears direct resemblance to the signified so there is less attention to the motivation for the sign. With higher levels of signification (connotations or myths), readers of signs require knowledge of the cultural or social motivation for the use of particular referents. Without this, the deeper meaning of messages may be lost to them; the higher the order of signification viewers can access, the deeper their engagement with the symbolism or codes in media messages. Yet, as varying depths of beliefs, attitudes and practices observed within groups will show, viewers connect to cultures at different levels of intensity. So viewing is conducted with varying levels of cultural capacity.

As Fiske and Hartley argue, the television sign is motivated: we 'must not [be] blind [...] to the equally central role of [socially based] convention in conveying its meaning' (2003: 25). TV messages rely on a range of audio-visual cues. These may harbour the unintentional aspects of the performance of identity. Television codes consist of performers' style of dress, gestures, camera angles, subject-to-camera distance, lighting and transitional devices. Its aural codes consist of sound effects, signature tunes, diegetic and non-diegetic sounds (background/mood music, incidental music). These are drawn (and can be read) from established cultural positions. Aural perspectives may also give indications of characters' positions within social structures. Perhaps the most evident cultural associations are found in speakers' accents and speech sounds, which have identifiable ethnic and national roots. These are deeply significant when characters bear the burden of group representation.

Programming flow also characterises the manner in which television is experienced. According to Williams (1990), rather than considering the television experience as a series of discrete moments, it is necessary to conceive of viewing as being part of a flow and to see its product as part of social relations within institutions that are shaped by the social context to which they belong. In spite of debates about the merit of this concept (see overview in Corner 1999: 60–9), Williams' argument remains relevant; it highlights factors crucial to the construction of meaning and worth.

The concept of flow shows that the position of a programme within a schedule, as attested by advertising and sponsorship pricing structures, indicates the value ascribed by the originating institution to the programme, the subject(s) treated in the programme and the intended audiences. Similarly, the time allocated to a programme is also an indication of value. These are nodes through which the ultimate meanings of television programmes and by inference, their subjects and intended audiences, are circulated. As noted by my earlier work (Esan 2008, 1993), audiences learn media industry conventions and make deductions from them about the place inscribed for them in society. To appreciate television's culpability in ethnic relations we must look at less studied aspects of programming, along with conspicuous aspects of TV messages. This chapter focuses on aspects on which audiences have remarked during viewing. These include preferred performers, dress, language, the politics of programme schedules and management practices. These have served as clues through which audiences discern societal power relations.

The Need for National Unity

Africa's partition in the 1880s resulted in the creation of the African states as they are known today. Incorporated into those states were independent, even if interrelated, ethnic groups. Each has histories, kinship ties, networks, trade links and other cultural affiliations, including shared myths of origin, yet some were separated by imposed boundaries. Communities also have records of acrimony; many of the political entities created in colonial times consisted of strange bed-fellows. Much cultural heritage, including memories of affinities and animosities, was transmitted through language and creative forms that constitute the content of television.

Illustrating its cultural diversity is the fact that Nigeria has more than 250 languages; there are 514 recorded living languages (Lewis 2009). Ethnic groups had existed as primordial nations, interrelating through migration necessitated by agricultural or trade pursuits. At times, contact resulted in conflicts: many tribal wars had been fought before contact with Europeans. Positive relationships informed high esteem in which groups were regarded. Links between Benin and indigenous Lagos is such that intergroup royal marriages are endorsed. Such approval is remarkable, since intergroup relationships are often haunted by ghosts of hostilities and acts of distrust. Knowledge of these is passed down through customs, myths, songs, poetry, taboos and other elements of oral culture. Taboos are also handed down through familial or clan instructions. These exclusions are not necessarily binding since some, due to contrary personal experiences, may resist them. However, the fact remains that political parties tend to be organised around such loyalties (as evidenced in the First Republic and the consequent Nigerian civil war (1967–70).

Ethnic sentiments have since combined with other (political, economic) aspirations, the most obvious being religious. A decade after the civil war (1980), the first of many violent clashes was ignited in the North. There have been more than 20 such episodes in 30 years, the latest being assaults by an Islamic fundamentalist sect, Boko Haram (Akaeze 2009). Though initially confined to six Northern states, their bombing operations spread to other parts, including Abuja, the Federal Capital Territory where there were attacks on police headquarters, the UN building and 2011 Christmas Eve church services. Evidently, religion, politics and the struggle for financial security now exploit and override primordial ethnic sentiments. Consequently, cleavages to ethnic groups are not as neat as initially suggested, yet their potential to divide the nation persists.

Pre-colonial rivalries intensified under British rule, exacerbated by disparities in colonial experiences. These were more pronounced at national level, between administrative entities and ethnic groups since northern Nigeria was administered by indirect rule, while southern Nigeria was subject to direct rule (Falola and Heaton 2008; Ajayi 2000). That arrangement meant northern elites were empowered to maintain feudal power, whilst the authority of traditional rulers in the south was undermined by colonial officers who were more actively involved in local life. It also meant that Islam, which had been introduced through the trans-Saharan trade routes, connecting peoples of West Africa's savannah lands with their North African neighbours, was allowed to thrive.[1] Islam consolidated its base in Nigeria through military conquests, particularly the Sokoto Caliphate. This obscured otherwise independent ethnic identities in northern Nigeria as it expanded (Esan 2009; Simpson and Oyetade 2008), firmly establishing the Hausa-Fulani hegemony and Islamic culture.

Traditional governance systems in Southern societies were more egalitarian, as seen in the cases of the Igbo and the Yorubas, with their political system of checks and balances. Colonial authorities in Southern Nigeria further contributed to such egalitarianism by promoting widespread adoption of Western education brought by Europeans, Christian missionaries and traders.[2] They had made in-roads through seaports along the Atlantic coast, such as Calabar and Lagos. Whereas missionaries in the south had relatively unfettered access to local peoples, this was not so in the feudal north. Islamic education remained privileged.[3] Differences in socialisation and cultures were continued in the staffing and administration of television stations established much later. Through established structures, like the Northern Elders' Forum, Arewa Consultative Forum, the northern elite are able to evoke the spirit of those native administrative structures and, with these, wield influence on the orientation of public services. They can steer the operations of national television in their domains, regardless of practices elsewhere. These disparities in colonial experiences, dominant religion and education account for much of the animosity and distrust that persist in present Nigeria.

In contemporary Nigeria, identity is also marked by state of origin; Nigeria has 36 states. They vary in their resource bases and their ability to provide physical infrastructure; these are indicators of progress. Groups are deemed backward or privileged from the existence of good transport links, hospitals, piped water, electricity, and such facilities, which shape ways of living. As these provisions are expected from governments, they are also indicators of *power*, or measures of political patronage. Physical development marks a sense of belonging, while absence of social infrastructure becomes evidence of neglect. These differences are often communicated through television footage, sometimes inadvertently. Seemingly innocuous footage thus becomes evidence of neglect or disparity in fortunes, fuelling intergroup resentment within the nation.

This discussion explains the disparate nature of many African societies and the need for social cohesion in these contexts. African communication systems that were effective in perpetuating ethnic identities in pre-colonial societies, described by Ugboajah (1985) as *oramedia*, find new life in the mass media, particularly television. Whereas oramedia were space-bound, through television they transcend physical boundaries and time. Television has creative ways to re-enact scenarios, thus evoking long-held memories. It also has a broad appeal, a domestic technology offering programmes that bring families and nations together. It is a useful tool for promoting social cohesion, modern lifestyles, appropriate attitudes and behaviours. Consequently, a high premium was placed on the establishment of television stations.

Television Industry: Structures and Disparities in Experience

From its inception in 1959, Nigerian television has been a tool of governance. The television industry consists of three types of station: those owned by the federal government, constituting the national network service; stations owned by state governments, which rival network affiliates, especially in democratic regimes; and independent (privately owned) stations. Certain audiences benefit from satellite and cable television services alongside the terrestrial service previously described. By viewing satellite stations, they may evade national broadcasts and programming planned for national unity.

There have been high aspirations for using television to educate audiences, transform society, offer entertainment and a view on the world. This required balance in programming, a distinction between the commercial imperatives of the television business and developmental motives necessitated by priorities of sponsoring governments. Being more affordable, entertainment programmes (both foreign and local) were favoured. The tendency to showcase folk productions (songs, dances) meant that particular ethnicities gained recognition. Attempts to reflect a federal programming character meant that at least three dominant groups featured regularly in network programmes. While shows like *Village Headmaster* (NTA, Lagos) and *Masquerades* (NTA, Enugu) acknowledged cultural diversity, *Magana Ja Rice* (NTA, Kaduna) was not as inclusive. In any case, characters reflected widely held ethnic stereotypes. Viewers may read cultural tolerance of states from these. Imported television programmes offered a common platform. Being sleek productions with portrayals of a better quality of life elsewhere, they called attention to the viewers' unsatisfactory realities. These had the potential to entrench disenchantment for the nation, while spreading affection for distant places.

Fostering unity begins with those who staff television stations, but this is a challenge when NTA's large size is considered. Staff are privy to disparate ethnic experiences, they even bear the burden of their groups as they compete to resource their local stations. The advertising revenue and public funds available to provincial broadcasters do not compare with that available at national headquarters or commercial centres. Similarly, because physical development across the nation is not uniform, location determines available infrastructural facilities. Disparities between the six zones (north-east, north-west, north central, south-east, south-west, south-south) tend to acquire political overtones, evoking ethnic sentiments and recalling other discontents. This is compounded when, as is inevitable in network television, imposed decisions are deemed to be in poor taste. Consequently, television supposed to promote patriotism inadvertently fuels parochial loyalties, even among television staff.

At the inception of a network service in 1976, Lagos was the operational headquarters. This held unsavoury connotations, when read along ethnic lines. While some saw Lagos as federal territory to which all citizens could have access and lay fair claim, others saw it as belonging to their particular region. The influx of others to their zone was tantamount to a usurping of their privileges. In spite of attempts to reflect federal character in appointments and promotions, the apparent dominance of staff from particular regions in senior management posts eroded confidence in fairness. This pattern mirrored what obtained in other public establishments, especially under military rule, thus it attested to claims that broadcasting was subjugated to the Northern hegemony. A corollary to this was the experience of those distant from Lagos, who regarded network news and current affairs programmes, due to heavy reliance on Lagos-based experts, as a deluge of information on events happening in and about Lagos. Resentment consequently bubbled away beneath a thin crust among television authority staff and audiences alike.

In the nation-building quest, news and schools broadcasts were meant to be a priority at federal government stations. Unlike news, which is politicised, educational programmes, if well planned, could bring enlightenment and detribalisation. However, as government priorities changed, the position of education on television schedules slipped; opportunities to offer broader-based enlightenment were reduced. News remains sacrosanct, a fixture on schedules; its scope increased as airtime was extended. A programme schedule for NTA Kano shows that, in the course of an eight-hour transmission day in 1979, almost two hours were devoted to news programmes. The bulk of this was in prime time (7.00 to 8.00 p.m. slot) for local news in English and Hausa. Network news was from 9.00 to 9.30 p.m. Even with the expanded (24-hour) service, news remains the most central programme on any television schedule. In 2008, a total of four hours in a 24-hour day was devoted to news alone. This, in addition to the established pattern noted above, included daytime slots and another half hour for world news at twilight (4.00 a.m.). That the four hours does not include bulletins accompanying network magazine shows, like AM Express, or other news and current affairs programmes, means more time was devoted to network transmissions of news or factual programming.

National network news should guarantee that uniform information is disseminated to nationwide audiences; local stations should get a chance to contribute to bulletins. In keeping with industry-wide conventions, these newscasts are scheduled as pillars of programming at key times of the day. Since time is an inelastic resource, even with a 24-hour service, not all local stations can be featured. Access to prime time thus reveals how local events are prioritised. In addition to network news, local stations have slots for local news in English and local language. Since it is meant to unify different groups, English, as the commonly understood language is preferred. Consequently, those with

little or no knowledge of English will be excluded, so news translations were essential. In the case of Nigerian Television Kano, the news
(*Labarei*) was translated into Hausa which is widely spoken in northern
Nigeria, a stark reminder of the Hausa-Fulani hegemony over marginalised ethnic groups. Complications arising from attempts to shake
this off were most evident in the case of NTA Jos. NTA Jos operates
in the highly diverse ethno-linguistic Jos plateau area. Since only five
of more than 40 languages spoken in the designated market area could
be accommodated on the weekly schedule, the effort to smooth ethnic
relations merely led to fresh dilemmas, notably the question of which
groups to exclude. In any case, the complications of such a multipli-
city of languages to be catered for aside, the fact remains that news
translations are inadequate. Simpson demonstrated this in his study
of radio news (1985) which showed that languages are not equivalent.
Yoruba, for example, requires more time (than English) to convey the
same ideas (1985: 139). Yet news translations tended to get less space
on broadcast schedules.

With the lack of language equivalence and the need to compress
news translations into briefer time slots than the main English-language
bulletins, bulletins in local languages are not as comprehensive. The
mission to keep local audiences well informed was thus hindered.
Though there was a higher chance of being on local (rather than
national) news, smaller minority groups were lucky to see themselves
(or events concerning them) in the news. The situation has improved
over the years, with network news now originating from more national
centres and remote locations following the acquisition of digital satellite transmission vans. However, the frequency, duration, thematic
patterns and slants of coverage in the news continue to be indicators
of the relative importance of different ethnic groups. If newsworthiness signifies what is important, then being on the news indicates the
importance of a news subject. By its features and oversight on particular issues and groups, (regardless of operational reasons for these)
television becomes culpable in perpetuating social exclusion within
society.

Through its wide range of fictional and factual programmes, TV
offers great opportunities for negotiating public issues. Via the variety of positions explored, audiences are confronted by similarities and
differences in their ways. Television viewing is thus more consequential

than viewers initially construe it to be. For instance, as shown in Esan (1993), it is regarded as a dispenser of justice by those who approach its courts of public opinion, seen in news, current affairs, ombudsman/ citizen rights programmes. Disparity in the experiences presented, when seen as ethnic discrimination, undermines national unity. Television remains a meeting point for various audience groups; it is a forum where different groups convene, especially for drama, football, festive specials and other media spectacles (Grade A broadcasts). If these shared experiences are refracted parochially, television's potential to unite is overturned. Television narratives reflect tensions and resolutions. In so doing, some Nigerians are shown to be more 'equal' than others. Like tabloids, TV offers information about social trends through entertainment programmes and sponsored reports of private events: town meetings, birthdays, weddings, and funerals. Big companies, their performance on the stock market and their products are also featured. It can be argued that the glaring display of affluence fans the embers of resentment amongst less privileged members of society. Though structured along lines of affluence, this pattern of inequality can often be read along ethnic/regional divides. In this case, television does not foster national unity. Yet since sale of airtime is a crucial funding stream, such programmes continue to be scheduled. This is another example of internal contradictions in television management. While it was meant to be utilitarian, television airtime goes to the highest bidder. The Nigerian television industry has witnessed many changes over the years, but remains strategic within the political, social and economic affairs of the nation. It mirrors the activities of leaders and those in government. This acknowledgement of its influence results in an unending quest for expansion. Agitation for new stations emerges as 'minority ethnic groups' seek to be recognised and new political blocs emerge. Given that television is highly cost-intensive, such proliferation exerts strains on lean resources. This takes its toll on output quality; programmes lose their appeal when they lack finesse. The national network, which went unchallenged under the military, is now regularly subverted under democratic governance. This is another paradox: in spite of liberalisation policies, the establishment of privately owned stations and the wide adoption of radical new media technologies, the national network is still maintained within a statist orientation.

'Performing' Ethnicity on National Television

Having examined how broader institutional practices work against national unity, let's return to the performance of the audio-visual aspects which are more familiar conduits of meaning. Studies informing this chapter show that inadvertent traps can be created in these when there is inadequate cultural sensitivity in the process of representation. Representation of ethnicity in television programmes can be gauged through on-screen performers, for example newscasters. There is evidence (Esan 1993) that audiences read the ethnic cultures of presenters and newsreaders (anchors, reporters, correspondents) by their names, speech and appearance. In Nigerian societies names, like accents, are more than labels. They betray peoples' ethnic origins and, by inference, their allegiances and the extent to which they should be trusted.

Performers can also be ethnically situated by their dress. Television audiences pay attention to these; they were fascinated by newscasters' traditional attires. The following are reminiscences from a veteran Nigerian newscaster in an interview about the distinctive caps for which he became known during his career.

> My screen outfit has a very interesting history behind it. You know, I was on the screen for about 10 to 11 years and three of us, Ikenna Ndaguba, Mike Enahoro and myself [Bode Alalade] were the regulars. Mike is from Edo State, Ike was pure Igbo and I was the only Yoruba, and we were allowed to [choose what to wear] you know, [but] anything you wear must be prim and proper. And they would wear a suit or a very good jacket [...] Then, Mike was always trying to be different. He would jerry – curl his hair, then wore *ifunpa,* a folklore arm charm.
>
> And so Festac 77 [International Festival of Arts and Culture 1977] was approaching and the then Head of State, Obasanjo, came with this order that since Nigeria was hosting the FESTAC [...] everybody must be dressed in traditional attire so that when visitors saw *us,* they would judge by what they see on television. [In] those days [...] the NTA ... [was the only operational television service ...] from then on, we were putting on our *native national* dresses [...] We [then] had to debate what was meant by national attire. *We know the Igbos had theirs, Edo isn't left out and so the Yorubas* [...] Up till now *people still recognise me with my Fila* (cap). (Emphasis added.) (Alalade 2009)

The intention in the directive that newscasters should don traditional attire was to promote national heritage, as though this were singular.

The excerpt above from a press interview reveals ethnic boundaries within dress. To visitors, differences between groups may have gone unnoticed, yet among Nigerians, and within the newsroom, the concept of a national outfit was subject to debate. Such debates were also conducted among audiences in the wider society, compounded by unbridled expressions of affiliations, taste and cultural preferences. The political insinuations drawn from extra-linguistic codes of dress were further coloured by religion. This was illustrated in the resistance expressed in certain quarters to the wearing of a hijab (headscarf) by the first prominent female network newscaster of Northern extraction (Hauwa Baba Ahmed). That act was read as a subtle incursion of Islamic values in a secular nation. Especially when read alongside the ethnic composition of those in authority (as is apparent in television management and news subjects), the attire was symbolic of brazen domination over other ethnic groups (southerners) by the (Hausa/Fulani) elite. This was in the 1980s when there were debates about the nation's membership of the Organisation of Islamic Cooperation.

It is evident from the quotation above the way language served as a conduit for ethnic sentiments. Particular concepts which were expressed in a local language (not English) conveyed particular ethnic connotations. To the Yoruba man, *ifunpa* is more than a mere armband. Indeed, the speaker goes on to qualify it as a 'charm', the sort encountered in folklore. Here is evidence that signs are read from viewers' own cultural repertoires.

In the following excerpt from a newspaper feature on another television broadcaster, the writer shows that even more usual items of dress (like caps) were subject to potentially divisive interpretation. Two points are underscored in this excerpt – the quality of voice and the newscaster's appearance. On this occasion, the voice, not other aspects of speech, like accent or intonation, was highlighted. It is evidence of the kind of details that viewers are routinely taught by media reviewers to assimilate. Television texts are often read along with other texts, like the press reviews cited here.

> You remember him with his booming golden voice, cutely dressed in *the typical Northern Nigeria or Hausa attire with a Maiduguri or Kano designed cap to match.* [Saying] 'Good evening I am John Momoh and welcome to network news and with me here tonight is Sienne All-well Brown.' (Emphasis added.)

Momoh on the tube, [with] his velvety voice picking the sentences as if it were specially designed for that purpose, was a beauty to behold [...] the man who sustained that velvety [voiced] tradition of the tube long after Mike Enahoros, the Ikenna Ndagubas and their like had left the stage. (Nwosu 2009)

Clearly, dress is critical to the performer's image, and the cap design can be associated with particular cities (as Scottish tartans are linked to particular families). It is safe to assume that most viewers may not be competent in decoding such specific details, but more general associations with areas of origin are widely known. On this occasion,

Figure 8.1   Bode Alalade in Yoruba cap

the reminiscence is positive, but the visual associations could also be negative if adoption of an item of clothing from the North by a presenter from the South is regarded as evidence of betrayal or domination.

When 'Seeing is Believing' – Conflicting Messages

When serving swathes of uneducated or semi-educated audiences, television's ability to simulate reality is an advantage. Even when the spoken word is incomprehensible, they can rely on the visuals to communicate. Likewise, when the nation was under repressive regimes, visuals offered creative and subversive ways of communication in the news and in other popular texts. As Kellner suggests, 'reading the spectacle of some popular texts of media culture helps to provide insights into current and emergent social realities and trends. Popular texts seize the attention and imaginations of massive audiences and are thus barometers of contemporary taste, hopes, fears, and fantasies' (Kellner 2003: 17).

On Nigerian television, popular texts such as 'light-hearted' entertainment programmes, comedies, musical shows feature prominently. Their popularity makes them commercially viable and earns them prominent schedule slots. By appearing innocuous, they seem to escape strict censoring reserved for news. These 'social diaries' are spectacles which showcase the private lives of leaders and influential members of society. The affluence shown contrasts sharply with the living standards of many, conflicting with public posturing about austerity and the need for probity. Even when there is no spoken reference to the affluence exhibited, audiences relying on extra-linguistic codes such as dress, wedding cakes, fleets of cars, grandiose venues and guests in attendance are quick to spot evidence of 'alleged' exploitation. Citizens cite this as evidence when they deliberate on social reality. Viewers have been known to cite such programmes as evidence of officials fleecing the national coffers, or their insensitivity to the lived experiences of the governed. The following is an example of comments to a photo report of a trip by Nigeria's First Lady to Ethiopia in January 2012. The fact that she had 32 people in her entourage was deemed wasteful and insensitive, especially as the trip occurred whilst protests were raging against the removal of government subsidy on fuel prices in a bid to cut costs. The offensive act was seen as enough reason to reject the President, and any others from his region (south-south) who may aspire to the office. These are indicative of TV audience responses to visual messages (Linda Ekeji's Blogspot 2012; emphases added).

> Nigeria should never elect [a] president from the South South again. (Anonymous, 28 Jan. 2012, 12.19 a.m.)
>
> *Look very closely at the picture and u will see* what our politicians ha[ve] turned our police men into. Is that not one of her security police man carrying her bag? and [he's] even saluting other senior officers by the side at the same time? (Unknown, 28 Jan. 2012, 9.50 a.m.)
>
> Wasteful spenders, she can't even *dress smartly* [...] (Anonymous, 28 Jan. 2012, 10.02 a.m.)

Though class divisions may be more important here, it is clear the privileged class is also viewed through ethnic lenses. Reaction may also be moderated by ethnic loyalties and access to extenuating explanations. Resentment against the privileged may be widespread, but it may not mitigate established ethnic rivalries.

Conclusion: Memories are Made of These

The chapter began by considering the social fabric and the need to weld the disparate groups that constitute Nigeria. Our attention focused on aspects of television, such as subjects' dress, language choice and the politics of programme scheduling. It has also called attention to staffing and resourcing issues, clues for discerning power relations in society. Given the medium's continued popularity, appreciating television practice is crucial to understanding the relative position of ethnic groups. As a socialising agent, television contributes to the construction of personal and group identity. It facilitates the social imagining of community through the shared experiences of regular features or special events. The media offer mental *milestones* which guide social relations, and televised media events are compelling. They justify more intense audience engagement while signalling the importance of events, issues and groups (Dayan and Katz 1992). They should be the pinnacle of the nation coming together, yet they do not guarantee national unity because there is no uniformity in the way texts are

Figure 8.2   Nigeria's first lady visit to Ethiopia, January 2012

decoded. Responses to media spectacles reveal fault lines in the social terrain (Fiske 1996). As shown here, these fissures did not occur suddenly. The central argument is that resentment, suspicion, distrust and consequent fragmentation occur gradually but consistently. Television can be divisive even in its routines; this is cause for serious concern.

The discussion here has focused on practices in the National Television Authority, since it bears the burden of fostering national unity, but the arguments can be applied to other state-owned stations to varying degrees, especially to those with ethnically diverse market areas. Television is a medium for fictional or factual stories. Its performers are profiled in ways that may exacerbate ethnic rivalries. By its peculiar modes of communication, it frames events and characters in particular ways, so the flow of messages produces a range of (ethnically) charged narratives that can trigger memories of other texts or experiences. As argued by McEachern (2002: p. xxii), media narratives reach from the past to the future, shaping newly formed perspectives. They 'operate as [...] expressive form[s] for constructing and reflecting upon identity, but also provide a means for re-contextualising and understanding meaning and significance of radical changes'. These narratives are thus relevant in the unending hegemonic struggles that occur in society.

Group (collective) memories and repertoires of knowledge about themselves and others are shaped through mediated encounters, especially where audiences are separated by vast distances, impossible physical terrain and consequently limited opportunities for direct experiences of other cultures. There is no doubt that television management and programming may be deliberately politicised to increase spheres of influence. As demonstrated here, ethnic sentiments are sometimes evoked inadvertently through seemingly innocuous elements of production or programming. Organisations may fail to recognise these flashpoints in their quest for what is convenient, popular and profitable.

This is an argument for decentralised operations; the closer stations are to their audiences the more aware of these nuances they are likely to be. Nigerian television broadcasting remains a prized tool of governance, yet it cannot foster national unity alone. It may take a cue from social media, in which common interests evolve organically and communities coalesce around these collaboratively determined interests. Commercialised aspects of television programming, particularly drama, music, talent shows, offer some hope in this regard. In these a fusion of cultures on mutually acceptable terms is emerging. Perhaps this marks a coming of age in the coexistence of ethnic groups, but it is evident, especially in a younger generation. Perhaps television stands a better chance when it is not orchestrated by external forces or infused by exploitative political sentiments?

Notes

1 Barnes (2010) notes that by deliberate policy of the colonialist British government, proselytization of Muslims (and later traditionalists) in northern Nigeria was prohibited.

2 It is on record that Portuguese Roman Catholics made contact in the fifteenth century, but it was not till the nineteenth century that any progress in evangelisation was sustained.

3 Islamic education arrived there earlier and accounted in part for the prestige of dominions such as the Kanem Borno Empire (ninth–nineteenth centuries) which in its height covered north-eastern Nigeria, parts of Cameroon, Chad Republic, Niger and southern Libya.

References

Ajayi, J. F. A. (2000) 'Ethnicity and nationalism in Nigeria', in Toyin Falola (ed.), *Tradition and Change in Africa: The Essays of J. F. A. Ajayi*, pp. 259–76, Trenton: Africa World Press.

Akaeze, Anthony (2009) 'From Maitatsine to Boko Haram', *Newswatch*, 28 Oct. <http://www. newswatchngr. com/index. php?option=com_content&task=view&id=1459&Itemid=1> (accessed Feb. 2012).

Alalade, B. (2009) 'This is Bode Alalade … NTA news' interview with Joke Kujenya', *The Nation* <http://thenationonlineng. net/web2/articles/20701/1/This-is--Bode-Alalade-NTA-News/Page1. html> (accessed Feb. 2012).

Anderson B. (1992) *Imagined Communities: Reflections on the Origins and Spread of Nationalism* (rev. edition), London: Verso.

Barnes, A. E. (2010) 'The great prohibition: the expansion of Christianity in colonial Northern Nigeria', *History Compass*, 8, pp. 440–54, doi: 10.1111/j.1478-0542.2010. 00686.X.

Barnier, A. (2001) *Sports Nationalism and Globalization*, Albany: State University of New York Press.

Butler, J. (1990) *Gender Trouble: Feminism and the Subversion of Identity*, London: Routledge.

Chothia, Farouk (2012) 'Who are Nigeria's Boko Haram Islamists?', *BBC Africa World News* <http://www. bbc. co. uk/news/world-africa-13809501> (accessed Feb. 2012).

Corner, J. (1999) *Critical Ideas in Television Studies*, Oxford: Clarendon Press.

Cottle, S. (2006) *Mediatized Conflict*, Maidenhead: Open University Press.

Curran, J. (2000) 'Television and the public sphere: television journalism, theory and practice – the case of *Newsnight*', in P. Holland (ed.), *The Television Handbook* (2nd edn), London: Routledge, pp 181–7.

Dayan, D., and Katz, E. (1992) *Media Events: The Live Broadcasting of History*, Cambridge, MA: Harvard University Press.

Esan, O. (1993) 'Receiving television messages: an ethnographic study of women in a Nigerian context', PhD thesis, University of Glasgow.

—— (2008) 'Appreciating Nollywood: audiences and Nigerian "Films"', *Particip@tion: Journal of Audience and Reception Studies*, 5/1 (online).

—— (2009) *Nigerian Television: Fifty Years of Television in Africa*, Princeton, NJ: AMV Publishing.

Falola, T., and Heaton, M. M. (2008) *A History of Nigeria*, Cambridge: Cambridge University Press.

Fiske, J. (1996) *Media Matters: Race and Gender in US Politics* (2nd edn), Minneapolis: University of Minnesota Press.

Fiske, J. and Hartley, J. (2003) *Reading Television* (2nd edn), London: Routledge.

Gillespie, M. (1995) *Television Ethnicity and Cultural Change*, London: Routledge.

Kellner, D. (2003) *Media Spectacle*, London: Routledge.

Lewis, G., and Phoenix, A. (2004) '"Race", ethnicity and identity', in Kath Woodward (ed.), *Questioning Identity: Gender, Class, Ethnicity* (2nd edn), London: Open University.

Lewis, M. Paul, ed. (2009) *Ethnologue: Languages of the World* (16th edn), Dallas, TX: SIL International <http://www. ethnologue. com>.

Linda Ikeji's Blogspot (2012) 'Comments on Nigeria's first lady arrives Ethiopia with 32 aides', posted on 27 Jan. <http://lindaikeji. blogspot. com/2012/01/ nigerias-first-lady-arrives-addis-ababa.html> (accessed Feb. 2012).

McEachern, C. (2002) *Narratives of Nation Media, Memory and Representation in the Making of the New South Africa*, New York: Nova Science Publishers.

Nwosu, Nduka (2009) 'Broadcasting in his blood', *This Day Online*, 26 Dec.

Simpson, A., and Oyetade, A. (2008) 'Nigeria: ethno-linguistic competition in the giant of Africa', in A. Simpson (ed.), *Language and National Identity in Africa*, pp. 172–98, Oxford: Oxford University Press.

Simpson, E. (1985) 'Translating in the Nigerian mass media', in Frank Ugboajah (ed.), *Mass Communication, Culture and Society*, pp. 133–52, Oxford: Hans Zell Publishers.

Ugboajah, F. (1985) 'Oramedia in Africa', in F. Ugboajah (ed.), *Mass Communication, Culture and Society*, pp. 165–76, Oxford: Hans Zell Publishers.

Williams, R. (1990) *Television, Technology and the Cultural Form*, London: Routledge.

9

INFLUENCING THE INFORMATION DOMAIN: THE UNITED NATIONS' INFORMATION INTERVENTION IN THE DEMOCRATIC REPUBLIC OF CONGO

Jacob Udo-Udo Jacob

Introduction

The genocide of the 1990s in Rwanda and in the Balkans led to consensus among a section of communication and conflict scholars that preventing genocide which can result from hate speech, ethno-nationalist propaganda and information deprivation in conflict areas is a justification for 'information intervention'. Metzl (1997) originally argued for an information intervention mechanism within a UN rapid deployment force to counter 'situations where media activities incite mass violence'. Price and Thompson (2002) have significantly built on Metzl's work on information intervention. They see information intervention as 'the extensive external management, manipulation or seizure of information space in conflict zones' (2002: 8). In *Forging Peace: Intervention, Human Rights and the Management of Media Space*, Monroe Price and Mark Thompson (2002) argue strongly on the rationale for information intervention as a form of humanitarian intervention in societies where the media are used as a tool for genocide or for humanitarian abuses. It is not necessarily a quick-fix media intervention programme but an intervention architecture with several mechanisms and actors – undertaken by states or IGOs in response to misuse of mass communication, especially when there is potential for mass violation of human rights. Strategies could range from providing counter-information that opposes harmful incitement to proscribing or suppressing the medium of harmful incitement itself.

This chapter explores what Metzl calls Phase II information intervention 'coming after the international community has established itself in a given conflict area' (quoted in Thompson 2002: 42). It examines the nature and impacts of the Information Intervention Operations of the UN Mission in the Democratic Republic of Congo. The chapter is broadly divided into three sections. The first provides the background to the UN Mission in the DRC (MONUC[1]) and the mission radio, Radio Okapi, and explains the nature of the partnership between the UN and Hirondelle Foundation. The second section explores the media philosophy of the two organizations. The final part discusses the empirical findings of the study and situates the work within the context of broader debates on strategic communications as an element of post-conflict stabilization in violently divided societies.

MONUC's Mandate and Radio Okapi

After the Lusaka Ceasefire Agreement was signed in 1999 by the six warring countries in Africa's Great Lakes Region (Democratic Republic of Congo, Angola, Namibia, Zimbabwe, Rwanda and Uganda) and belligerent forces in the Democratic Republic of Congo, the UN Security Council deployed UN liaison personnel in August 1999 to support and monitor compliance with the ceasefire agreement. The liaison office became the UN Organization Mission in the Democratic Republic of Congo (MONUC). Acting under Chapter VII of the UN Charter, UN Resolution 1291 (2000) expanded the size and mandate of MONUC. But like most UN Mission mandates, the Resolution did not clearly articulate any public information responsibility to inform the Congolese on the peace process. Although the mandate authorized MONUC to support and cooperate closely with the Facilitator of the Congolese National Dialogue (para. 7h), the mission was not empowered to provide information to the Congolese on the proceedings of the national dialogue. At this time, the DRC, about the size of Western Europe, did not have any national radio or television station. So there was clearly a huge information gap between Kinshasa – tenuously held by government forces – and the other regions controlled then by different rebel groups and guerrilla entrepreneurs. Aware of the potential dangers such an information gap posed to the peace process, and how long it would take the UN to authorize and set up a radio station, then Assistant Secretary General on Humanitarian Affairs, Mr Sergio Vieira de Mello, enquired from Jean-Marie Etter and his associates at Swiss-based NGO Hirondelle Foundation if they could set up a radio station in the DRC as quickly as possible – between 15 days and one month. Hirondelle Foundation had extensive experience of running radio projects in areas of conflict, including Liberia, Kosovo, Central African Republic (CAR) and in East Timor where they had worked with the UN Mission to jointly produce radio programmes for Timor refugees. Jean-Marie Etter and his colleagues accepted the challenge and in December 2001 a Memorandum of Understanding (renewed yearly ever since) was signed between the UN and the NGO to set up Radio Okapi in the DRC. The station was launched in February 2002. Radio Okapi is run by Hirondelle Foundation but the programmes are under the general authority of the UN Secretary General's Special Representative in the DRC. This collaboration offers a refreshing model for post-conflict information intervention. Indeed Price (2000) has previously made a case for UN collaboration with NGOs in information intervention as partners or as watchdogs.

However, UN collaboration with an NGO is not without its own problems. Indeed, the UN and NGOs do not necessarily see eye to eye ideologically. IGOs generally and the UN in particular have philosophies that are different from those of NGOs and they adopt different ideological approaches to dealing with conflicts, especially where the UN Mission has a Chapter VII mandate. In the DRC, although the UN and Hirondelle Foundation have worked together since 2002, this study shows that they have asymmetric approaches, caused not only by differences in ideologies but also differences in operational objectives. In-depth personal interviews with staff of the two collaborating organizations indicate that they have contending public information philosophies. While Hirondelle Foundation favours an 'information approach', MONUC's Public Information Department favour what I have chosen to call a 'strategic communications approach'. Strategic communications in this sense implies the deliberative design of communication contents to persuade a predefined audience to take up a form of behaviour that supports the strategic interests of the source. These contending approaches are evident in two flagship intervention programmes broadcast on Radio Okapi, *Dialogue entre Congolais* (*Dialogue* hereafter), produced by Hirondelle Foundation, and *Gutahuka*,[2] produced by MONUC.

Different Backgrounds, Contending Philosophies

Radio Okapi's information approach is derived from the organisation's ethical values developed over the years from its experience in crisis states. This was stressed by Jean-Marie Etter during an interview with the author.[3] Hirondelle Foundation's media ideology is driven by the primary objectives of providing information and creating a platform for responsible and civic-minded exchange of opinions and dialogue. Their approach is rooted in their belief that objective information eliminates or reduces fear and creates a platform for citizens to be engaged with transformational or conflict resolution processes. Their approach is evident in its flagship programme *Dialogue,* a political magazine programme. It was originally designed as a space for the Congolese to express their opinions on any subject discussed at the political negotiations at Sun City in South Africa to end the Congolese conflicts (Taunya 2004). The objective was to popularize the Sun City Dialogue Inter-Congolais talks so that Congolese citizens that were not participating directly in the talks could still be involved in the process. The programme initially bore the same name as the talks, but the name was subtly changed to *Dialogue entre Congolais* (dialogue between Congolese) after the talks ended in chaos. The programme lasts for 45 minutes and is broadcast twice daily during weekdays – from 7.15 p.m. to 8 p.m. and from 4.15 a.m. to 5 a.m. The scheduling of this programme is instructive. Mano (2005), Hendy (2000) and Ellis (2000) have all written eloquently on the implications of broadcast programme scheduling. They affirm that scheduling suggests a deliberate positioning and sequencing of programmes to attract specific audiences at specific times. Indeed as Mano has noted, broadcasters 'consciously seek to find appropriate programme for particular and relevant moments in an already existing schedule' (2005: 95). In South Kivu, sundown (between 6 and 9 p.m.) is a critical programming moment because it is the time that families, friends, age-grade associations among others sit together at the end of the day to banter and listen to radio. It is a prime time for achieving group listenership. The repeat slot at 4.15 am follows *Gutahuka*, which is broadcast from 3.45 a.m. to 4.15 a.m. on weekdays. This sequence is meant to get *Gutahuka* listeners to also listen to *Dialogue* and to reach early-risers and lone listeners. In South Kivu, eastern DRC, where this study was conducted, it is not uncommon for residents to tune to radio late at night or very early in the morning for the main purpose of listening to news or to music as radio is the major and sometimes only accessible mass medium. The two slots of *Dialogue* therefore are intended to reach as many listeners as possible – both group and lone listeners.

On the other hand, as would be expected, MONUC's public information operation is intimately linked with its mission operational objectives in the DRC. One of MONUC's key mission objectives has been to disarm and repatriate foreign combatants in the eastern region of the country. To achieve this objective, MONUC has adopted a 'push and pull' strategy, involving the application of military pressure while offering voluntary disarmament and repatriation for armed combatants belonging to the elusive but deadly Democratic Forces for the Liberation of Rwanda (FDLR) – a predominantly Rwandan Hutu armed group in eastern DRC. As part of its 'pull' strategy, MONUC has deployed one of the most sophisticated information operation campaigns in UN history. The objective is to convince thousands of individual combatants and commanders of the FDLR to voluntarily disarm and join the UN's Demobilisation, Disarmament Repatriation Resettlement and Reintegration programme (DDRRR). The UN Mission's communication approach to DDRRR is novel and, because of the unique nature of the DRC conflict, it has not been modelled after any previous UN public information operations. Whereas in previous cases, the UN's Disarmament, Demobilisation and Reintegration (DDR) activities involved troops within the countries of operation; in the DRC, DDR involves additional components of Repatriation and Resettlement of foreign combatants to home or third countries. Although the UN has partnered with the Congolese armed forces (by providing logistic support – such as food rations, helicopters, etc.) to engage the FDLR militarily, success has been minimal compared with the civilian casualties and the political ramifications thereof. The FDLR do not have any well-defined location or territory of control or communications installations that can be targeted and neutralised. They either operate in the dense forests in eastern DRC or live among civilian Hutu populations. Previous military attempts (such as Operations Umoja Wetu, Kimia II and Amani Leo) to neutralise the FDLR have resulted in disproportionate civilian casualties. Also, the terrain is inaccessible by road, hence providing an ideal operational environment for guerrilla-style armed groups to successfully operate and evade capture. With these unique challenges, it became a strategic necessity for MONUC to deploy a strategic communications architecture to appeal to armed combatants, particularly militants of the FDLR, to voluntarily disarm and join the DDRRR process. To achieve this, the UN designed the radio programme *Gutahuka* to reach individual combatants and persuade them to come out of hiding and return 'home' to Rwanda. *Gutahuka,* has been broadcasting since 2002. It has become an integral part of the planning and deployment of the UN's DDRRR operations. Unlike other programmes on Radio Okapi, *Gutahuka* is produced directly by the Audio and Video Production Unit of MONUC's Public Information Department. The production team travels regularly to the reintegration camp in Motubo, Western Rwanda, and other parts of Rwanda to meet and interview repatriated ex-combatants in reintegration camps and family members of fighters. MONUC officials interviewed for this research said the purpose of *Gutahuka* is to speak to 'individual combatants' of the FDLR in particular and Rwandan Hutus in the DRC in general, encouraging them to lay down their arms and return home. According to MONUC's spokesman Madnodje Mounoubai, *Gutahuka* is an 'alternative to military pressure' and was designed to fulfil the DDRRR mandate of the mission. He said the programme is

> a response to the difficulties to reach the FDLR combatants and an attempt to get information to non combatants [...] to provide them with information on how they can go back to their country on a voluntary basis. (Madnodje Mounoubai, online interview with author on 9 March 2010)

On Radio Okapi, *Gutabuka* is broadcast daily on weekdays and on Saturdays between 3.45 a.m. and 4.15 a.m. Various other radio stations and mobile broadcast units in South Kivu broadcast the programme at different periods, but mostly early mornings and late evenings.

By interviewing ex-combatants and extended family members, *Gutabuka* ties perceived norms to the group identity of not only the FDLR network but also the Hutu ethnic group. It appeals, as it were, to their sense of oneness, not only as a rebel network but also as a family – an ethnic group. In every edition of *Gutabuka,* MONUC

Table 9.1   Tale of two intervention programmes: *Dialogue* and *Gutabuka* represent the ideological leaning and operational objectives of their producers

	Gutabuka (Go back Home {in Kinyarwanda})	*Dialogue entre Congolais* (Dialogue between Congolese)
Production	Produced by MONUC's Public Information Department	Produced by Radio Okapi (Hirondelle Foundation)
Form	Talk-show format	Multiple/competing participation frame involving town-hall style discussion format involving moderator and panellists.
Message	Single narrator: 'You really need to return to Rwanda before it is too late'. Interviews with ex-combatants who typically encourage combatants to repatriate.	Debate on a range of topics relating to governance, politics, corruption, economy, security, conflict, peace and development.
Target Audience	FDLR militants, Hutu civilians and refugees in eastern DRC.	Congolese population, particularly opinion leaders, cultural leaders, local journalists, etc.

seeks to fulfil Rimal and Real's definition of descriptive norms in seeking to influence perception about 'individuals' beliefs about how widespread a particular behaviour are among their referent others' (2003: 185).

Various other sensitization activities, including direct phone calls, one-to-one contacts, in addition to military and political pressures, combine to buttress *Gutahuka*'s message. MONUC has, in addition, dropped several thousands of leaflets on known FDLR positions. Messages on the leaflets urge combatants to 'come out of the bush and go home'. The messages also inform FDLR combatants and their dependants of the option of voluntary repatriation and seek to persuade them to 'abandon hard-line leaders and a hopeless future in the bush' (MONUC 2009). The leaflets contain phone numbers of MONUC's DDRRR staff for those that wish to call, and information on how to listen to *Gutahuka*.

Generally, repatriation successes have been modest compared with the number of FDLR combatants, including those that have on their own stopped fighting and integrated into Hutu civilian communities either on a permanent basis or temporarily. From 1 January to 21 May 2010 MONUC's DDRRR Unit demobilized and received a total of 664 FDLR combatants. In 2009, 1,564 FDLR foreign combatants were repatriated, along with 2,187 dependants. As shown in Figure 9.1, repatriation was modest in 2010 up to 21 May when the last data were obtained for the research.

There is no reliable information on the actual number of FDLR fighters in combat at the time the above data were obtained, or the number of ex-combatants that have integrated into civilian life in eastern DRC. But estimates of FDLR fighters in 2010 ranged between 3,000 and 15,000 fighters.[4]

Brief Notes on Methodology

In assessing the nature of impacts of the two programmes, 'influentials' among Congolese autochthons and Rwandan Hutus across four towns or contexts in South Kivu of eastern DRC were selected using a refinement of Eric Nisbert's (2006) engagement model of opinion leadership. Participants aged between 18 and 48 were selected from various sections of the autochthon and Hutu communities – they included

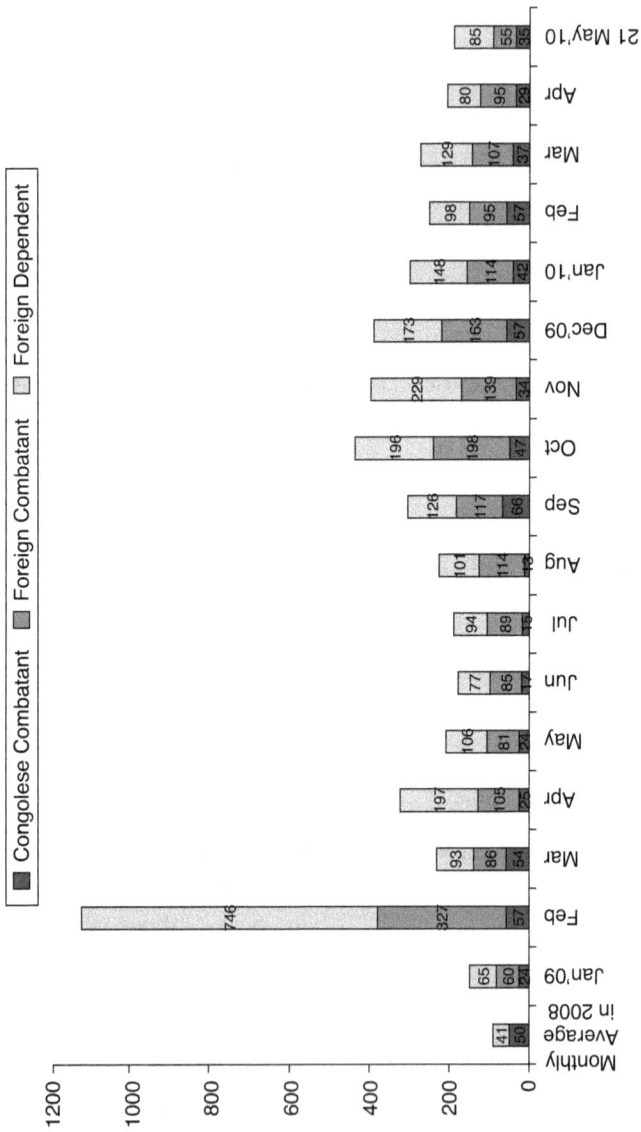

Figure 9.1   DDR/RR of FDLR elements

women and former combatants. From the influentials' pool, a matched randomization technique was used to assign Hutus and autochthons in South Kivu to listen to either one of the two radio programmes within their naturalistic contexts for a period of 13 months starting from December 2008. A similar methodological approach combining field observational and experimental methods was used by Paluck (2009) in her study of media and inter-group prejudice in Rwanda. Autochthon control groups listened to *Gutahuka*[5] while Hutu control groups listened to *Dialogue*. Peer researchers, selected from the participants, were trained to monitor listenership for the entire period.

At the end of the treatment, outcomes of perceptions of barriers to peace, perceptions of descriptive and prescriptive interventions, perceptions of victimhood and villainy, perceptions of opportunities for personal development and civic engagement, and attitudes toward members of other ethnic groups were assessed in a total of 16 focus groups moderated and recorded by the peer researchers. Focus group comments from the four contexts of study (which were recorded verbatim) were analysed and integrated to show patterns and interrelationships across contexts and networks and subsequently interpreted within the larger structure of the study. At the first level of analysis, comments from Rwandan Hutu groups across the four contexts of study were categorized and coded to show participants' beliefs about consequences of returning to Rwanda. The intention was to identify specific elements of normative beliefs shared/unshared by participants across contexts and listening groups. The next section discusses findings and the emerging implications thereof.

Undesirable Consequences of Repatriating to Rwanda

Across Hutu listening groups, the most recurring undesirable concept was participants' perception of the Gacaca justice system in Rwanda. Six out of eight focus groups (in both *Gutahuka* and *Dialogue* listening groups), expressed the undesirability of the Gacaca justice process as a consequence of repatriation. Participants feared that the Gacaca justice system was designed to persecute Hutus that returned. This fear was expressed in all *Gutahuka* groups and two out of four *Dialogue* groups. Its prevalence in all contexts suggests that this fear is not treated in *Gutahuka*. Invariably, it is a factor that participants seriously cared about and they would need to be convinced that if they returned they would not be victimised. *Gutabuka* as a programme does not guarantee that returnees would not be prosecuted in the Gacaca courts, but it gives assurances that returnees will be given a fair hearing if ever referred to the traditional courts. Among Hutu communities in South Kivu, there are rumours of returnees being convicted by the courts based on false testimonies. Such rumours have thrived because of insufficient or inadequate and unreliable information on exactly what the courts are for and the processes involved in their judgments.

Ajzen (1988) has written that among beliefs that ultimately determine intention and action is a set that deals with the presence or absence of requisite resources and opportunities. These beliefs, according to him, may be based in part on previous experiences or influenced by second-hand or socially transmitted information by friends or close others. This seems to be the case in Hutu participants' thinking about the Gacaca courts. Although participants did not have any direct experience of the Gacaca justice system, as they obviously are yet to return to Rwanda, their behavioural beliefs about the system is influenced by their exposure to second-hand information about the traditional courts. *Gutabuka* has not succeeded in treating or correcting this (mis)information, as evident from the pattern of prevalence of this behavioural belief across all Hutu *Gutabuka* listening groups. Behavioural intention, or in this case, intention to repatriate, is not supported by adequate information that can treat the fear generated by second-hand influences on perceptions about Gacaca. Ajzen corroborates that behaviour is a function 'of salient information, or beliefs, relevant to the behaviour' (1988: 134).

In summary (see Figure 9.2), through its creative representation of the personal successes of Hutu repatriatees *Gutabuka* is more successful in convincing listeners that personal development is not an undesirable consequence of returning. By regularly interviewing former combatants and commanders that have gone on to occupy key political positions in Rwanda, *Gutabuka* sends two categories of messages: first, that in Rwanda, there is no discrimination against Hutus and, secondly, that there are enabling conditions for combatants to return and achieve their personal development goals. Indeed, one of those regularly interviewed is Major General Paul Rwarakabije, the former Commander in Chief of the FDLR and now a Commissioner of the Rwanda Demobilisation

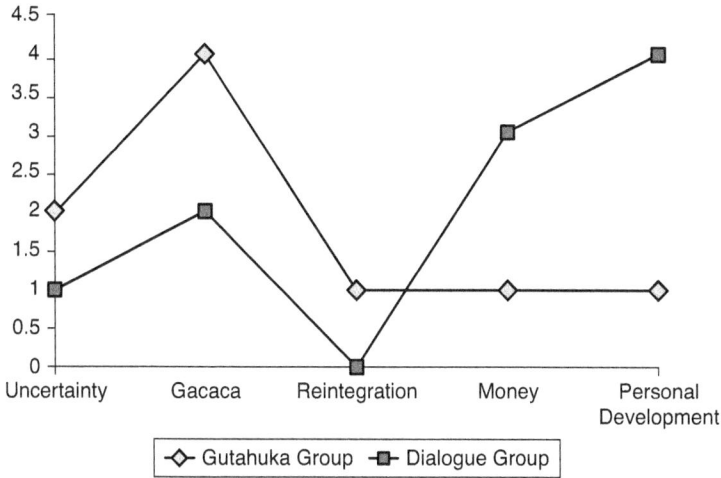

Figure 9.2   Undesirable consequences of repatriating across listening groups

and Reintegration Commission. His success is consistently represented as proof that any combatant can return to Rwanda and obtain a senior position irrespective of ethnic group or social status.

Although there have been significant political changes in Rwanda and indeed in the DRC, the highly polarising politics that created divisions between Hutus and Tutsis in the 1980s and early 1990s are consistently retold in Hutu communities in South Kivu, hence even those who were too young then to understand and those who were not born then have strong feelings about ongoing political events and the ones that impelled the genocide.

Dialogue and Reconciliation

Dialogue is based on a model that illustrates mass communication as a horizontal or transactional process. By creating a platform for rigorous debates of key issues that confront the community as a whole, the pro-gramme encourages audiences to participate in evaluating the current political situation, to perceive the current situation based on the different positions debated and to interpret the debates in a way that fits their own peculiar episteme. On the other hand, Congolese autoch-thons exposed to *Gutahuka* expressed more awareness of the ethnic and political divisions that could deter future social and political inter-relationships. Across the four contexts studied (Uvira, Walungu, Fizi and Mwenga), except in Fizi with its peculiar socio-cultural blend of Hutus and autochthons, *Gutahuka*-exposed autochthons were pessimistic about possibilities of a unified Congolese army involving all the ethnic groups including settled Rwandan Hutus. A salient pattern of difference in beliefs between the two autochthon listening groups is that *Dialogue* listeners showed more empathy towards Hutus than listeners of *Gutahuka*. In discussing their perceptions of victimhood, autochthon listeners of *Gutahuka* did not see Hutus as victims of the conflict, whereas autochthon *Dialogue* listeners across all contexts believed Hutus were among the main victims of the conflict, implying a greater sense of empathy towards the Hutus.

It had been envisaged at the beginning of the research that exposure to the Other's programme would potentially deepen mutual understanding and empathy with the Other's issues, but the reverse has been the case in autochthon listeners of *Gutahuka*. They perceived Hutus as the problem and expressed the normative appeal in *Gutahuka* that peace in the DRC was linked to the repatriation of FDLR militants (embedded in Hutu communities) to Rwanda. This has implications for contentious debates on the impacts of exposure to contents meant for the Other, particularly in deeply divided societies, and for the overarching debates on the role of the media in reinforcing dominant power relations in society. Indeed, Barak (1994) has observed how media contents identify heroes, villains and neutral characters and associate them with specific traits, beliefs or forms of behaviour, and in other cases label and stigmatise certain activities and individuals or groups as antisocial, deviant or undesirable. He posits that such associations have implications for social control. Also, Mutz (1998) has written brilliantly on the 'impersonal' nature of influence by media portrayals of attitudes, beliefs or experiences of collectives outside an individual's personal life space. She has rightly argued for 'impersonal influence' to be taken more seriously because of its potential to expand contemporary understanding of social influence processes from media portrayals of indirect associations. Findings provide important evidence within the spheres of Barak's (1994) 'symbolic deviance' and Mutz's (1998) 'impersonal influence'. By constantly calling on FDLR militants to repatriate, *Gutahuka* labels or stigmatizes Hutus in general as deviant and undesirable. This is because there is a social reality that associates the FDLR with Hutus and vice versa, which in turn creates unspoken assumptions and cognitive framing of the Hutu Other as 'foreign', 'unwelcome', 'deviant' and 'undesirable' among autochthon listeners of the programme. Although autochthons are not the target audience for the programme, they are as exposed if not more exposed to it as the targets themselves – more exposed because FDLR militants in the forests are prevented by their commanders from listening to the programme for fear they would be convinced to surrender. Obviously radio is not selective in its reach; hence audiences who are not targets of a particular intervention programme but are exposed to it do end up consuming the programme. In the case of *Gutahuka*, although MONUC presents the programme in Kinyarwanda – the language spoken among Hutus in Rwanda, several Congolese in the Kivus understand and speak Kinyarwanda fluently, having lived side by side with Rwandans for several years. For non-targets, *Gutahuka*'s messages construct 'symbolic deviance' – involving unspoken assumptions, associations and framing of the FDLR combatant as an unwelcome or undesirable Hutu. This in turn affects non-targets' perception of the Hutu Other. The 'Otherisation' of Hutus is further deepened by media reports of joint military activities against the FDLR. An autochthon *Gutahuka* group member in Mwenga, in one of the focus groups, said of Hutus: 'there must be a problem with you when everybody is pursuing you'. The result is what Barak (1994) terms 'symbolic punishment' through stigmatization or labelling of the Hutu Other as antisocial, deviant or undesirable. Such negativity may not be expressed explicitly in *Gutahuka* but dynamic interactions of *Gutahuka*'s messages and implicit normative appeals with unspoken assumptions rooted in an epistemic association of the FDLR with Hutus and vice versa lead to the construction of symbolic deviance not intended by the programme creators. Although *Gutahuka*'s messages and normative appeals are intended to restore peace in South Kivu by achieving voluntary repatriation of FDLR elements and Hutu civilians, they do have negative implications for social relations between autochthons and the Hutu Other when considered against the backdrop of a social reality or discursive formation that associates the FDLR with Hutus and vice versa – an association taken for granted or unaccounted for in the programme. By problematising the FDLR-Hutu, *Gutahuka* creates or at least intensifies animosity towards Hutus among autochthon listeners in three of four contexts researched.

Indeed, the programme reinforces dominant power relations by depicting the FDLR as the problem and not the breakdown in social relations and other structural causes of the conflict. The result has been a 'we–they' cognition and expression of relations between the autochthon 'self' and the Hutu Other. This is evident in a comment by an autochthon *Gutahuka* listener in Walungu:

> They [Hutus] have raped thousands of our women, killed thousands of our young men, stole everything they can steal, they are the ones that have kept us where we are today.

It had also been envisaged at the beginning of the study that any potential impacts of the programmes would be weakened within contexts of intercommunal interactions between the two ethnic groups. However, findings show that, in some of the contexts where Congolese autochthons lived close to and had regular interpersonal interactions with Hutus, perception of Hutus seem to be influenced more deeply by media representations of the FDLR/Hutus than by their day-to-day interactions with them. This corroborates Mutz's position that people respond 'to a media-constructed pseudoenvironment – rather than their immediate personal experiences or those of friends and acquaintances' (1998: 6). Because of the media's expertise in matters that are beyond the realm of citizens' personal experiences, they are perceived as more reliable sources of information.

Indeed, in violently divided societies, citizens are exposed to a communicative sphere that draws on four contending realities with varying degrees of potential impacts on interpretation and engagement with media contents: historical reality, objective reality, subjective reality and mediated reality (see Figure 9.3).

Communication patterns of groups researched were overwhelmingly rooted in their memory or socially acquired knowledge of previous conflicts, events or interrelationships. Historical realities define the epistemes within which metaphors, discursive practices and communication patterns of each network are negotiated. Hugh Miall (2004) has argued that collective memory is a salient element that should be of stronger interest to conflict transformers because memories of past conflicts determine groups' expectations in future relationships

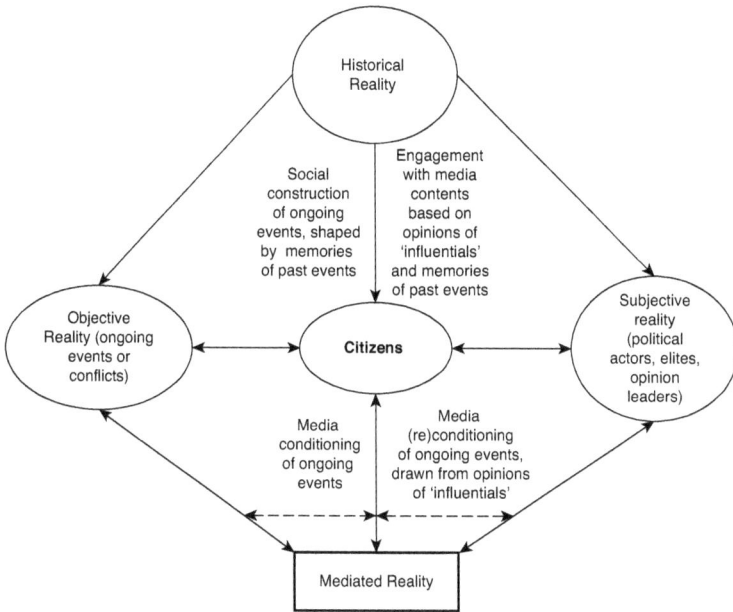

Figure 9.3   Contending realities in conflicts settings

and significantly determine their behaviour toward the Other and how meaning is shared. In this study, key influentials or purveyors of subjective realities were themselves influenced by historical realities, which in turn infected their communication patterns. Participants in the focus groups were at the intersection of a triad of realities that in addition to other factors influenced their perceptions. Those exposed to a mediated reality that did not provide a platform for objectively engaging and debating with the historical and subjective realities in the triad were subjected to the normative influences of those realities in their engagement with media contents. Exposure to the Others' media contents within a communicative sphere or intersection that is hostile to the Other created a stronger negative opinion of the ethnic Other. The tendency to blame the Hutu-Other for the misfortune of the autochthon-self was intensified with exposure to the Hutu-Other's behaviour change messages.

In each context studied, historical realities influenced how participants expressed their views, how programme messages were interpreted and the various ways they sought alternative mediated or socially transmitted information that met their peculiar needs.

Exceptions were found among participants exposed to a programme where the contending realities were confronted and debated. Through the programme *Dialogue*, Radio Okapi performs more than mere cognitive functions of providing objective information. The programme also undertakes interpretative functions including analysis, evaluation, assessments and comments. Discussants in some cases are not only the authors of the cognitive and interpretative elements of *Dialogue* but are also the authors of the very issues they seek to interpret. Through the programme, they are able to present their arguments within their own narrative frameworks. Their narrative frameworks are different from the narrative frameworks in Radio Okapi's news discourses with its inherent gate-keeping appendages. Arguably, this represents the liberal democratic role of Radio Okapi in the DRC. By mediating objective realities of ongoing events and subjective realities purveyed by political elites, *Dialogue* provides elites with a raw forum to criticise policy decisions and to comment on other issues of popular concern.

Conclusion

In conclusion, in violently divided societies, conflicting groups constantly co-evolve with the social and political environments and the emerging imperatives or dynamics of their relationships with other groups. The nature of information each group need in their co-evolution processes and how they engage with such information is equally co-evolving. When conflicts arise with other groups, behaviour and responses are negotiated in line with not only the contending issues but also with their evolving perception of the other. An understanding of the factors that shape perceptions of the other is an important element to note when designing information intervention contents for transforming intergroup conflicts.

In crisis societies, historical and contextual metaphors influence how citizens express their views and engage with programme contents. In this case, they influence how Congolese autochthons and Rwandan Hutus deconstruct *Gutahuka* and other DDRRR sensitization activities and the various ways and means through which network members seek alternative mediated or socially transmitted information to affirm or repudiate their normative beliefs and intentions. Metaphors and associated inferences that underlie internal communication patterns of Hutu ethnic networks are not the same as those that underlie their communication with cultural outsiders, even within the same contexts and also with spatially distant referents even within the same ethnic network. For the ethnic Hutus in Congo, these metaphors include a discursive history of war, of guilt, of genocide, of displacement, of asylum, of fugitivity, of refugeeism, of dialectical shibboleths that restrict citizenship and its rewards, of constantly struggling against resistance from autochthonous groups and the haunts of a Tutsi-dominated Congolese army. Though unexpressed, these metaphors make up the discursive formations that interfere with the contents of *Gutahuka*'s normative appeals. Former combatants that have returned to Rwanda and have gone on to occupy key political positions in Rwanda do not necessarily share these discursive formations with Rwandan Hutus that are still in the DRC in terms of place and time. Hence using them as normative referents in *Gutahuka* is less than effective, and could indeed be counter-productive. Though they are 'fellow' Hutus, in the contexts studied, they are 'cultural outsiders'.

Two critical implications emerge. First, 'cultural insiders' are not necessarily those that live within the same spatial context, or that belong to the same ethnic group or speak the same dialect. Indeed, contextually associated individuals or even ethnically associated groups in violently divided societies do not always have homogeneous interpretation, perception and/or decoding of media messages. Central to influencing the information domain, is the ideological orientation of messages audiences are exposed to and how they interact with local epistemes, including historical and subjective realities on ground at each conflict phase. Another implication is that hate contents are not only the ones that are overtly hateful. Messages targeted at specific groups for the purpose of achieving behavioural change can lead to alienation and hostility toward the target group by the other (non-target) groups exposed to the messages. The implication is that media intervention contents that purvey a narrative without first understanding how it interacts with epistemic narratives, metaphors and historical realities on ground run the risk of deepening rifts between groups and escalating the conflict (see Jacob 2010).

In the DRC, Rwandan Hutus are more open to information which they could use to collectively (re)negotiate their own future, behavioural intentions and even survival as a people. For them, information is a key element in their survival kit. Indeed, some Hutus spend a substantial part of their income on strong-signal radio sets and batteries so they can listen to the BBC World Service and Radio France International for information they normally would not be able to access on the local news sources. An approach that rigorously provides information to fulfil this basic survival need is essential.

For targets that are already keen to return, *Gutahuka* does offer hope and reassurance that it is the right decision to make – *those that made the same decision previously are happy about it; that help is available – MONUC is on hand to extract them and take them safely to Rwanda where they would be reinserted into their communities;* and that there is no need to delay – *repatriation has to be done now before it is too late. Gutahuka* however had limited impacts on targets that were yet to make a decision about whether to voluntarily repatriate or not. For these, the knowledge and information which they could use to make an informed decision to repatriate seem lost in the messages of *Gutahuka*. A prudent approach to convincing Rwandan Hutus to voluntarily repatriate can potentially be achieved from two fronts – *informational* and *referential*. First, participants' behavioural intention is influenced not only by group pressures but also by a collective sense of uncertainty about what the Rwandan homeland holds for them. This can be treated with rigorous and objective information. Furthermore, rigorous information to dispel the myths and false stories about Gacaca justice system in the Rwandan homeland can also provide a useful resource for achieving impacts. Secondly, interveners can work from the 'inside' through social means of information sharing. Opinion leaders, family heads, pastors, priests, leaders of age-grade and other self-help associations have the potential to exert more normative influence on behaviour and attitudes than the physically and socially distant referents used in *Gutahuka*.

Notes

1 On 28 May 2010 (when the research work was coming to an end) the UN Security Council adopted Resolution 1925 (2010) to extend the mandate of MONUC until 30 June 2010. Effective 1 July 2010, Resolution 1925, renamed the Mission as the United Nations Stabilisation Mission in the Congo (MONUSCO). Still acting under Chapter VII of the UN Charter, MONUSCO places more emphasis on supporting and stabilising the DRC's

military, law enforcement and justice institutions and consolidating the peace. Throughout this chapter, the old acronym MONUC is used to refer to the UN Mission in the DRC mainly because the research was conducted while the Mission was so named.

2 *Gutahuka* means 'go back home' in Kinyarwanda.

3 15 August 2007, Lausanne, Switzerland.

4 These figures depend on who you ask. UN and other GoDRC sources estimate that the number of FDLR fighters (as in December 2009) is between 2,000 and 4,000 fighters, whereas FDLR sources put the number at between 10,000 and 15,000.

5 Autochthon participants selected to listen *Gutahuka* were fluent in Kinyarwanda – the language of the broadcast.

References

Ajzen, I. (1988) *Attitudes, Personality, and Behavior*, Milton-Keynes and Chicago, IL: Open University Press and Dorsey Press.

Alleyne, M. D. (2003) *Global Lies? Propaganda, the UN and World Order*, Basingstoke: Palgrave Macmillan.

Barak, Greg (1994) 'Media, society and criminology', in Greg Barak (ed.), *Media, Process, and the Social Construction of Crime: Studies in Newsmaking Criminology*, pp. 3–45, New York and London: Garland Publishing.

Berkeley, B. (1994) 'Sounds of violence: Rwanda's killer radio', *New Republic*, 21/8–9, pp. 18–19.

Ellis, J. (2000) 'Scheduling: the last creative act in television?', *Media, Culture and Society*, 22/1, pp. 25–38.

Hendy, D. (2000) *Radio in the Global Age*, Cambridge: Polity Press.

Jacob, J. U. U. (2010) *Rethinking Information Intervention in Violently Divided Societies: MONUC's Public Information Operations in the Democratic Republic of Congo*, Leeds, UK: University of Leeds.

Keohane, R. O. (2002) *Power and Governance in a Partially Globalized World*, London: Routledge.

Kirschke, L. (1996) *Broadcasting Genocide: Censorship, Propaganda, and State-Sponsored Violence in Rwanda 1990–1994*, London: Article 19.

Lederach, J. P. (1996) *Preparing for Peace*, New York: Syracuse University Press.

—— (1997) *Building Peace: Sustainable Reconciliation in Divided Societies*, Washington, DC: United States Institute of Peace.

Lindley, D. (2004) 'Untapped power? UN public information operations', *International Peacekeeping*, 11/4, Winter, pp. 608–24.

Lusaka Ceasefire Agreement (1999) Democratic Republic of Congo: Lusaka Ceasefire Agreement, 10 July.

Mano, W. (2005) 'Scheduling for rural and urban listeners on bilingual Radio Zimbabwe', *Radio Journal: International Studies in Broadcast and Audio Media*, 3/2, pp. 93–106.

Metzl, J. F. (1997) 'Information intervention: when switching channels isn't enough', *Foreign Affairs*, 76/6, pp. 15–20.

Miall, H. (2004) 'Conflict transformation: a multi-dimensional task', in A. Austin, M. Fischer, and N. Ropers (eds), *Transforming Ethnopolitical Conflict: The Berghof Handbook*, pp. 3–45. Berlin: VS Verlag für Sozialwissenschaften.

MONUC (2009) 'Surrenders and repatriations of FDLR combatants increase as MONUC step up DDRRR efforts', press release, 28 Sept.

Mutz, D. C. (1998) *Impersonal Influence: How Perceptions of Mass Collectives Affect Political Attitudes*, Cambridge: Cambridge University Press.

Nisbert, E. (2006) 'The engagement model of opinion leadership: testing validity within a European context', *International Journal of Public Opinion Research*, 18/1, pp.3–30.

Paluck, E. L. (2009) 'Reducing intergroup prejudice and conflict using the media: a field experiment in Rwanda', *Journal of Personality and Social Psychology*, 96, pp. 574–87.

Price, M., and Thompson, M. (2002) *Forging Peace: Intervention, Human Rights and the Management of Media Space*, Edinburgh: Edinburgh University Press.

Price, M. E. (2000) 'Restructuring the media in post-conflict societies: four perspectives. The experience of intergovernmental and non-governmental organizations', *Cardozo Online Journal of Conflict Resolution*, 1/31.

Rimal, R. N., and Real, K. (2003) 'Perceived risk and efficacy beliefs as motivators of change: use of the risk perception attitude (RPA) framework to understand health behaviors', *Human Communication Research*, 29/3, pp. 370–99.

Taunya, J. N. (2004) 'Public Information and the media: Radio Okapi's contribution to the peace process in the DRC', in Mark Malan and Joao Gomes Porto (eds), *Challenges of Peace Implementation: The UN Mission in the Democratic Republic of the Congo*, Pretoria: Institute for Security Studies, pp.53–65.

Thompson, Allan (2007) *The Media and the Rwandan Genocide*, London: Pluto Press.

Thompson, M. (2002) 'Defining information intervention: an interview with Jamie Metzl', in M. Price and M. Thompson (eds), *Forging Peace: Intervention, Human Rights and the Management of Media Space*, Edinburgh: Edinburgh University Press, pp.53–5.

United Nations Official Documents

UN Doc A/RES/13(i), ANNEX I (1946) *Recommendations of the Technical Advisory Committee on Information Concerning the Policies, Functions and Organisation of the Department of Public Information*.

UN Doc A/Res/3/217D (1948) *Publicity to be Given to the Universal Declaration of Human Rights*, GA Res 217 D (III). 3rd Sess.

S/INF/56 (2000) *The Situation Concerning the Democratic Republic of the Congo*, SC Res. 1291, UN SCOR, 55th Sess.

10

'THUS SAITH THE PROPHET': THE MEDIA, ETHNIC MYTHS AND ELECTORAL POLITICS IN KENYA

Duncan Omanga

Introduction

Van Gorp (2007) argues for the centrality of a cultural item in identifying media frames. Adopting the frequently quoted definition of framing by Entman (1993) as a project in which framing is argued to highlight and make salient aspects of a communication text in such a way as to 'promote a particular problem definition, causal interpretation, moral evaluation, and/or treatment recommendation for the item described' (1993: 52), the constructionist approach subsumes the primacy of culture in the extraction of frames. In this particular paradigm, culture is thought to be the primary base from which knowledge is constituted, and meaning and comprehension of the outside world made (Hall 1997). In fact, culture might be defined as the empirically demonstrable set of common frames exhibited in the discourse and thinking of most people in a social grouping (Entman 1993).

With this assumption, this paradigm becomes critical in understanding how the framing of a key ethnic myth in western Kenya came to play a critical role in the 2007 general elections. Elijah Masinde, a self-declared prophet, had years before foretold how the Luhya (a conglomeration of about 21 subtribes but still Kenya's second largest ethnic group) would have as one of their own[1] ascend the country's presidency by first supporting a Luo presidency, Kenya's fourth largest ethnic group. Among several other factors, this chapter argues that this particular prophecy was pivotal in galvanising the historically diverse and disparate Luhya subtribes, especially the Bukusus and the Maragoli (the two biggest subtribes among the Luhya) into supporting a Luo candidature in the hope that power would naturally come to the Luhya through succession. This prophecy was revived after the then leading Luo candidate, Raila Odinga chose as his running mate a Luhya, Musalia Mudavadi, pitting themselves against incumbent president Mwai Kibaki who chose to run without a running mate.

The constructionist approach to framing deployed in this chapter shows how the media lent themselves as a site for the construction, dissemination and also contention of an ethnic myth that was believed to manage latter-day succession politics in Kenya. The focus of the framing is on Kenya's two leading newspapers, *the Daily Nation* and *The Standard*. The two were chosen because of their dominance in terms of circulation and their longevity in Kenya's media space. The analysis involved 20 news commentaries and a few news reports. Although there was extensive use of pictures, these are only mentioned briefly.

Following Van Gorp (2007), this study extracts frames through a deep reading of the coverage of the 'Elijah Masinde prophecy' by looking at the relationship between the framing and reasoning devices through textual analysis. The unit of analysis is the sentence. According to Gorp (2007), upon exposure or interaction with a media text, the frame will manifest itself in the text through several framing devices. These devices include, but are not limited to: word choice, metaphors, exemplars, descriptions, arguments, visual imagery, visual metaphors, stereotypes, catch phrases, dramatic characters, graphics and lexical choices. Gamson and Stuart consider these devices more like signature elements that 'suggest the core frame in shorthand fashion' (1992: 60). Secondly, the core frame has 'reasoning devices', which scholars agree (Taylor 2008; Van Gorp 2007; Gamson and Lasch 1983) are related to the four functions of framing as conceived by Entman (1993), namely to define a problem, assign responsibility, pass a moral judgment and reach possible solutions. In other words, reasoning devices are the product of the interaction between the reader and framing devices in the text that enable the reader to deduce justification, see the 'causes and consequences in a temporal order' (Van Gorp 2007: 64).

Ethnicity, the Media and the Pre-Election Period

In 1992, the Kenyan parliament passed a bill that required a presidential candidate to garner 25 per cent of the votes in at least five provinces (Kenya has eight provinces). The passage of the law was also meant to ensure that a particular candidate had support from across the country. In 2007, the swing vote apparently seemed to be safely located within the disparate Luhya subtribes, an ethnic conglomeration that rarely voted as a bloc. The battle for this constituency was an obvious hunting ground for the two leading candidates as it held the keys to a sure victory. Part of this contest would involve wrestling with and contesting the interpretation of Elijah Masinde's prophecy, with the media appearing more and more as the adjudicators of this political contest.

The importance of the Luhya vote lies on the fact that they are the second most populous tribal group in Kenya, consisting of about 21 different sub-tribes,[2] most of whom have only a tenuous linguistic and cultural similarity. Among the Luhya subtribes the two most populous are the Maragoli and the Bukusu. The rivalry between these two has dominated Luhya politics and has been the single reason why political unity among the Luhya has become so elusive. Unlike other populous communities like the Kikuyu, Kalenjin and the Luo who vote as a bloc, since 1963 the Luhya have a history of spreading their votes in a way that reflects the voting patterns of these two most populous Luhya subtribes. Come 2007, the Luhya vote held the balance of power. Way back in 2002 this was not a major problem as both Kibaki and Raila were in the same coalition and both had substantial Luhya opinion shapers in their midst. This time the erstwhile friends were now locked in a gruelling campaign for the hearts and minds of the Luhya. While Kibaki had the advantage of incumbency complete with several Luhya ministers behind him, Raila Odinga had the challenge of uniting disparate supporters across the country. Courting the Luhya vote with its diverse subtribes demanded an approach that would appeal to all the subtribes and unite them behind a Luo candidate, Raila Odinga. This was not going to be an easy task considering the sharp social cultural differences among the Luhya and the Luo. In spite of all this, Raila's party ODM overwhelmingly won the Luhya vote, winning about 80 per cent of the vote. This chapter argues that, among several reasons for Raila gaining favour with the Luhya, such as pervasive disillusionment with the Kibaki regime, marginalisation of the Luhya and a yearning for fundamental change, the Luhya overcame cultural barriers and subtribal differences to overwhelmingly support a Luo candidature partly because of the prophecy made by Elijah Masinde. What is more, a near sensationalist approach to the coverage of the events surrounding the appropriation of the prophecy legitimised the Raila-Mudavadi axis as the most natural, logical and authentic (through authority and expert opinion) manifestation of the revered prophecy.

Elijah Masinde, Ethnicity and Political Prophecies

Elijah Masinde was an enigmatic Bukusu 'prophet' and founder of the Dini ya Msambwa – a politico-religious cult combining Christianity with African traditional rituals and customs. Masinde was born around 1908–10 in Maeni village, in western Kenya. According to Wipper (1977), Elijah Masinde's headstrong personality, a little madness and defiance to authority in a colonial context, a background comprising forced labour, land dispossession, tribal warfare and Christian mission work, formed fertile ground from which the *dini* (Swahili word for sect) flourished like foliage. In the 1940s evidence of the *dini* began to be noticed on the foothills of Mount Elgon, western Kenya. Masinde created the *dini*, turning it into a politico-religious group that sought not only traditional worship but also the expulsion of the white man and the restoration of land to Africans. According to Bellers (2009), an open defiance of colonial authority was to be a key element of the Dini ya Msambwa and its subsequent appeal to the Bukusu.

After a sojourn in the forests of Mount Elgon in the 1940s he alleged that his ancestors (Bisambwa) appeared to him in a dream and urged him to lead his people back to the old ways of worship (Wipper 1977). Dini ya Msambwa was born, which loosely translated means the religion of our ancestors. Borrowing heavily from Christianity and mixing traditional practices, Masinde's sect denounced Christianity as a religion of the imperialist and perceived missionaries as agents of foreign domination. His blatant and sometimes public clashes with authorities and white settlers led to frequent arrests in the pre-independence period. His frequent arrests, rearrests and releases led to myths of him walking through prison walls. His most memorable release in May 1961 was greeted by a rapturous welcome in his Bukusu homeland, with politicians falling over themselves to tap into the publicity and euphoria surrounding his return.

In 1964, President Kenyatta revoked the law proscribing Dini ya Msambwa and it was subsequently registered. This did not last for long. After several violent incidences from his followers, the *dini* was deregistered as the then Vice President Moi felt that it was a political party masquerading as a religion. Impatient and disillusioned with the pace of reforms during Moi's presidency, an ageing Masinde led his adherents in denouncing Moi's rule and was subsequently arrested in 1985 but released shortly after. Moi felt Masinde was now too old for prison. Elijah Masinde died on 8 June 1987 and was buried in his Maeni village. By the time of his death, he had acquired a larger-than-life image of a prophet, a political leader and a tribal hero all rolled into one. Before his death, Masinde had also built a reputation as a prophet and subsequently etched himself into the annals of Bukusu history when some of his numerous prophetic pronouncements were said to be confirmed with the passage of time. However, it is worth noting that these prophetic utterances were not religious but were all political in nature. This is partly because of Masinde's primary focus on challenging the establishment, coupled with politicians' exploitation of the pronouncements for political gain, and a local media that has kept regurgitating the pronouncements and keeping them alive every election year.

According to Macarthur (2008), Masinde's stature as a prophet was secured when a string of his prophecies came to pass. For instance, upon his deportation to Lamu he said he would not remain there for long, confirmed when the colonial administration moved him to Marsabit. Upon the death of President Kenyatta, which Elijah Masinde was said to have prophesied would come in 1978, there was a high-level behind the scenes tussle for who would succeed him. The political manoeuvres to succeed Kenyatta had begun when it was clear to those very close to the presidency that he was ailing. In warning Masinde Muliro (not related to the 'prophet' but a fellow Bukusu), then Luhya's most senior politician, to keep away from the succession politics, Elijah Masinde stated:

Omwana wefwe alichaa amihe, ne Muliro akhapanila bali ele khu sisala sya Kenyatta tawe. Alekha busa okundi elekho, eye kamafuki khundebe ng'eneyo. Mala owililekho oyo, aliaahachililisia babandu barekane mumaya.[3]

(Our son will rule one day, and Muliro should not fight for those who will take Kenyatta's seat. Let him leave it for someone else, the seat is bloody. And whoever will take that seat will incite people to fight among themselves.)

No immediate bloodletting ensued, as power transferred smoothly from Kenyatta to Moi. However, it was during Moi's reign that the country began to have predictable tribal violence every five years during election time. Some adherents and sympathisers of Elijah Masinde argued that the ethnic clashes in the early 1990s and beyond were accurately foretold in Masinde's warning that the seat of the presidency is bloody.

Despite widespread appropriation beyond his native Bukusu, his prophecies were mostly based on ethnic relations, ethnic othering and a peculiar Bukusu ethnocentrism. For instance, he is recorded to have predicted that during the regime of Moi the Luhya region, with specific reference to the Bukusu in Bungoma, would suffer political marginalisation and come to the brink of economic ruin, saying 'Khuuba ne Barwa nende Baswahili, Papa, aba olinga oweikame mumurongoro, efula ekwaa Soli munju ta' (My friend, to work with Kalenjins and Swahili is like shielding under a tree when it is raining. You are not inside a house.) In the 24-year reign of President Moi, a Kalenjin, the populous western province of Kenya had some of the lowest poverty levels in the country. The worst hit was Bungoma and the neighbouring Kakamega Districts that had little in terms of infrastructure or industries and recorded very high poverty levels and very high infant mortality rates (Warren and Liambila 2004).

Some of his prophecies were interpreted in the light of the wider regional politics. One of the most memorable prophecies was made at the height of his fugitive years when he went into hiding in Mount Elgon. The Kenyan authorities intensified a search for him, forcing him to venture into Uganda where the then Ugandan President Milton Obote had him arrested. He was to spend the next few months in jail. Upon his release, he bizarrely took a fallen tree and dragged it along to the Kenyan side of the border; according to him this was a kind of symbolism of the political fate that was to befall Obote and Ugandans in general. 'Omulang'o emwalo sye e Matore, mbone karurire khu Bwami. Lundi mbone karerire kamafuki musibala. Chia mwekesie ba Befwe e Mbale' (The Lang'o (Obote) in the land of Bananas (Uganda) has left authority. And he has brought bloodshed in the land. Go ye forth and educate (save) our people in Mbale.) Shortly after, Army General Idi Amin toppled the Obote government in a bloody coup in 1971, ushering the country into an epoch of bloodshed that was to last almost a decade. Some among the Luhya saw this as a fulfillment of Elijah Masinde's prophecy and a kind of punishment meted on the Ugandans for mistreating 'a prophet'.

While incidences of a trans-ethnic interpretation of his pronouncements existed as previously indicated, this was an exception rather than the norm. Most of his prophecies were reflective of Kenya's ethnic politics where the ascendancy of a member of a community to the highest seat of power is interpreted as tantamount to the advancement of members of that tribe. This has meant that ethnicity has come to play a crucial role in voter behaviour in Kenya. Accordingly, the Luhya have long cherished the prospect of one of their own 'sons' ruling Kenya one day. With this in mind, Elijah Masinde had something to say on Luhya leadership in the country. In 1965/6, in a town called Kimilili, he announced that 'Nabone omwana aselukhe mu Babukusu. Omwana mwenoyoo aliamiha' (I have seen a son has come of age among us. It will come to pass that this son will come to rule). Here he made the most politicised of his prophecies, declaring that 'Bubwami bukhamile khunyanja' (leadership will come from the lake). By suggesting that leadership for the Luhya will come through the 'lake', a word he used to refer to the Luos, he set the stage for what would be one of the strongest grounds for Luo and Bukusu (and later entire Luhya) ethnic collaboration in contesting political power in Kenya. However, according to Wafula Buke, Elijah Masinde's prophecy was made in a context in which he was simply trying to read Kenya's political landscape just like any other political analyst. In an article published in the *Daily Nation,* he argues that 'the God who gave Masinde the prophecy of a Luhya winning the presidency after a Luo understood the dynamics of post independent Kenya'. In other words, one can also conceive these prophecies as simple political astuteness that comes easily with studying Kenya's politics. Still, this prophecy has been potent in political mobilising. In 1992, the Bukusu overwhelmingly supported for the presidency Raila's father, the late Jaramogi Oginga Odinga, who had appointed the late Michael Wamalwa, a Luhya from the Bukusu subtribe, as his running mate, an arrangement interpreted as fulfilling the aforementioned prophecy. The quest failed mostly because of a lack of support from other major ethnic groups and in particular the other Luhya subtribes who scattered their votes among other contenders, eventually sealing Moi's victory. Another factor was how the media framed the two polls. In 1992, the prophecy received extremely scant media coverage and was seen as Bukusu-specific, despite attempts by Wamalwa to convince the Luhya otherwise. But as the next section reveals, in 2007 the media became extremely pivotal in constructing the frame of a Luhya nation held together and united by Masinde's prophecy.

The Media, Ethnic Myths and Regional Politics

In 2007, both Kibaki and Raila were keen to capture the votes of the rich western province. For Raila being a Luo came with the advantage of drawing on Elijah Masinde's prophecy. The ODM's key message to the voters of western province was that Kibaki had had his time, and it was now the time for Masinde's prophecy to be fulfilled. According to ODM, a Luo (read Raila) would first have to 'cleanse' the seat in order to pave way for a Luhya presidency. With Musalia Mudavadi picked as Raila's running mate, himself a Luhya from the Maragoli subtribe, the message of Luhya ascendancy to power soon found fertile ground. The Kenyan media took it up and began an intensive scrutiny of the role of prophetic pronouncements on the prevailing political realignments, and their impact on ethnic voting patterns. The focus was most intense between September and October 2007, which coincided with intensive campaigns from both sides of the political divide concentrated in western province, the homeland of the Luhya.

The public broadcaster, the Kenya Broadcasting Corporation, and the two leading privately owned television stations, The Kenya Television Network (owned by the Standard group) and the Nation TV (owned by the Nation group) all put considerable focus on the role of the prophecy in galvanising ethnic identities in western province. However, it was the newspapers that gave the most extensive coverage of the prophecy and its role in the forthcoming polls. In fact, the two papers virtually dedicated a couple of Sunday editions[4] in September and October to more in-depth coverage and analysis of the nexus between the prophecy and electoral politics. It was precisely for this reason that the newspapers became the focus of this study. This chapter argues that, while the media may be seen as simply purveying what politicians were appropriating for selfish gains, the media played a critical role in conferring and denying legitimacy to the political players involved, as far as the prophetic pronouncements were concerned. Worth noting, there were a few issues that made the media more culpable in ascribing and denying legitimacy. First, when Elijah Masinde made the so-called prophetic announcements, it is right to argue that the prophecy was specific to the subtribe of the Bukusu. Since Kenya had attained independence the two dominant subtribes of the Luhya, the Maragoli and the Bukusu, rarely saw each other eye to eye politically, and would almost always vote opposite ways. Indeed, although the Bukusu had had a presidential candidate before, Wamalwa Kijana, he could barely garner votes in Maragoli land, much less the rest of the country. But with the choice of Mudavadi as Raila's running mate, coupled with opinion polls indicating an ODM win, opinion began shifting towards an acknowledgment that perhaps Elijah Masinde's prophecy was not Bukusu-specific. While this is probable, the manner in which the media framed the events firmly legitimised the Raila–Mudavadi duo as the rightful heirs and the perfect manifestation of this much cherished prophetic pronouncement of Elijah Masinde.

On 9 September 2007, *The Standard* newspaper allocated extensive coverage to a biographical report of Elijah Masinde. In the background was a big picture of a smiling Masinde and underneath, inset into the larger avuncular image of the prophet, were pictures of Raila Odinga and Musalia Mudavadi locked in an embrace. The picture pointed to an overbearing influence of the late prophet on the two politicians, who appear as though emerging from Masinde's shadow. The message was compelling and striking. The headline reinforced this: 'Elijah Masinde and the Prophecy'. The story went on to describe how the candidature of the duo against incumbent Kibaki had roused memories of the age old prophecy.

The emergent frames from the news commentary reveal a sense of expectancy, suggesting that this may have been what voters from the region had been waiting for. It is important to note that the paper totally fails to mention that, being a Maragoli, there was the possibility that Mudavadi may after all not be eligible to lay claim to the prophecy. This temporary construction of the Luhya as a unified

Figure 10.1.   Photo of Elijah Mafinde published in *The Standard* on
9 September 2007

unit played down and blurred serious subtribal differences among the
21 Luhya subtribes that later produced a rare manifestation of a Luhya
voting bloc. In addition, the news commentary anchored legitimacy to
the frame by suggesting that 'elders' themselves had confirmed that the
prophecy was indeed about to come to pass. Culturally, the mention of
the opinion of elders is significant, as it adds not only legitimacy but
authority to the story, as elders are considered to be the right opinion
formers in as far as interpretation of such a culturally laden issue is
concerned. As a result, the ODM party was framed as simply the natural and more obvious fulfillment of the prophecy. This particular
frame of Raila and Mudavadi as the *natural heirs* of Masinde's prophecy
was introduced through the following lines:

> The nomination of Lang'ata MP Raila Odinga as the Orange
> Democratic Movement (ODM) presidential candidate with former
> Vice-President Musalia Mudavadi as his running mate has sparked
> off a debate in western Kenya [...] memories of a prophecy by Elijah

Masinde have been rekindled in words uttered many decades ago. A number of elderly people in Western province think the prophecy is about to be fulfilled albeit through another generation. They say the prophecy by the founder of Dini ya Msambwa, is slowly becoming a reality. (*Sunday Standard*, 9 Sept. 2007)

By legitimising this particular frame, coupled with a repetitive focus, the media over time helped create a Luhya ethnic identity built around the prophecy of Elijah Masinde. Macarthur (2008) reveals that, on a weekly basis, starting in September 2007, the press reported on the Masinde prophecy, its meanings, its adherents and political consequences. It is worth noting also that, as much as the Masinde prophecy existed in the minds of the people of Western Kenya, the media foraged through Masinde's history and related it to the developments in national politics as the 2007 poll drew close. However, even more effective was the determination of politicians to 'claim' Masinde's prophecy and the subsequent media coverage.

The next month, the *Daily Nation* also gave substantial coverage to the meaning of the prophecy and its relationship to the Raila–Mudavadi candidature. The *Daily Nation* also accorded legitimacy to the duo as perhaps the most accurate representation of the prophecy by Elijah Masinde. Citing evidence on the ground, the paper produced a rather different frame to that of *The Standard*, focusing not on the 'natural' nature of the relationship between the candidacy and the prophecy, but rather on Mudavadi and his fortuitous appointment as Raila's running mate. Appearing in the *Daily Nation* on 12 October 2007, news commentary traced the reasons for the emergence of ODM in a hitherto hostile Bungoma District (home of the Bukusu) as the product of two main factors. One was the nomination of Musalia Mudavadi as Raila's running mate. This piece was quick to acknowledge that on his own Mudavadi had never had any substantial following among the Bukusu, and that something beyond him must have made him gain the legitimacy of the influential Bukusu subtribe, and by extension the entire Luhya ethnic group.

In framing the Raila–Mudavadi candidature as the *logical heirs* to prophecy, the report deployed a causal ideological frame that simply argued that the prophecy made by Elijah Masinde was responsible for the acceptance of Mudavadi, a Maragoli Luhya, in a predominantly Bukusu-Luhya region. Following the success of this particular media frame, the ODM incorporated Dini ya Msambwa at the heart

of its campaigns in Bungoma, in an attempt at 'owning' a potentially powerful cultural institution that the Luhya had come to
identify with. Further, in an obviously media choreographed event,
Mr Mudavadi visited the shrine of the late Masinde at Maeni in
Bungoma East District and met with a delegation of its current leadership. Here, he met and consulted with the family of the late Elijah
Masinde and sought their blessings in seeking political power. In subsequent political campaigns, the biggest of which was held in Uhuru
Park in Nairobi, Dini ya Msambwa leaders were regularly invited to
offer opening prayers alongside mainstream church leaders. This particular strategy was meant to secure the ethnic Luhya constituency in
a battle that would focus more on the essence of Masinde's prophecy
and the artefacts of the *dini* left behind by Elijah Masinde.

As time went by, prominent Bukusu politicians who were not in ODM
discovered that there was a gradual shift of opinion among their electorate from PNU to ODM. According to them, the only logical reason
for this was to be found in the appropriation of Masinde's prophecy. As
expected, a battle over the interpretation of the prophecy ensued, with
politicians on both sides of the political divide making incessant visits
to the family and the shrine of the late Masinde in an attempt to own
the prophecy. The media captured this battle with glee by constructing
a binarism of winners and losers of Elijah Masinde's political 'blessings'.
On one side was the Raila–Mudavadi candidature and on the other was
Mwai Kibaki's PNU, whose point man in Luhyaland was a Bukusu cab-
inet minister, Musikari Kombo. Kibaki had failed to name a running
mate, as a post-election bargaining chip if he needed to form a coalition.
Nevertheless, Kombo went around telling Luhya voters that he would
be appointed vice president after the elections, and the Luhya would still
have their number two slot in a PNU government. When this argument failed to resonate with the voters, Kombo attacked Mudavadi's
legitimacy in appropriating Masinde's prophecy. But the media, both
The Standard and the *Daily Nation*, fortified the legitimacy of the Raila-
udavadi duo after Mudavadi paid yet another visit to the home of the
late prophet, with a horde of print and electronic journalists to immor-
talise and circulate the news. An article in *The Standard* announced what
seemed like the outcome of a tussle replete with cultural symbolic lexical items that legitimised the candidature of Raila and Mudavadi as the
winners of the Elijah Masinde prophecy:

at an elaborate ceremony presided over by a prominent elder, Patrick Chaka, at the shrine (of the late Elijah Masinde), Mudavadi beat Kombo (Bukusu, PNU politician) to the game by sitting on the special stool. The late Masinde Muliro (most prominent Bukusu politician in the 70s and 80s) and the late Vice-President, Michael Wamalwa also sat on the stool signifying their new role as leaders of the Bukusu and the Luhya community as a whole. (*The Standard,* 15 Oct. 2007)

As seen, by suggesting that the event was elaborate, and using triumphant expressions, the frame of legitimacy through *authority* is constructed. This is made even more powerful by the symbolism of the stool, which connotes leadership and power. In addition, this legitimacy through authority frame is further fortified by the journalist emphasising that the ceremony was presided over, not merely by an elder, but one who was prominent, which could be interpreted variously. The impression conveyed is that of an elder who is well known, widely respected and regarded as a custodian of cultural capital in that particular region. The acme of the event is illustrated by the stool sitting, an event loaded with cultural meaning. The fact that the two most prominent Bukusu politicians (now deceased) sat on this stool legitimises the candidature of Raila–Mudavadi, with Mudavadi seen as the new leader of the Bukusu, and the Luhya as a whole. This suggestion that Mudavadi was now the leader of the Luhya as a whole was one of the many strategic constructions that the media circulated that may have been instrumental in constructing a Luhya identity. The media frame of legitimacy through *authority* was also manifest through news commentary that supposedly included accounts from professionals drawn from the community. The most obvious reason for inclusion of expert and 'leading' opinion is to send the message that this particular myth transcends class and educational boundaries, further suggesting that the narrative of the prophecy was not simply an idle or fringe opinion, but a largely pervasive and cross-sectional one. In a Sunday news commentary on the politics column of the *Sunday Standard*, the following excerpt formed part of a wider frame constructing the legitimacy of the Raila–Mudavadi axis authoritatively, through the so-called expert opinion:

Leading community leaders including Moi University lecturer Prof Bonventure Kere, Lugari MP Dr Enock Kibungunchy, (a medical doctor) lawyer Eugene Wamalwa and the chairman of Kenya Sugar Board Mr Saulo Busolo are in agreement that Raila's presidential candidature has serious political connotations and bearing on the Luhya [...] the community cannot ignore the prophecy of Masinde. It is the gospel that is preached by the many locals. (*Sunday Standard*, 9 Sept. 2007)

The choice of a university professor, a medical doctor, a lawyer and the chief executive of a major industry is very instructive at this point, for it attempts to give authority, through opinion leaders and the elite members of the Bukusu ethnic group, to the notion of a Raila– Mudavadi candidacy. Although the frame attempted to entertain a counter-hegemonic opinion, in which another professional differed, arguing that the prophecy would have little impact in Luhya, his lone voice was marginalised and subsequently drowned by the news commentary through the marshalling of superior and diverse framing elements against this feeble counterframe. Indeed, the suggestion that these are the 'leading' community leaders also adds legitimacy to their opinion on the matter while delegitimising other counterframes. This article also failed to mention is that Mudavadi was not a Bukusu, and that he could not, strictly speaking, appropriate the sought of privileges he was harnessing.

It was therefore not long before the prophecy and its interpretation were contested among political rivals, each attempting to attach an interpretation convenient to them. Government minister Kombo protested at the manner in which ODM were 'hijacking' and misappropriating the prophecy. Realising that the Bukusu voters were trooping towards ODM, Kombo held campaigns in and around Bungoma telling voters that Masinde's prophecy was Bukusu-specific and insisting that Mudavadi's visit to the shrine was an 'abomination'. He insisted that 'a follow up visit' (of course led by him on behalf of PNU) to the shrine was necessary to 'cleanse' the shrine of the pollution left by outsiders.

Meanwhile, the media and several journalists camped at the late Elijah Masinde's home, seeking answers from close friends, elders and his family on the emerging confusion. Kombo's plea to his fellow Bukusus met serious obstacles from the onset. It seems that his political fate was sealed when Elijah Masinde's family and the Dini ya Msambwa elders came out strongly in defence of Raila and Mudavadi. Dismissing claims of shrine defilement, they affirmed that their blessing on the ODM leadership was final. All the while, the unfolding duel for Masinde's prophecy between the two sides grabbed media headlines. A frame that delegitimised Kombo's perspective emerged in the *Daily Nation* of 12 October 2007. Family members were quoted as saying that Kombo's intention to make a follow-up visit to cleanse the shrine was met with outrage from Elijah Masinde's family.

> Masinde's family has told Ford-Kenya to consult with them before visiting the shrine. The family spokesperson, Mzee Lucas Watta, warned that the party leaders were not welcome to the shrine. 'We have blessed the Orange family and given Musalia the baton to be the third Luhya leader. We cannot alter this and (Kombo) must be ready to carry its own burden,' said Watta. (*Daily Nation*, 12 Oct. 2007)

However, this statement did not seem to deter Kombo and his team in contesting the precious prophecy. To illustrate the seriousness of the suggested shrine infringement, a court order was sought to bar any ODM member from visiting the shrine, in a suit filed by alleged Dini ya Musambwa spiritual leaders Mr Maloba Joseph, Mr Manyasi Situma and Mr Barasa Namasaka. Things did not turn out as they had expected when the case was thrown out on 2 November 2007.[5] This contest and the court drama that followed became a media bonanza in both the print and the electronic media. It was at this point that the ODM leadership made another visit to the late Masinde's home, perhaps with the intention to settle any doubts of ODM's claim to the prophecy. As usual, a battery of journalists was in tow to capture the proceedings. On 12 November 2007, the *Daily Nation* had the following report on what transpired:

> The family of *Dini ya Msambwa* sect leader Elijah Masinde on Sunday said that they would support ODM presidential candidate Raila Odinga in the December General Election. The announcement was made by Masinde's widow, Mama Sarah Nanyama Masinde, 105, after Mr Odinga and his running mate Musalia Mudavadi held a closed door meeting with the family of the sect's spiritual leader at Maeni in Kimilili constituency in Bungoma North. (*Daily Nation*, 12 Nov. 2007)

The publication of this story (which was also aired on television) had potential ramifications for the ethnic voter behaviour in western province. But even more powerful is the framing of the Raila–Mudavadi legitimacy through *authority*, which both the politicians and the media helped to construct. The fact that it was Masinde's widow who made the announcement must have been both strategic and effective. Moreover, the media's emphasis on her age, and the fact that they held closed-door meetings, is a subtle media-constructed frame of legitimacy to ODM through *authority*.

Soon after the triad of the Masinde family, the ODM leading politicians and the media settled the issue of who the rightful beneficiaries of the prophecy were, the ODM made began campaigns in Luhyaland that looked more and more like victory marches rather than pre-election campaigns. For instance, while speaking in Bungoma Raila Odinga promised that an ODM government would erect a mausoleum in Elijah Masinde's honour. He also promised that Masinde would be recognised as a national hero and his impoverished family would be taken care of. These pronouncements struck a positive chord with Bukusu electorate. In the company of Luhya leaders and the Dini ya Msambwa leadership, Raila reiterated that Elijah Masinde's prophecy was about to be realised through him. Several PNU civic and parliamentary politicians defected *en masse* to the ODM party, as many feared losing in the subsequent polls. This hit Kombo and the wider PNU fraternity hard. It came as no surprise when Kombo himself, a three-term MP and leading Bukusu politician, lost his legislative seat. He had, as it were, dared the 'gods'.

Conclusion

31 January 2007 remains a day many Kenyans would rather not remember. The country imploded following the announcement that Kibaki had controversially secured a second term. As the country descended into anarchy, the Rift valley regions of Eldoret, Nakuru, Naivasha and the cities of Nairobi, Kisumu and Mombasa witnessed the lion's share of the mayhem. While this was predictable, the so-called 'peaceful marches' that were always a precursor to street confrontations in these towns quickly spread into what was almost becoming a civil war. The sleepy towns of Bungoma, Kitale and Webuye (Bukusu zones) were drawn into the conflict. While it is true that electoral fraud precipitated the initial uproar in the Bukusu region, it is equally true that Elijah Masinde's prophecy gave the violence a legitimate and moral

platform. Following the media construction of the Raila–Mudavadi candidature as the most natural, logical and most genuine outworking of Masinde's prophecy, many residents may have felt that the electoral system had robbed them of what had been 'accurately foretold' in the 1960s by their legendary son. In an interview with Wafula Buke on 14 October 2009 in Nairobi, the prominent activist had this to say concerning the role of Elijah Masinde's prophecy in the ensuing violence in Bungoma;

> absolutely, Masinde's influence was pervasive in the whole scheme of things [...] one has to remember that in Bukusuland, Elijah Masinde was the first among no equals. He is first. His is the gigantic personality standing long after all 'boys are separated from the man'. He is the preeminent in all political conduct in Bukusuland to this day. He is our hero.

These statements notwithstanding, it makes more sense to argue that perhaps only a very tenuous relationship exists between the violence in parts of Bukusuland, the entire Luhyaland and Masinde's prophecy. What is important to draw from the foregoing discussion is that a relationship between the media, political behaviour and the prophecy were all at work to construct a potent Luhya ethnic voting bloc that overwhelmingly voted for Raila Odinga as president. This does not mean that the prophecy worked in isolation, or that it had the strongest influence. Indeed, it is much more prudent to argue that there was a desire for change among the Luhya too, who had grievances of political isolation and unemployment just like other ethnic groups. Still, the ramifications of the circulation and mediatisation of the prophecy can be seen at two levels. At the first level the prophecy proved effective as one of the most successful devices to galvanise the diverse ethnicities represented under the overarching Luhya generic category. Indeed, this was arguably why the media pushed so hard in affirming Luhya identity, whose disparate subtribes lack a single unifying identity, not even a language. Secondly, the influence of the prophecy can be seen in the fact that for the first time in the history of Kenya's voter behaviour, the Bukusu supported a Luo presidential candidate whose running mate was not an ethnic Bukusu, and did so by referring to Masinde's prophecy, 'Bubwami bukhamile khunyanja' (leadership will come from the lake).

Unfortunately, the 2007 general elections were marred with controversy and the Luhya will have to wait a little longer to see Masinde's
prophecy come to pass. The ODM is now in a grand coalition with
PNU, where Kibaki remains president, Raila is prime minister and
Mudavadi is a deputy prime minister in the same government. The
arrangement was crafted in a bid to manage the ethnic conflict that
was threatening to tear the country apart. But still, the Luhya are hopeful that their turn to rule, probably through Mudavadi, will come. In a
Daily Nation report on 27 September 2008, barely a year after the election, House Speaker Kennneth Marende, a Luhya from the Bunyore
subtribe, gave hints of a Raila–Mudavadi second shot at the presidency
arguing that 'the prophecy by Elijah Masinde that ascension to leadership by the community would be through Lake Victoria would (still)
be fulfilled (in 2012)'. So far, political events in Kenya seem to have
transgressed Elijah Masinde's prophetic script.

Acknowledgements

The author wishes to thank Joseph Musakali of Moi University, School
of Information Sciences and Magdalene Wafula of Moi University for
their contribution in translating the 'prophecies' made by the late Elijah
Masinde. The author also extends his gratitude to Pamela Omanga for
offering useful insights, and Wafula Buke, a community mobiliser in
Bukusuland, for providing useful information on Elijah Masinde's role
in contemporary ethnic politics in Bukusu.

Notes

1 The ethnic based politics in Kenya has always been interpreted as a means
  of advancing the interests of a particular community. Accordingly, politicians campaign mostly on the basis of ethnic interests and will almost always
  invoke discourses that suggest that it is a particular community's turn to rule.
2 See the Kenya National Bureau of Statistics 2010 for details.
3 Elijah Masinde's words were recorded by some of those who knew him, walked
  with him and were together with him as members of his sect. Some were simply
  his friends. All the quotations in the original Bukusu were reproduced courtesy
  of Prof. Mukwana, W. J., who is now based in Australia and was a close friend
  of the late Elijah Masinde. A full dossier and more details of his life from one
  who knew him can be found on the online Luhya blog *The Lumboka Star*.

4 Sunday editions are normally bulkier, with more room for analytical and commentary news than news reports. Being an election year, the extensive focus on the prophecy in a Sunday edition must have also meant that the same issue was the most significant political event the previous week, at least according to the media.

5 The true sponsors of the suit were of course Musikari Kombo and the PNU Luhya political elite who felt that ODM was reaping substantial cultural and political capital following the frequent visits to the 'shrine' (Elijah Masinde's home). The trio that filed the suit was possibly cobbled up from one of the many breakaway groups of the *dini*.

References

CIA (2009) *CIA World Factbook* <https://www.cia.gov/library/publications/the-world factbook/geos/ke.html>.

CIPEV (2008) *Final Report*, Nairobi: Commission of Inquiry into the Post Election Violence.

Bellers, V. (2009) <http://www.britishempire.co.uk/article/sanders/sanderschapter21.htm>.

Buke, W. (2009) Interview with Wafula Buke at the Kasarani Sports View Hotel, Nairobi, Oct.

Entman, Robert M. (1993) 'Framing: towards clarification of a fractured paradigm', *Journal of Communication*, 43/4, pp. 51–8.

Ezekiel, Alembi (2000) *Elijah Masinde: A Rebel with a Cause*, Nairobi: Sasa Sema.

Gamson, W. A., and Lasch, E. Kathryn (1983) 'The political culture of social welfare policy', in S. Spiro, and Ephraim Yuchtman-Yaar (eds), *Evaluating the Welfare State: Social and political perspectives*, New York: Academic Press.

Gamson, W. A., and Stuart, D. (1992) 'Media discourse as a symbolic contest: the bomb in political cartoons', *Sociological Forum*, 7/1, pp. 55–86.

Hall, Stuart (1997) 'The work of representation', in S. Hall (ed.), *Representation: Cultural representations and signifying practices*, London: Sage.

Kenya National Bureau of Statistics (2009) *Population and Housing Census*, Nairobi: Bureau of Statistics.

Macarthur, J. (2008) 'How the West was won: regional politics and prophetic promises in the 2007 Kenya elections', *Journal of East African Studies*, 2/2, pp. 227–41.

Mukwana, W. Julius (2004) 'Elijah Masinde, Omubichachi', *The Lumboka Star*, 27 Nov.

Taylor, I. (2008) 'Surveying the battlefield: mapping the different arguments and positions of the Iraq War debate through frame analysis', *Westminster Chapters in Communication and Culture*, 5/3, pp. 69–90.

Van Gorp, B. (2007) 'The Constructionist Approach to Framing: Bringing Culture Back', *Journal of Communication*, 57, pp. 60–78.

Warren, C., and Liambila W. (2004) *Safe Motherhood Demonstration Project in Western Province: Approaches to Providing Quality Maternal Care in Kenya*, Nairobi: Population Council.

Wipper, Audrey (1977) *Rural Rebels: A Study of Two Protest Movements in Kenya*, Nairobi: Oxford University Press.

Selected Newspaper References

Bogle, C. (2007) 'How Western Province is likely to vote', *The Standard*, 16 Sept.

Buke, W. (2007) 'Raila to fulfil Luhya dream of ascending to presidency', *The Standard*, 21 Sept.

Daily Nation (2007) 'Scramble for Western vote in top gear', 23 Sept.

—— (2007) 'Honour all freedom heroes, says Mudavadi', 27 Sept.

—— (2007) 'Leaders Extol Mudavadi, King of Western', 27 Sept.

Kabaji, E. (2007) 'Myths and stories that will shape how we vote', *The Standard*, 15 Oct.

Kapchanga, L., and Barnabas Bii (2007) 'Masinde family supports Raila', *Daily Nation*, 12 Nov.

Kinyungu, C., and Wanyonyi, R. (2007) 'Kombo masses troops to counter Orange wave in Bungoma', *Daily Nation*, 14 Oct.

Obonyo, O., and Ojwang, Anderson (2007) 'ODM wins case in shrine visitation row', *The Standard*, 4 Nov.

Ojwang, A., and Kisia, Allan (2007) 'Elijah Masinde and the Luhya Prophecy', *The Standard*, 9 Sept.

Ojwang, A., and Makabila, S. (2007) 'Mudavadi's position divides Bukusu elders', *The Standard*, 16 Sept.

Wanyeki, Muthoni (2007) 'Remembering our real hero(in)es', *The East African*, 12 Oct.

Wanyonyi, R. (2007) 'Sect founder's kin disown ceremony', *The Standard*, 11 Oct.

11

A CRITICAL VIEW OF THE KENYAN MEDIA SYSTEM THROUGH THE LENS OF THE JOURNALISTS

Elisabet Helander

Introduction

Following the eruption of violent political clashes after the 2007 Kenyan presidential election, a commission set out to investigate underlying causes. The commission, led by Judge Phillip Waki, produced a report which apportioned part of the blame for the ethnically driven violence to Kenyan media (Waki 2008). This stirred debate among Kenya's media practitioners, causing some self-criticism among journalists, which was echoed in responses that were given in the research for this chapter. However, the question of ethnic tension relayed in the media appears to be partly the problem of a partisan media, which impacts on journalism practice. The structure of the Kenyan media system appears to result in many media outlets becoming direct political instruments during election campaigns, when politicians appeal to ethnicity to win votes. By interviewing ordinary journalists and editors who work in print, TV and radio, the focus is on how they perceive their own practice within the structure.

The media's role in a transitional democracy was the starting point for this research. Kenyans have seen broadcasting expansion with new independent channels and some press growth in the past decade. About 21 per cent of Kenyans have internet access. A new constitution was enacted in 2010, and was widely praised for extending press

freedom and information access (Freedomhouse 2011). Are more pluralist media the source of reliable information and a forum for open
political debate? Although Kenya has a more pluralist media and a
less oppressive legal environment, the influence of the government
still looms large. Freedom of expression is still regulated through the
Law on Sedition, as well as by criminal libel and defamation cases,
where the burden of proof rests with the accused. The Statutory Media
Council, established by the 2007 Media Act, regulates the journalists'
conduct.

The Media Council is appointed by the Ministry of Information
and media stakeholders, which puts its independence in some doubt
(Freedomhouse 2011). The Media Act has caused heated debate
among media practitioners (Makali 2010b). However, Kenyan journalists surveyed emphasised a number of other factors, which also
play a role in their independence, e.g., their collective professional
status and media owners' financial and political interests. What fore-
grounds in this context, is the media organisations' corruption and
the manipulation of news in favour or disfavour of politicians. As
Kenya is regarded as having a well-developed and fast-growing media
industry (Makali 2010a), it is pertinent to analyse the media system's
weakness.

Conditions for a Habermasian public sphere – a comprehensible
discourse based on truthful information – are only fulfilled among
an elite in African society (Berger 2002). Many Kenyans are serviced
by either government-controlled media, or by privately owned media,
which sometimes have a direct connection to a political party. In
this environment, more open and free political debate takes place on
the media margins, in specialist publications and on internet blogs,
something to which several of the interviewees give witness. In the
Kenyan case both government and business leaders may be keen to
feed the public with nothing subversive to their interest and power
(Nyamnjoh 2004). A related question is how standards are set for political reporting and opinion making in mainstream media. The case
study shows that this is unclear in a newly liberalised media system,
because common professional standards are not being upheld through
any trusted formal institutions.

The case study is based on individual semi-structured interviews
with people working in different parts of the media. It aimed to find

what factors impact on how stories are covered, and how journalists view their professional situation and working conditions. The responses help to illustrate the relation between the structure of the media system, and journalism practice in a recently liberalised environment. The issues that run through most of the interviews are: aspects of the political economy of mainstream media, the ethical problem of bribery in journalism and the problem of politics being linked to ethnicity.

Historic Background and Outline of Kenya's Mass Media

Kenya is a former British colony that gained independence in 1963 and adopted a constitution and legal system similar to that of the United Kingdom. Since the country held its first multi-party elections in 1992, Kenya's media has gradually opened up to more independent voices. The right to freedom of expression and the liberalisation of broadcasting was called for as an integral part of the development of democratic rule.

As part of liberalisation, the Communications Commission of Kenya allocated 224 FM and 89 TV frequencies. About 60 radio frequencies are in use, which indicates how quickly both local and national radio has grown. There are 14 TV channels in Kenya, which only use a small portion of the number of frequencies allocated (CCK 2005, in Maina 2006). The allocation process for broadcasting licences and frequencies was not transparent and has been criticised in Kenyan media debate. The accusation is that it was based on political patronage and some frequencies are being hoarded illegally (Makali 2010a). Most broadcasting licences awarded during the Moi administration in the 1990s were based on relationships with government officials, according to Ogola (2009).

The *Daily Nation* is the largest paper in terms of readership, and the second largest is the *East African Standard*. The *Daily Nation* was founded in 1960 by the Aga Khan and is now owned by the Nation Media Group, of which the Aga Khan is the principal shareholder. The three dominating media houses Nation Media Group, the Standard Group and Royal Media have so-called cross-media ownership, which means that they own influential TV and radio channels as well as a range of papers. The state-owned broadcaster, Kenya Broadcasting Corporation, has countrywide coverage and is partly financed by advertising revenue (Maina 2006).

Although Kenya has enjoyed economic growth in the last decade, the media market is relatively small and economic constraints have an effect on journalism practice. Specialised reporting is rare, as the case study exemplifies. The papers and radio stations do not employ enough staff, but rely instead on freelancers' contributions, especially for coverage outside the capital.

Theoretical Framework

Although the Kenyan media has been liberalized, and is no longer state dominated, it is now susceptible to both political influence and commercial pressure. In this aspect, Kenyan mainstream media do not differ from media in the Western world. There are, however, socio-political conditions with certain implications for journalism practice in a developing country going through a transition to democracy (Skjerdal 2009). There are values and norms that transcend journalistic practices in all mass media. Indeed, comparing comments from Kenyan journalists with my own experience working as a Swedish foreign correspondent shows that there are universal issues that affect most journalists.

Political economy theories developed in the Western media context are in some ways applicable when analysing Kenyan journalism. A great number of the case study's interviewees talk about the political interests reflected in their medium, as well as the influence of business advertisers who, in turn, support political parties. Different theoretical works on the political economy of the media by, for example, Herman and Chomsky (1994), McChesney (2004) and Curran (1996) point to the same issues found in the Kenyan case. The theoretical ideas of the more libertarian strand have great resonance when interviewees talk about their journalistic ideals, many emphasising unbiased and informative reporting.

An article by Rønning (2009) notes an African culture of gifts, and the idea of a favour for a favour, which are used to make a system work smoothly. In the same article, Rønning states that many Africans have come to accept petty corruption as part of their daily lives. Although the bribery phenomenon is spoken of as being widespread, the Kenyan journalists do not accept petty corruption as normal. Several lament it vehemently and would like to change it.[1] The corruption impacts on the relatively poor majority of the population and has a demoralising influence on the whole society, as it undermines trust in all institutions.

Rønning's article focuses on media's role in curbing public sector corruption and only touches upon the issue of corruption in the media itself (2009). The effect of corruption is that it can undermine institutions' legitimacy, including that of the media. The media are often presumed to be holding government officials to account and to be able to expose corruption in public administration. What person or organisation is exposed and when may become something interested parties will try to influence by bribery or by co-opting journalists and editors in some other way.

The problem of corruption in a transitional democracy often stems from the many interest groups in the intermediate class who are vying for power over government bodies and the economy. The lack of institutional legitimacy leads to weak institutions, which leads to contestation over the rules and gives scope for corrupt practices – a negative spiral. Both sociologists and economists have picked up the concept of civil society in developing countries, including the independent media as potential crusaders against corruption. Political corruption is often part of a set of exchanges within patron–client networks through which elites construct compromises with interest groups who would otherwise threaten the system's political stability (Khan, 1998). Mass media, representing different interest groups in the intermediate class in Kenya, become involved in such patron-client networks. Far from solving the corruption problem, the civil society in developing countries may be part of that problem.

This argument falls into line with analysis by the South African media scholar Guy Berger (2002) who stated that the roles of civil society and independent media are being unduly romanticised. Private media, instead of being a democratic champion, can be part of the problem when, for example, there is the practice of 'journalism for sale' or so called 'brown envelope journalism' (Berger 2002). Interviewees were acutely aware of corruption's undermining effect in the media, but did not see how they, individually or collectively, could change the trend. Their professional position is weak because they feel exposed to various threats, such as job dismissal, physical violence and police harassment.

In arguments on African media there has been too much emphasis on the state having undue influence over the media sphere, with the only antidote being seen as privatisation or an opening up to market forces. Little attention has been paid to the media's relation to citizens' rights, i.e., the importance of a regulatory framework that sets out clear rules on such matters as defamation, hate speech, undue editorial influence and ownership interests in the whole media sector. What appears to have been under-emphasised is that a media regulation system should promote press freedom, but should also define what responsibility the media has to citizens (Rønning 1994).

In spite of the deregulated media market, and the expansion of pluralist media, journalists find themselves curtailed in their work by commercial pressures and outside influences from both business and political interests. The broader question about how the political economy and inadequate regulation of media affect journalists' and editors' work are reflected in the interviews. Several journalists are noticing a certain change of focus, away from worries about government control and more towards market control.[2] When analysing the mass media in more established democracies, their role can appear passive or, at worst, as undermining the democratic system's functioning. This is the case when, for example, media simplify a complex issue, or omit to report on topics that are expensive and difficult to cover. James Curran exemplifies several problems in his critique of free market media (2000), which has relevance to study of the current development of Kenyan media.

The liberal model assumes that, if the media is publicly rather than state funded, it will also hold allegiance to the public rather than the state. However, these assumptions fail to take into account the wider power relations in which the media is situated. In Africa it is often the case that a private media proprietor toes the government line or downplays a controversial story for fear of repercussions to their business interests. Ownership concentration can also limit media market competition and lead to a narrowing of public debate (Curran 2000). This is particularly important in Kenya, where the market is still small in financial terms and ownership is concentrated in only three dominating media companies (Maina 2006).

Those who take a more critical view of the commercially driven media worry about consequences for the practice of journalism. The commercial media model holds an inherent risk of marginalising the new, the critical and the radical in McChesney's (2004) view. Nyamnjoh (2004) echoes this in his analysis of African media when he states that more radical or critical views can only be expressed in the weekly or monthly press, rather than in mainstream mass media. One respondent mentioned that the problem of the main paper, the *Daily Nation*, is that it is bland and careful to the point of saying almost nothing.[3]

This article focuses on Kenyan journalism practice to gauge its role in a recently established democratic system. The aim was to scrutinise the media's ability to promote widespread egalitarian participation in a rational and critical discourse around political issues in society, one of the basic political issues raised by Habermas in his theory of the public sphere (Calhoun 2002).

Hallin and Mancini developed an extensive model to compare different types of media systems and to analyse the media–state relationship. It is built on the basis of research into media systems in western Europe and North America (Hallin and Mancini 2004). Part of this theoretical framework is relevant to understanding the relationship between journalistic professionalism and political parallelism in the Kenyan media and its historical context. Hallin and Mancini's theoretical model may only cautiously be applied to transitional democracies in the global South due to their different economic and political context.

The three media and politics models are (a) the liberal model, (b) the democratic corporatist model and (c) the polarized pluralist model.

The polarized pluralist model, which displays a lower level of journalistic professionalism, a recent history of state intervention or the central role of government in the media, lower mass circulation newspapers, and a high degree of political parallelism, can be found in Spain and Greece, for example. Mancini and Hallin (2004) also include a number of political system variables that define the three models. They suggest that the polarized pluralist model will be widely applicable in Africa. Some of what is relevant in their analysis of Southern Europe, including the role of patron–client networks, the history of state intervention and autocratic rule, media use as an instrument for political and business interests, limited development of the mass circulation press and a lack of common professional norms, is found in Kenyan media systems. Their analysis of professionalism will be explored with reference to interview responses.

Ogude (2009) has explained very well how ethnic or tribal rhetoric easily gains ground in competitive politics, especially when people live under constrained economic conditions. Administrative structures have functioned along ethnic lines since the colonial era and continue to be used to dispense state resources in exchange for political support. Ogude (2009) provides an interesting analysis of how Kenyan literature reflects the concept of *the state as a site of eating*, which helps explain why ethnic consciousness overrides other forms of solidarity in times of economic hardship.

Legal, Regulatory and Employment Conditions

The Media Council of Kenya was an industry body which began to function in 2004 to apply self-regulation and defend the media's freedom and independence. It was developed by the Media Industry Steering Committee (MISC), formed in 1993 by media stakeholders, like the Media Owners' Association, the Kenya Union of Journalists, the Editors' Guild, the Kenya Correspondents' Association, media NGOs, training institutions, state media and the alternative press. Although the Media Council of Kenya formulated a comprehensive Code of Conduct for journalists, its regulating role is weak when it comes to enforcement (Maina 2006). Interview respondents recognize that the self-regulation system does not appear to work well.

With the enactment of the 2008 comprehensive Kenya Media Law, the Media Council came under statutory rather than voluntary dispensation, which makes it more powerful. Mudhai (2007) argues that it should promote industry, and that there is a need to establish credible sanctions against those who break the conduct code. The new Media Law of 2008 and the Information and Communication Act of 2009 have added new regulation. Amongst many other things, the Media Law includes a detailed code of conduct prohibiting journalists: 'accept gifts, favors, or compensation from those who might seek to influence coverage' (*Kenya Gazette Supplement* 2007).

Since 2008 the Media Council has received over 70 complaints, most of which have been dismissed for different reasons, suggesting that it lacks the power to enforce compliance to the code of conduct. This may relate to insufficient funding. A statute law of 2009 provided the Media Council with funding from the exchequer, rather than relying on the media owners and unions for its budget (Makali 2010b). This recent change may result in a more effective institution as long as it can remain independent of government and keep its credibility with media practitioners. Its success depends on council members' integrity as they partly represent media owners (Mudhai 2007).

The Kenya Union of Journalists is not held in very high regard among the journalists interviewed in the case study. It has a weak position in relation to the employers and cannot give much practical support to its members. The largest paper, the *Daily Nation*, actively hinders new employees from joining the union, which further undermines it (Makali 2010a). It is also significant that about 80 per cent of journalists in Kenya are not permanent employees but are referred to as correspondents. The correspondents depend on payment per story or per word. Their professional position is precarious and this has a bearing on their integrity and independence.

A Thematic Analysis of the Interviews with Kenyan Journalists

By thematically analysing 15 interviews with various journalists in Nairobi, it is possible to shed light on a number of issues affecting the quality and content of their work. The sample consisted of one-third broadcast journalists and two-thirds print journalists and interviews took place in different Nairobi locations in 2009. Three of the journalists worked freelance for a number of different media. A fixed set of questions was used in all the interviews and interviewees were made to understand that their names and the material would be treated confidentially. Some of the journalists were, in spite of this assurance, quite self-conscious when talking about sensitive matters, for example, about ethnic bias, during the recorded interviews. Considering the worries about their safety that some expressed, it is likely that they were careful when talking of sensitive issues.

Most of the journalists genuinely cared about the Kenyan media and wanted to engage in debate about it. The employed journalists were more constrained and less outspoken compared with those who worked freelance or for alternative or aid-funded media. The use of interviews for research is, in spite of possible flaws, a useful way to explore the relation between structure and practice in media production.

The different media practitioners who contributed to the research did it independently of each other. The fact that so many brought up the same issues in regard to journalism practice may be an indication of an influential debate taking place among a relatively small journalist community. However, overlapping responses help to support the hypothesis that a liberalised media in Kenya has not led to independent and varied political coverage in the mainstream media. In other words, the media system is not as pluralist as it may appear.

Interview questions:

What is your job day to day?
How do you see your role as a journalist?
What are the changes that have taken place in media during the last decade?
Are you a member of a union?
What sort of stories are you mostly doing?
How do you get your information?
What do you have to think about when you do a story?
Do you ever find that you can't do the story that you would like to do?
Do you think the owner of your medium has direct editorial influence?
Are you proud of the job that you do?
Are you often worried for your safety or losing your job?
Who do you ask when you are unsure of what you can say in a story?

The Independence of Mass Media are Compromised

Several respondents spoke about positive changes that have taken place regarding freedom of speech in the last ten years.

> There is greater latitude, more room, to actually express yourself. But, most importantly, there were stories that would be killed because of government, and they can now be told.[4]

A journalist working for a news agency refers to the development of the media as a commercial market by saying 'people are investing a lot of money in the media, whereas before it seemed unviable'.[5] There are also a number of journalists who comment that 'there is a lot of competition'.[6] The increased competition between media outlets is seen as both good and bad from the general public's viewpoint.

In spite of the media's liberalisation and growth, the same journalists state that many impediments to free speech remain. 'The media is compromised' is a phrase that several journalists used in interviews, and they explain the factors that curtail the independence of journalists and editors. One journalist describes the current climate of fear, which leads to self-censorship at two of the main broadsheets, the *Daily Nation* and *The East African Standard*. 'They are deliberately vague on certain things, and it's because editors don't want to get in trouble'.[7] The threat of being sued for libel is taken very seriously by most interviewees. The papers have teams of in-house lawyers who go through all political articles for possibly libellous statements. This coincides with the general trend in Africa, where media are faced with governments' use of libel laws in ways that contradict democratic governance and the constitutional provision of press freedom (Murphy 2007). Such repressive legal frameworks are upheld by lawmakers, who perceive journalists as potential troublemakers (Nyamnjoh 2005, 2010).

The issue of the media owner having direct editorial influence is another aspect which is brought up by those working for private mass media.

> During the election violence, the company that I work for was taking one side, with the PNU. There are unspoken rules that you cannot go against. It's not there consciously, but it's there, and you look out for your job. Ethics and beliefs are being compromised.[8]

Another example is a respondent who saw the media owner's influence as something unavoidable. 'This newspaper is partly owned by politicians so of course there will be that interference and political influence'.[9] The presumption that private media will hold allegiance to the public rather than the state fails to take into account the relations of power in which media are situated (Curran 2000). The editor of a non-commercial publication sums up the position of Kenya's media very simply. 'It's an economic entity and it has to curry favour with the few corporate powers. But they are also very closely linked to the political powers.'[10]

A journalist working for one of the main papers in 2007 lamented the way election coverage inflamed ethnic tensions.

> Why didn't we see it coming, shouldn't we have risen up to a different role of conflict resolution before it exploded? I speak about responsibility, play down the conflict, not just report what politicians say [...]
>
> But not just that – we flaunted the rules – we took sides and became tribal journalists, partisan journalists and contributed to the ethnic tension to puff up a particular party. I know you can't be objective 100 per cent, but we reneged on our responsibility.[11]

As a consequence of heightened ethnic tension, many journalists could not report from certain areas of the country. One journalist told how he used to do investigative stories without fear.

> Now I have to pretend to be of another group than Kikuyu, which is very hard to do when you need to immerse yourself in order to get a good story, and I have to rely on the guide to some extent.[12]

The main papers and broadcasters are historically aligned with either side of the political arena. According to many interviewees, these outlets are used as instruments for political and business interests. This historical pattern has implications for the democratisation process. It is not just a matter of lifting censorship and holding multi-party elections, but involves a transformation of the media, and of relations among political, social and economic institutions (Hallin and Papathanassopoulos 2002, in Blankson and Murphy 2007). I will return to the question in a discussion about professionalism and regulation.

A small number of the journalists interviewed bring up the problem of the media ignoring actual issues behind a politician's statements and posturing, while the 'bigger stories on socioeconomic issues, life for us Kenyans, are not the main stories in the news bulletins at night'.[13] Most are more conscious of advertisers and other business interests as a hindrance to independent journalism, as illustrated by the following examples.

An article, which included some criticism of Kenya Airways, had grave consequences for the paper's advertising revenue.

Kenya Airways cut all their advertising and went to the *Nation*. I think it was for over a year. Then we had to write a very favourable story about them in order to get the advertising back.[14]

A television producer explained how advertisers influence television programming content. It will often be the case that a company approaches a TV station and threatens to pull all advertising for a month unless they stop pursuing or airing a specific story with any negative material about the company. If it is broadcast it can also have consequences for the individual journalist.

I know for a fact that journalists have been fired for doing such stories. They just pick up the phone and say: 'If this person doesn't go then you will not be getting this business'.[15]

The liberal media model has advantages not only for greater variation in types of media but also for business opportunities and market access. A liberalised and deregulated media system leaves more room for different companies to influence consumers, as the political economy theory suggests (McChesney 2004). There are also examples of the medium owner's financial interests having influence on content. 'The Nation would be very careful when covering issues to do with investments done by Aga Khan, its owner', according to interviewee No. 1. The question of direct influence by media owners is possibly even more important with radio broadcasting. According to a journalist, in practice there are no limitations to who can own a radio station. 'There is a law against MPs owning a station, but it's not being followed'.[16]

It was surprising how many journalists spoke of the issue of 'killing a story' by means of bribes. One commented that 'properties and bank accounts would tell you a lot about the editors', regarding the amounts of money and assets gained by editors through bribes. Another journalist spoke about a publication, *The People*, which survives solely through political patronage. This type of press is referred to in Kenya as 'the gutter press' and most articles are published under pseudonyms.

The People started as a very serious investigative weekly and had become very successful, running insider stories on the previous Moi regime. The owner decided to turn it into a daily, but then couldn't afford to run it. He had all these reporters in there whose wages weren't being paid, and the standard plummeted. Some very good journalist stayed and lost their self-confidence. It then became all about political patronage, some of the journalists now depending directly on payment by politicians.[17]

It is impossible to gauge the exact extent of corrupt practices and 'brown envelope journalism' in Kenya. The phenomenon of payment in exchange for favourable coverage or for no coverage was talked about spontaneously in many of the interviews. Corruption within the media has to do with the way media organisations are structured and journalists' behaviour and practices when sourcing and reporting. It is unusual for someone to be exposed as a corrupt journalist, as their ranks close to protect their own. This is how several journalists explained why it is very rare that journalists or editors face the consequences of their illicit relations.

According to a seasoned print journalist, the reporters covering parliament routinely pick up a brown envelope from the party spokesperson.[18] The corruption ranges from petty sums to influence journalists to more serious cases of large bribes for specific stories. Typically, the journalists will lament the incidence of corruption among their colleagues but do not know where to turn. A few cases have been exposed, and those involved have owned up, but mostly the corruption is not proven (Mudhai 2007).

Lack of Common Norms and Standards

In transitional democracies there is a need for the media to develop vocational principles and responsibilities (Blankson 2007). Who decides when media codes of conduct have been breached? The libel laws are being misused to stop a story from being pursued further, according to an editor. By filing a claim for libel, the subject matter cannot be followed up by the media until the case has been settled.[19] That appears to be the most commonly used form of media regulation in Kenya.

The journalist's trade union has a relatively weak position in supporting journalists' rights or in enforcing a code of conduct. A seasoned print journalist, a member of the journalist's union in Kenya says, for example, that 'they have not been able to articulate our issues and in fact are not journalists themselves'.[20] The lack of support from the union or any other organisation relates immediately to their sense of insecurity.

Most interviewees were not journalist's union members, because there was no practical need for it and some regarded the union with great suspicion. A journalist working for a news agency criticised it for 'being compromised by the government, ineffective, and only bargaining for collective wage agreements'. On the other hand, one journalist at the dominant Nation Media Group explained that the company actively discourages trade union activity and forbids new employees from joining the Kenyan Union of Journalists.[21] This is likely to undermine union's possibilities of supporting and fostering professionalism.

Kenyan journalists are led by their editor's instructions rather than a common code of ethics to which everyone can refer. The Media Council now has a statutory status, giving it greater power to implement regulation. However, among journalists, this development was seen as more worrying than anything else. Media Council members are too closely connected to the government, according to one radio journalist, who also says that: 'there is a thin line between independence and dependence'.[22] The government decided to strengthen the Media Council's regulatory power in order to better control the media and to hinder a repeat of the ethnic incitement that took place at the 2007 general election. A TV journalist lamented that: 'parliament blamed the media for all this ethnic violence, when it was actually they who called the tribal lines [in the election campaign]'.[23] When MP candidates campaign by speaking to one specific ethnic group, addressing their grievances to win their votes, it is also reflected in mass media's political reporting.[24] Two of the interviewed journalists accuse politicians of relying heavily on the support of an ethnic group, rather than promoting a more general political programme benefiting people more widely.

The acute awareness of threats to journalists and the lack of faith in government institutions were mentioned by a number of respondents. A news reporter was found murdered a week before the interviews and two journalists saw it as likely to be connected to the reporter's work. They did not think the murder case would be thoroughly investigated, either by the police or the press.

> People are losing faith in our politicians! They don't have faith in our judicial system. We don't even go to the police. The media council are

people who are rich, are people who have connections. They cannot relate to the normal reporter.[25]

It is possible to see how the group structure of Kenyan society has, until recently, been organised and monitored by the state, which means that the new political dispensation was partly born from a weak and contrived institutional organisation. The suspicion against government authority and any organisation vaguely connected to it, like the journalist's trade union or the Media Council, is a recurring theme in interviews. Transition to democratic governance is hampered by the absence of sustainable social organisations which hold some respect among the public. Politics is volatile and personalised and those who have the financial resources to influence media have the advantage (Bennett 1998). 'We have a very big issue with accountability', says a journalist of many years' experience working for both local and international publications.[26]

It is clear that there is a need for regulation to govern the media in its relations with other organisations and its obligations to the public, but it remains to explain why the existing code of ethics is not adhered to. Hallin's and Mancini's analysis of different levels of professionalism is useful in this context. Their starting point is Weber's definition of a rational-legal authority as a form of rule-based adherence to formal and universal rules of procedure. In this system, individuals and organisations act according to procedures seen as serving the society as whole, or a common good. Where this type of rule-bound authority is strongly developed, the agencies that regulate broadcasting and press are likely to be more autonomous and more respected by media practitioners (Mancini and Hallin 2004). This type of respected authority has not fully developed in Kenya, which may be why journalists interviewed in this case study kept referring to their lack of trust in so many of the institutions governing them. The inability to keep journalistic professional norms and form a united professional collective stems from this problem.

When placing Kenya within the Mancin and Hallin analytical framework outlined earlier, it would fall into the 'polarized pluralist model' category. By comparison, in Scandinavian countries the media are expected to strictly stick to common norms. Sweden, for example, would fall into the category 'democratic corporatist model', characterised by strong institutions, among other things. A good example is that of a journalist sacked from his prominent job as a foreign correspondent because of suspicion of a connection to organised crime in Sweden. A suspected criminal claimed in private to be getting favours from the journalist. While nothing was proved, the Swedish journalist will never be able to get a job in mainstream media again, according to the Swedish editor Peter Felman.[27] The collective voice of journalists, often represented by the union, works here to maintain media credibility by excluding erring journalists. This type of automatic exclusion would, according to journalists interviewed in Nairobi, not happen in Kenya. They seldom see negative consequences for journalists who overstep ethical norms. There is no trusted collective professional voice expressed within the media's structure. Such a voice should function in media self-regulation.

The Gap between Ideals and Practice in Journalism

The interviewees have different backgrounds in terms of their amount of experience and their type of education. Younger journalists had recently graduated from journalism school, and had textbooks fresh in their minds when responding to some questions. In spite of the variation, they all had similar ideas about what constitutes independent journalistic judgement and what relevant information is. However, there is a wide gap between the reporting journalists think they should do and what they are expected to do by their employer. One problem widely recognised by interviewees is that the mass media is city-centred and ignores the issues of rural areas.

> I want to reverse the trend of Nairobi-journalism, go local, and de-centring. We need to learn, enter an age of discovery, we think we know what's going on, but we are part of an élite nationalist project going around like missionaries telling people what's right and wrong.[28]

For example, to scrutinise a policy issue by talking to people who will be affected takes time and resources, which is often not affordable. This is one weakness of commercially driven media in a developing country. Another journalist complained that 'people don't know their rights. I want to start a program to educate'.[29] Basic information and education is not given airtime because it is not deemed commercially viable. There is also a great frustration over being unable to follow up a story due to a lack of public information. Most of the journalists had ambitions to be a 'professional journalist', which meant being objective and neutral in their work. They believe they should have the role of 'a watchdog' in society. A young radio presenter also emphasised the role of informing listeners objectively. Many of the journalists' statements exemplify how they are hemmed in by a lack of information and thereby they risk speculation.

A problem with the simple call for independent media and freedom of speech as a catch-all solution is that it ignores the journalists' position and that of the readers/listeners/viewers. Communication is sustained and produced by interpreting subjects acting within a context, in itself partly constructed by the media. It is important to recognise that individuals are 'situated interpreters' and not all-knowing subjects (Keane 1996). Points made are relevant in Kenya, where liberalisation of the media has taken place and yet is not classified as free, nor has it served the role to truthfully inform the public during the election campaigns (Kadhi and Rutten 2001). Kenyan journalists and their editors are 'situated interpreters' who will exercise self-censorship when faced with certain information and will also serve as propagandists or become polarised when, for example, the heat of an election campaign affects them.

Conclusion

By analysing interviews conducted in Nairobi in 2009, it is possible to understand the background and context of the media system within which they work. It is difficult for the journalist to play the role that they would like, in supporting the democratic process and a well-informed and balanced debate. The mass media is described as being compromised by a number of different interests, such as business advertisers, the government or media owners. They describe in detail all the different aspects of the problem, including corruption, which undermine media's credibility as an institution. Although several journalists have great ambitions it was found that many were despondent about their ability to influence matters. Their sense of professional pride was not strong, nor their sense of job or personal safety. Several media theorists, including Hallin and Mancini (2004), provide useful theories to explain this phenomenon's political and historic context. Kenya's recent history of autocratic rule still looms large over the society as a whole and the media system specifically.

There is a need for some regulation to govern the media in relation to other organisations and their obligation to the public. Kenya's media are regarded as very good when compared to many other developing countries. However, this paper suggests that although Kenya has a pluralist and growing media system, it still has clear deficiencies in providing an open forum for debate based on independent political reporting. Development in the last two decades has set the stage for more manipulation of public opinion through media, while both corruption and biased reporting continues unsanctioned. As political leaders have so far sustained their support through co-option and patronage of local ethnic groups, it is difficult for Kenyan journalists to remain immune to the division (Ogude 2009).

Notes

1   No. 1 interviewed 8 Feb. 2009 and No. 2 interviewed 9 Feb. 2009.
2   No. 7, interviewed in Nairobi, 11 Feb., and No. 8 and No. 10, interviewed in Nairobi, 13 Feb. 2009.
3   No. 14, interviewed in Nairobi, 14 Feb. 2009.
4   No. 4, interviewed in Nairobi, 9 Feb. 2009.
5   No.15, interviewed in Nairobi, 11 Feb. 2009.
6   No. 1, interviewed in Nairobi, 8 Feb. 2009.
7   No. 13, interviewed in Nairobi, 14 Feb. 2009.
8   No. 2, interviewed in Nairobi, 9 Feb. 2009.
9   No. 7, interviewed in Nairobi, 11 Feb. 2009.
10   No. 14, interviewed, 12 Feb. 2009.
11   No. 9, interviewed in Nairobi, 13 Feb. 2009.
12   No. 14, interviewed in Nairobi, 12 Feb. 2009.
13   No. 4, interviewed in Nairobi, 9 Feb. 2009.
14   No. 7, interviewed in Nairobi, 11 Feb. 2009.
15   No. 4, interviewed in Nairobi, 9 Feb. 2009.
16   No. 2, interviewed in Nairobi, 9 Feb. 2009.
17   No. 13, interviewed in Nairobi, 14 Feb. 2009.
18   No. 9, interviewed in Nairobi, 13 Feb. 2009.
19   No. 6, interviewed in Nairobi, 11 Feb. 2009.
20   No. 1, interviewed in Nairobi, 8 Feb. 2009.
21   No. 10, interviewed in Nairobi, 13 Feb. 2009.
22   No. 2, interviewed in Nairobi, 9 Feb. 2009.
23   No. 4, interviewed in Nairobi, 9 Feb. 2009.

24   No. 2, interviewed in Nairobi, 9 Feb. 2009.
25   No. 2, interviewed in Nairobi, 9 Feb. 2009.
26   No. 13, interviewed in Nairobi, 14 Feb. 2009.
27   Stated in conversation in Stockholm, 11 Sept. 2009.
28   No. 13 interviewed in Nairobi, 14 Feb. 2009.
29   No. 2 interviewed in Nairobi, 9 Feb. 2009.

References

Bennett, L. (1998) 'The media and democratic development: the social bias of political communication', in P. O'Neil (ed.), *Communicating Democracy*, pp. 195–208, Boulder, CO: Lynne Rienner.

Berger, G. (2002) 'Theorizing the media-democracy relationship in Southern Africa', *Gazette: The International Journal for Communication Studies*, 64/1, pp. 21–45.

Blankson, I. A. (2007) 'Media independence and pluralism in Africa', in I. A. Blankson and R. Murphy (eds), *Negotiating Democracy*, pp.15–33, New York: State University of New York Press.

Calhoun, Craig, ed. (2002) *Dictionary of the Social Sciences*, Oxford: Oxford University Press. Accessed in 2011 on http://www.freedomhouse.org/report/freedom-press/2011/kenya.

Curran, J. (2000) 'Rethinking media and democracy revisited', in J. Curran and M. Gurevitch (eds), *Mass Media and Society*, pp. 120–153, London: Arnold.

Hallin, D. C., and Mancini, P. (2004) *Comparing Media Systems: Three Models of Media and Politics*, Cambridge: Cambridge University Press.

Herman, E and Chomsky, N. (1994) *Manufacturing Consent: The political Economy of the Mass Media*. London: Vintage Press.

Ismail, A. J., and Deane J. (2008) 'The 2007 general election in Kenya and its aftermath: the role of local media', *International Journal of Press/Politics*, 13, p. 319.

Kadhi, J. and Rutten, M. (2001) 'The Kenyan media in the 1997 general elections: A look at the watchdogs'. In M. Rutten, A. Mazrui and F. Grignon, (Eds.), *Out for the Count: The 1997 General Elections and Prospects for Democracy in Kenya* (pp. 315–380). Kampala: Fountain Press.

Kadhi, J. S. M. (1999), 'Anglophone Africa: journalists – puppets of the proprietors', in M. Kunczik (ed.), *Ethics in Journalism: A Reader on the Perception in the Third World*, Bonn: The Division for International Development Cooperation of Friedrich-Ebert-Stiftung, pp. 82–133.

Keane, J. (1996) *Media and Democracy*, Cambridge: Polity Press.

Kenya Gazette (2007) Act No. 3, Supplement No. 93, Nairobi.

Kenya Human Rights Commission (1997) *Shackled Messengers: The Media in Multiparty Kenya*, Nairobi: Kenya Human Rights Commission.

—— (2008) *A Report on the 2007 General Elections*, 27 Feb., Nairobi: Kenya Human Rights Commission.

Khan, M. (1998) 'The role of civil society and patron-client networks in the analysis of corruption', in *Integrity Improvement Initiatives in Developing Countries*, New York: UNDP, Management Development and Governance Division, pp. 111–128.

Maina, L. W. (2006) *African Media Development Initiative: Kenya Context*, London: BBC World Service Trust, UK.

Makali, D. (2010a) 'What is wrong?', *Expression Today* (Nairobi: Media Institute of Kenya), March.

—— (2010b) 'Watchdog or spectator', *Expression Today* (Nairobi: Media Institute of Kenya), April/May.

McChesney, R.M. (2004). 'The political economy of international communicatioin'. In P.N. Thomas and Z. Nain (eds.), *Who owns the media?: Global trends and local resistances* (pp. 3–21) Penang, Malaysia: Southbound.

Mudhai, F. (2007) 'Time to harvest? Media, corruption and elections in Kenya', *Ethical Space: The International Journal of Communication Ethics*, 4/4, pp. 30–5.

Murphy, R. (2007) 'Introduction', in I. A. Blankson and R. Murphy (eds), *Negotiating Democracy*, New York: State University of New York Press.

Nyamnjoh, F. B. (2005) *Africa's Media, Democracy and the Politics of Belonging*, London: Zed Books.

—— (2004), Media ownership and control in Africa in the age of globalisation. In P. N Thomas,. and Z. Nain (eds). *Who owns the media?: Global trends and local resistances* (pp. 119–134). Southbound, Penang, Malaysia.

—— (2010) Keynote address for the Racism, Ethnicity and the Media in Africa conference, 25–6 March, London.

Ochieng, P. (1992) *I Accuse the Press: An Insider's View of the Media and Politics in Africa*, Nairobi: ACTS Press.

Ogbondah, C. (2002) 'Media laws in political transition', in G. Hyden, M. Leslie, and F. F. Ogundimu (eds), *Media and Democracy in Africa,* ch. 3, Uppsala: Nordic Africa Institute.

Ogola, G. (2009) 'A Media at Cross-Roads', *Africa Insight*, 39/1, June.

Ogude, J. (2009) 'The state as a site of eating', *Africa Insight*, 39/1, June.

Rønning, H. (1994) *Media and Democracy: Theories and Principles with Reference to an African Context*, PLACE: SAPES Books, seminar chapter series, 8.

—— (2009) 'The politics of corruption and the media in Africa', *Journal of African Media Studies*, 1/1.

Skjerdal, Terje S. (2009) 'Between journalism "universals" and cultural particulars: challenges facing the development of a journalism program in an East African context', *Journal of African Media Studies,* 1/1.

Tomaselli, K. G. (2009) 'Repositioning African media studies: thoughts and provocations' *Journal of African Media Studies*, 1/1.

Waki, P. (2008) *The Waki-Report*, Nairobi: Commission to investigate causes of violence in the 2007 election.

12

THE RISE AND FALL OF THE UGANDAN ANTI-HOMOSEXUALITY BILL IN DOMESTIC PRESS: A STUDY ON THE IMPORTANCE OF INTERNATIONAL ALLIES

Cecilia Strand

Introduction

In mid-October 2009, a private member bill by Member of Parliament David Bahati from the ruling National Resistance Movement party of Uganda caused an outcry among human rights organisations and development partners (Strand 2011). The proposed Anti-Homosexuality Bill of October 2009 was criticised on a range of issues, but particularly contentious was the proposal of imprisonment for life for anyone convicted of 'the offense of homosexuality' (Bahati 2009: clause 2), and the introduction of the term 'aggravated homosexuality', for which the Bill sought to impose the death penalty (Bahati 2009: clause 3). As section 145 of the Uganda Penal Code Act already states that sodomy is punishable by life imprisonment, and sections 146 and 148 similarly state that attempted sodomy is punishable with penalties of up to seven years in prison (Hollander 2009), the proposed Bill sought to strengthen existing laws on homosexuality.

After being dormant for ten months, the Bill suddenly re-appeared a second time when it was re-tabled in Parliament on 7 February 2012 (Amnesty International 2012).

A recent study (Strand 2011) analysed the attempts made by local human rights defenders to sensitise the Ugandan public on the implications of the proposed Bill in 2009, by combining interviews with content analysis. Local Ugandan organisations quickly condemned the proposed Bill (Sexual Minorities Uganda (SMUG) 2009; International Gay and Lesbian Human Rights Commission (IGLHRC) 2009a), and formed the Civil Society Coalition on Human Rights and Constitutional Law, a coalition of 28 Ugandan organisations. The main purpose of this Coalition was to prevent the draft Bill from being enacted, and it consequently approached various stakeholders in order to sensitise them on the Bill. The study found that, despite the local human rights defenders' concerted efforts and quick response to the proposed Bill, they were initially unable to access editorial space and influence the domestic media's framing of the Bill as anti-public health, anti-human rights and, ultimately, a piece of legislation affecting all Ugandans and not only sexual minorities. Consequently, the Coalition had to use paid space in order to publicise their statements (Civil Society Coalition on Human Rights and Constitutional Law 2009a, 2009b).

The domestic media's reluctance to cover the Bill and even provide space for paid statements was attributed to a range of factors, such as the history of state-supported discrimination against lesbian, gay, bisexual and transgendered individuals (Human Rights Watch 2008; Tamale 2009; Dicklitch et al. 2012), past incidences of sanctions against the media for attempting to cover sexual minorities (British Broadcasting Corporation 2004; Johnson and International Gay and Lesbian Human Rights Commission 2007; Human Rights Watch 2010) as well as the Ugandan public's negative sentiments on sexual minorities (Pew Research Center Project 2007). Recent research on Ugandan journalists' experiences in covering the Anti-Homosexuality Bill and homosexuality highlight significant and multiple hurdles in the form of audiences' negative perceptions and direct interference by government officials and media owners which makes providing sexual minorities fair and balanced coverage a precarious task, in particular for journalists based outside the capital (Borlase 2011).

The content analysis did however reveal that coverage of the Bill itself, as opposed to Coalition's framing of it, increased substantially – measured as frequency and prominence – in December 2009 (Figure 12.1). Indeed the media coverage of the Bill increased fourfold in

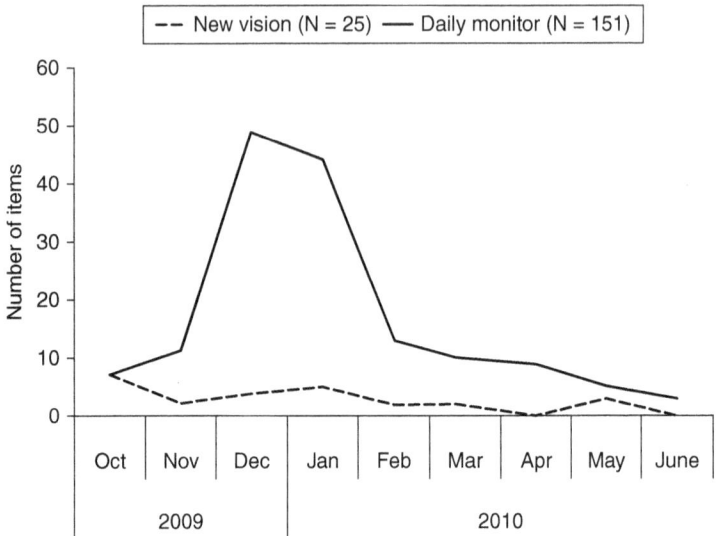

Figure 12.1   Number of items (n=176) by month

December 2009. Human rights defenders' self-attested difficulties in accessing editorial space, combined with the content analysis showing that Ugandan civil society actors were seldom referred to as a source, indicate that domestic human rights actors were not responsible for getting the media to provide the Bill with substantial coverage.

This study will revisit the newspaper coverage of the Anti-Homosexuality Bill in an attempt to understand what caused the initially reluctant journalists to revise their position, at least in the privately owned media, and begin to award the proposed Bill both salience and prominence, i.e., a higher frequency, as well as front-page coverage. This chapter will thus attempt to understand the processes whereby a socially contentious issue such as the Ugandan Anti-Homosexuality Bill gains salience and prominence on the media agenda, and eventually is textually defeated, in the sense that it is framed as a problematic and ultimately an unnecessary piece of legislation.

As the Bill was signed into law by President Museveni on 24 February 2014, the textual defeat in itself did not result in the Bill's real-life demise. Nevertheless, the successful reframing of the Bill could still be regarded as *one* important battleground for human rights activists in terms creating a more multidimensional grasp of the Bill as a social policy option. Understanding how a socially-contentious issue first emerges onto the domestic media agenda, despite the media's initial reluctance to cover it, and then is critically discussed even through a range of diverging perspectives makes it possible to not only inform future human rights advocacy of sexual minority rights in Uganda, but assist organizations fighting similar battles elsewhere in Africa.

This study is inspired by agenda-setting theory and departs from an underlying assumption that the media's coverage of social issues and current events matters in the sense that it influences, but does not determine its readers/listeners/viewers' understanding of the covered issue. Agenda-setting theory proposes that the overall frequency of an issue, combined with the duration of that issue's presence in the coverage, will to a large extent influence the reader's, listener's or viewer's perception of the same issue's importance (McCombs 2004, 2005). Agenda-setting theory assumes that the media have agenda-setting effects also at the attribute level, i.e. how an issue is framed. According to McCombs (2004: 88) a frame can be defined as 'dominant perspective on the object – a pervasive description and characterisation of the object'. Weaver (2007: 142) summarises, 'Whereas the "first level" of agenda setting is focused on the relative salience (usually operationally defined as perceived importance) of issues or subjects, the "second level" examines the relative salience of attributes of issues'. In short, by their selection and framing of the selected issues, the media influence how social issues such as a piece of legislation are regarded as important and how they are to be understood.

Agenda-setting theory has however not paid sufficient attention to the processes that precede an issue's emergence on the media agenda. Walters et al. (1996) argue that agenda-setting theory has gone too far in simplifying matters and that more attention needs be paid to *how* an issue becomes part of the media's agenda. Issues do not simply arise from nowhere, but are often the result of lobbying by grassroots movements, formal and informal civil society groups and/or business interests, as well as a range of contextual factors on the micro and meta levels. McCombs (2005: 548) also calls for more research on the question 'if the press sets the public agenda, who sets the media agenda?'

The closely related framing theory has suffered similar criticism. Carragee and Roefs (2004) argue that framing theory has failed to pay sufficient attention to the complex process through which media frames are actually created and gain popularity. Entman (2003)'s *cascading network activation model,* that was created to explain how the White House successfully spread interpretive frames on the 9/11 attacks to the network of non-administration elites and news organisations, their texts, and finally the public, indicates that the media agenda is the result of a complex interplay and competition between actors' framing of issues and events. Framing according to Entman (2003: 417) entails '*selecting and highlighting some facets of events or issues, and making connections among them so as to promote a particular interpretation, evaluation, and/or solution.* The words and images that make up the frame can be distinguished from the rest of the news by their capacity to stimulate support of or opposition to the sides in a political conflict' (Emphasis added). Entman's research highlights the intricate interplay between multiple actors that influence the frame production process.

Although this study is limited in scope, it does seek to contribute to our understanding of how a socially contentious issue gains salience as well as a deeper understanding of the multiple actors that influence the frame production process. Furthermore, the Ugandan case highlights the need to include not only domestic actors in an analysis of how an issue emerges onto a local media agenda, and how the same issues are framed and reframed during the issue's life cycle. Rather, in an interconnected world, issue emergence and frame creation processes are likely to be the result of not only domestic actors but multiple regional and international actors.

Methodology

In order to understand the process whereby the Anti-Homosexuality Bill was established on the domestic media agenda, as well as the subsequent frame and reframing of the proposed Bill, this study combines an analysis of external actors' agenda-building efforts in relation to the Bill and qualitative content analysis of the Ugandan print media. Although agenda-setting studies often rely heavily on quantitative measures, this study merely uses the basic salience measurement as a compass to guide the analysis of the discursive features of the media texts.

Sample

The print material was sampled in several steps. First, all the items in the two largest English-language newspapers – the government-owned

newspaper the *New Vision* (*NV*), and the largest privately owned newspaper, the *Daily Monitor* (*DM*) – containing one of the following words
were included in the initial sample stretching from 14 October 2009 to
30 June 2010: 'Anti-Homosexuality Bill', 'homosexual', 'homosexuality',
'homo', 'gay', 'gays', 'gayism', 'kuch', 'bisexual', 'lesbian' and 'transgendered'.
This search generated 237 items from the *Daily Monitor* and 69 items
from *New Vision*, which were sorted manually in order to identify only
the items that specifically dealt with the Anti-Homosexuality Bill. That
process generated a sample containing 151 *DM* items and 25 *NV* items.
The term 'item' here refers to the various types of texts produced and
controlled by the editorial teams of the newspapers, such as news articles
and analysis, interviews, the editorial, columns and opinion pieces and
purchased international newswire material, as well as Letters to the Editor.
Paid supplements or public statements on paid space, i.e., texts that are
produced and controlled by the paying organisation were not included.

A basic frequency assessment was done on the 176 items which generated an overview of how the coverage of the proposed Bill fluctuated over
time. This study attempts to first understand which actors appear to have
caused the fourfold increase in coverage and potentially influenced the
readers' perceptions of the Bill as an important piece of legislation, and
second the media's framing of the Bill from introduction to textual defeat.
So the final sample was limited to the period from 14 October 2009 until
the last week of January 2010, when coverage sharply decreases.

The Analysis of Print Media

The content analysis was inspired by narrative content analysis.
Narratives analysis 'permits a holistic approach to discourse that
preserves context and particularity' (Riessman 1993, in Smith 2000).
Narratives are a fundamental and universal form of expression and
characterised by the narrator's *perspective* and *context*. Perspective refers
to the fact that a narrative contains a point of view towards what has
happened, and an interpretation of what was significant about that
event (Smith 2000). Context, in this study, refers to the external factors
that influence the narrator's construction of his/her narrative.

Each item was first identified as news, media initiated analysis,
which includes interviews and features, the editorial, opinion columns
pieces or Letter to the Editor. Secondly each item was summarised
into a short narrative. The narrative consisted of *who* the primary and

secondary actors are in the text and what actions the main character/s are engaged in, in relation to the proposed Bill. Special attention was paid to whether the actor was framed as being opposed to or supportive of the proposed Bill, or rather appeared to discuss parts or the Bill in its entirety in a balanced manner. In short, each item was thus turned into a bare-boned mini-story. These mini-stories assisted in visualising how the domestic media's framing of the Bill changed over time, as well as who was awarded agency in relation to the Bill.

A separate supplementary analysis of the external context was conducted. As a previous study had indicated that domestic human rights activists had had limited influence over the framing of the proposed Bill (Strand 2011), this contextual analysis focused solely on international actors and their actions in relation to the Bill. Source material consisted of statements, speeches, analysis, reports and press releases, as well as WikiLeaks cables from the US Embassy in Kampala, international human rights organisations and religious leaders.

Results

The following section is divided into three periods of media coverage of the proposed Bill. Each period signifies a shift in the coverage, which also for the most part coincides with shifts in external actors' response to the proposed Bill. Although the periods are characterised by different numerical frequencies, ranging from low in October–November 2009, high in December 2009, to declining in January 2010, each period also signifies a change in the dynamics and narratives around the Bill. Each period is visualised through a number of quotes from the two newspapers, with a clear dominance of *Daily Monitor* quotes.

Introduction of the Bill: A Domestic Affair
(14 October–16 November 2009)

On 14 October 2009, the Bill was tabled in parliament. Local human rights defenders, both individually and through the newly founded Civil Society Coalition on Human Rights and Constitutional Law, attempted to raise awareness around the Bill and get the local media to include their concerns by directly approaching them (Strand 2011). They revert to releasing a first statement 'Anti-homosexuality or anti-human rights bill?' on 23 October in paid space, as they had failed to access editorially controlled space. International human rights organisations were also quick to vocally oppose the Bill (Human Rights Watch 2009; Amnesty International 2009; IGLHRC 2009a, 2009b).

The Domestic Media's Narratives of the Newly Introduced Bill

During this first phase of the coverage, the small number of articles (Figure 12.1) coming from both the government-owned *New Vision* (*NV*) and the privately owned *Daily Monitor* (*DM*) indicate that neither editorial team considered the Bill to be an important news item.

The primary proponents of the Bill were its author, Member of Parliament David Bahati, Ethics and Integrity Minister Nsaba Buturo, Speaker of the Parliament Edward Ssekandi and local religious leaders, as well as private citizens. The Bill's main proponents portray the Bill as a long overdue and much needed protection against threats against traditional family life. 'We are trying as much as we can to protect the traditional heterosexual family. It is under threat. Anybody who says it is minor underestimates the damage being done' (MP David Bahati, *DM*, news item, 30 October 2009). Nsaba Buturo voiced similar concerns and claims that Uganda is ' "under siege" [...] The proposed law would "make Uganda a leader" in efforts against gay culture in Africa, Dr Buturo said' (*DM*, news item, 30 October 2009). Religious leaders from a range of faiths are constructed as a third group of supporters, with one reservation. 'Leaders from the Church of Uganda, Orthodox, Pentecostal, Seventh Day Adventist, and the Uganda Muslim Supreme Council, unanimously supported the Bill, but called for a change in the penalties'. Religious leaders were quoted requesting Parliament quickly enact the Bill into law (*DM*, news item, 29 October 2009). This item not only carries a first reference to domestic reservations on the death penalty in the news section, but a reference to international objections: 'Ethics and integrity minister James Nsaba Buturo revealed that there was pressure from the international community not to implement the Bill' (*DM*, news item, 29 October 2009).

The government-owned *New Vision* only carried items that were either neutral or supportive of the Proposed Bill. Letter of the week was:

I would like to commend the MPs who took a brave step to table the anti homosexuality Bill. It is a firm reminder on Uganda's stand. There are some things we are not ready to accept and homosexuality is one of them. This step serves to notify the world that Ugandans are not pro-homosexuality even if some Ugandans are involved in it. I am very sure some human rights bodies and the Western world will come out to intimidate us to support homosexuality. (NV, Letter to the Editor, 16 Oct. 2009)

At the end of October Member of Parliament Margaret Muhanga stated in an opinion piece:

Africa will stay an enslaved continent as long as the Western world provide dime to the poor and hungry and propagates all their wishes [...] October 23 was one of the worst days of my life when I woke up to read, with disbelief a one-and-a-half page press release in The New Vision titled; 'Antihomosexuality or anti-human rights Bill' by a coalition of civil society organisations on human rights and constitutional law.

The MP ends with 'Ugandans must rise up and fight all sources of evil no matter how much money the West sends. Human dignity must be protected' (NV, Column. 23 October 2009). The privately owned newspaper the *Daily Monitor* did early on include voices of dissent, but only on space earmarked for opinion and social commentary. 'Law and policy makers would be better advised to address the more pressing and endemic problem' (DM, Letter to Editor, 16 October 2009).

Gay people are not the only ones who should fear the new bill criminalizing homosexuality. Measures which make who you are a crime are easy to manipulate [...] How will the new law be enforced? Arrests and prosecutions will almost always result from denunciations. Since you can't tell a gay man or woman just by looking, everyone is at risk. (DM, Column, 19 October 2009)

The Bill fundamentally undermines numerous human rights and has rightly been denounced by a group of 17 local and international human rights organisations, who have called for its immediate withdrawal. One of the gravest provisions in the Bill is the new offence of 'aggravated homosexuality', which states that anyone who commits the offence of homosexuality against a person under the age of 18 years, against a person with a disability or when the offender is HIV positive shall be liable on conviction to suffer death. This provision is unjustifiably draconian in nature. (DM, Column, 26 October 2009)

Most significant is the fact that the provisions of the other four substantive new clauses blatantly violate Uganda's Constitution and many other regional and international instruments. And for those who think that the Bill is only directed against 'homosexuals', they should look again [...] Those sitting back and thinking, 'Get them Bahati!', may be shocked one day when it is them that this law throws in jail [...] Politicians find that homosexuals are a great scapegoat or red herring to divert attention to more pressing issues that affect the ordinary Ugandan such as unemployment, corruption, poor health facilities, reform of electoral laws and so forth. If we are to be absolutely honest with ourselves, we should ask whether there are not more pressing issues of moral violation in other areas such as domestic violence, torture and corruption. None of these areas have specific laws outlawing their practice. That is where the likes of Hon. Bahati should expend their energies. (*DM*, Column, 3 November 2009)

Even if local human rights activists are not included in the two papers' regular news reporting, responses to their campaigning efforts are.

Efforts by Civil Society Organisations (CSOs) to persuade women MPs to denounce the Anti-homosexuality Bill hit a dead end as the legislators vowed to ensure that it is passed. While addressing a press conference on Friday, Uganda Women Parliamentarians' (Uwopa) chairperson Jane Alisemera (Bundibugyo, NRM) told journalists that they have been approached by several civil society organisations asking them to denounce the Bill. 'These people have been sending us phone messages, writing to us letters telling us to denounce the Bill but we are in support of the Bill because in this country we cherish families and children.' (*DM*, News, 9 November 2009).

In this first phase of the coverage, the Bill's main supporters dominate the news space in both newspapers. The Bill is constructed as a piece of legislation that will protect traditional Ugandan family life, Ugandan culture and social mores. On news space the Bill, is predominantly constructed as unproblematic, with the exception of its provision for the death penalty. Although there are fleeting references to international concerns about the Bill, international actors are nameless and faceless, and the Bill is constructed as a local matter and as an instrument to solve local challenges. The Bill's detractors are only visible in the privately owned media's spaces earmarked for social commentary. Towards the end of October 2009, *New Vision* seizes almost all coverage of Bill, whereas the *Daily Monitor* appears to make a different editorial decision. There is thus no inter-media agenda setting as of mid-November 2009.

An Onslaught of International Protests
(17 November–22 December 2009)

As of mid-November a first round of international public figures raised their concerns about the Ugandan Bill. One of the first leaders was the former President of Botswana and current chairman of Champions for an AIDS-free generation, Festus Mogae, arguing that the Bill undermined ongoing HIV prevention efforts. The former UN envoy Stephen Lewis condemned the Bill at the yearly Commonwealth meeting in 2009, stating that

> There are deeply offensive sodomy laws and homophobic statutes on the books of many other Commonwealth countries, particularly here in the Caribbean. But nothing is as stark, punitive and redolent of hate as the Bill in Uganda; nothing comes close to such an omnibus violation of the human rights of sexual minorities. [...] The entire bill confounds rationality. In fact, the legislation has a powerfully Orwellian flavor. (Lewis 2009)

These international actors were followed at the end of November by the Swedish minister for development cooperation, Gunilla Karlsson (Sveriges Radio/Studio Ett 2009) as well as the Canadian prime minister Stephen Harper (Cobb 2009), and UK prime minister Gordon Brown (Chapman 2009).

International criticism would however intensify even further, in the sense that important development partners publicly opposed the Bill. On 3 December 2009 the EU Commission through the EU Presidency and the local troika in Uganda met the acting Foreign Minister/State Minister of Foreign Affairs to hand over a démarche, voicing its concerns with the Bill and reminding Uganda that its domestic legislation must be consistent with its international human rights obligations (European Parliament 2010). The EU was followed by an even more important donor, the United States. In mid-December 2009, US President Barack Obama (Eleveld 2009) and Secretary of State Hillary Clinton voiced the US government's strong concern on separate occasions. Clinton voiced her concern in a speech, saying 'governments should be expected to resist the temptation to restrict freedom of expression when criticism arises, and be vigilant in preventing law from becoming an instrument of oppression, as bills like the one under consideration in Uganda to criminalize homosexuality would do' (Clinton 2009). On 17 December the EU Parliament issued the European

Parliament resolution of 2009 on 'Uganda: anti-homosexual draft legisla-tion', a strong worded statement against it (European Parliament 2009). Besides condemning the Bill and reminding the Ugandan government of its obligations to protect universal human rights, it included a refer-ence to potential implications should Uganda move forward with the Bill by stating 'that international donors, non-governmental organisations and humanitarian organisations would have to reconsider or cease their activ-ities in certain fields should the bill pass into law' (EU 2009). Besides the various official communications on the Bill, behind the scene dip-lomatic pressure was also applied on Uganda. Diplomatic cables from the US Embassy in Kampala show that the US opposition towards the Bill is made clear, but that outside inference is rejected. In a meeting between the US Embassy staff and MP David Bahati, he 'criticized inter-national donors for short circuiting Uganda's democratic procedures when it is in their interest, said demands to withdraw the legislation outright are unacceptable, and ridiculed recent threats by Sweden to cut its assist-ance' (US Embassy 2009). Bahati attributed international criticism to a misreading of the text and a misunderstanding of the 'situation on the ground' in Uganda (US Embassy 2009).

The Bill was not only criticised by important donors and development partners, but also by religious leaders. The Anglican Church's Archbishop of Canterbury spoke out against the Bill on 12 December: 'Overall, the proposed legislation is of shocking severity and I can't see how it could be supported by any Anglican who is committed to what the Communion has said in recent decades. Apart from invoking the death penalty, it makes pastoral care impossible – it seeks to turn pastors into inform-ers'. He added that the Anglican Church in Uganda opposed the death penalty but, tellingly, he noted that its archbishop, Henry Orombi, who boycotted the Lambeth Conference the previous year, 'has not taken a position on this bill' (Williams 2009). The Catholic Church, through the Vatican's legal attaché, the Reverend Philip J. Bene, released a statement on 17 December 2009, stating to a United Nations panel that it was opposed to 'unjust discrimination' against gay men and lesbians.

Editorial Narrative U-Turns: The Bill as a Source of Conflict

During this phase of intense international criticism media coverage is transformed not only numerically in the privately owned media, but in terms of how it is framed for its readers. The Bill moves from the back-end of the *Daily Monitor* into the news section and several front page covers. Another interesting feature is that the newspaper appears to be liberated by the international criticism, in the sense that it allows severe criticism to be voiced in all sections of the paper. Furthermore it starts to produce media-initiated analysis of the Bill, where the newspapers invite individuals of opposing opinion to discuss various aspects of the Bill and its potential implications. The 26 November 2009 *Daily Monitor* carries the first of many media-initiated analysis of the Bill – 'How relevant is the anti-gay bill' – where MP Bahati discusses the Bill with a local human rights lawyer.

Besides these structural changes in the coverage, the Bill itself is reframed to its readers. The main actors in relation to the Bill change from solely domestic to a mix of domestic actors and international public officials, political leaders, development partners as well as international media. The change of primary agents in relation to the Bill solidifies the framing of the Bill as no longer a domestic matter.

The Bill is further reframed as a source of conflict as opposed to a solution to Ugandan problems, and coverage begins to revolve around the international criticism and domestic actors' responses to it. The Government of Uganda's response to the international criticism is initially framed as defiant. 'The government yesterday responded strongly to international criticism over the proposed anti-gay law, saying the process would continue uninterrupted. Speaker Edward Ssekandi told *Daily Monitor* that it was necessary "to do whatever we can to stop" homosexual liaisons in Uganda' (*DM*, News, 30 Nov. 2009).

> The government yesterday reiterated its opposition to homosexuals and said donors were free to withdraw their funding if they wish. Ethics and Integrity minister Buturo was responding to a daily monitor story that Sweden has joined other countries that are pressuring the government to discard a proposed law that would severely punish homosexuality in the country. 'Homosexuality will not be promoted, encouraged or supported in Uganda'. (*DM*, News, 4 December 2009)

The Bill is further constructed as a source of conflict by coverage highlighting the mobilisation of a new range of supporters.

> At least 200 senior religious leaders in Uganda have thrown their weight behind the government backing it not to 'yield to pressure' from donor countries that are demanding the withdrawal of the

Anti-Homosexuality Bill before Parliament. Under their umbrella organisation of the Inter-religious Council of Uganda (IRC), the clerics have recommended that the government should think of cutting diplomatic ties with countries that are bent on forcing homosexuality on Ugandans. (*DM*, News, 10 December 2009)

Support for the Bill is reported to have been a central component of most Christmas sermons (*DM*, News, 26 Dec. 2009). Besides religious leaders, cultural leaders, the Bunyoro-Kitara King (*DM*, News, 21 Dec. 2009), and the Rwenzururu King, Charles Wesley Mumbere Iremangoma (*DM*, News, 28 Dec. 2009) as well as parents' associations (*DM*, News, 18 Dec. 2009) called on Members of Parliament to enact the Bill when it was presented to Parliament again.

International media outlets interest and extensive coverage of the Bill merge as a new frame in late December 2009. International coverage of the Bill becomes part of the *Daily Monitor*'s media news section and is discussed by social commentators.

However, the Bill does not cease to appear on space earmarked for social commentary. On the contrary, support or opposition is continuously agitated in columns and Letters to the Editor. But besides the highly polarised debate on the pros and cons of the Bill, a growing focus is the international pressure. Interestingly enough both supporters and those who oppose the Bill reject the mounting international pressure coming from political leaders and development partners around the world. 'As the debate on the anti-gay bill continues, I feel disgusted with foreign countries like Sweden that are trying to intimidate Uganda to back off the bill in its current form' (*DM*, Letter to the Editor, 6 Dec. 2009). 'Ugandans should guard own cultural and social values. I wish to express my dismay about the statements made by Sweden's Development Assistant Minister, Ms Gunilla Carlsson [...] I find Sweden's position an abuse to our culture and social sovereignty' (*DM*, Letter to the Editor, 11 December 2009).

> The question of the Anti-Homosexual Bill is a serious moral issue that should not be confused with 'human rights.' We (Uganda) have a Parliament to decide the fate of the country objectively and lead us into a good direction! And I don't think fear of 'sanctions' should turn us into animals. If foreign powers now want to choose for us a destiny then, I think that is moral imperialism that we must not accept. (*DM*, Letter to the Editor, 21 December 2009)

Towards the end of the second phase of coverage, the Bill in itself is no longer the centre of the debate, but has rather been replaced by a debate about the mounting pressure and attempts to interfere in what is perceived as a domestic process.

In mid-December the first report surfaces indicating that President Museveni and the Government of Uganda have begun distancing themselves from the proposed legislation. In an opinion piece in the government-owned *New Vision* by senior presidential adviser John Nagenda, the reframing of the Bill is tested on the public. The opinion piece draws parallels between MP Bahati and McCarthyism, as well as the Inquisition period, where people who deviated from current beliefs were tortured to death by priests. He continues 'I believe, and I am raising the bar, that we must laugh at this MP and others like him: laugh and stay sane. What crime have same-sex lovers committed, per se, by being who they are?' He finishes the piece with 'Parliament should not pass this Bill'. The reframing of the Bill from being a welcomed and fairly unproblematic piece of legislation to being problematic and unwanted is also visible in the *Daily Monitor*. In mid- and late December 2009, the Government of Uganda is framed as indecisive when senior public officials claim it has no official position on the Bill (*DM*, News, 12 and 27 Dec. 2009).

The Unnecessary and Unwanted Bill (8–30 January 2010)

A week into 2010, a new round of international criticism commences. The UN Special Rapporteur on Health, Anand Grover, raised his concerns, saying the Bill is 'not only a violation of the fundamental human rights of Ugandans, but will also undermine efforts to achieve universal access to HIV prevention, treatment, care and support' (United Nations High Commissioner for Human Rights 2010). UN High Commissioner for Human Rights Navi Pillay also voiced her concerns in mid-January 2010. US Senator Ron Wyden applied another type of pressure. In a letter addressed to United States Trade Representative Ron Kirk and Secretary Hillary Clinton, Senator Wyden argued that Uganda's status as beneficiary of the African Growth and Opportunity Act (AGOA) should be revoked should the country proceed with the Bill. 'There are few words that could adequately express the barbarity of the Ugandan proposal [...] I strongly urge you to communicate immediately to the Ugandan government, and President Yoweri Museveni directly, that Uganda's beneficiary status under

AGOA will be revoked should the proposed legislation be enacted' (Wyden 2010). Wikileaks cables indicate that international pressure has had the intended effect. In a meeting between the US Ambassador and President Museveni, the Ugandan President stated that the Bill's provisions for sentencing to life in prison or death are ' "unacceptable" ', and that the bill will be significantly amended or perhaps shelved completely. The President stressed that he is handling the issue and urged the U.S. to give him space to deal with the legislation internally. Museveni's comments echoed those of Foreign Minister Sam Kutesa, who told the Ambassador on January 21 that the bill will likely "die a natural death"' (US Embassy 2010).

Media Narratives on the Unwanted Bill

As of 2010 the privately owned media continue to frame the Bill as problematic and even a hindrance to foreign policy, both in news space and space earmarked for opinions. News coverage includes senior government officials signalling distance and in some cases even outspoken opposition to the Bill. 'The State Minister for Investments, Mr Aston Kajara, yesterday said the government was looking at the Bill with the possibility of withdrawing it. "The government's official position is that we have enough laws to cover homosexuality acts," Mr Kajara said. "Government did not sponsor this Bill. It is a private member's Bill" (DM, News, 8 Jan. 2010). Furthermore, the previous framing of government as defiant is replaced by a media discourse where the government is seen to recognise the importance of development partners' opinions.

> The president made the revelation today while opening the National Executive Conference of the ruling National Resistance Movement at State House Entebbe. Mr Museveni told the delegates that despite the fact that Uganda, has to protect its values and cultures, there is need to exercise extreme caution on the anti-gay bill. He said that the anti-gay bill is already impacting negatively on Uganda's foreign policy. (DM, News, 12 Jan. 2010)

Other key actors in Ugandan society are also framed as having revised their position on the Bill.

> The titular head of the Catholic Church in Uganda has weighed in on the proposed anti-homosexuality law, saying he rejects it because it is 'at

odds with the core values' of Christians. But while Kampala Archbishop Cyprian Lwanga's opposition to the 2009 Anti-Homosexuality Bill is based on compassion, the cleric retains the view that homosexuality is immoral and violates God's will. (*DM*, News, 12 Jan. 2010)

The media narrative does contain several examples of opposition towards the changing discourse. Speaker of the Parliament Edward Ssekandi is reported to have said, 'There is no way we can be intimidated by remarks from the President to stop the Bill. This Bill was officially tabled in Parliament and was subsequently committed to a committee for scrutiny. The President has a right to express his views like any other people who have petitioned me' (*DM*, News, 15 Jan. 2010).

Who really is Museveni serving, Ugandans or foreign interests? How could he refer to the matter as a sensitive foreign policy issue? Is he trying to deflate the power of Parliament? Are we really free people who can legislate good laws for our people without fear of foreign powers? I think it is time we tried local traditional institutions if they can safeguard our values. (*DM*, Letter to the Editor, 15 Jan. 2010)

'It appears we are being subjugated in the fight against homosexuality by donors and some world leaders. It is also discernible that the gays Bill is losing the support of the President [...] I am filled with shock that the proponents of this idea cannot respect our cultural way of life and they are persuading our President to embrace homosexuality when it is very obvious we detest and it. (*DM*, Letter to the Editor, 15 Jan. 2010)

The previous framing of the Bill as a source of conflict and polarisation appears at the end of January to be gradually replaced by a more sober and contemplative approach from even its sternest supporters. The Ndorwa West MP David Bahati

had told this newspaper that he was ready to listen to the ministers' input but added that being a Private Member's Bill, they would not do much to it although 'if they want to amend some clauses, I can do it'. When contacted, Information Minister Kabakumba Masiko said they had decided to form a sub-committee to discuss the Bill and 'see if we can amend it'. (DM, News, 21 Jan. 2010)

The Bill is thus finally reconstructed as a piece of legislation in need of revision, even by its author. The Bill has been textually defeated, in the sense that it is not framed as a viable option in its current format, or has the unequivocal backing by its supporters.

As the Bill and the processing of it becomes a bureaucratic procedure, and the intense international and domestic campaigning against it begins to trail off in mid-January 2010 the Bill appears to no longer warrant neither the same amount of coverage nor front page coverage. In addition, the Bill itself or its potential consequences are no longer the main theme in all the items that carry a reference to the Bill. Instead, as of the end of January 2010, the Bill starts being referred to only in passing.

Discussion

After the Bill had been reviewed by the Legal and Parliamentary Affairs Committee in 2010, it resurfaced briefly as an item on the Uganda Parliament Order Paper, but failed to be processed before the 8th Parliament was dismissed. After a dormancy of ten months, the Bill resurfaced a second time when it was retabled in Parliament in February 2012, but failed to make it for a vote (Amnesty International 2012). In December 2013, the Bill re-appeared once more in Parliament and a slightly less harsh version of the Bill was passed four years after it was introduced. Despite heavy international criticism and threats of withdrawal of aid, President Museveni signed the Bill into law in late February 2014.

Returning to the media discourses on the Bill, it is important to remember that media narratives should never be treated as accurate description of *what really happened* (Earl et al. 2004; Oliver and Maney 2000; Barranco and Wisler 1999). Media texts should rather be seen as the narrations, i.e. the journalist or commentators' point of view and an interpretation of what was significant about that event. Accordingly, as tempting as it might be for human rights activists and others to argue that the media's reframing of the Bill led to its extended 'burial by committee', one should refrain from such conclusions. Claims of linear causalities between media coverage and policy outcome are most likely too simplistic descriptions at best and outright erroneous at worst. They are also likely to miss the complex interplay between local and international actors' lobbying efforts outside the media. This chapter suggests a complex interplay between international actors' efforts to push the Bill onto the media agenda and facilitate a domestic debate in and outside the media sphere, parallel to applying political pressures tied to development corporations, which lead to a temporary reassessment of the Bill.

In conclusion, media narratives should be regarded as the product of organised interests and pressure groups, including international media. In Uganda, various international actors' appear to have played a significant role in the process whereby the Bill gains salience and prominence in the privately-owned media, as well as o have introduced alternative frames for understanding the Bill. Furthermore, although it was not included in this study there are indications of international inter-media agenda setting. International media organisations' coverage of the Bill became a part of the domestic media's coverage. Borlase's (2011) research on Ugandan journalists' experiences of covering sexual minorities and the Bill indicates that international media and their coverage of the Bill cued Ugandan media and in a sense dictated how much attention the Bill received at home.

Finally, the Ugandan case does bring to our attention the importance of including a range of actors, domestic *and* international from multiple fields in order to approach the pertinent question: If the media influence the public's agenda, who influences the media agenda? Although this chapter has not conclusively addressed all actors' influences on the framing of the Bill, it does bring to our attention the need to cast a wide net and include non-domestic actors in the analysis.

References

Amnesty International (2009) Anti-homosexuality bill threatens liberties and human rights defenders, press release, 15 Oct. <http://www.amnesty.org/en/for-media/press-releases/uganda-%E2%80%98anti-homosexuality%E2%80%99-bill-threatens-liberties-and-human-rights-de> (accessed Oct. 2009).

—— (2012) 'Uganda: anti-homosexuality bill is re-tabled in Uganda' <http://www.amnesty.org/en/library/asset/AFR59/001/2012/en/2de6dc7c-50a7-4347-9602-efe5ba371433/afr590012012en.html> (accessed June 2012).

Barranco, J., and Wisler, D. (1999) 'Validity and systematicity of newspaper data in event analysis', *European Sociological Review*, 15, pp. 301–22.

Borlase, R. (2011) 'Global journalism, local realities: Ugandan journalists' views on reporting homosexuality', M.Sc. in Media, Communication and Development, London School of Economics and Political Science.

British Broadcasting Corporation (2004) 'Fine for Ugandan radio gay show' <http://news.bbc.co.uk/2/hi/africa/3712266.stm> (accessed June 2010).

Carragee, K. M., and Roefs, W. (2004) 'The neglect of power in recent framing research', *Journal of Communication*, 54, pp. 214–33.

Chapman, J. (2009) 'Gordon Brown caught up in gay rights storm as Uganda debates death penalty for homosexuals', *Daily Mail*, 30 Nov.

Clinton, Hillary Rodham (2009) 'Remarks on the human rights agenda for the 21st century', 14 Dec., Georgetown University's Gaston Hall, Washington, DC.

Civil Society Coalition on Human Rights and Constitutional Law (2009a) 'Anti-homosexuality or human rights bill?', press statement, 23 Oct., Kampala <www.ugandans4rights.org/publications.php> (accessed Oct. 2009).

—— (2009b) 'Embrace diversity; end discrimination in Uganda!' Human Rights Day press statement, 10 Dec., Kampala <http://www.ugandans4rights.org/publications.php> (accessed Dec. 2009).

Cobb, C. (2009) 'Harper slams Uganda's anti-gay bill', *National Post* (Port of Spain) <http://network.nationalpost.com/np/blogs/posted/archive/2009/11/30/359927.aspx> (accessed Dec. 2009).

Dicklitch, S., Yost, B. and Dougan, B. M. (2012) 'Building a barometer of gay rights (BGR): a case study of Uganda and the persecution of homosexuals', *Human Rights Quarterly,* 34, pp. 448–71.

Earl, J., Martin, A., McCarthy, J. D., and Soule, S. A. (2004) 'The use of newspaper data in the study of collective action', *Annual Review of Sociology*, pp. 65–80.

Eleveld, K. (2009) 'White House condemns Uganda Bill', *The Advocate* <http://www.advocate.com/news/daily-news/2009/12/12/white-house-condemns-uganda-bill> (accessed Dec. 2009).

Entman, R. (2003) 'Cascading activation: contesting the White House's frame after 9/11', *Political Communication*, 20, pp. 415–32.

European Parliament (2009) Resolution of 17 December 2009 on Uganda: anti-homosexual draft legislation. P7_TA(2009)0119 ed. Strasbourg: European Parliament.

—— (2010) 'Answer given by Mr Piebalgs on behalf of the European Commission' <http://www.europarl.europa.eu/sides/getAllAnswers.do?reference=E-2010-2603&language=RO> (accessed June 2012).

Hollander, M. (2009) 'Gay rights in Uganda: seeking to overturn Uganda's anti-sodomy laws', *Virginia Journal of International Law*, 50, p. 219.

Human Rights Watch (2008) *This Alien Legacy: The Origins of 'Sodomy' Laws in British Colonialism,* PLACE: HRW.

—— (2009) 'Uganda: anti-homosexuality Bill threatens liberties and human rights defenders', 15 Oct., <http://www.hrw.org/en/news/2009/10/15/uganda-anti-homosexuality-bill-threatens-liberties-and-human-rights-defenders> (accessed Jan. 2010).

—— (2010) 'A media minefield increased threats to freedom of expression in Uganda'.

International Gay and Lesbian Human Rights Commission (IGLHRC) (2009a) 'Uganda action alert: dismiss the Anti-Homosexuality Bill', 16 Oct. <http://www.iglhrc.org/cgi-bin/iowa/article/takeaction/partners/989.html> (accessed Oct. 2009).

—— (2009b) 'Uganda: Proposed legislation attacks LGBT people and their defenders', statement, 7 Oct. <http://www.iglhrc.org/cgi bin/iowa/article/takeaction/partners/982.html> (accessed Oct. 2009).

Johnson, C. A., and International Gay and Lesbian Human Rights Commission (2007) *Off the Map: How HIV/AIDS Programming is Failing Same-Sex Practicing People in Africa*, New York: International Gay and Lesbian Human Rights Commission.

Lewis, S. (2009) Remarks by Stephen Lewis, Co-Director of AIDS-Free World delivered at the Commonwealth People's Forum on the eve of the Commonwealth Heads of Government Meeting.

McCombs, M. (2004) *Setting the Agenda: The Mass Media and Public Opinion*, Cambridge: Polity Press.

—— (2005) 'A look at agenda-setting: past, present and future', *Journalism Studies*, 6, pp. 543–57.

Oliver, P. E., and Maney, G. M. (2000) 'Political Processes and local newspaper coverage of protest events: from selection bias to triadic interactions1', *American Journal of Sociology*, 106, pp. 463–505.

Pew Research Center Project (2007) 'World publics welcome global trade – but not immigration'.

Sexual Minorities Uganda (SMUG) (2009) 'Condemn the tabled Anti-Homosexuality Bill', statement, 15 Oct. <http://www.iglhrc.org/cgi-bin/iowa/article/takeaction/partners/988.html> (accessed Oct. 2009).

Smith, C. P. (2000) 'Content analysis and narrative analysis', *Handbook of Research Methods in Social and Personality Psychology*, pp. 313–35.

Strand, C. (2011) 'Kill Bill! Ugandan human rights organizations' attempts to influence the media's coverage of the Anti-Homosexuality Bill', *Culture, Health and Sexuality*, 13, pp. 917–31.

Sveriges Radio/Studio Ett (2009) *Lag mot homosexualitet i Uganda* (Law against homosexuality in Uganda), Stockholm: Sveriges Radio/Studio Ett.

Tamale, S. (2009) 'A human rights impact assessment of the anti-homosexuality Bill', public dialogue, 18 Nov., Makarere University, Kampala <http://pambazuka.org/en/category/features/61423> (accessed June 2012).

United Nations High Commissioner for Human Rights (2010) 'Top UN rights official urges Uganda to do away with 'anti-homosexuality bill' <http://www.un.org/apps/news/story.asp?NewsID=33491&Cr=discrimination&Cr1> (accessed June 2012).

US Embassy Kampala (2009) 09KAMPALA1413, 24 Dec. in US State Department, Wikileaks.

—— (2010) 10KAMPALA45, 28 Jan. in US State Department, Wikileaks.

Walters, T. N., Walters, L. M. and Gray, R. (1996) 'Agenda building in the 1992 presidential campaign', *Public Relations Review*, 22, pp. 9–24.

Weaver, D. H. (2007) 'Thoughts on agenda setting, framing, and priming', *Journal of Communication*, 57, pp. 142–7.

Williams, Rowan (2009) Archbishop of Canterbury Rowan Williams' statement <http://www.archbishopofcanterbury.org/articles.php/2037/dr-rowan-williams-taking-a-break-from-canterbury-travails-daily-telegraph-article> (accessed June 2010).

Wyden, R. (2010) Letter to the Honorable Ron Kirk United States Trade Representative and the Honorable Hillary Clinton on the subject 'Uganda anti-homosexuality proposal violates human rights standards', 12 Jan. <http://www.wyden.senate.gov/news/press-releases/state-dept-to-wyden-uganda-anti-homosexuality-proposal-violates-human-rights-standards> (accessed June 2012).

13

SAKAWA – THE SPIRIT OF CYBERFRAUD: ANALYSIS OF A RUMOUR COMPLEX IN GHANA

Felix Riedel

Introduction

In early 2009, the United States Department of Justice listed Ghana among the global top ten production sites of cyberfraud.[1] At that time, the majority of Ghanaians could not afford internet access.[2] Nonetheless the media showed high concern about the issue, regarding it as important as armed robbery, littering and corruption. A series of films fanned rumours about occult rituals connected to cyberfraud. The result was an unprecedented national obsession with internet fraud.[3] This chapter will outline the expansive process of rumours and suggest a situated content analysis of the six most popular films of that genre (Adorno 1972: s. 62). As Pamela J. Steward and Andrew Strathern have written, rumours tend to appear as a complex with 'confluences, nuances and even contradictions' (2004: 177).

After an introductory description of the process of expansions and the media content, this chapter will highlight a selective set of social rifts connected to the films. The main focus is on the effects and conditions of normative propaganda. In short, the film genre tends to utilise prevalent mystifications of a modern medium to promote social norms and resentments. While the public reception of the films defined them as critical and educational, their ramifications were actually affirmative and deceptive. Economic contradictions and ambivalences were racialised and projected onto white people, Nigerians, the wealthy and people suffering from psychosomatic disorders or diseases.

From Cyberfraud to Rituals

Cyberfraud is organised according to specific local modes of production and cultural patterns. Daniel J. Smith (2007) and Harvey Glickman (2005) analysed cyberfraud in Nigeria; Jenna Burrell gained insights into the practices of fraudsters in Ghana.[4] The most common form of fraud in Nigeria and Ghana is the credit card scam.[5] More specialised types of deception include sham business proposals, exploitive pen pal relationships and calls for donations to false NGOs. According to Burrell, these scams capitalise on negative stereotypes of Africa (compare Smith 2007: 32). She also observed that Ghanaian fraudsters prefer to target philanthropists while Nigerian approaches tend to focus on commerce (Burrell 2008: 18).

Though cyberfraud is not new to Ghana, several official sites and public media – including the *Ghanaian Times* and the *Daily Graphic* – now place it constantly in their headlines.[6] A major concern was a high student dropout rate allegedly caused by a widespread predilection for cyberfraud. The predominant authoritarian approach invoked the government to deal with the problem for the sake of the children. The second most critical concern was Ghana's international reputation. Unlike other crimes, cyberfraud could access its victims globally. The result was a mortified patriotism, which incited a public discourse about white people, wealth, technology and morals.

The first strategy to protect national integrity was the introduction of an alien term to redefine cyberfraud and the associated practices. Both the term *cyberfraud* and the common Nigerian Code 419[7] were almost entirely replaced by the Hausa word *Sakawa*. My native friends and informants translated it as 'putting something inside'.[8] It almost totally replaced the term 419 which had once expanded its content from fraud to 'an all-encompassing signifier in Nigerian discourse for any behaviour that relies on dissimulation, illusion, or some other manipulation of the truth in order to facilitate gain or advantage' (Smith 2007: 20).

Sakawa was soon a catch-all phrase used for drug-trafficking, for criminal acts, for greed and 'quick money' in general. On 15 July 2009 Metro-TV portrayed an official complaining in disgust about this trend: 'Now everything is [called] *Sakawa!*'

Where cyberfraud is concerned, *Sakawa* remains very spe-cific: it merged the mundane act of cyberfraud with occult and ritual murder. To summarise, under the influence of the media and public discourse, the word *Sakawa* first signified cyberfraud associated with occult rituals, and later on referred to any deviant behaviour yielding monetary benefits. This process reveals the nodes the original theme offered and its connectivity to everyone's experience.

The Films and their Rituals

Films provided the main source for rumour and communal know-ledge of non-users[9] (i.e., those not involved) about *Sakawa*. According to street vendors, the first films about cyberfraud – *Café Guys*[10] and *Sakawa Boys*[11] – were bestsellers. The widespread visibility of post-ers and available copies confirmed their statements. This success even generated its own *Sakawa*-myth. It was insinuated that the first stocks of copies were either stolen or bought by *Sakawa Boys* to quell the truth or to make more money from it.[12]

After the success of these films all renowned film companies created their own versions. *Sakawa Girls I + II*[13] was followed by *The Dons in Sakawa I–IV*[14] and *Agya Koo – Sakawa I + II*.[15] Agya Koo even starred another *Sakawa* film: *Sakawa – 419 I–IV*.[16] *Sakawa Boys*, *Sakawa Girls* and *Agya Koo – Sakawa* still promise further sequels. Returning in May 2011, I found the mania had cooled. Some posters in Tamale advertised a new film, *Sakawa in Western Region I + II*.[17] However, traders at Opera Square in Accra did not even remember specific movies anymore, making snide remarks about the former hype. Nonetheless, *Sakawa* was still a common term for occult money-rituals and fraud, at least in the media.

Before I introduce the variations in the original cyberfraud-based *Sakawa*-theme, I want to differentiate them from the copycat-versions which rather occupied the vogue for the label to suggest a no-tech version of *Sakawa*:

- *Sakawa Girls I + II* is rather a *Mami-Wata*[18] film: There is only one initial reference to cyberfraud and this shows a young woman's failure to extract money from dupes. She then conjures a blonde sea goddess to the shore, who assists her in turning a Ghanaian husband into a Sugardaddy against his will. The film even deepens the technological gender-bias inherent in the other films.

* *Agya Koo in Sakawa I + II* and *Sakawa 419 I–IV* are conventional *Sikaduro* films with occasional references to white people but none to cyberfraud. In both films, joining a secret society of ritualists is the precondition of a tainted yield.

Only the three films *Sakawa Boys I–IV*, *Café Guys I + II* and *The Dons in Sakawa I + IV* have the internet as the main arena and all portray a male youth suffering tremendous pressure.

In *Café Guys*, the hopes of the students Samme and Kobi for a successful life are shattered along with their self-esteem: 'Have you ever seen a hungry man thinking straight?' At the same time, two women are leaving the lectures. One of them complains: 'I can't date one man. I would be the loser if I would do that. I need about four men. One buys me a car, the other a house'. A wealthy man passes by and invites the women into his Jeep. Later on he introduces Samme and Kobi to cyberfraud and to the blonde goddess, 'Bina'. She kills Kobi, but Samme succeeds and joins a team of fraudsters. As a rich man he ridicules his father's moral demands and pampers his mother with gifts.

Figure 13.1   419 poster displayed on a building; photo by Felix Ridel

In *The Dons in Sakawa*, a graduate computer genius called Hakeem is unemployed and is unable to provide for his own means, nor to pay the rent of his mother and sister. At home, he catches his girlfriend sleeping with her boss. She mocks him: 'This is just a job strategy. Grow up, Hakeem, grow up!' Hakeem almost strangles her in fury. Imprisoned for that, he is bailed out by relatives. Indebted and desperate he leaves his family in tears and reluctantly joins a team of professional fraudsters. One of them campaigns: 'For crying out loud, you are the best in our group, you finished with a fucking first class and here you are living like a peasant. Listen! There are endless opportunities to make money on the internet'.

Sakawa Boys is introduced by three crises. An asthmatic mother needs her medicine, while being unable to pay either rent or school fees. The sister of another young man suffers from heart disease, which has to be treated at a cost of 'USD 50,000'. She eventually dies after her brother's futile attempts to force a rich uncle into payment. A third young man is desperately trying to meet the demands of his girlfriend in competition with other men.

The initial conflict is most often one between male and female roles. In two films the father seems absent or has a weak position. While the young male is expected to provide for female relatives or partners, his economic condition does not allow him to fulfil his duty. To solve this crisis, all the young men start to engage in cyberfraud and initially fail: 'The mugus are not calling!'[19] After their initiation into a cult, their success is tremendous. They are portrayed as persistently chatting in internet cafés, performing phone-calls with white people, carelessly splurging on shopping sprees and dressing up in the most eccentric ways. Additional rituals are required to ensure ongoing success or to please the gods after breaking taboos that were bonded to the luxury.

Here are all the rituals portrayed in the films:

1. Sleeping in a coffin, or carrying a coffin in *Sakawa Boys* and *The Dons in Sakawa*.
2. Staying away from water for three months in *Café Guys*.
3. Raping a virgin woman and taking the so-caused blood in *Café Guys*.
4. Extracting blood through biting the throat of unconscious children in *Sakawa Boys*.
5. Swallowing a frog, a giant spider and a ring in *The Dons in Sakawa*.

6. Bringing menstrual blood (as an alternative to sacrificing one's 'manhood') to the Mallam in *Sakawa Boys*.
7. Killing an only brother and providing a bottle of his blood to the leader of the occult brotherhood in *Agya Koo in Sakawa*.
8. Eating rotten food from a dump yard, sleeping upside down and mating with a goat for three weeks or three months in *Agya Koo in Sakawa*.
9. Eating one's own faeces, maggots from a public toilet and house-flies in *Sakawa 419*.
10. Walking around naked at night in *Sakawa 419*.
11. Killing one's pregnant wife and eating the unborn child with the occult brotherhood in *Sakawa 419*.
12. Sleeping with 'mad women' in *The Dons in Sakawa* and in *Sakawa 419*.

The initiation ritual can be classified as one against disgust or fear. Isolation from society plays a major role: sleeping in a coffin and avoiding bathing for weeks might point at the difficulty to gain distance from society. At the same time, these initial rituals tend to repeat the former economic and emotional humiliation in an auto-aggressive and masochistic act. Later on this aggression turns against society, as the dynamics of the cursed wealth and its interrelation with human behaviour demand further rituals. In *Sakawa 419* the aggressive act of homicide, infanticide and cannibalism is considered to be effective while the auto-aggressive act of eating faeces and maggots is a futile task. In the other films, the auto-aggressive ritual is considered effective but it serves just as a door-opener with invisible strings attached to it. The cult's demands always cut through family ties and partnerships. In *Café Guys*, Kobi is splashed with tabooed water by his sister who could not stand his stench. He eventually dies from a rash infesting his catatonic body. Several other fraudsters develop mental disorders. In *Sakawa Boys* two children are killed or stunned through the extraction of their blood. In *Sakawa Boys* the father of a fraudster dies from fire in the new house the fraudster bought for his parents. In *The Dons in Sakawa* the fraudster Hakeem is forced to violate a taboo to rescue his sister after an accident – he dies on the spot. In *Café Guys* Samme refuses help to his friend Kobi. Both have betrayed their best female friend Maame Akua to make ritual use of her virgin blood. Samme is shot by the police in the end.

In general, the rituals associated with *Sakawa* resemble familiar notions about *Sikaduro* or *Juju*. These Ghanaian versions of occult economies[20] are by no means new.[21] William C. Olsen retraced the impact of windfalls in the Ghanaian cocoa industry in the early twentieth century. Shrines were imported from the north, thriving upon the fears of the wealthy and the needs of the poor. Wealth was interpreted as a reward from shrine worship but the gains – farmland, children and health – were supposed to be consistently threatened by envious acts of 'witchcraft' (Olsen 2002). Past shrine-taboos were in balance with social norms: stealing, adultery and cursing were prohibited and only the conformist was rewarded with riches (see Olsen 2002: 548). However, notions about present-day money rituals include human sacrifice, typically of close relatives or children. Shrines, once a legitimate source of wealth creation and protection from witchcraft, are now perceived as totally deviant and evil. As they forbid help and solidarity, their taboos are antisocial and mock the initial impulse of the fraudsters. According to my informants between Accra and Cape Coast, the money produced in *Sikaduro* is always *quick money*: it is expected to turn into leaves after a while. In *Sakawa Boys* this legend is repeated: money turns into empty paper after the breach of an antisocial taboo. Other legends say that after some years of tremendous luxury the money ritualists will become handicapped, spastic or lunatic.[22] Concepts of *Sakawa* originate from traditional ideologemes. As film-fantasies connected these 'traditional' rituals to cyberfraud, they stretched the frame of reference.

Rumours and the Media

Rumours were inspired by different enforcements from the media. Three actors gave an interview on TV-Africa. One actor 'confessed' his former complicity in *Sakawa*. After his salvation through Jesus Christ he went straight to the producer of the film because he felt it was his moral responsibility to inform the public about this menace: 'We want to educate the public about those things, that the northern countries know about those things and that we generate possibilities for the youth so they won't go into Sakawa'.[23] The audience accepted this confession as particularly believable because the born-again actor publicly stated he had committed criminal and even occult activities. Another actor boasted similar insider information in a documentary by the online magazine *VICE*.[24]

Others felt this educational urge and the yield it promised. On one day in early June 2009, I passed at least four different newspapers dealing with different obviously made-up incidents and pictures of *Sakawa*-rituals and their evidence: 'human snakes', blood-covered shrines, missing children. The more renowned newspapers wrote about *Sakawa* at least every week between May and August. While soccer-championships and Barack Obama's visit were important issues during my stay in Ghana from February to October 2009, *Sakawa* outclassed all. In public places dozens gathered around *Sakawa*-posters, which showed variations of the film-themes along with a collage of cars, computers, bank notes, shrines, white women, mutilated corpses,[25] naked men and photoshopped 'evidences' of therianthropy. Once I gave in to the urge to challenge the obvious fabrications: the audience remonstrated.

Oral rumour played an essential role in the transformation of media contents into communal knowledge. I want to illustrate this through two anecdotes.

Akos worked full-time at a run-down hotel for GhS 90 a month. When Akos was informed by Kwabena and Prince that *Sakawa Boys* would steal used tampons to produce a money ritual from the blood it contains, she expressed surprise and horror: she had never thought of such an infamous way to steal her blood and she regarded it as a real threat. This rumour was new in town and it was believable. The very same ritual was depicted in the film *Sakawa Boys*. One of the two men must have watched the film and then used it at this specific moment to distress the woman in front of me and other men. Pretending care and information, it emotionally exploited this specific 'spiritual' vulnerability of women. The paranoia among relatives Margareth J. Field found widespread was likely to increase.[26] Rumours were not only spread but used for individual purposes and in specific situations.

Akos dreamt about her own shop. She needed GhS 1,300 for the start-up but she was afraid of asking a bank for a loan. Occasionally we discussed the idea and she joked: '*Sakawa*! If I don't have the money, I'll do *Sakawa*! I'll turn you into a lizard and then you vomit money like this: Ough, Ough! I kill you!'[27] Kwabena and I started laughing about her overacting a cut with the finger across the throat and vomiting. I asked them: 'Will it work? Will a person become rich through rituals?' Both became very serious. Of course it works. One could see it every day. Kwabena informed me:

Somehow they use the spiritual world to get the money. Once they went to Swedru, you know the place, to do some rituals, to kill someone and get the power to get money from the bank or something. But now they use it also in the internet to get money. I don't know how they do it, but somehow with the spiritual world. I've seen some of them, young men driving around in big cars.[28]

I heard this identification of fraud and cars more often. Cars were the most celebrated property of fraudsters in films and posters.

This suggests a specific kind of wealth is a 'violation of a moral economy rooted in kinship' (Smith 2007: 164). A young person in a new car attacks the traditional order and provokes envy against the person who has escaped traditional obligations. Already Meyer Fortes stated: 'Ashanti people are full of jealousy. Whenever they see that someone who is below them in age or rank succeeds in doing any great thing, they become envious and wish him ill, and then find means to kill him.[29]

In another example, I asked a young lady if she owned the bookshop she was working in. Her answer was sardonic laughter: 'In Ghana here, a young person can't own a shop'. Another young woman did not claim her inheritance of some yam fields as she was too afraid of jealous witchcraft performed by older relatives against her. It is dubious whether the young generation is capable of achieving economic prosperity in tandem with appeasing the traditional obligations. Smith states: '419 men are often despised precisely because they fail to fulfil many of the duties that are expected of big men' (2008: 144).

According to *Sakawa* mythology, it is possible for African youths to manipulate the authority of white people. This challenged the age-hierarchy (compare Van der Geest 2002). A new middle class of young people, through fraud or legitimate means, threatens older members of society, the traditional holders of economical and spiritual power. All films and posters point to this conflict with the age-hierarchy: young people who lust for Western commodities and wealth suffer heavy punishment. One poster depicts a '*Sakawa*-Boy' with a severed head. Another picture shows a '*Sakawa*-Girl' who morphed from a beach-beauty into a hog. To go for sex, beauty, style and cars is regarded as an violation of the traditional and spiritual order and results in symbolised castration and monstrous metamorphosis. Explicit castration sustains hierarchies in the films. In *The Dons of Sakawa* success is only guaranteed through obedience towards 'Lord Califa', who is said

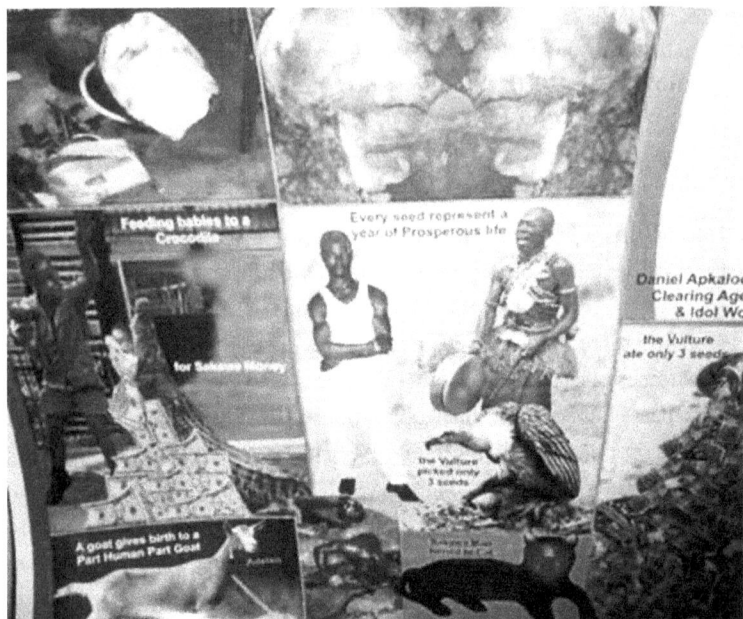

Figure 13.2   *Sakawa* film posters; photo by Felix Ridel

Figure 13.3   *Sakawa* film posters showing boy with severed head;
photo by Felix Ridel

Figure 13.4   *Sakawa* film poster on display; photo by Felix Ridel

to 'provide for his children' but taboos solidarity with relatives. This forces Hakeem into self-sacrifice. His corpse is successfully claimed by the cultists against the will of the pastor, who keeps at least the soul.[30] In *Sakawa 419* the god *Osepetreku* (leopard) causes infertility, ulcers and impotence in exchange for wealth. The 'great Sakawa' in *Sakawa Boys* likewise threatens life, mind and 'manhood' of the young men.

A naïve critique of ideology could deduce a conspiracy of traditional forces behind this castration threat. However, Adorno et al.'s study of authoritarian ideologies offers the concept of the 'authoritarian' syndrome, which enables us to think of this threat as produced and used within the mindset of the youth:

> Stereotypy, in this syndrome, is not only a means of social identification, but has truly 'economic' function in the subject's own psychology: it helps to canalize his libidinous energy according to the demands of his overstrict superego. Thus stereotypy itself tends to become heavily libidinized and plays a large role in the subject's inner household.' (2003: 474ff., 475)

This subconscious level of African occult fantasies is comparable to anti-Semitic ideology, which similarly involves 'sado-masochistic resolutions of the Oedipus complex' (ibid., p. 474), 'retrogression to the anal-sadistic phase' (ibid., p. 476) and obsessions with rigid community norms.[31] The desired is destroyed, as Smith noted from riots in Nigeria: 'Rather than targeting people who symbolized the constraints of traditional hierarchies, the rioters and the subsequent accusations focused on those who had escaped and abandoned the traditional obligations of patron-clientism' (2007: 144).

Rumour and propaganda do not form a logical pattern, they play on the level of the subconscious and therefore they are allowed to be inconsistent.[32] African rumours could also be interpreted as a *radio trottoir*, which serves as mouthpiece for social critique and information during times of censorship (compare Bourgault 1995: 203). Rumour contents would then be metaphors and not contradictory projections (compare Stewart and Strathern 2004: 76). But ethnographers have documented the deep belief into occult rumours (Smith 2007: 156), which alone forbids a reading as 'metaphors'. The 'fantastic forms of popular criticism' (ibid.: 153) are not chosen in a conscious escape from censorship, but effects of distorted drives within the individuals. Nonetheless, there is a critique against social ills and the current economic recession presented in the rumour complex. Unemployment was named as the primary reason why young people engage in occult rituals and cyberfraud. A broadcaster lamented: 'The youth is too poor so they do *Sakawa*'. Similar opinions could be read in many online comments. Unlike the terrifying *Sikaduro*, *Sakawa*-rumours were not only used for jokes but also for class struggle rhetoric against government and elites. Marlene deWitte (2009) even interprets the mythological picture of money as a poignant criticism of capitalism. This downplays the aggressive components of rumours[33] and it overlooks the inherent elements of bourgeois ideology.

The classical ideology of capitalist societies tries to repress any remembrance of violence of primitive accumulation (see Marx 1973: 741ff.) alongside the historical, psychological and cultural embeddings of the modes of production. It negates violence and luck and emphasises individual work and acumen. *Sakawa*-ideology inverts this concept. It aggressively minimises skills, luck and labour while it highlights and overrates violent and spiritual modes of accumulation. At the same time, *Sakawa*-myths provide not only an inverted but a concentrated form of bourgeois ideology: the ideal of sacrificing workers and saving is condensed to intensified ritual sacrifice. The reward is expanded to instant and lush wealth.

The coffin-rituals embody sacrificed labour in a concentrated form. Sleeping in a coffin allows the practitioners to enter the spiritual realm, where a scornful laughing skeleton fills two of the three coffins with money. One of three fraudsters does not come back from his spiritual journey, he remains in his coffin. His spirit is wandering around in the dark, carrying the coffin.[34] Sacrifice also spoils glorified consumption (Wendl 2004: s. 22). The 'great *Sakawa*' forbids accumulation. In *Sakawa Boys* money is earmarked for 'fun', not 'to own any property' – which means investments in legal business. '*Sakawa*-money' induces dependency on the criminal activity.[35] Through this dependency the fraudsters are finally forced to 'bring blood' – again a symbol for labour. This visible evidence of a consumption that breeds horrendous risks and consequences redeems those who neither have riches nor are sacrificed for it.

This ideology expresses amazement about the relative stratification of bourgeois societies. The traditional hierarchies profiting from ongoing primitive accumulation were never really contested by bourgeois revolts.[36] As a result, the imagination of such an instant stratification is accompanied by a mixture of desire, guilt and fear (also see Smith 2007: 145). Unstable class identification is then stabilised through imaginary threats.[37] Under these preconditions, ideologemes about the 'happy poor' are fostered by the terrified and not by the powerful subject. Kwabena told me in a conversation: 'I've been thinking. See, *Sakawa*, you know, the Mallams, they make so many people so very, very rich. But if you see their houses they are always shacks. Why don't they use their powers to make themselves rich? It's not logic'. He hesitated and continued: 'So maybe they know something, that it is not good to be rich'.[38]

Nationalism and Projection

Sakawa-ideology tends to discriminate three groups: the white victims of cyberfraud, those mistaken for criminals, and the real criminals and individuals with symptoms identified as the side-effects of rituals.

The three classical *Sakawa*-stories celebrate a revolt against a white subject. *African science*, as occult rituals are often called, forces greedy whites to give away their money. This collective narcissistic fantasy gains momentum. The tendency to display white dupes as greedy and therefore to blame for their loss was earlier popularised through the resourceful Nigerian film *The Master*,[39] an obvious point of reference of *Sakawa Boys*. The final monologue about colonial exploitation and justified fraud is imitated in *Sakawa Boys* and both films refer to fraud as a 'game' in the music theme. A young woman was humming and singing the refrain of the *Sakawa Boys* theme in my presence: '*Sakawa* is not a crime, it's a game, we happen to find, yeah'.[40] In a discussion with her female co-worker she insisted that *Sakawa* was not a crime, enjoying the identification with the fraudsters. When I asked a young friend, what *Sakawa* is, he became angry all of a sudden: 'It is because you whites are too greedy-oh!' (See also Smith 2007: 37). Here is one characteristic online comment:

> I am not a racist. However, I think 419 is good if it is aimed at white people who themselves used various 419 means to rid Africa of its riches and glory. The average Whiteman thinks that Africans are 'FOOLS'. Is this not one of the ways to hit them back and tell them, 'We are smarter than you thought?' Let's pay them back in their own coin.[41]

Crime is understood as a way to fight racism, blurring the category 'white' into a 'racist' and 'greedy' entity. As Smith notes for Nigeria, the focus on international cyberfraud 'obscures the fact, that the primary victims [...] are [...] not foreigners' (2007: 28). But many if not most Ghanaians were aware of the destructive effects of cyberfraud on their own economy – in general, blaming whites was mixed with pity and just occasionally brought up old resentments.

In the virtual sphere guilt was most often put on Nigerians. A online article concerning cyberfraud commented:

> These Nigerians are not operating only in Ghana; they're everywhere duping unsuspecting victims around the globe. We've lost our guard; we've allowed these criminals to swamp our cyber cities to taint our beautiful pride and image. Govt should wake up clamp up on these criminals.
>
> We need to weed the criminals out of our system. That's the only way we could build our reputation back in the eyes of the rest of the world. It's time to act and swiftly![42]

The phenomenon was restricted to the internet in my observation. I have in no case met such aggressive resentments in personal discussions. Fraudsters were highlighted as they were now charged with crimes far more severe than cyberfraud. Also common internet users were now under suspicion of criminal activity.

People with the symptoms portrayed as effects of rituals in films and posters could feel offended. Their suffering was interpreted in the films as just punishment for evil deeds (Riedel 2012; also see Olsen 2002: 523). The outcome of many Ghanaian films is an inverted psychosomatic aetiology (compare Riedel 2008) where the audience interprets specific symptoms as clear signs of money rituals. Anyhow, there was no notice-able maltreatment of mentally ill persons after the *Sakawa*-films.

Pathic projections[43] are prone to violent aggression. According to Smith, the 'Owerri riots' against prosperous citizens in Nigeria were guided by rumours about 419 and related occult rituals including child-murder and human sacrifice (2007: 140). I have never heard or read about any violent mob related to *Sakawa*. In films and posters, punishing aggression was delegated to gods. However, the extent of critical reflexion on the rumours remains too unexplored to draw further conclusions.

The Racialised Supremacy of Media Technology

The *Sakawa* mythology contains a strong reference to the literacy gap (Field 1960: 53). The intimate and elitist society of internet-users, with their strong insider-outsider attitude (intensified through Facebook) fosters the presumption of a 'modern secret knowledge' (compare Krings 2007: 126), well-known from popular Western resentments against the so-called *Nerd*. The gap between illiterates and literates grows through the advent of a new medium which requires height-ened literacy. This medium is at the same time an instrument for the production of value and knowledge. Several films depicted reading the words of a traditional god as outclassing the mental skills developed from modern learning. These films compensate illiterates and semi-literates for feelings of inadequacies in real life. Films propagate that 'powers' from internet access, internet cafés serving as 'modern day shrines', could only be superseded by the authoritarian and intrusive public sphere of the Christian congregation with its oral practices.

Sakawa ideology also introduces concepts of new media and their production. Matthias Krings (2007: 126) interprets African vampire-films as reflections on new body-concepts, medicinal techniques and labour division. Similarly *Sakawa*-films reflect technological and

economical gaps arising with the internet. Heike Behrend sharpened the thesis that during times of technological upheaval the new
medium is likely to be associated with sorcery and magic (2003:
287). She highlights the magical use of media through Europeans
in Africa. Photographs were used by European journalists and missionaries as 'magic charms' in a manipulative way. Using unfamiliar
media generated power was reported to have a disturbing effect on
many Africans (Behrend 2003: 287ff.). They developed strategies to
counteract Western arrogance – new media were downplayed as a variation of African spiritual techniques (Behrend 2003: 288, 298). In
Sakawa-films, manipulating the distribution of commodities is attributed to ambiguous priests, shrines and gods. This inversion marks
triumph of the local over the global modes of production (compare
Comaroff and Comaroff 1998: 291). According to Behrend, after the
interferences caused by the introduction of new media and the related
technological supremacy of the West, the hybridisation of former and
new media seeks to deal with the disturbance in a productive way.
Through becoming enchanted, the new media is de-enchanted. The
supremacy of the West is therefore diminished and local empowerment takes place (Behrend 2003: 298).

But many Ghanaians have ambivalent feelings about this new
technology. A stereotypical comment from Ghana is: 'You whites
use witchcraft in a positive way to produce phones, laptops, cameras'
(compare Harnischfeger 2004 in Wendl 2004 196). On the other
hand, 'African science' was boasted as primordial: 'Our ancestors
took a chewing stick and turned it into a plane or a phone, if they
wanted'.[44] Both statements are interrelated – the second is a narcissistic compensation of the technological mortification expressed in
the idiom of 'witchcraft'. It does not necessarily consist of agency –
it is an ideologeme. The mythomanic retrojection 'our ancestors'
preserves a technologically skilled 'we' which counters indigenous
racist notions enforced on many African individuals by the racialised appearance of technological disparities. Not the usage of new
media, but its invention and production are mystified by both the
obscured accumulation of knowledge through scripture and the
imbalance of production sites. Therefore, the occult in *Sakawa*-
films is not a reference to the virtual. The frame of reference is
rather the supremacy of media technology and the role of the occult

as 'African science' invented and controlled by the 'Juju-Man'.[45] The theme song of *Sakawa Boys* states:

> Gone were the days, when Africa was blind
> We were blind, but now we can see-yeah
> Sakawa is not a crime
> It's a Game we happen to find-yeah
> Yahoo dot com, (hey, hey) yahoo dot com, heehee [...]'

The racialised 'stigma of primitiveness' (Behrend 2003: 293) is subverted through the alliance of 'African science' with current technology. This 'counter-discourse' is fragile. One woman told me in an internet café:

> Your white Scientists have second eyes. They use it to invent. I'm train-ing mine, so I can invent something. Second eyes, yes, you can't see them! I want to invent at the bank, on Sundays, you can't bring money there, but if I sold on Saturday evening, where should I bring it that it will be save if armed robbers come at night to my house? I want to invent an ATM, to bring in money and to get the receipt.[46]

She grumbled as I told her that this gadget exists and is standard in Western banks. She equates creativity with magic, but she was not aware of the operational and experimental sequences in the production and invention of technology. The limited but existent supremacy of Western technology was not only abused by colonial agents, it contin-ues to pose an epistemological problem for many Africans. While the usage of technology might become de-spiritualised over the years, the shrouded means of production remain to induce mythologies. Narcissistic mortification tends to be filled by plombages consist-ing of occult fantasies but not solved if not by the realities creating it. Jonathan Haynes (2000: 34) draws the conclusion: 'Commodities, as Marx said, obscure the social relations that created them; this is doubly so when they are imported into a radically different society and invested with meanings never imagined by the manufacturer'.

Conclusions

Sakawa-films play on wishes for luxury, safety and advancement. They defraud the audience of an elaborate theory of economy[47] and tech-nology as they affirm traditional mythologies about value generation and media invention. Rituals serve as distorted imaginations of contradictions between the demands of both economy and society. Surprisingly, the projections against constructed outgroups did not translate into open aggression. Racialising remained auto-aggressive or tried to compensate technological disparities through mythomanic fantasies. Read as a critique of hedonist ideologies of culture industry,[48] *Sakawa*-films might expound the problem of the antagonisms between 'fun' and bliss and between private and public. But at the same time the ideology promotes daily grind.[49] 'We were better off poor', says Agya Koo in *Sakawa 419*. Extreme punishment awaits those who want to overcome poverty and the traditional order. The prevalent global social modes of production and the traditional order are contested, but re-established in the end. *Sakawa*-films offer no other viable solution than staying poor, faithful, honest and obedient.

Notes

1   US Department of Justice (ed.) 2009: "Internet Crime Report": 8. http://www.ic3.gov/media/annualreport/2009_IC3Report.pdf (accessed Feb. 2011).
2   Returning in 2011 I found it popular among the youth to sport a Facebook profile through mobile phone connections.
3   Data were gathered during nine months of field research, located mostly in Cape Coast in 2009 and 2011.
4   Burrell 2008; 2010. Burrell reports and analyses rumours among users about success in cyberfraud but none referred to occult rituals that granted success. It is therefore likely that these rumours were not existent at that time.
5   Conversation on 9 Sept. 2009.
6   I collected about 10 articles and observed maybe three dozen more during the first half of 2009.
7   After the section of the Nigerian law concerning cyberfraud, see Smith 2007: 19.
8   Compare Oduro-Frimpong 2011: 2. Joseph Oduro-Frimpong's discussion of its linguistic origins leads one to the conclusion that the Akan elements *kawa* (ring), and the Hausa word *Sakawa* were in one case blended: The sub-heading of the film *Sakawa Boys* is '*Mallam Issa Kawa*', which was translated as 'Mallam Issa's Ring'.
9   Compare Burrell's study on rumours among users and fraudsters which were by that time not concerned about rituals or magic: Burrell 2010.
10   Director: Uriel Adjin-Tettey, 2009.
11   Director: Sokrate Safo, 2009.

12 'Sakawa Boys buy movie about them' <http://themorningpost.wordpress. com/2009/06/10/Sakawa Boys-buy-movie-about-them> (March 2009).

13 Director: Kafui Dzivenu, 2009.

14 Director: Moses Ebere, 2009.

15 Director: James Aboagye, 2009.

16 Director: Samuel Nyamekye, 2009.

17 Director: Teddy Ansah, 2010.

18 About Mami-Wata see Wendl 1991.

19 'Mugu' means (white) 'dupe'.

20 See Comaroff and Comaroff 1998. They and successive authors connect the phenomenon to neo-liberalism and a supposed modernity accompanied by social upheavals. Nonetheless, the history of rumours is far older than neo-liberalism and capitalism itself and is situated in many different economic contexts, from anti-Semitic blood-libels to South American urban legends about murderous human fat traders. See also: Riedel 2008: 97ff. Phenomenological approaches translate these ideologemes into a scientific terminology, but conclusive analytical explanations, especially on the individual psychological level of choice, remain rare.

21 Stewart and Strathern also argue: 'It is not necessary, or even cogent, to suppose that these situations are unique to the late twentieth or early twenty-first century or to postmodernity' (2004: 192).

22 An informant of Field utters similar fears: 'I remember thirty or forty men in Akwapim who started building big houses, but they died before they were finished' (Field 1960: 112). Note that a common punishment for theft is lynching or at least being brutalised by the mob.

23 TV-Africa: 10 June 2009. Quoted analogously from notes. The TV show simultaneously advertised the films and the Christian ritual of confession.

24 'The Sakawa Boys' on 'Motherboard' <http://www.vice.com/motherboard/ mbd-vbs-the-Sakawa Boys> (Jan. 2012).

25 While ritual murder is a reality in Africa, I suspect all of these pictures to be either shot at traffic-accidents or downloaded from online sources.

26 Field 1960: 87. A German woman with Ghanaian parents told me she was warned against taking any food from relatives in Ghana. It might have been poisoned for no obvious reason.

27 Conversation on: 19 July 2009.

28 Conversation on: 6 June 2009.

29 Meyer Fortes 1945, after Olsen 2002: 535. In my presence, many Ghanaians explained their social problems in similar words, suspecting witchcraft or witchcraft accusations as results of envy.

30 K. T. Busia (1951) also suggested the solidarity of the matrilineage contested through the cocoa boom of the early twentieth century (cited in Olsen 2002: 536). This is also an element in *Sakawa* films as relatives from

the matrilineage demand solidarity that is tabooed by some films. I leave this complex issue to better informed analysts.

31   Riedel 2008: 97ff. See also Adorno and Horkheimer 1969: 181.

32   This is the main argument of Adorno's study about astrology: Adorno 2003 (1957).

33   Compare Stewart and Strathern 2004: 201. Compare Geschiere's critique of the post-modernist sympathies for witchcraft beliefs as critiques of modernity: Ciekawy and Geschiere 1998: 3.

34   Two strangers see him and run away in panic. According to the director this was an accident: The two passengers interpreted him as an omen of death. 'The Sakawa Boys' on 'Motherboard' <http://www.vice.com/motherboard/mbd-vbs-the-Sakawa Boys> (Jan. 2012). This scene might also be a reference to traditional coffin-rituals. M. J. Field mentions a ritual in which the carriers of a coffin take it to the supposed witch or evil-doer who had killed the deceased (Field 1960: 77).

35   Contradictory to this behaviour are statements Burrell collected among fraudsters in Accra, who stated their wish to invest the money in legal businesses to gain independence from fraud. See Burrell 2008: 20; Riedel 2012: 242.

36   Nonetheless, the feudal order was crumbling in the late nineteenth century: Olsen 2002: 526–7.

37   A comparison with the concept of the 'misfit bourgeois' would be worthwhile. Compare Adorno 2003 (1950): 309ff.

38   Conversation on: 27 July 2009. 'Not good' does not imply morals but punishment and conflict.

39   Director: Andy Amenechi, 2004.

40   Conversation on 30 June 2009.

41   18 Aug. 2009: 'Ghana rated among top 10 Nations in Cyber Crime' <http://mobile.ghanaweb.com/wap/comment.article.php?ID=167017> (March 2011).

42   Ibid.

43   Pathic projection is a psychological concept, which includes more sexual layers than scapegoating- and blaming-theories. Compare the discussion of projection-theories of Adorno/Horkheimer 1969: 196ff; 201.

44   Conversation on: 2 June 2009.

45   Wendl compares the Juju-Man with the image of the 'mad scientist' in Western movies (Wendl 2004: 20).

46   Conversation on 2 June 2009.

47   Adorno/Horkheimer 1969: 49. My translation.

48   Adorno/Horkheimer 1969: 149.

49   Compare Adorno/Horkheimer 1969: 156ff.

References

Adorno, Theodor W. (1968) *Ohne Leitbild: Parva Aesthetica*, Frankfurt/Main: Suhrkamp.

—— (1972) *Erziehung zur Mündigkeit,* Frankfurt/Main: Suhrkamp.

—— (2003) *Soziologische Schriften (II.1. und II.2),* Frankfurt/Main: Suhrkamp.

—— et al. (2003 [1950]) *Studies in the Authoritarian Personality,* in *Soziologische Schriften* (II.1), pp. 237–509, Frankfurt/Main: Suhrkamp.

—— et al. (2003 [1957]): *The Stars down to Earth,* in *Soziologische Schriften (II.2),* pp. 7–120, Frankfurt/Main: Suhrkamp.

Adorno, Theodor W. and Horkheimer, Max (1969 [1947]) *Dialektik der Aufklärung: Philosophische Fragmente,* Frankfurt/Main: Suhrkamp.

Behrend, Heike (2003) 'Call and kill: Zur Verzauberung und Entzauberung westlicher technischer Medien in Afrika', in Erhard Schüttpelz and Albert Erhard (eds), *Signale der Störung*, pp. 287–300, Munich: Fink.

Bourgault, Louise M. (1995) *Mass Media in sub-Saharan Africa*, Bloomington, IN, and Indianapolis: Indiana University Press.

Burrell, Jenna (2008) 'Problematic empowerment: West African internet scams as strategic misrepresentation', *Information Technology and International Development*, 4/4, pp. 15–30.

—— (2010) 'User agency in the middle range: rumors and the reinvention of the internet in Accra, Ghana', *Science, Technology and Human Values*, 36/2, pp. 139–59.

Comaroff, Jean, and Comaroff, John (1998) 'Occult economies and the violence of abstraction: notes from the South African postcolony', *American Ethnologist*, 26/2, pp. 279–303.

Ciekawy, Diane, and Geschiere, Peter (1998) 'Containing witchcraft: conflicting scenarios in post-colonial Africa', *African Studies Review*, 41/3, pp. 1–14 <http://www.jstor.org/stable/525351> (accessed Jan. 2012).

deWitte, Marlene (2009) 'Financial crisis worldwide: Sakawa money in Ghana', <http://standplaatswereld.nl/2009/11/26/financial-crisis-worldwide-5-sakawa-money-in-ghana> (accessed Dec. 2012).

Field, Margareth J. (1970) *Search for Security: An Ethno-Psychiatric Study of Rural Ghana*, New York: W. W. Norton & Co.

Glickman, Harvey (2005) 'The Nigerian "419" advance fee scams: prank or peril?', *Canadian Journal of African Studies,* 39/3, pp. 460–89.

Harnischfeger, Johannes (2004) 'Die Realität des Okkulten', in Tobias Wendl (ed.), *Africa Screams: Das Böse in Kino, Kunst und Kult,* pp. 189–97, Wuppertal: Peter Hammer.

Haynes, Jonathan, ed. (2000) *Nigerian Video Films*, Ohio: University Center for International Studies.

Krings, Matthias (2007) 'Afrikanische Video-Vampire – Wiedergänger zwischen den Kulturen', in Silke Seybold (ed.), *All about Evil: Das Böse*, pp. 120–7, Mainz: Philipp von Zabern.

Marx, Karl (1973 [1867]) *Das Kapital: Kritik der politischen Ökonomie*, MEW 23, Berlin: Dietz.

Meyer, Birgit, and Pels, Peter (2003) *Magic and Modernity: Interfaces of Revelation and Concealment*, Stanford, CA: Stanford University Press.

Oduro-Frimpong, Joseph (2011) *Sakawa. On occultic rituals and cyberfraud in Ghanaian popular cinema. Working paper*. Available: http://media-anthropology.net

Olsen, William C. (2002) ' "Children for death": money, wealth, and witchcraft suspicion in colonial Asante', *Cahiers d'Etudes Africaines*, 42/167, pp. 521–50 <http://www.jstor.org/stable/4393235> (accessed Jan. 2012).

Riedel, Felix (2008) *Die modernen Hexenjagden im subsaharischen Afrika: Darstellung und Vergleich mit dem Antisemitismus aus der Perspektive der Kritischen Theorie*, Göttingen: Sierke.

—— (2012) ' "When will you whites give us the real internet?" Zum Verhältnis von unerreichter Nähe, technischem Rückstand und Internetbetrug in Ghana', in Pablo Abend, Tobias Haupts, and Claudia Müller (eds), *Medialität der Nähe*, pp.213–245, Bielefeld: Transcript.

Sartre, Jean-Paul (1994 [1954]) *Überlegungen zur Judenfrage*, Reinbeck bei Hamburg: Rowohlt Taschenbuch Verlag GmbH.

Schüttpelz, Erhard (2009) 'Die medientechnische Überlegenheit des Westens: Zur Geschichte und Geographie der immutable mobiles Bruno Latours', in Jörg Döring and Tristan Thielmann (eds), *Mediengeographie: Theorie, Analyse, Diskussion*, pp. 67–110, Bielefeld: Transcript.

Smith, Daniel Jordan (2007) *A Culture of Corruption: Everyday Deception and Popular Discontent in Nigeria*, Princeton, NJ, and Oxford: Princeton University Press.

Stewart, Pamela J., and Strathern, Andrew (2004) *Witchcraft, Sorcery, Rumors, and Gossip*, Cambridge: Cambridge University Press.

Van der Geest, Sjaak (2002) 'From wisdom to witchcraft: ambivalence towards old age in rural Ghana', *Africa*, 72/3, pp. 437–63.

Wendl, Tobias (1991) *Mami Wata oder ein Kult zwischen den Kulturen*, Münster: Lit.

—— (2004) 'Africa screams: Spurensuche für eine Archäologie des Bösen und des Schreckens', in Tobias Wendl (ed.), *Africa Screams: Das Böse in Kino, Kunst und Kult*, pp. 11–29, Wuppertal: Peter Hammer.

Filmography

Aboagye, James (2009) *Agya Koo – Sakawa I–II*. Ghana.
Adjin-Tettey, Uriel (2009) *Café Guys I–II*. Ghana.
Amenechi, Andy (2004) *The Master*. Nigeria.
Dzivenu, Kafui (2009) *Sakawa Girls I–II*. Ghana.
Ebere, Moses (2009) *The Dons in Sakawa I–IV*. Ghana.
Nyamekye, Samuel (2009) *Sakawa 419 I–IV*. Ghana.
Safo, Sokrate (2009) *Sakawa Boys I–IV*. Ghana.

14

BLACK AFRICAN DIASPORIC CINEMAS: IDENTITIES AND THE CHALLENGE OF COMPLEXITY

Daniela Ricci

How do the filmmakers of the black African diasporas deal with identity and racial issues as witnesses to the existential quest in today's post-post-colonial hybrid world? How do their life experiences, in terms of migration and, especially, of their confrontation with 'otherness', even after colonialism, influence their work and 'film objects'?

We need to consider identity's importance on a personal and social level in today's increasingly complex and interconnected world. In this respect, I believe that contemporary black African diasporic directors are highly privileged observers, capable of offering us a variety of multifocal standpoints. Their positioning is also marked by the fact that they are black, with all the complexity that 'blackness' brings with it.

The longing to know oneself, to situate oneself in relationship to others, has always been at the centre of human experience. From Socrates to Pirandello (1941), passing through Amin Maalouf (2001) and his 'belonging to the human adventure', the great spiritual works and artistic expressions of every era bear witness to this search for identity.

'Who and what are we? Good question!' exclaims Aimé Césaire in *Cahier d'un retour au pays natal*. Césaire, one of the promoters of the *Négritude*, asks a question that brings with it racial issues. Do these existential questions still carry the same meaning today? We have to wonder if nowadays the individual isn't likely to be exploring identity issues in relation to a more 'liquid' sense of collectivity and belonging – to cite Zygmunt Bauman's expression.[1] It is much more complex now, since our sense of belonging is often multiple, lacking in rigid boundaries, and is in continuous dynamic transformation. Indeed, each of us could define him/herself according to various identity aspects that depend on the context. Nevertheless, the 'black condition'[2] is often the most evident characteristic and can condition perceptions and representation. We know the consequences of racism on people's perceptions and psychologies, as Frantz Fanon described so well (Fanon 1952). My intention is to analyse how filmmakers of the black African diasporas tackle these themes in their 'film discourses'.

The art works of some Sub-Saharan African directors who have tackled this subject provide a valuable insight into the issue of the search for individual identity. We presume that these ancestral questionings of the human soul are more urgent for those whose collective history is marked by slavery and colonialism, experiences that have left a sense of self-contempt, to quote Burkinabe historian Joseph Ki-Zerbo[3]. Paul Gilroy also sees in the common historical past of the slave trade the emblem of his new concept of the black diaspora. Its main representatives are black artists from former colonies who bear witness to this concern for identity.

Homi K. Bhabha states that 'hybridity' began with the 'ambivalence of the object of colonial discourse – that "otherness" which is at once an object of desire and derision, an articulation of difference contained within the fantasy of origin and identity' (Bhabha 1994: 96). According to Bhabha, we can go beyond the dual logic of Edward Said who, nevertheless, did sow the seeds of non-Eurocentric dialogue (Said 1979). While revising Du Bois' concept of 'double consciousness', Bhabha speaks of cultural 'hybridity', interstices, negotiations, 'being in the beyond'.

As regards cinema, I shall focus on some black African feature films – leaving aside the prolific Nollywood film industry – touching on various kinds of film production and underlining the many differences identifiable on the African continent and even within one individual country. According to Jean-Pierre Esquenazi, we believe that the fictional universe can become a sort of reference for consideration of the real world, in much the same way that the philosopher Arthur Danto speaks about literature. Fiction may indeed be an essential contribution to the construction of a 'collective imagery' that helps us comprehend reality (Esquenazi 2009).

The reappropriation and redefinition of identity by these black, diasporic 'culturally hybrid filmmakers, whose cinema Olivier Barlet has called 'nomadic cinema', becomes particularly important (Barlet 2005). The exploration of self-consciousness is typical of many black populations[4] who have suffered oppression which can lead to a certain feeling of self-contempt, as seen in the films by Isaac Julien, or by Trinidad's Horace Ové. Let's take the example of *Pressure* (1975), the first full-length black British feature film, which also inspired Barbados' Menelik Shabazz in the making of *Burning an Illusion* (1981). In the same genre, films by Ghanaian John Akomfrah and those filmmakers with whom he founded the 'Black Audio Film Collective' explore the problems of black identities in Great Britain.

Sub-Saharan African filmmaking germinated at the time of political independence and naturally became part of this search for identity – a liberated voice from within, in an ambivalent relationship with former settlers. It could not be otherwise, considering that various generations of filmmakers mostly consisted of expatriates (e.g., Med Hondo, Haile Gerima, Abderrahmane Sissako, Dani Kouyaté, Jean-Marie Teno, Mama Keita, Balufu Bakupa-Kanyinda, Jean Odoutan, Newton Aduaka, John Akomfrah, Mweze Ngangura, Oswalde Lewat, Cedric Ido, Daouda Coulibaly and Soussaba Cissé).

It is important to analyse how the status of black African diasporic directors affects the subjects and the aesthetics of their films and their artistic approaches. From the viewpoint of the sociology of film, it's important to consider the film object as a process, that 'at each stage can be transformed, and that the sum total of these movements constitutes the journey's symbolic value' (Esquenazi 2007: 120).

The ways in which the black diasporic filmmakers are perceived in their host societies influences their artistic production also. In fact they stand in some interstitial spaces between different cultures, from where they have a privileged, critical point of view. In any case, I feel it is important to bear in mind that a film is essentially a piece of art, a 'symbolic object'.

> The art object touches us, not because it is an inspired exception to a mediocre world, but because it is etched with our history and filled with the cries, the fears, the joys of our existence. (Esquenazi 2001: 9)

For this reason, too, I believe it is necessary to avoid a merely ethnographic point of view. In fact, the issue of identity has always been pivotal to African filmmaking. Africa (and Africans) had previously been merely a backdrop for many foreign films: colonial filmmakers depicted Africa in an exotic, if not fossilized and racist key, reinforcing stereotypes and foregrounding the Western 'civilized' world's mission. In the post-colonial period particularly, in their urgency to reaffirm themselves, black African filmmakers immediately began to ask the questions: 'Who am I? Who are we?' This concern is echoed even in the titles of their films: *Concerto pour un exil, A nous deux la France, Identité, Les princes noirs de Saint-Germains-des-Près, Heritage... Africa!, Exilé, Immigré en France, Comédie exotique, Nationalité immigré, Immatriculation temporaire, Pièces d'identité* – to cite but a few. The contemporary *Identité malsaine* by Congolese Amog Lemra is also meaningful.

After having been 'folklorised', Africans had to reappropriate their points of view, their history and their self-awareness because, as the saying goes, 'hunting stories always sing the praises of the hunters because the lions have no *griots*'. To that point, African imagery had been viewed from the outside, as in the ethnographic cinema of directors such as Jean Rouch, for instance. There was little room for inner reflection, since the Laval Decree[5] prohibited any filming in the French colonies without authorization. On this, Manthia Diawara wrote:

> 'Unlike the British and the Belgians, who had colonial African film units, the French had no policy for producing films that were especially intended for their subjects in Africa. The only decision made by the French concerning films in the colonies was the implementation of a law in 1934 called 'Le Décret Laval'. [...] The purpose of the Laval decree was to control the content of films that were shot in Africa and to minimize the creative roles played by Africans in the making of films. [...] Although historians of African film agree that Laval's decree was rarely applied against filmmakers, they also believe that it had the effect of postponing the birth of Francophone African film. (Diawara 1992: 22)

Jean Rouch[6] agrees with this when he points out that the Laval Law, which 'almost never applied to French filmmakers, served as a pretext to deny young Africans the right to film. Although rarely applied, its existence was enough to fix the games'.[7] In the former Belgian colonies an analogous law was in force. It is significant that the film *Afrique*

Sur Seine,[8] considered the first Sub-Saharan African film,[9] was filmed in Paris as a result of the Laval Law.

The enigmatic ellipsis contained in the title of Sembène Ousmane's *La Noire de… (The Black Girl from /of…)* (Senegal/France, 1966), the first black African full-length film (actually around 60 minutes in length), is emblematic of the dual obsession of all migrants: self-consciousness and belonging. The fact that the title declares that the main character is black is in itself meaningful. The emblematic annihilation of 'the other' is celebrated in the humiliating existence of Diouna, a young Senegalese housemaid brought to Antibes, in France, by her French 'masters', which culminates in her suicide. Another significant element is the confusion surrounding Sembène's name – the very essence of each individual's identity. Ousmane was his first name, Sembène his surname, but he was called Sembène Ousmane, according to the inversion that French colonization had imposed upon the people. He always wanted to reinvert the two names, saying that he would 'straighten them out' on the day that Senegal became independent and there were no more French street names in Dakar. He died in 2007 without ever having been able to turn his name around (Dia 2008). In Sembène's Socratic belief that one had to know oneself in order to know someone else, his militant definition of cinema was 'école du soir, école du soi' ('night school, school of self').

Similarly, in the documentary Joseph Ki-Zerbo *Identités, identité pour l'Afrique* by Dani Kouyaté (2005), Ki-Zerbo and others, mixing personal and collective issues, say:

> 'Identity must be constructed, with a hard and often ferocious fight. This is why we say that we cannot carry our identity around like a medal or a decoration. We must model it and construct it day by day […] Africa is branded with plural identities which sometimes clash and conflict, individual, familial, collective identities [...] Identity cannot be acquired passively. […] The best way for people to develop is to start with the central paradigm of their own culture, but 'open to all breaths of the world.'[10] (citing Césaire)

Many films echo this same concern to seek oneself and one's own roots, to emerge from behind the camouflage, to go forward, opening oneself up to the other. 'The new is born of the old', says the *griot* of *Niaye* (Sembène Ousmane, 1964) and 'The future is born of the past', states the *griot* of Keita (*Keita, l'héritage du griot*, Kouyaté, 1995), to quote some examples. 'You know, we cannot actually move forward if we don't look back to see what has affected us. Why are we behaving the way we are behaving today? How did we start?' asks Kwaw P. Ansah. We find a similar message in *Sankofa* (Gerima 1993), which, in the Akan language, means 'returning to the past in order to go forward'.

The migration experience strongly marks the existence of each of the filmmakers of the black African diaspora who, once settled in Europe or North America, often underwent culture shock themselves. This has a particular resonance when coupled with the colonial and racial phenomenon.

Mweze Ngangura declares: 'If I had not moved to Europe, if I did not live in Europe, in Belgium, to be exact, I never would have had the idea for *Pièces d'identité*. I think the work we produce, the work we make, is always related to the life of the person making it. Even if we are not aware of it, it's true'.[11] It is interesting to observe how the encounter with 'otherness', and self-consciousness, influence their artistic process.

The encounter and the confrontation with 'otherness' is central to many films, such as *L'Afrance* (Alain Gomis, Senegal, 2001), inspired by *The Ambiguous Adventure* by Cheick Hamidou Kane. A comparative analysis between *L'Afrance* and *Teza*[12] by Haile Gerima would be inter-esting. In their own very different ways, both films discuss the theme of the return to his home country of the intellectual from overseas. For Gomis, born in France, it is his Senegalese father's recollections which he has made his own, such as the dream of 'coming back'; whereas for Haile Gerima, *Teza* is a sort of cathartic exorcism of broken dreams and a way to find new paths. We can find the issue of return – even if for only 24 hours, but enough to discover the worst tragedies – in *L'absence* (Mama Keita, 2009), which I will consider later.

The French-born Alain Gomis has to 'fend for himself', to find his way in the melting pot that is today's world. He carries with him, as evidenced by the very title of his film, *L'Afrance* – a fusion of the words Afrique and France – the same dual cultural belonging that charac-terizes the movie, which begins with a collage of images of Paris and Dakar.

In a different way, *Teza* is full of autobiographical references and real-life events; Gerima tells the story of young intellectuals though the words of the protagonist, Anberber, who left to study in 'modern' Germany, full of dreams of going back home to help his country. He goes home and is quickly disheartened, observing the violent 'changes' the country is undergoing. He does not recognize himself, feeling out of place and with no points of reference. Only when he returns to his village, to his mother and he starts to reassemble fragments of his memory, does he begin to heal. The *Tebel* at the church where he had served as a boy exorcises more than the demons the village believes responsible for his nightmares and sickness.

Teza reveals the disappointment of a generation of intellectuals who, for a variety of reasons and circumstances, never realized their dream of a better Ethiopia. The film purposefully shares with the spectator the brutality of upheaval. Viewers are bombarded with political, social and silent violence to the point that they are forced out of their comfort zone, realizing the purpose of such films is to make us question, not simply observe, as in the Esquenazian notion of the fictional text as a *paraphrase* of reality (Esquenazi 2009). Gerima's style is not linear, but echoes the Ethiopian narrative tradition of weaving allegory, fact and circumstance together to create stories that transcend space and time. According to Gerima, filmmaking is telling stories, 'making memories' and taking on a fight, making one's own contribution toward revolution.

In the United States Gerima was alienated culturally until he found himself in the African American community. It was in the embrace of this black community that he found his way home. His films are journeys of self-discovery, storytelling, *griot*-like, that provides him with a path to an Africa that at times no longer exists.

> In the United States I realized that, for me, therapy for my alienation was to remember history. For Africans it's so important to reaffirm their identity and that which can come through the reconstruction of historical memory. (Ricci 2009)

Another film among the many that deal with the confrontation with 'otherness' is *Keita, the Heritage of the Griot* (Kouyaté, Burkina Faso, 1995), which alternates French with the Bambara language. Dani Kouyaté puts the spectator before the dilemma of young Mabo who looks for a balance between the two different approaches, on the one hand, he is fascinated by stories of his heritage and the myth of Sundjata Keita, told by the *griot* Djeliba (actually played by Sotigui Kouyaté, the father of the filmmaker, who was a real *griot* and well-known actor), and on the other, placed into a French school system that denies his identity: 'our ancestors were like gorillas, their intelligence was not developed, then the homo sapiens came',[13] the young boy studies. It is interesting to notice that the film aesthetics is exactly based on a mix of oral story-telling and modern cinema, with continuous transitions from reality to the imagination, and from the present to the past.

The magnitude of the identity issue is amply witnessed by Kouyaté's last documentary *'Souvenirs encombrants d'une femme de ménage'* (France/Guadalupe 2009). The Burkinabe director transposes into the cinema screen a theatrical drama about the life of the elderly black Guadalupe Thérèse Bernis, who plays herself in the film. Having come to France from Guadalupe she has worked all her life as a housemaid. Mother of six children, always abandoned by their fathers, she has slept on the street and struggled to get by. The confessions of her very hard exist-ence, while they help her to free her mind of the misfortunes of her life, also lead the audience to ponder the same questions on freedom, equality, existence and identity.

> We West Indians, we are immigrants, even if we are not like African immigrants. But African or West Indian immigrants, it's all the same, nig-gers are niggers, jumbled in the same bag. I am French. That's what they say. But I don't know how. I'm not French like you, people of France.'

Kouyaté, like others, invites the audience to have the courage to take on the complexities of the realities that are interconnected by their differences.

Kouyaté is himself a good example of this synthesis: a *griot* in Sweden, who chose cinema as a way to tell the stories of his traditions, filtered through a critical eye, as he does, for instance, in his film *Sia, le rêve du pyton* (2001). He is quoted as saying: 'I had the good fortune of living during the era of cinema, what a fabulous instrument for a *griot*!'[14] An emblematic anecdote that refers back to the film *Sia*,[15] but which is also true on a wider scale, relates to language, which we know is not just a means of expression, but also a structure for meaning, an important fea-ture of cultural identity. The film script was written in French, mostly because Bambara is a very complex language, but also in order to allow the producers to read it. They used it to determine the film's length but when it was filmed in Bambara, the dialogues were much longer, creating production problems. This is not just an expenses problem relating to the amount of film footage needed, but rather emblematic of the complexity of choosing a language when expressing oneself, an issue that many intellectuals (Mongo Bety, Boris Boubacar Diop, Chinua Achebe, Ngugi Wa Thiong'o, amongst others) have explored. These writers highlight the very complex issue of deciding which audience an art work is meant for. This concern is even more pregnant if we consider that the receiver participates in the construction of the meaning of the fictional discourse; the process of filmmaking doesn't end with its production, but continues with the audience's interpretation, which also depends on social context. What's more, as Esquenazi states, 'the "real life" of a fiction, which makes it into a filmic work, begins with the audience's appropriation of it' (Esquenazi 2007: 129).

Economic issues and financial market regulations are the biggest constraints for production. Another major problem for African films, associated with the audience, is distribution.[16] Few films make it out of the realm of film festivals or special film reviews. Such issues are well described in the documentary *Sacred Places* by Cameroon's Jean Marie Teno (2009).[17]

Returning to the problem of funding these films, it seems that they often originate either as independent productions or with the help of funding from the former colonial powers: a new form of dependence upon these powers, a phenomenon unique in the world. I believe, for instance, that a good example of independent cinema would be *Rage* by Newton Aduaka (UK, 1999) which tells the story of the dreams and comparative realities of life in London for 'Rage', a mixed-race young musician and his two friends, one white, the other black, searching for their identity. *Rage* was released in 1999 in many theatres in Great Britain. Going beyond civil rights or black power movements, these directors came to an acceptance of their knowledge of their own hybrid identities. Olivier Barlet wrote, on the occasion of Fespaco 2003:

> It is not so much that the new generation of filmmakers rejects their predecessors, but rather that they affirm the fact that they belong to a hybrid world, a cultural half-way house that resists globalization in the sense that blending into the world does not mean losing one's specificity. This cinema avoids getting trapped into preconceived notions about what is or isn't 'African'. It explores a territory of roaming, of the fringes, in other words, Africa's future at present. (Barlet 2003)

The concept of hybridity brings to mind Mama Keita, born in Senegal to a Guinean father, who was in the French military, and a Vietnamese mother, and raised in France. His works centre on the search for self in the midst of cultural confusion, and he has told[18] that the main characters of his films are often multiracial, a choice he has made almost without realizing it. His works are filmed for the most part in Europe, Africa or the United States, and they immerse the spectator in uncertainty as well as a feeling of always being absent, as his film *L'absence* reminds us.

Finally, I would like to dwell a moment on Jean Odoutan and his cinema as an expression of identity search. He emigrated to France from Benin at a very young age and, after a series of vicissitudes that included living for a while on the streets and being handed over to the French social services (DASS), later being raised in the home of a French family, he became a filmmaker involved in contributing to the development of his home country. So his passion for cinema finally led him back to his roots. He began his approach to the camera as an extra, then as an actor in the movies of various filmmakers, such as Michel Blanc, Eric Woret, Luigi Comencini, Marco Ferreri, Bertrand Tavernier, Frédéric Schoendorffer, Pierre Schoendorffer. Tired of playing the 'negro character', he decided to move to the other side of the lens. He says that it was during the months spent shooting *Dien Bien Phu* in Vietnam with Pierre Schoendorffer, as Assistant Director, that he learned about filmmaking and decided to do it himself.

He began with several short films and video clips. He is also a musician and composer and was able to express what he felt as a young African student in France. He states: 'I am from Benin, but I make French films, which are considered Beninese'.[19]

> I had a chance to learn about black Benin culture from my parents and also about the white French culture, so I think that in my work there is an interaction of both cultures. I don't ask myself who I am anymore, mine is a hybrid culture that nourishes me, it is rich and I'm proud of it.[20]

Belonging to both cultures, his social comedies – a rather rare genre – are steeped in Africa. He has shot many films in only a few years: *Barbecue Pejo* (Benin, 2000), *Djib* (France, 2000), *Mama Aloko* (France, 2002), *La valse des gros derrières* (France, 2004), *Pim Pim tché* (Benin, 2009). 'I like to make social and people-oriented movies; I like *"art"* cinema, but why not "mass audience" movies? Anyway, I like films that make you think and reflect. I also like intelligent madness, and I like when fiction meets intelligent madness'.[21] You could say he is really the author of his own life, a self-made artist who has built his career block by struggling block. He often says that 'each film is an act of faith'. Indeed, he does everything in every one of his movies: from script to direction, but also the casting, acting, music composition, production and distribution. His comedies – which he himself defines with humour as 'une banlieuserie nègre' (a negro tale of the suburbs), or 'une joviale béninoiserie' (a jovial trick Benin style) – are social messages, almost as though he were consciously aiming to help black Africans acquire a better knowledge of themselves.

These feature films have an epistemological and pragmatic function. They hold a truth that concerns the real world, and operate as a sort of tool to help us to better comprehend our universe (Esquenazi 2009). As an example, in *La valse de gros derrières* Odoutan poses several questions. The character he plays himself encourages black women to leave their passive roles behind and to achieve their own goals, seeking cultural realization and not blindly serving their husbands like maids. At the same time, he urges all black people, all human beings, to be themselves. This message is particularly direct, almost didactic, in *Djib*.

He also underlines the fact that there are very few black Africans on French movie screens. This issue is relevant, even though, back in the 1980s, Med Hondo and some other filmmakers were already saying that 'One cannot defend his dignity if he is not shown on the screen [...] if the African can't see himself in these images he is dominated and alienated'.[22] Jean Odoutan's almost autobiographical film, *Djib,* is emblematic and is a true paraphrase of some of the aspects of his reality. For the viewer, his characters are a kind of intermediary with a fictitious world, to apply the theoretical thinking of Kate Hamburger. *Djib* is his second feature-length film, made immediately after he spent several months in Benin shooting *Barbecue Pejo*. The movie tells the story of a young black boy living in the outskirts of Paris, in search of himself and an honest life, defending the dignity of being 'negro'. ('I'm Dijbril Toure, an authentic ebony negro!' he declares). He lives with his grandmother (Laurentine Milebo), his hyperbolic and rude language revealing his deep lack of affection. Through Djib's love story with a young North African girl, Odoutan reveals the conflict there often is between different immigrant communities. The movie is set in the area where he lives, which he knows very well. Djib decides to leave his trafficking to try to make an honest living. 'I want to treat my girl to a change of ozone! A real vacation on my scooter! And be straight with myself with an honest job!' His motto is 'Never let anyone except a black call you a nigger, otherwise it's the worst insult'. In his films, Odoutan speaks in people's language with intelligence – even if at times he can be a bit overly didactic. His cinema is ironic and mocking. He likes to play on words and to entertain and amuse his audience as he transmits his messages.

Djib's conversation with his grandmother in emblematic. She says to him:

> You make us Blacks ashamed. Because of you, folks don't respect us, because of you, they call us monkeys, because of you even the folks at home laugh at us, wondering why we're in a White Man's Land. Do you know what it means? Never let anyone except a black call you a nigger.

Djib completes the sentence:

> It's the worst insult! Scold me for anything, except that. I hate being called a nigger by anyone except a Black. When he says 'nigger', he thinks 'slave', when he says 'nigger', he thinks 'dirty', when he says 'nigger', he thinks 'monkey', when he says 'nigger' he doesn't think intelligent, but I'm intelligent even more than him.

Then Odoutan makes the grandmother say: 'If you want to be someone, be yourself, don't copy others, or follow ill-bred sons in the streets with their "I'm a rapper and I fuck your mother" ... Don't do as your parents shouting their hatred louder than the Whites, where are they today?'

Olivier Barlet writes about Odoutan's interesting farcical social portraits of community life:

> Whilst all African filmmakers struggle for years to make their films, Odoutan has the nerve necessary to bring out punchy, rough-and-ready films that have ended up seducing certain critics. *Libération* and even the *Cahiers du Cinéma,* extol this Beninese director's typically suburban cocky humour and verve. He overflows with energy. [...] The humor is omnipresent, yet we don't laugh because the situations are dramatic and extreme. We stay glued to the screen, both fascinated and irritated, as this cinema is more serious than it at first seems and Odoutan is more gifted than he likes to let on'. (Barlet 2002)

Although he lives in France, in order to contribute to the development of his home country, Odoutan felt the need to create the Cinematographic Institute of Ouidah (ICO) and Quintessence International Film Festival in Benin. This festival shows important films from all over the world. Like Bazin, in fact, he believes that artistic quality can help to emancipate people. 'There is a cinema culture to be developed in Benin and that is what we hope do through Quintessence'.[23] This quest for cultural and personal identity that we find in many films, which attempts to resist acculturation, is best described by the Quintessence Festival's motto: 'La culture sans ma culture m'acculture' (Culture, without my culture, acculturates me).

These are just a few examples of how these black African filmmakers, each in a different and individual way, transpose their plural and displaced points of view to the screen, along with the complexity of contemporary reality, both as a social phenomenon and the result of their personal histories, in touch with their own roots.

Notes

1 See *Liquid Modernity* (2000), *Liquid Love: The Frailty of Human Bonds* (2003), *Liquid Life* (2005).

2 I borrow the expression from Pap Ndiaye, *La condition noire*, Paris: Gallimard, 2009é.

3 *Joseph Ki-Zerbo. Identité, identités pour l'Afrique*, by Dani Kouyaté, 2005.

4 I believe that, even with many and important differences, we can see Black people as a transnational group, because of the historical weight of the injustices and dominations they have suffered.

5 The Laval Decree, 1934, took its name from the contemporary governor of the colonies. It banned 'prises de vues en Afrique occidentale Francophone, sans l'accord du gouverneur'. Filming images was only allowed with 'un scénario préétabli, et en présence d'un représentant de l'autorité'.

6 My translation from French.

7 The first French filmmaker affected by the Laval Decree was René Vautier, when he shot 'Afrique 50' (1950) in the Ivory Coast. It was a condemnation of French colonialism, which he was able to later make secretly in France. The film was first censored, then it was awarded a prize by the Minister of Foreign Affairs as proof of the anti-colonialist feelings of those times. Source: DVD extra (insert of *L'Humanité, Afrique, les temps des indépendances*, hors série, April 2010).

8 By Robert Caristan, Jacques Mélo Kane, Mamadou Sarr, Paulin S. Vieyra, 1955.

9   According to Gariazzo, this was not actually the first film. Vieyra had already
    made *C'était il y a quatre ans*, as *film de fin d'études* in Paris, 1954. However,
    there were also other movies, e.g. *La leçon de cinéma*, made by the Congolese,
    Albert Mongita, in 1951; *Les pneus gonflés*, made by the Congolese, Lubalu,
    1953; *é Mouramani*, made by the Guinean Mamadou Tourém, 1953; *Aventure
    en France* in France, by the Cameroonian, Jean Paul N'Gassa, 1962. In 1963
    the Cameroonian, Thérèse Sita Bella, made *Tam-tam à Paris*. (According to
    Alessandra Speciale and Frank Ukadike she was then the only woman film-
    maker.) However, it seems the very first film was *La morte de Rasalama* (or
    just *Rasalama*; 1937 or 1947, depending on the source) by the Madagascan,
    Raberono.

10 My translation from French. The intellectuals concerned in this quotation
    are : Joseph and Jacqueline Ki-Zerbo, Ekilia Mbokolo, Iba Der Thiam.

11 *Cinematografias de Africa: Un encuentro con sus protagonistas.* A film by Gabriel
    Rosenthal, Casa Africa, Spain, 2010.

12 *Teza* (Ethiopia, France, Germany, 2008) took Gerima 14 years to make. It won
    many prizes around the world, amongst which were 'The Jury Award' at the
    Venice Film Festival and the 'Tanit d'or' at the Journées Cinématographiques
    de Carthage, Tunisia, 2008, 'Etalon d'or' de Yennenga at Fespaco, Burkina
    Faso, 2009, Africa's two main international film festivals.

13 My translation from French.

14 www.dani-kouyate.com. My translation from French.

15 Dani Kouyaté met during the Festival Uno Sguardo all'Africa (A Glance at
    Africa), Savona, Italy, Nov. 2010.

16 On this subject, King Ampaw tells Ukadike (*Questioning African Cinema –
    Conversations with Filmmakers*, University of Minnesota Press, Minneapolis
    2002) that his first film, *They Call it Love*, was never distributed and it
    remained locked in a university library in Germany. The same destiny seems
    to have been in store for Sembène's first film *L'empire du Sonrhaï* (or *du Songhay*),
    which some, like Paulin Vieyra and Guy Hennebelle, argue has never been
    shown. Jean Rouch confided to Pierre Haffner that Sembène had told him
    about this film, but he thought that it was a legend. (See also Dia 2009.)

17 Similar questions about the place of African cinema, and cinema in general,
    are not new. We find them considered in the works of Chad's Mahamat
    Saleh Haroun and the Cameroon's Jean Pierre Bekolo and Jean-Marie Teno,
    in their films *Bye Bye Africa* (Haroun, Tchad, 1999), *Le complot d'Aristote*
    (Bekolo, Zimbabwe, Cameroun, 1996).

18 My interview with Mama Keita, Paris, June 2010.

19 www.45rdlc.com. My translation from French. (Accessed on 20 November
    2010).

20 Interview with Jean Odoutan, Paris, June 2010.

21 Interview with Jean Odoutan, Paris, June 2010.
22 From 'Caméra d'Afrique', a film by Férid Boughédir, Tunisia, 1983.
23 www.45rdcl.com. My translation from French.

References

Barlet Olivier (2002) 'Le phénomène Odoutan' <www.africultures.com> 1 Feb. (accessed 20 Oct. 2010).

—— (2003) 'Fespaco 2003: the onus on cinematic creation: A critical overview of the festival, the complete selection, the official competition winners and special awards' <www.africultures.com> 1 May (accessed Oct. 2010).

—— (2005) 'Defense of African film' <www.africultures.com> 23 March (accessed Oct. 2009).

Bhabha, Homi K. (1994) *The Location of Culture*, New York: Routledge.

Césaire, Aimé (1956) *Cahier d'un retour au pays natal*, Paris, Présence Africaine.

Dia, Thierno I., ed. (2008) 'Sembène Ousmane (1923–2007)', *Africultures*, 76.

Diawara, Manthia (1992) *African Cinema, Politics and Culture*, Bloomington, IN: Indiana University Press.

Dubois, William Edward Burghardt (1994 [1903]) *The Souls of Black Folk*, New York: Dover.

Esquenazi Jean Pierre (2001) *Hitchcock et l'aventure de Vertigo: L'invention à Hollywood*, Paris: CMRS Editions.

—— (2007) 'Eléments de sociologie du film', *Cinémas: revue d'études cinématographiques/Cinémas: Journal of Film Studies in Cinémas*, 17/2–3 <www.erudit. org>.

—— (2009) *La vérité de la fiction: Comment peut-on croire que les récits de fiction nous parlent sérieusement de la réalité?*, Paris: Lavoisier.

Fanon, Frantz (1952) *Peau noire, masques blancs*, Paris: Edition de Seuil.

Gariazzo, Giuseppe (2001) *Breve storia del cinema africano*, Turin: Lindau.

Gilroy, Paul (1987) *There Ain't No Black in the Union Jack* (new edn), London: Routledge.

—— (1993) *The Black Atlantic: Modernity and Double Consciousness* (Cambridge, MA: Harvard University Press).

Maalouf, Amin (2001) *Les identités meurtrières*, Paris: LGF Editeur.

Pirandello, Luigi (1941 [1926]) *Uno, nessuno e centomila*, Milan: Arnoldo Mondadori.

Ricci, Daniela (2009) 'Ancora su Teza', *Lo straniero*, 13/108, June.

Rouch, Jean (1967) *Catalogue Films ethnographiques sur l'Afrique noire*, preface by Jean Rouch, Bruges: Les presses Saint-Augustin.

Said, Edward W. (1979) *Orientalism*, New York: Vintage Books.

Speciale, Alessandra, ed. (1987) *La nascita del cinema in Africa nera 1963–1987*, Milan: Fabbri Editori.

Ukadike, Nwachukwu Frank (1994) *Black African Cinema*, Berkeley, CA: University of California Press.

15

RACE AND THE REPRODUCTION OF COLONIAL MYTHOLOGIES ON LAND: A POST-COLONIAL READING OF BRITISH MEDIA DISCOURSE ON ZIMBABWE

Wendy Willems

The history of racism in Africa in many ways coincides with the history of colonialism. Colonialism was based on the social construction of racial categories which were made to appear natural and self-evident. On the African continent, settler colonialism created a bifurcated state with on the one hand, a category of white citizens enjoying full civil, political and economic rights and, on the other, a category of black subjects who were denied these fundamental rights (Mamdani 1996). While post-colonial governments have made attempts to break with this colonial legacy, race continues to be an important marker of identity. For example, while the post-independent Zimbabwean government adopted a policy of reconciliation towards its white settler community at independence in 1980, race and the colonial experience re-emerged as central features of official imaginations of the Zimbabwe nation in the early 2000s (Gandhi and Jambaya 2002; Raftopoulos 2004, 2007). The emergence of a narrow, exclusionary version of 'patriotic history', mediated by the ZANU-PF government, demonstrated that nationalism in Zimbabwe was not able to transcend the racialised paradigm introduced by the colonial government (Ranger 2004; Bull-Christiansen 2004; Kriger 2006; Tendi 2008).

The production of racial categories, however, was not only part of the introduction of colonial governance on the African continent but also played a crucial role in the legitimisation of colonial rule in the 'motherland'. As Said (1985) and Mudimbe (1988) have demonstrated so powerfully, the construction of a primitive, uncivilised 'Other' in a range of Western discourses strongly contributed to the justification of colonial rule in both the 'Orient' and Africa. In his book *The Invention of Africa*, Mudimbe (1988: 69) distinguishes three kinds of imaginations which have been important in Western representations of Africa:

> In fact, from a more general historical frame, one can observe three complementary genres of 'speeches' contributing to the invention of a primitive Africa: the exotic text on savages, represented by travellers' reports; the philosophical interpretations about a hierarchy of civilisations; and the anthropological search for primitiveness. The complementarity of these speeches is obvious. It is perceived as a unity in the Western consciousness. The exotic text dominates in the seventeenth century. In the eighteenth century, it complements Enlightenment classifications of peoples and civilisation. In the nineteenth century, an ideology of conquest appears in explorers' sagas, anthropologists' theories, and the implementation of colonial policy.

Mudimbe argues that the knowledge produced by these discourses proved to be an important instrument of the West to obtain control over African populations. New branches of knowledge, such as anthropology, confirmed and maintained the old image of the 'primitive' and the 'savage' Africa, under the guise of science, and herewith served to maintain and justify colonial rule.

Historians, of colonialism have pointed to the role of propaganda in maintaining and justifying British colonial rule (August 1985; Carruthers 1995; Morris 2000) and the role of popular media, such as cinema, radio, theatre, literature, photography and the colonial exhibitions, in shaping Europe's superior self-identity (MacKenzie 1986; Pratt 1991; Nederveen Pieterse 1992; McClintock 1995; Coombes 1997; Maxwell 1999). For example, McClintock (1995) argued that, during the height of colonialism in the late nineteenth century, advertising functioned as a key site through which superior images of Europeans were circulated in the colonies, while inferior images of 'the colonised' found their way into the colonial 'motherland'.

This chapter offers a post-colonial reading of constructions of race in British newspaper reporting on Zimbabwe, focusing particularly on the *Daily Telegraph* newspaper. While many analyses in the field of media studies consider media representations as the product of a set of professional routines that are inherently part of media institutions, I interpret these texts primarily through a post-colonial lens, thereby tracing the remnants of earlier colonial constructions of race and thus contributing to emerging post-colonial approaches to media (Shohat and Stam 1996, 2003; Fernandez 1999; Shome and Hedge 2002; Brunt and Cere 2010). As Barthes (1972: 11) has argued, media are constantly involved in silencing and masking the genealogy of the texts they produce: 'the "naturalness" with which newspapers, art and common sense constantly dress up a reality which, even though it is the one we live in, is undoubtedly determined by history' (cited in Campbell 1995: 11). Similarly, Ferguson (1998: 53) has pointed out that '[t]he history of the media representation of blackness, for instance, is full of examples of the ways in which white imperial society has undertaken ideological work to eradicate certain key historical issues in order to eternalise its own claim to dominance as part of the natural order of things'.

By considering contemporary media texts as intertextual adaptations of the three types of historical 'speeches' that Mudimbe identified, I examine the way in which British media discourse on Africa builds on past colonial discourses. Instead of merely considering newspapers as products of institutional routines and news cultures, thereby reflecting ownership ideologies, I am interested in identifying the traces of preceding historical discourses in present-day media texts. The key focus in this chapter is then on the way in which British media discourse on Zimbabwe has contributed to the reproduction of colonial mythologies on land. As I have pointed out elsewhere (Willems 2004, 2005), the land issue gained significant political importance in Zimbabwe in the early 2000s. Land did not only carry material weight but also had a strong symbolic meaning which effectively enabled the Zimbabwean government to remind its former coloniser, Britain, of its role in occupying the territory now known as Zimbabwe.

Britain's links to Zimbabwe date back to the early 1890s when the British South Africa Company (BSAC) began to venture into the province now known as Mashonaland in present-day eastern Zimbabwe. The BSAC was established in 1889 by Cecil John Rhodes, an English-born mining magnate who had made his fortune in the diamond mines of Kimberley, South Africa. Through the BSAC, Rhodes hoped to find mineral resources such as gold and diamonds that would enable the British Empire to finance an extension of its reign. Gold was known to exist in Mashonaland. Hence, in May 1890, Rhodes sent a force known as the 'Pioneer Column' from South Africa to Mashonaland in order to explore the region's mining potential. When it arrived in Salisbury (Harare at present) in September 1890, the Pioneer Column claimed Mashonaland for the British Empire. In 1891, an Order-in-Council from the British government declared both Mashonaland and Matabeleland (what is currently western Zimbabwe) a British protectorate under BSAC rule.

Rhodesia, as the country became known, formally broke its ties with Britain in November 1965 when the reactionary Rhodesian Front (RF) government declared unilateral independence of Rhodesia from Britain. After a long, protracted liberation struggle, the country finally obtained black majority rule in April 1980 and became known as Zimbabwe. While formally Britain's links with Rhodesia came to an end in 1965, Britain remained heavily involved in the Lancaster House negotiations that eventually resulted in Zimbabwe's independence in 1980. Throughout the 1980s and 1990s, the British government offered various degrees of support to the country's land reform exercise but it could be argued that interactions between the two countries intensified in the early 2000s when a number of commercial, white-owned farms were occupied. Informed by the countries' long-term ties, media coverage by global institutions such as BBC and CNN constituted an important platform in which the contested interactions between the British and Zimbabwean governments took shape.

In the 1990s, social geographers, anthropologists, environmental historians and literary theorists began to treat landscapes as texts inscribed with social meanings which are by no means self-evident but which gain significance in a particular discursive formation (Cosgrove 1988; Barnes and Duncan 1992; Bender 1993; Mitchell 1994; Hirsch and O'Hanlon 1995). Similarly, a considerable number of scholars researching Southern Africa have studied colonial, scientific and literary representations of land (MacKenzie 1988; Beinart and Coates 1995; Fortmann 1995; Darian-Smith et al. 1996; Beinart and MacGregor 2003; Wolmer 2007; Hughes 2006, 2010).[1] Land was thus not only forcefully and violently expropriated by the colonisers but claims to land were legitimised through discourse and language. Many of the studies referred to above have highlighted how both colonial governments and white farmers in the post-colonial setting justified their claims to land through a discourse of conservation in which they presented themselves as custodians and protectors of the environment, while Africans were presented as responsible for the incidence of ecological crises, often seen as caused by the usage of 'inferior' agricultural techniques. Whites considered themselves to have contributed to the transformation of wild landscapes into economically productive land, whereas blacks were constructed as ultimately responsible for the land's ecological degradation. As I demonstrate in this chapter, these highly racialised interpretations of landscapes were reproduced in some British media reporting on Zimbabwe.

Arguably, the media operate as a crucial site through which dominant ideologies on race are reproduced and articulated (Hall 1981, 1997; Campbell 1995; Shohat and Stam 1996, 2003; Gandy 1998; Gabriel 1998; Ferguson 1998; Downing and Husband 2005). As Hall (1981: 35) has argued, 'the media construct for us a definition of what race is, what meaning the imagery of race carries, and what the "problem of race" is understood to be. They help to classify out the world in terms of the categories of race'. The British newspaper the *Daily Telegraph* became a crucial space in which racialised, colonial mythologies on land were reproduced. Before analysing media representations of Zimbabwe in the early 2000s, I will provide a brief historical background of the *Daily Telegraph*.

Empire and the *Daily Telegraph*: A Historical Reconstruction

As Couldry (2006: 182) has argued, by virtue of its object of study, media studies has adopted a form of 'centrism' which he defines as 'the automatic assumption that media are central to explaining the dynamics of contemporary societies'. By adopting media texts as the central object of study, media scholars have closed 'down the field of media we analyse and (in so doing) [it] reinforces its own validity in an endless self-fulfilling prophecy' (Couldry 2006: 182). In practising media-centrism, media scholars have often presented the media as analytically separable from society. In conventional analyses of media representations, texts are seen as products of journalistic routines, institutional

rules and economic imperatives but this approach has somewhat under-
valued the way in which newspaper discourse is embedded in a broader
social, political and cultural context and bears traces of many preceding
texts. This section therefore situates the history of the *Daily Telegraph*
within a broader historical context in which the emergence of newspapers very much coincided with the rise of the British Empire.

The history of the *Daily Telegraph* is inextricably caught up with
the expansion of British imperialism, although this official history is
largely silenced in the paper's current corporate identity. There is no
historical profile on the website and not even a mission statement that
spells out the newspaper's main values. This is in strong contrast with,
for example, the *Guardian,* which profiles an elaborate history on its
homepage. The *Daily Telegraph* was established in June 1855 by Colonel
Arthur B. Sleigh, and supported 'liberal' and 'progressive' causes,
including a campaign against capital punishment.[2] After the paper
lowered its price to one penny (thereby becoming Britain's first penny
newspaper), it quickly rose in popularity and was able to compete with
other contemporary popular newspapers, such as *The Times* (which cost
7 pence) and the *Daily News* and *Morning Post* (which both cost 5 pence).
By 1856, the *Daily Telegraph*'s circulation had reached 27,000, outnum-
bering the 10,000 which *The Times* circulated at the time.

In 1873, Edwin Arnold became the new editor of the *Daily Telegraph*
and this significantly changed the newspaper's editorial line. Arnold was
a strong advocate of British imperialism and a loyal supporter of the
Conservative Party. He managed to persuade the newspaper's proprietor
to co-sponsor, together with the *New York Herald,* a trip by the British
explorer Henry Morton Stanley to Africa to trace the course of the River
Congo. According to the *Daily Telegraph,* the aim of the expedition
was 'to complete the work left unfinished by the lamented death of Dr
Livingstone; to solve, if possible, the remaining problems of the geography of Central Africa; and to investigate and report upon the haunts of
the slave traders' (quoted in Stanley 1988: 3). The paper hoped that 'very
important results will accrue from this undertaking to the advantage of
science, humanity and civilization' (quoted in Stanley 1988: 3). Between
1874 and 1877, Stanley had a column in the newspaper to keep readers
posted on his travel experiences. Writing in 1922, the Victorian explorer
Sir Harry Johnston noted that Stanley's letters 'gave some definite
impulse to British minds to establish an uninterrupted British control

over South, Central, East and North Africa which might link up with Egypt in a series of peaceful, prosperous, well-governed states' (quoted in Merrington 2001: 330). In 1876, the newspaper's editor, Edwin Arnold, also published a pamphlet in which he introduced the idea of a British Empire that would stretch from the 'Cape-to-Cairo', and Arnold thereby invented to an influential concept that was later to be adopted by Cecil John Rhodes, the founding father of Rhodesia, current-day Zimbabwe. In 1884–5, the *Daily Telegraph* also supported Sir Harry Johnston's exploration of Mount Kilimanjaro, and in 1899–1900, it supported Lionel Decle's journey from the Cape to Cairo.

In 1928, the paper came into the hands of William Berry, the First Viscount Camrose. His family remained involved in the management of the newspaper until 1987, when the Canadian-born right-wing newspaper magnate, Conrad Black, took over. While Black did not initially interfere much in the newspaper's editorial line, he appointed staff who were in general sympathetic to his stance. In 1989 he became more concerned about what he called the *Daily Telegraph*'s 'flirtation with incorrect thinking about Ulster and about South Africa' (Curran and Seaton 2003: 72–3). It was the editor, Max Hastings, who particularly came under fire from Black and eventually left the newspaper in 1996. Black was dismissed in 2004 by his company Hollinger Inc. on allegations of corruption, and the company was sold in June 2004, to British businessmen, the twin brothers Sir David and Sir Frederick Barclay.

Under Black, the *Daily Telegraph* firmly supported the Conservatives, which gave the newspaper its well-known nickname, the 'Torygraph'. However, the Barclay brothers commented in an interview that the *Daily Telegraph* would not automatically support the Conservatives. As they noted about another newspaper which they owned, *The Scotsman*: 'In the last election [in 2001], and I think the one before [in 1997], *The Scotsman* supported Blair, and we were very happy about that. Where the government are [sic] right, we shall support them'.[3] While Conrad Black was a loyal member of the Conservative Party, the Barclay brothers did not openly reveal their party preference. However, in the run-up to the 2005 general elections, the newspaper still largely endorsed the views of the Conservative Party and, according to an opinion poll taken in 2004, 61 per cent of *Telegraph* readers would vote for the Conservative Party in the 2005 elections.[4] Overall, the *Daily Telegraph* arguably represents the voice of 'middle England', a section of British society that historically did not radically contest the activities of the Empire and in many ways worked with it rather than against it.

Imagining Zimbabwe: A Post-Colonial Reading of the *Daily Telegraph*

Bearing in mind the historical context in which the *Daily Telegraph* emerged, it is now imperative to discuss how the paper imagined events unfolding in Zimbabwe.

In its reporting on the causes of the 'crisis' of the early 2000s, the paper was straightforward and largely attributed the events that were unfolding to President Robert Mugabe's implementation of disastrous economic policies which ultimately served to keep him in power:

> For 18 months now we have watched one of the most productive of African nations slide down the economic waste pipe, with starvation threatening thousands, and ruin tens of thousands. Neighbouring countries, South Africa particularly, could be destabilised by population movement. It is the sort of situation that could become genocide, and it has been engineered by one man, with one aim: to keep himself in power.[5]

Zimbabwe provided the textbook example of 'bad African governance'. According to the *Daily Telegraph*, the main causes of the crisis were to be sought in Zimbabwe's economic and political mismanagement, with the land occupations central in this regard since they had resulted in major food production and foreign currency losses. The profiling of Mugabe as the sole cause of the crisis gave legitimacy to the reactionary and racist myth that 'Africans are not able to govern themselves', which was often invoked before independence in order to justify colonial rule and, of course, fitted well with the 'right-of-centre' ideology that the newspaper wished to convey. This became even more apparent in the *Daily Telegraph*'s coverage of the death of the Rhodesian Front leader, Ian Smith, in November 2007. For example, in an article on Smith, reporter Graham Boynton describes a meeting between Smith and Mugabe in April 1980, the day after Mugabe took office as Prime Minister of Zimbabwe. Boynton writes that, after this meeting, Ian Smith 'rushed home in a state of excitement, and, over lunch, told his wife, Janet, that perhaps he had been wrong about a black government being incapable of running his beloved Rhodesia'.[6] Smith had apparently expressed his confidence in the new leader to his wife. Boynton uses this example to demonstrate that 'Ian Smith had sadly been proven right', which is also the title of the article. As Boynton narrates:

> The point is Mugabe was not the sophisticated, balanced, sensible man Smith had briefly hoped for. [...] The sensible chap, in fact, turned out to be the type of African leader that 'good old Smithy', as his support-ers called him, had campaigned against throughout the UDI years. He became the embodiment of corrupt, violent, amoral African dic-tatorship – just as Smith had warned his supporters [...]. It was easy to mock Ian Smith, but he was right – both about the betrayals and about the quality of most African politicians.[7]

This article portrays 'bad leadership' as something that comes with being 'African' and, arguably, 'black'. It suggests that Africans somehow have a higher propensity to being 'corrupt dictators'. This essentialist and racist assumption serves to gloss over the injustices perpetrated by the colonial government under Ian Smith and almost implies that Smith's rule could be characterised as 'good leadership'. This is reinforced by the author's comparison between Smith and Mugabe, where Boynton backs up his comparison by arguing that 'if you were to go to Harare today and ask ordinary black Zimbabweans who they would rather have as their leader – Smith or Mugabe – the answer would be almost unanimous. And it would not be Mugabe'. Articles in the *Daily Telegraph* frequently compared Smith and Mugabe and mostly came to the conclusion that 'Smith wasn't whiter than white, but he was no Mugabe', as the paper's columnist, Bill Deedes, wrote in an article in August 2001:

> One difference between Smith and Mugabe is that, whereas the former built Rhodesia up for a time, the latter is pulling Zimbabwe down. Smith was able to defy the world for 14 years because he made Rhodesia more self-sufficient. I remember being astonished by the extent to which the country turned to producing for itself what international sanctions stopped it from importing [...]. I am not dressing him in a white sheet. His Republican Front included one or two thoroughly unpleasant char-acters. Smith began efforts to bring the blacks into government and to find a suitable black leader too late. But to put Smith in the same stable as Mugabe is to stand history on its head – and, before someone writes a film on those lines, it is well to assert as much.[8]

While the Rhodesian economy at the macro-economic level may have survived sanctions relatively well, the newspaper did not, dwell on how wealth was distributed during the colonial period, nor did it consider the political freedoms which were denied to Africans during Smith's regime. Constructions of Rhodesia or Zimbabwe as a 'paradise lost' beg the following question: 'for whom was it a paradise?' In putting the blame for the Zimbabwe crisis on Mugabe, the *Daily Telegraph* largely mirrored New Labour's framing of the situation as a 'crisis of governance' that had been solely caused by Mugabe.

Particularly at the beginning of the crisis in 2000 and 2001, the *Daily Telegraph* foregrounded the economic impact of farm occupations and the plight of white commercial farmers. The newspaper considered the land occupations and concomitant violence as crucial to what was unfolding in the country. In its representation of the situation in Zimbabwe, the *Daily Telegraph* painted a picture of a battle between irrational black mobs and innocent white farmer victims (Willems 2005). In its reporting on Zimbabwe, the *Daily Telegraph* emphasised the 'drama' unfolding on the white-owned commercial farms. Numerous reports narrated how farmers had lost their lives or their farms. Extensive coverage on the funerals of farmers who had been killed was provided, and obituaries would herald them as heroic figures, often having been benevolent towards their workers and contributed in important ways towards agricultural production in Zimbabwe.

With regard to those occupying the farms, the *Daily Telegraph* generally described occupiers as aggressive and the paper did not make attempts to find out from the occupiers what motivated them. Instead, the newspaper assumed they were merely showing their support for Mugabe and following his instructions, rather than expressing their discontent about the lack of access to land. Descriptions typical of the paper's coverage of the occupiers were, for example: 'encouraged by President Mugabe [...], mobs wielding spears and axes have terrified farmers' families',[9] and 'drunken mobs of pro-Mugabe squatters have threatened to kill some farmers'.[10] The majority of articles included quotations from white farmers and their experiences of the occupations, portraying them as victims of the occupiers, who were encouraged or motivated to occupy land by President Mugabe. White farmers were accorded the right to speak about events, and occupiers was denied agency in representations which were reinforced through descriptions of them as 'drunk' or 'drugged'. Occupiers were presented as not being genuinely interested in land, but merely as following the orders of

their President. Readers themselves were left to interpret what motivated these 'angry mobs'. Occupiers were simply portrayed as pawns
of the Mugabe regime, sent by the ruling party to frighten the white
minority. While the Zimbabwean government often presented the
occupiers as veterans of the 1970s liberation war who would finally
redress the 'land issue', the *Daily Telegraph* sought to delegitimise this
by stressing that many of those occupying the farms were too young to
be war veterans. As the newspaper noted: '[m]any of the invaders are
not war veterans, but rather paid thugs and peasants hoping to receive
a plot of land. Most are too young to have fought in the war in the
1970s'.[11] The *Daily Telegraph* thereby implied that, if they had been
'true' war veterans, they would have been entitled to the land; mere
peasants and youths were not eligible to receive a piece of land.

In its reporting on the farmers, the *Daily Telegraph* fell back on positive images of farmers as benevolent, paternal employers, or as pioneer
heroes transforming virgin bush land into productive farming acres,
thus reproducing colonial stereotypes of the white settler. For example,
on the rare occasion that the *Daily Telegraph* gave voice to farm workers, it quoted them as praising farmer Alan Dunn, who had just been
assaulted by six men and who subsequently died of his injuries:

> Forlorn workers huddled together yesterday, mourning an employer
> who they said was 'a good man who cared for us'. A tractor was driven
> out to tend his fields, while some recalled how Mr Dunn would help
> the black farmers whom the government had settled on nearby land by
> giving them free fertiliser and transport. Mr Mahoso [a farm worker]
> fears for the livelihood of the 180-strong workforce. He said: 'What are
> we going to do? We don't know our future now that Mr Dunn has been
> taken from us. Whenever we had a problem, he would help us. We have
> all cried today, even that small child, he has cried for Mr Dunn.'[12]

Instead of victims of an exploitative white farmer, farm workers were
portrayed as beneficiaries of a benevolent employer. The farmers were
represented as acting in the best interests of their workers, providing
them with decent housing and adequate salaries, thereby 'developing'
and positively contributing to the lives of farm workers. Reinforcing
this positive image was the representation of white farmers as harmless
victims of the state that was behind the violence inflicted on them and
thereby deprived farm workers of their main livelihood.

The second positive image that the *Daily Telegraph* invoked was that of the farmer as über-masculine pioneer hero. This image was brought up in coverage of the growing emigration of white farmers to other African countries such as Mozambique, Zambia and Nigeria:

> Driven off their land in Zimbabwe, scores of white farmers are trekking into neighbouring Mozambique to carve out new lives in a country recovering from years of civil war and appalling floods. The pioneering excitement felt by the new arrivals is soon tempered by the tough conditions where everything has to be built from scratch. Forced to spend months in tents on remote plots of land, the farmers are being struck down by more virulent strains of malaria than they are used to back home in Zimbabwe.[13]

White farmers were presented as hard-working individuals who had the ability to transform virgin bush land into productive farms. The colonial image of the pioneer hero taming and bringing order to the empty, chaotic and wild African bush landscape was evoked.[14] The farmer was portrayed as the creator of something positive out of nothing.

This colonial perspective relates to the third positive image which the *Daily Telegraph* invoked: the white farmer as productive farmer contributing in a major way to the economy. Productivity was often presented as an inherent characteristic of white farmers, and suggestions were made that black farmers were incapable of establishing productive and well-run farms. For example, the newspaper regularly reported on how the government's land reform efforts, both in the past and the present, had failed because newly resettled farmers had not been able to match the production figures of the white farmers who had previously owned farms acquired for redistribution:

> What was once a pleasant garden is now littered with the wrecks of burnt-out cars and weeds have submerged the ruins of the farmhouse. The fate of Grazley Farm, one of the first acquired under President Mugabe's land redistribution programme, is seen by Zimbabwe's white farmers as a chilling warning of what could befall their properties after yesterday's vote in parliament. [...] Until its acquisition by the state in 1981, Grazley was one of the most productive dairy farms in Zimbabwe. Ben Harding, the owner, employed almost 100 people and the community living on his land exceeded 500. Today, about 20 people scratch a living amid the dereliction and decay. [...]

Few signs of cultivation are visible among the rolling green hills that offer some of the best farming land in Africa. Here and there a clump of maize shows where a few people live in poverty. Surrounding them are tracts of wild, unkempt land and vandalised storehouses.[15]

The orderly and productive Grazley Farm under Harding's management was contrasted with the chaotic, unproductive and vandalised remains of Grazley Farm after resettlement. The article considered the example of the farm as archetypical for what would happen if black farmers were given access to the land. White farmers were here presented as having a legitimate claim to land because they had the capacity to turn it into productive land. Black farmers were represented as destructive farmers who should not be entitled to 'the best farming land in Africa'. These images clearly draw from the colonial stereotypes of black and white farmers that were discussed earlier in this chapter. While portrayals of blacks as destructive farmers were used by the colonial administrators in the 1950s to obtain control over these farmers through the Native Land Husbandry Act, similar images in the *Daily Telegraph*'s coverage of the land occupations served to discredit land reform. White farmers were presented as indispensable and as being irreplaceable by black farmers.

Apart from challenging the impact of land reform on productivity, the newspaper also dispelled the myth that land redistribution in Zimbabwe had resulted in a more equitable distribution of land, emphasising the amount of corruption involved in the land reform exercise. The newspaper highlighted how land was parcelled out to 'Mugabe cronies' who had neither the capacity nor the interest to farm. Land was presented as a resource that enabled Mugabe to remain in power. For example, an article in April 2000 wrote that 'The new owners of the Marula block [a farming area in Matabeleland South, Zimbabwe] are not white farmers but a collection of government officials, ministers and high court judges who were given the land as part of the scheme of political patronage used to keep President Mugabe and his ruling party in power'.[16] Another article noted that '[m]ore than one million acres of land compulsorily purchased from white farmers has [sic] been distributed to a group of well-connected Zimbabweans, many of them political allies of President Mugabe'.[17]

While corruption has indeed been a problem under the land reform programme, the *Daily Telegraph* tended to focus on the A2 resettlement model part of the fast track land reform programme. The main objective of this scheme was not to provide landless subsistence farmers with a piece of land, but instead it aimed to increase the participation of 'black indigenous farmers' in commercial farming. In order to become eligible for the scheme, potential beneficiaries had to prove their experience in farming or provide evidence of sufficient resources to invest in commercial farming. The model A1 scheme, which had a deliberate social justice objective and aimed to resettle 'landless peasants in the communal areas', received virtually no attention from the newspaper. The *Daily Telegraph* therefore only told readers part of the story of land reform. This is not to say that the A1 scheme was successful and unaffected by corruption, but by not highlighting the different objectives of the government's land reform programme, the *Daily Telegraph* undermined the credibility of both past and present land reform efforts.

Conclusion

As Hall (1981: 38) has argued, '[r]acism has a long and distinguished history in British culture. It is grounded in the relations of slavery, colonial conquest, economic exploitation and imperialism in which the European races have stood in relation to the "native peoples" of the colonized and exploited periphery'. While the construction of race in British media is often naturalised in a form of covert, inferential racism, this chapter has demonstrated through a close reading of media reports on Zimbabwe that race still forms a crucial part of the post-colonial encounter between Western discourses and the 'Other'. In its reporting on Zimbabwe in the early 2000s, the *Daily Telegraph* reproduced a series of myths which were quite clearly informed by colonial discourses on land and agricultural productivity. Offering positive images of white settlers as the benevolent employer, pioneer hero and productive farmer, the paper implicitly justified their claim to land, while constructing blacks as unproductive, if not destructive, peasant farmers who were undeserving of land ownership. While race continues to be a crucial identity marker in social relations in many African nation states, it also profoundly shapes the popular national imaginaries of former colonial powers. As Said (1994: 9) has argued, '[i]mperialism still casts a shadow over our time [...]. In the present [imperialism] still lingers and exhorts influence where it has always been, in the political, ideological, economic and social practices'. Given the continued skewed flow of information between North and South, these agenda-setting Western representations of Africa also have the potential to impact on African media discourses which often heavily draw their copy from European newspapers and news agencies.

Notes

1   See also special issue of the *Journal of Southern African Studies*, 15/2 (1989) on the politics of colonial conservation in Southern African Studies, and a special issue of *Journal of Historical Geography*, 31/2 (2005) on landscape, politics and historical geography in Southern Africa.

2   'Messenger with a new Telegraph', *Observer*, 19 Nov. 2006 <http://media.guardian.co.uk/presspublishing/story/0,,1951605,00.html> (accessed Oct. 2011).

3   David Leigh, '*Telegraph* could back Labour says Barclay', *Guardian*, 20 Jan. 2004 <http://business.guardian.co.uk/story/0,3604,1126875,00.html> (accessed Feb. 2012).

4   Ipsos MORI, 9 March 2005, 'Voting intention by newspaper readership', <http://www.ipsos-mori.com/researchpublications/researcharchive/poll.aspx?oItemId=580> (accessed Feb. 2012). As part of this poll, 21,727 adults above 18 years old were interviewed between July and Dec. 2004.

5   Alan Judd, 'Why is "'ethical'" Britain still silent over Mugabe's brutality? The Government's continuing refusal to condemn the corruption and violence in Zimbabwe makes nonsense of its claim to an ethical foreign policy', *Daily Telegraph*, 26 Nov. 2001.

6   Graham Boynton, 'Ian Smith has sadly been proven right', *Daily Telegraph*, 22 Nov. 2007.

7   Ibid.

8   W. F. Deedes, 'Smith wasn't whiter than white, but he was no Mugabe', *Daily Telegraph*, 20 Aug. 2001.

9   David Blair, 'White farms face more invasions in Zimbabwe', *Daily Telegraph*, 13 March 2000.

10   David Blair, 'Mugabe warns farmers of "severe" violence', *Daily Telegraph*, 30 March 2000.

11   Anton La Guardia, 'Retired colonels condemn thugs in farm attacks', *Daily Telegraph*, 19 April 2000.

12   David Blair, 'Workers mourn farmer beaten to death by mob', *Daily Telegraph*, 9 May 2000.

13   Tim Butcher, 'Farmers quit Zimbabwe to be pioneers once more', *Daily Telegraph*, 2 Nov. 2002.
14   See also Rutherford (2001: 81–6) on the role of 'pioneer stories' in white farmers' oral history narratives.
15   David Blair, 'Ruined state farm gives grim warning of disaster', *Daily Telegraph*, 7 April 2000.
16   Peter Foster, 'Despair in the Matabeleland bush over distribution of land', *Daily Telegraph*, 27 April 2000.
17   David Blair and Christopher Lockwood, 'Mugabe gives white farms to his cronies', *Daily Telegraph*, 29 March 2000.

References

Alexander, K., and Muzondidya, J. (2005) 'The ghost voters, the exiles, the non-citizens: an election of exclusion', *Cape Times*, 31 March.

August, T. G. (1985) *The Selling of the Empire: British and French Imperialist Propaganda, 1890–1940*, Westport, CT: Greenwood Press.

Barnes, T. J., and Duncan, J. S. (1992) *Writing Worlds: Discourse, Text and Metaphor in the Representation of Landscape*, London: Routledge.

Barthes, R. (1973) *Mythologies*, London: Granada.

Beinart, W., and Coates, P. A. (1995) *Environment and History: The Taming of Nature in the USA and South Africa,* London: Routledge.

Beinart, W., and MacGregor, J. (2003) *Social History and African Environments*, Oxford: James Currey.

Bender, B. (1993) *Landscape: Politics and Perspectives*, Oxford: Berg.

Brunt, R., and Cere, R. (2010) *Postcolonial Media Culture in Britain*, Basingstoke: Palgrave Macmillan.

Bull-Christiansen, L. (2004) *Tales of the Nation: Feminist Nationalism of Patriotic History? Defining National History and Identity in Zimbabwe*, Uppsala: Nordic Africa Institute.

Campbell, C. P. (1995) *Race, Myth and the News*, Thousand Oaks, CA: Sage.

Carruthers, S. L. (1995) *Winning Hearts and Minds: British Governments, the Media, and Colonial Counter-Insurgency, 1944–1960*, London: Leicester University Press.

Coombes, A. E. (1997) *Reinventing Africa: Museums, Material Culture, and Popular Imagination in Late Victorian and Edwardian England*, New Haven, CT: Yale University Press.

Cosgrove, D. (1988) *The Iconography of the Landscape: Essays in the Symbolic Representation, Design and Use of Past Environments*, Cambridge: Cambridge University Press.

Couldry, N. (2006) 'Transvaluing media studies: or, beyond the myth of the mediated centre', in J. Curran and D. Morley (eds.), *Media and Cultural theory*, pp. 177–94, London: Routledge.

Darian-Smith, K., Gunner, L., and Nuttall, S. (1996) *Text, Theory, Space: Land, Literature and History in South Africa and Australia*, London: Routledge.

Downing, J., and Husband, C. (2005) *Representing 'Race': Racisms, Ethnicities and Media*, London: Sage.

Ferguson, R. (1998) *Representing 'Race': Ideology, Identity, and the Media*, London: Arnold.

Fernandez, M. (1999) 'Postcolonial media theory', *Third Text*, 13/47, pp. 11–17.

Fortmann, L. (1995) 'Talking claims: discursive strategies in contesting property', *World Development*, 23/6, pp. 1053–63.

Gabriel, J. (1998) *Whitewash: Racialised Politics and the Media*, London: Routledge.

Gandhi, D., and Jambaya, L. (2002) *Towards a National Agenda on ZBC: Vision 30 Revisited*, Harare: Media Monitoring Project Zimbabwe.

Gandy, O. H. (1998) *Communication and Race: A Structural Perspective*, London: Arnold.

Hall, S. (1981) 'The whites of their eyes: racist ideologies and the media', in G. Bridges and R. Brunt (eds.). *Silver Linings: Some Strategies for the Eighties*, pp. 28–52, London: Lawrence & Wishart.

—— (1997) 'The spectacle of the "Other" ', in S. Hall (ed.), *Representation: Cultural Representations and Signifying Practices*, pp. 223–97, London: Sage.

Hirsch, E., and O'Hanlon, M. (1995) *The Anthropology of Landscape: Perspectives on Place and Space*, Oxford: Clarendon Press.

Hughes, D. M. (2006) 'Hydrology of hope: farm dams, conservation, and whiteness in Zimbabwe', *American Ethnologist*, 33/2, pp. 269–87.

—— (2010) *Whiteness in Zimbabwe: Race, Landscape, and the Problem of Belonging*, New York: Palgrave Macmillan.

Klotz, A. (1993) 'Race and nationalism in Zimbabwean foreign policy', *Round Table*, 327, pp. 255–79.

Kriger, N. (2006) 'From patriotic memories to "patriotic history" in Zimbabwe, 1990–2005', *Third World Quarterly*, 27/6, pp. 1151–69.

McClintock, A. (1995) *Imperial Leather: Race, Gender, and Sexuality in the Colonial Contest*, New York: Routledge.

MacKenzie, J. M. (1986) *Imperialism and Popular Culture*, Manchester: Manchester University Press.

—— (1988) *The Empire of Nature: Hunting, Conservation and British Imperialism*, Manchester: Manchester University Press.

Mamdani, M. (1996) *Citizen and Subject: Contemporary Africa and the Legacy of Colonialism*, Princeton, NJ: Princeton University Press.

Maxwell, A. (1999) *Colonial Photography and Exhibitions: Representations of the 'Native' and the Making of European Identities*, London: Leicester University Press.

Mitchell, W. J. T. (1994) *Landscape and Power*, London: University of Chicago Press.

Moore, D. S., Kosek, J., and Pandian, A. (2003) *Race, Nature, and the Politics of Difference*, Durham, NC: Duke University Press.

Morris, K. (2000) *British Techniques of Public Relations and Propaganda for Mobilizing East and Central Africa during World War II*, PLACE: Edwin Mellen Press.

Mudimbe, V. Y. (1988) *The Invention of Africa: Gnosis, Philosophy, and the Order of Knowledge*, Bloomington, IN: Indiana University Press.

Nederveen Pieterse, J. (1992) *White on Black: Images of Africa and Blacks in Western Popular Culture*, New Haven, CT: Yale University Press.

Phimister, I., and Raftopoulos, B. (2004) 'Mugabe, Mbeki and the politics of anti-imperialism', *Review of African Political Economy*, 31/101, pp. 385–400.

Pratt, M. L. (1991) *Imperial Eyes: Travel Writing and Transculturation*, London: Routledge.

Raftopoulos, B. (2004) 'Nation, race and history in Zimbabwean politics', in B. Raftopoulos and T. Savage (eds), *Zimbabwe: Injustice and Political Reconciliation*, pp. 160–75, Cape Town: Institute for Justice and Reconciliation.

Ranger, T. (2004) 'Nationalist historiography, patriotic history and the history of the nation', *Journal of Southern African Studies*, 30/2, pp. 215–34.

Reed, W. C. (1993) 'International politics and national liberation: ZANU and the politics of contested sovereignty in Zimbabwe', *African Studies Review*, 36/2, pp. 31–59.

Said, E. W. (1985) *Orientalism*, Harmondsworth: Penguin.

—— (1994) *Culture and Imperialism*, New York: Vintage.

Shohat, E., and Stam, R. (1996) *Unthinking Eurocentrism: Multiculturalism and the Media*, London: Routledge.

—— (2003) *Multiculturalism, Postcoloniality and Transnational Media*, New Brunswick, NJ: Rutgers University Press.

Shome, R., and Hegde, R. S. (2002) 'Postcolonial approaches to communication: charting the terrain, engaging the intersections', *Communication Theory*, 12/3, pp. 249–70.

Tendi, B.-M. (2008) 'Patriotic history and public intellectuals critical of power', *Journal of Southern African Studies*, 34/2, pp. 379–96.

Willems, W. (2004) 'Peaceful demonstrators, violent invaders: representations of land in the Zimbabwean press', *World Development*, 32/10, pp. 1767–83.

—— (2005) 'Remnants of empire? British media reporting on Zimbabwe', Westminster Papers in Communication and Culture, special issue on Zimbabwe, Oct., pp. 91–108.

Wolmer, W. (2007) *From Wilderness Vision to Farm Invasions: Conservation and Development in Zimbabwe's South-East Lowveld*, Oxford: James Currey.

16

REPRESENTATION OF OTHERNESS: AFRICANS AND CRIME IN THE NORWEGIAN MEDIA

Martin Nkosi Ndlela

Introduction

Increased immigration and globalisation is significantly changing the fabric and fundamentals of the Norwegian society, which for many years has been perceived as relatively homogeneous. The most visible elements of these transformations are the demographics in schools, neighbourhoods, labour market and law and order. This chapter is mainly concerned with the latter. The mainstream media have a fundamental role in mediating discourses pertaining to immigrants, framing and interpreting issues where immigrants are involved, predicting outcomes, and thereby influencing public perceptions and broad assumptions. The connection between immigrants and crime has been one of the most contentious issues in the Norwegian media discourses. Focusing on visible immigrants, especially of African origin, this chapter examines the relationship between the media and perceptions of crime as represented in the main discourses. It looks at the mainstream media's role in mediating differences focusing mainly on the issue of security, crime control and discrimination.

Media, Ethnicity and Crime

The mass media play a significant role in interethnic relations, fostering common (mis)understandings, integration, or isolation of immigrants. Hence 'the role of mass media in creating a social environment conducive to interethnic coexistence cannot be minimized' (Liu 2005: 366). The media provide exposure and insights on the lives of immigrants and provides a lens through which mainstream perceptions of the population are shaped. However, several works in media sociology argue that the reality presented in the mass media is a socially constructed one, hence a symbolic social reality. Berger and Luckmann (1967) argue that individuals and groups interacting in a social system over time form concepts or mental representation of each other's actions, which over time become institutionalised and the meanings become embedded in society. Therefore reality is socially constructed. As argued by Adoni and Mane (1984) the reality presented by the media is a socially constructed one, a symbolic social reality. These theoretical underpinnings suggest that crime is also socially constructed mainly by the mass media.

Several works in media sociology have studied the construction of reality in the mass media (Fishman 1980; Galtung and Ruge 1970; Golding and Elliot 1979). These studies have also shown that news production is part of a complex of professional routines for the management of possible sources, the interaction among journalists and the possible 'formulations' of reality (van Dijk 1983). News texts should therefore be seen as a manifestation of a complex process in which knowledge, beliefs and opinions are matched with existing or incoming information about events, the social contexts of news production and representations of the reading public (ibid.). News production is not a direct representation (biased or not) of events, but rather some form of discourse processing. News reports can be understood as a narrative combining both factual elements and information embedded within a meaningful context, and also carrying implicit messages. An interpretative commentary attends to the content of news reports. As noted by Galtung and Ruge (1970), the (re)construction of news reports involves an active (re)interpretation and representation in accordance with the selective perception of both journalists and readers. News reports are a reconstruction of available discourses and are frequently drawn from shared narratives and myths which resonate with larger social themes.

Media texts therefore do not merely reflect the reality on the ground, they also recreate and reshape it through signifying practices and representation. As Hall has argued, representation does not entail a straightforward presentation of the world and the relationships in it (Hall 1997). It implies the active work of selecting and presenting, of structuring and shaping; not merely the transmitting of already existing meaning, but the more active labour of making things mean (Hall 1982). One way of making things mean is through stereotyping – a process of selection, magnification and reduction. Media representations reduce, shrink, condense and select/reject aspects of intricate social relations in order to represent them as fixed, natural, obvious and ready to consume.

The media play a significant role in the construction and reproduction of images of African immigrants. Images are constructed, produced and reproduced through everyday language use in the media. Text and visual images may stress the prevailing conceptions about African immigrants or might contest them. Readers are generally sensitive to contextual cues given in the narratives and their explanation and conception of issues such as crime is critically dependent upon the particular reference points furnished in the media. The majority of ethnic Norwegians derive their understanding and images of visible immigrants from the media. Few ethnic Norwegians have direct contact with immigrants, but the picture is gradually changing. Statistics show that contact amongst the adult population has increased gradually from 67 to 75 per cent (or three in four) between 2002 and 2009 (Blom 2010: 133), but most of the images and knowledge they have is mediated. Newspapers, together with other mass media, therefore play an important role in the intertextual chaining through which images and discourses of African immigrants are disseminated. Understanding how these newspapers portray African immigrants is important because research has shown that peoples' attitudes towards foreigners can be influenced by the media's framing of issues related to immigration or immigrants. For example, Statistics Norway's research on attitudes towards immigrants and immigration policy reveal that during the period 2001–7 these were stable, but may have been partially influenced by recurring changes[1] (Blom 2010).

Reporting Crime and Crime Statistics

Discourses in the media to a greater extent contribute to the construction of 'otherness' and typologising discriminatory practices. The media play a central role in this *othering* process, especially with regards to crime reporting. Reporting on crime and immigrants intensified in the Norwegian media during the late 1990s. In the late 1990s and early 2000s, crime has been extensively covered in the Norwegian media, and in most cases where immigrants appear in the daily press, it has to do with their involvement in crime. Fjeldstad and Lindstad, two free-lance journalists who have for many years worked on questions related to foreigners, have noted in their study (2005) carried out between 30 April and 1 June 2003 that if you remove the sports pages the immigrant you meet in the newspaper articles is a criminal. Immigrants involved in positive work, other than football, rarely appear in the daily press. The dominant picture in the media discourse then was that of a criminal immigrant rather than a law-abiding one. Consequently ethnic Norwegians are bound to have negative attitudes towards all foreigners, as shown in a survey by Statistics Norway (Blom 2004: 115). In the European Social Survey on relations between immigrants and crime, Norway lies in the third position after the Czech Republic and Greece (Blom 2004: 116). Three in every four Norwegians believe that increased immigration has contributed to an increased crime rate. The perception that increased immigration leads to increased crime in society is higher among Norwegians than that the inhabitants of other European countries with higher numbers of immigrants. 2010 results from Statistics Norway show that one in three believes that immigrants are a source of insecurity (Blom 2010: 133). Perceptions are highly dependent on the prevailing social conditions and how those conditions are mediated in the media. One of the reasons for the negative percep-tions in Norway is increased media coverage of immigrants involved in crime, as well as the exploitation of this coverage by right-leaning parties in their quest to attract 'worried voters'.

According to statistical records and media discourses people of non-Western origins are over-represented in the crime statistics. Some politicians have publicly stated that foreigners are more criminal than Norwegians. This is the same perspective found in the media. Some researchers have disputed the statistics, arguing that they don't reflect the real crime trends in Norway. It might be true that criminal statistics show an over-representation of immigrants in the light of their proportion of the population. But one has to view with a critical eye the method-ologies used in arriving at those statistics before putting all foreigners in negative light. As Lie has argued, 'statistics give a simplified picture of reality where different aspects are accentuated. Different ways of categorisation are used and labels are attached to the categories. To categorise people on the basis of selected criteria and labels represents a simplification and generalisation' (Lie 2002: 13). It can be argued therefore that some categorisation can be more exclusionary than others depending on the intentions of the researcher. Ulla Haslund of Statistics Norway takes note of this when she points that in the media and amongst the public sometimes there is blending of registered foreign residents and non-registered foreigners, especially when it comes to crime. She wonders if it is justified to blame all foreigners for crimes committed by non-resident foreigners (Haslund 2004: 114). The media represents a generalised view of immigrants on the basis of these categorisations.

Another notable problematic is that statistics presented in the media only tell the reader that immigrants are over-represented in crime statistics, but does not distinguish whether there is a big number of immigrants involved in criminal activities or that there are just a few active criminals amongst immigrant populations who commit crime repeatedly. Placing people into categories is one method of exclusionary representation. Statistics on immigrants often create or uphold a distinction and division between 'us' and 'them'. Østby has argued that 'ideally the categories should not be given more meaning than was necessary to create them' (2001). The presentation of statistics is clearly very problematic in that it is unanalytical in nature.

Another problem with the reporting of statistics is that there is a general discrepancy between figures given by Statistics Norway and figures supplied by the police. These are the two main sources of statistical information on crime. The difference on, for example, murder statistics, is that the police (Kripos) and Statistics Norway operate on different figures. While both statistics are based on only murder in accordance with criminal law §233 paragraphs 1 and 2 and don't include attempted murder or grievous bodily harm which results in death, figures from Statistics Norway are based on reports at the time of crime registration, while police figures are continually updated (Kripos 2005: 31).

In the past year, the subject of crime and immigrants has graced the newspaper columns and dominated political debates aired on television. Newspapers have reported on the involvement by people of foreign origin in criminal activities ranging from serious crimes such as murder, armed robberies, rape to petty crimes such as traffic offences and shoplifting. According to police murder statistics, 31 people were murdered in Norway in 2004. The number was seven less than the ten-year average of 38 murders per year. Of these murders, 30 per cent were carried out by foreign citizens (six persons) or people of foreign origin (six persons). According to the police these represented a marked percentage increase in comparison to 2003 (24 per cent). The discourses in the media magnify the statistical over-representation of immigrants, and disregard the fact that murder cases have gone down significantly in the past year. The decrease in total numbers is not highlighted in the newspapers analysed, but what is highlighted is the percentage increase of the accused murderers who are either foreigners or of immigrant background. What the media have emphasised is that the perpetrators who are either foreign citizens or have a foreign background are over-represented in the murder statistics in relation to their percentage of the overall population. This is a strikingly uncritical presentation of problematic statistics. First of all, foreign citizens are not part of the immigrant population in Norway. These can be short-term tourists or visitors not permanently resident in Norway. In this case, immigrants have the extra burden of blame for crimes committed by non-resident foreigners. The blending of categories obviously affects the outcome of the statistics results.

Also absent from the media discourses are some of the facts given by the police: that in the majority of murder cases, the victim and the murderer were known to each other, the murderers were mainly man, and almost half of the murderers were under the influence of alcohol or drugs during the incidents (Kripos 2005).

Why Immigrants Dominate Statistics

Another question that can be asked regarding the criminal statistics is why non-Western immigrants are over-represented in registered crime statistics. Is it because immigrants are more criminal than ethnic Norwegians or is it because of the higher possibilities of them being caught and prosecuted? As advocate Abid Q. Raja, has argued, not all committed crimes are uncovered or registered. If all violations in Norway were reported or investigated and the right person caught or convicted, then the crime statistics would give us a correct answer on how crime is distributed amongst different ethnic groups (*Aftenposten*, 27 April 2004). These views are also echoed by criminologist Nils Christie who argues that 'crime statistics show more what society has chosen to criminalize, and importantly, who we have chosen to control' (ibid.). Another criminologist, Elisabeth Myhre Lie raises the same question when she asks whether in reality foreigners are more criminal than Norwegians. She cautions against rushing to conclusions and comparisons, because given the settlement patterns of immigrants and of Norwegians, there 'is a risk of comparing the crime frequency of young immigrant men in towns with older women in the countryside' (Lie 2000).

Another hypothesis that can be advanced is that visible immigrants are more observed than ethnic Norwegians and are therefore more likely to be arrested. This hypothesis is backed by a leader article in *Dagbladet*, 'Politikvittering' (19 April 2003), where the writer notes that darker skinned immigrants are stopped and checked time and again, even if they haven't done anything wrong. The writer cites the case of an African man who holds the highest record of being stopped – 17 times within three weeks – because he had a new and expensive bicycle. The result of excessive surveillance is that crime committed by immigrants is much more likely to be uncovered and registered than that committed by ethnic Norwegians.

Most of the statistical reports which show that crime is higher amongst non-Western immigrants are based on the number of arrests rather than on convictions. Earlier statistics by Statistics Norway have shown that, out of these arrests, 64 per cent of the cases in which immigrants are involved do not end in convictions.

Besides all these arguments presented above, there are other factors which account for the high propensity of criminality amongst immigrant groups. High unemployment amongst immigrants, weaknesses of the Norwegian integration programmes, socio-cultural differences amongst immigrant groups, past experiences of refugees as well as the global nature of crime, are some of the factors that have accounted for increased crime in Norway. Even when these factors are alluded to in the media, there is a conscious or unconscious tendency to present crime in a stereotyped disposition, whereby crime is a natural trait amongst immigrants, especially visible non-Western immigrants. Crime has become a main characteristic of branding and stigmatising non-Western immigrants. The functional aspect of crime discourses in the media is to influence changes in immigration policies and justify stringent discriminatory visa requirements. These discourses are likely to have consequential effects on how ethnic Norwegians perceive foreigners, create social barriers, and exclusionary or discriminatory reactions.

Othering through Brutalisation

Elsrud (2008) uses the phrase 'constructing brutal others' to describe one of the components in the subtle and complex process of 'othering'. Brutalisation of the ethnified other is portrayed in text and pictures in the newspapers. The randomly selected articles used in this chapter are qualitatively analysed for clues on discourse and interpretations attached to these texts. A critical approach perspective is applied in order to capture meanings, signification and values attached to the texts. These are texts about various forms of crime such as rape, violent robbery, gang activities, stabbings where African are directly or indirectly referred to.

Reporting cases and statistics of different variants of rape is very much a contested area, fraught with different frames of interpretation, distortions and stereotyping. The first challenging element pertains to the media's understanding of the different categories of rape used by the police, as well as the breadth and variations of registered police reports. The second challenge pertains to the subsequent associative meanings given to the figures. There is a marked tendency for selective focus and exposure, where the media focus mainly on one or two particular forms of rape (usually assault rape) and one group of perpetrators (mainly a weak group in society). This highlights the alleged links between non-Western immigrants and crime and provides unconsciously negative associations about the ethnified other. In their report, Grytdal and Sætre (2011) warn against causal conclusions, in particular with respect to the variable of 'ethnic background'/'country of origin'. The media's coverage and public debates unduly provide an interpretative framework where cultural background from outside Norway represents in itself an increased risk of rape. The construction and framing of rape in the media involves brutalisation, with the creation of a potentially brutal masculine other – non-Western men (including Africans) – and victimised innocent Norwegian girls. There have been several incidents of rape where victims were young Norwegian girls and the offenders were visible immigrants.[2] In some way inferences are made through a civilised–primitive binary which is in turn imbued with gendered and racial meanings and stereotypes. This civilised–primitive binary can be illustrated by media drawing upon tragic incidences in Africa where women are brutally raped. For example, in a number of articles and TV programmes a Congolese girl, Héléne Laba Kamama was invited to Oslo by the Norwegian Church Aid to share her cruel and heart-breaking experiences at the hands of the rebels in Congo. The invitation came amidst an increase in rape cases during the autumn of 2011. The documentary also shown on national TV NRK described how Kamama 'experienced and survived some of the worst conceivable' when at 13 she was kidnapped and raped by armed soldiers in the '*jungles'* of 'the so-called Democratic Republic of Congo'. The jungle has been used metaphorically in many narratives about Africans, be it in literature, history textbooks and the media as a signifier for primitiveness. There are therefore negative associations represented by the words. The brutality of the other is in some instances emphasised by drawing associations to predators. Describing the actions of the convicted serial rapist of Togolese origin, one victim used the following terms, 'he was like a predator going after people',[3] words which formed the title of the article appearing in *Aftenposten* (5 Nov. 2011). The perpetrator blamed his action to the powers of 'voodoo', the forces of darkness. References to the jungle, comparisons with predators and reference to the forces of darkness (voodoo) invoke 'the ubiquitous cultural figure of the savage primitive rapist' (Bederman 1995: 181).

Coverage of rape cases and the meanings linked with possible perpetrators, and the over-representation of the ethnified other in statistics, increase perceptions of increased risk and heighten the level of fear of the other in society. Certain phrases and images have added to the sense of loss of control. The media have repeatedly utilised the phrase 'rape wave' to denote the increased instances of rape. For example, in 2010 the media quickly labelled Oslo a 'rape capital' in Scandinavia, even though the police statistics showed that in same year Oslo had fewer reported cases of rape or attempted rape per 100,000 residents than Stockholm and Copenhagen. The police data challenged the prevailing claims in the media which singled out non-Western men as perpetrators of the crime. In autumn 2011 Norway was again hit by what media described as a 'rape wave', increased incidences of rape, mostly in Oslo. Non-Western men, including Africans, featured prominently as suspected perpetrators named by victims or wanted by the police. In Oslo, 54 assault rapes were reported in 2011, against 24 in 2010, an increase highlighted by the media. Meland (2012) points out that several people have been critical of what they thought was a media-created panic used to stigmatise an entire group. The police also report on new sexual cultural traits. Again through media coverage and public discourse, a causal link is established and asylum seekers are singled out. The link between rape and asylum seekers is not supported by the police data, but nevertheless panic-like coverage in media demands immediate action to contain the 'wave'. Consequently senior politicians, including the mayor of Oslo, Fabian Stang, proposed closing refugee reception centres and restricting the movement of inmates, on grounds that this group is overrepresented in the rape statistics. The proposal to restrict the movements of a specified social group on the basis of criminal actions committed by a few members of the same group is a clear illustration of what Sætre (n.d.) refers to as demonisation of a weak group in society. Elsrud (2008) in her conceptualisation of 'othering through brutalization' shows that this brutality is portrayed in blunt ways, including frequent use of such terms as 'crime wave'. Fear images are based on selective use of statistics, misinterpretation and old myths.

The newspapers have also carried stories in which immigrants were involved in violence and stabbings. Non-Western immigrants have not only been the visible perpetrators but have also been the victims of stabbing. News reports on stabbings were prevalent in 2004, with stories such as '21 year old stabbed at Grunerløkka in Oslo';[4] 'Sentenced to four years for knife stabbing';[5] 'Charged for Murder – threatened with murder';[6] 'Washed away blood trail'.[7] However, the most infamous stabbing reported in the newspapers is the murder in the tram (*Trikke-Drapet*), where a psychologically sick Somali went berserk inside a tram and stabbed to death a 23-year-old Norwegian and also stabbed five other passengers in August 2004. The incident was extensively covered in the media and the discourses on this gruesome murder concentrated not just on the murderer's mental illness but also on the triangular discourse on immigrants, crime and immigrant politics. The murder in the tram evoked strong anti-immigrant sentiments and aroused fear towards dark-skinned immigrants.

As Baglo argued in an article published four months before the murder took place, 'murder and violence committed by an immigrant is immediately connected with ethnicity and specific national groups' (*Dagbladet*, 9 April 2004). The same applies to this murder, as focus and blame was immediately directed specifically towards Somalis. A representative of the Somali people in Oslo, Khalid Osman, expressed this concern in an article 'Tram Murder: Fears ticking bomb', when he said that 'we have noticed already that people look strangely at us and that fear of strangers is on the increase' (*Dagbladet*, 6 Aug. 2004). He also stressed the point that the murder was not the fault of all Somalis. The public reaction is also captured in a comment by a police sergeant, Finn Abrahamsen, in an article in *Dagbladet*, 'Tram Murder: I feel ashamed for racism'. He describes how following the incident foreigners were shouted at in the streets of Oslo and fellow passengers in public transport immediately left their seats each time a dark-skinned person sat next to them. There is no doubt that the media partly contributed to this reaction. While one cannot blame the media for public reaction, the media are not innocent bystanders. The images and explanations they bring to the incident have a bearing on contextualisation and in arousing fear. In an article in *Dagbladet*, 'Tram-murder – Rambo knife is in practice a killing machine', the knife used in the murder is described in detail as being of a 'Rambo First Blood' make (6 Aug. 2004).

Articles about armed robberies of post offices, banks, petrol stations and supermarkets also dominated the media discourses in 2004. *Aftenposten* ('Total robberies in Oslo doubles; Wave of Robberies of Oslo shops', 31 March 2004) gives an overview of all the robberies in Oslo. The frequency of these robberies is shocking. For example, criminals carried out eight robberies in January, twelve in February and nine in March. Altogether there were 29 robberies in Oslo alone, double the figure for the same period the previous year. Perhaps the biggest armed robbery in 2004 was the bank robbery in Stavanger on 5 April 2004, where the robbers went off with millions of dollars and left one policeman dead and others injured. The initial reporting on this robbery gave the impression that it was carried out by 'dark-skinned people', a reference to visible immigrants. This expectation is linked to discourses in the media that such robberies could only be carried out by 'Others'. The Stavanger robbery illustrates a much more complex picture than that given in the newspapers. Organised crime cuts across races and nationalities, a fact that is often overlooked in the Norwegian crime discourses. The media give the impression that crime is committed within ethnic parameters, with names applied such as Kurdish, Iraqi, Islamic, Iranian, Somali, Yugoslavian, Pakistani, Vietnamese or Albanian. The lexical use of *miljø* (milieu) in the media connotes shady activities within immigrant communities. These criminal milieus are perceived to be organised and dangerous. The criminal activities of these groups have a higher chance of being covered and discussed in the media than any other incidents or events involving immigrants.

In an article headed 'New report with a clear warning: Criminality amongst immigrants can lead to Mafia like situation in Norway', the reporter, citing research carried by NIBR (Norsk Institutt for by – og regionsforskning), plays on the fears of the Norwegian audience (*Aftenposten*, 25 Aug. 2004). The audience, which is already well informed about immigrants and crime, is strongly warned in the headlines that if action is not taken by the authorities and society in general, the criminal environment in Norway will soon be organised along the lines of infamous mafia groups operating in the USA. The mafia, well-known to the Norwegian audience for its brutal criminality, has been reported extensively in the media, fiction and sometimes overdramatised in film. Can the so-called Pakistani and Somali gangsters in Oslo be compared to the American mafia, the real or the reconstructed mafia? This comparison is made regardless of the nature of crimes committed. Yet the mafia came from a geographical and historical period different from that of the Norwegian immigrants. The article mentions that 19-year-old immigrant youths are over-represented in criminal statistics in certain districts of Oslo, like Furuset, Stovner and Gamle Oslo.

The article also indicates that the Norwegian authorities have been caught napping and not prepared in the wake of mass immigration ('i kjølvannet av masseinnvandringen til Norge'). The lexical use of the phrase 'mass immigration' clearly gives the picture that Norway is receiving an uncountable number of immigrants each year, yet figures from Statistics Norway show that in 2004 there was a dramatic decrease in asylum seekers. In the media there is a clear correlation between the rise of crime and the rising numbers of immigrants. The article clearly indicates the beliefs and opinions of the writer, which are also substantiated by the researcher. Of particular interest is the choice of lexical items used to denote the young immigrants involved in crime, especially in Oslo.

In another article in *Aftenposten*, 'Police must be tougher' (27 Oct. 2004) the writer describes drug trafficking in one of Oslo streets by young immigrant boys. Africans are clearly visible in the drug market. Framing of the article is in such a way that the drug problem is an extension of problems associated with immigrants. Therefore the article is quick to point out that immigrant youths are involved in drugs. This article has a number of omissions, in that it does not attempt to explain why these boys are involved. These young boys are obviously not the main importers of drugs but merely runners.

In 2011, a series of media reports focused on Oslo's narcotics market where illegal immigrants (mainly without IDs) and asylum seekers dominate the street sellers, with Nigerian and central Africans dominating Akerselva riverwalk and North Africans operating along the Skippergaten street near the central train station. The dilemma with these groups is that most of them don't have identity papers and therefore cannot be returned to their home countries. Even when they are arrested, they return to the same spots as soon as they are released. The discourse in the media has focused exclusively on the sellers, ignoring the majority ethnic Norwegians who constitute the largest numbers of consumers. The discourses created in the media built on already existing stereotypes on immigrants and their relations to drugs, especially Africans and Pakistanis. The media give the impression to their readers that the drug problems faced by Norway can be blamed on non-Western immigrants and therefore the police have to be tough on this group.

Conclusion

The framing by the media of any event or issue to a large extent decides the framing of the public debate (Tuchman 1978). The discourse on crime in the Norwegian press is in an a way declaring the visible immigrants as the Other, and stressing that what makes immigrants dissimilar from and opposite from the ethnic Norwegians is their disposition to criminal activities. Criminality is much more than a mere stereotypical representation of visible immigrants, it amounts to a construction of the Other. The concept of the Other is prominent in post-colonial theory (Said 2003; Bhabha, 1996). In many ways the concept is similar to stereotyping but carries larger and more symbolic meanings. The Other refers to the people who are classified by the dominant groups as being inherently different. In the Norwegian case race is the defining marker used by those able to construct the Other or are engaged in the process of othering. Cultural values, norms and religion are some of the markers often used in the media. However, in the discourses on crime, skin colour is the dominant marker. In the media people perceived as the other – visible minorities – are aggregated into groups based on the underlying characteristics that they are perceived to share and are presented to the dominant group through stereotypical images. Negative representation of visible immigrants, the erasure of their voices and experiences and the repetition of images and discourse, fuels the 'othering' process.

The analysis in this chapter does not question the authenticity of crime statistics, but rather the manner in which they are selected, uncritically interpreted and represented. The argument raised is that the media presents a simplified version of an otherwise complex issue. The impression given by the media is that crime is a trait of non-Westerners, explained solely on the basis of ethnicity, and passes over other factors that have been cited in many years of research on immigrants. One can only speculate that the main reason for this oversimplification is to stigmatise visible immigrants and set up a 'control frame'.

Not all news reports are negative, but the choice of language and emphasis is that increased immigration has led to increased crime levels. It has become difficult to avoid perceiving the link between non-Western immigrants and the problem of inner-city crime. Yet no satisfactory evidence has been produced to show that increased immigration into Norway has resulted in an increase in crime. Figures presented by Statistics Norway which suggest that people of foreign origin are over-represented in crime statistics are highly dependent on definitions used and variables such as age, reclassification of the nature of crimes, number of arrests versus number of prosecutions. Crime within immigrant communities is even more harmful to the immigrants than it is to the natives. The media representation of crime and visible immigrants has the far-reaching consequence of convincing the public that 'immigrants equals crime', thereby racialising the crime problem and increasing support for xenophobic campaigns against immigrant communities.

Notes

1   <http://www.ssb.no/vis/emner/02/sa_innvand/sa119/main.html>.
2   '16-year-old could not pay: forced to have sex with a taxi driver' (*Dagbladet*, 6 Jan. 2004).

3   'Han var som et rovdyr som gikk etter folk' title of an article in *Aftenposten*, 5 Nov. 2011.
4   '21 year old stabbed at Grunerløkka in Oslo' (*Dagsavisen*, 6 Aug. 2004).
5   'Sentenced to four years for knife stabbing' (*VG*, 23 Dec. 2004).
6   'Charged for murder – threatened with murder' (*Dagsavisen*, 18 Dec. 2004).
7   'Washed away blood trail' (*Dagbladet*, 17 Dec. 2004).

References

Adoni, H., and Mane, S. (1984) 'Media and the social construction of reality: toward an integration of theory and research', *Communication Research*, 11/3, pp. 323–40.

Bederman, G. (1995) *A Cultural History of Gender and Race in the United States 1880–1917*, Chicago: University of Chicago Press.

Berger, P.L., and Luckmann, T. (1967) *The Social Construction of Reality: A Treatise in the Sociology of Knowledge*. New York, Garden City.

Bhabha, Homi K. (1996) *Locations of Culture: Discussing Post-Colonial Culture*, London: Routledge.

Blom, S. (2004) 'Holdninger til innvandrere og innvandring', in K. Tronstad (ed.), *Innvandring og innvandrere*, Oslo: Statistics Norway.

—— (2010) 'Holdning til innvandrere og innvandring', in K. Henriksen, L. Østby, and ?. Ellingsen (eds) *Innvandring og innvandrere*, Oslo-Kongsvinger: Statistics Norway.

Elsrud, T. (2008) 'Othering through genderization in the regional press: constructing brutal others out of immigrants in rural Sweden', *European Journal of Cultural Studies*, 11, p. 423.

Entman, R. (1991) 'Framing U.S. coverage of international news: contrasts in narratives of KAL and Iran Air incidents', *Journal of Communication*, Autumn, pp. 6–27.

Fishman, M. (1980) *Manufacturing the News*, Austin, TX: University of Texas Press.

Fjellstad, Ø., and Lindstad, M. (2005) *Av utenlandsk opprinnelse: Nye Nordmenn i Avisspaltene*, Kristiansand: IJ-forlaget.

Gaultung, J., and Ruge, M. H. (1970) 'The structure of news', in J. Tunstall (ed.), *Media Sociology*, London: Constable.

Goffman, E. (1974) *Frame Analysis*, New York: Harper & Row

Golding, P., and Elliot, P. (1979) *Making the News*, London: Longman.

Grytdal, V., and Sætre, M. (2011) 'Voldtekt i den globale byen- Endringer i anmeldte voldtekter og seksualkultur i Oslo', Oslo Politidistrikt <https://www.politi.no/vedlegg/lokale_vedlegg/oslo/Vedlegg_1309.pdf> (accessed Feb, 2012).

Gullestad, M. (2001) 'Imagined sameness: shifting notions of "us" and "them" in Norway', in L. Ytrehus (ed.), *Forestillinger om 'den andre': Images of Otherness*, Kristiansand: Norwegian Academic Press.

Haslund, U. (2004) 'Kriminalitet: straffende innvandrere', in L. Østby (ed.), *Innvandrere i Norge – Hvem er de, og hvordan går det med dem?*, Oslo: Statistics Norway.

Jensen, K. B. (1987) 'News as ideology: economic statistics and political ritual in television network news', *Journal of Communication*, Winter, 37/1.

Kripos (Kriminalpolitisentralen): Årsrapport 2004

Lie, B. (2002) *Immigration and Immigrants 2002*, Oslo: Statistics Norway.

Lie, E. M. (2000) 'Innvandrere og kriminalitet', *OP Magasin*, 1, Oslo: Politikammer.

Liu, S. (2006) 'An examination of the effects of print media exposure and contact on subjective social reality and acculturation attitudes', *International Journal of Intercultural Relations*, 30, pp. 365–82.

Martinez, R., and Lee, M. (2000) 'The nature of crime: continuity and change', *Criminal Justice*, 1.

Meland, A. (2012) 'Overfallvoldtekter', *VG*, 5 Jan. 2012 <https://web.retriever-info.com/services/archive.html?method=displayDocument&documentId=0550162012010544795177&serviceId=2>.

NSD (2004) 'Tre av fire nordmenn mener innvandring gir økt kriminalitet' <http:/www.nsd.uib.no/nsd/oppslag/innvandring_kriminalitet.html>.

Østby, L (2001) 'Hvorfor fokusere på innvandrere?', *Samfunnsspeilet*, 2, Oslo: Statistics Norway.

Politidirektoret (2005) *Kommenterte STRASAK-tall 2004*, Oslo: Seksjon for analyse og forebygging, Jan.

Sætre, M. (n.d.) 'Voldteksbølge i mediene' <http://www.phs.no/Documents/Nyhetsdokumenter/Kronikker/Marianne%20S%C3%A6tre_voldtekt.pdf> (accessed Feb. 2012).

Said, Edward (1994) *Culture and Imperialism*, New York: Vintage Books.

Stubbs, M. (1983) *Discourse Analysis: The Sociolinguistic Analysis of National Language*, Oxford: Basil Blackwell.

Tuchman, G. (1978) *Making News*, New York: Macmillan.

Van Dijk, T. A. (1983) 'Discourse analysis: its development and application to the structure of news', *Journal of Communication*, Spring, 33/2.

Weedon, C. (1997) *Feminist Practice and Poststructural Theory*, Oxford: Blackwell Publishers.

White, P. (1997) 'Death, disruption and the moral order: the narrative impulse in mass media "hard news" reporting', in F. Christie and J. R. Martin (eds), *Genre and Institutions: Social Processes in the Workplace and School*, London: Cassell.

INDEX

Page references to illustrations are set in italics.

Abrahamsen, Finn, 325–326
L'absence (film), 292
Achebe, Chinua, 7
Adamu, Bala, 145
Ader, C. R., 123
Adio, Waziri, 145
Adoni, H., 317
Adorno, Theodor W., 270
Aduaka, Newton, 291
affirmative action, 19, 65
L'Afrance (film), 288
African Commission, definition of
    indigenous, 29
African identity, 7–9
African National Congress
    (ANC), 15
'African science', 273–274, 276–277
Afrikaans press
    discursive strategies for denying
        racism, 61–71
    repositioning of after apartheid,
        57–60
Afrikaans University of the Free
    State (UFS) racism case and
    media discourse, 61–71
Afrikaner *Weerstandsbeweging*, 47
Afrikaners
    racial attacks by, 61–62, 70, 71
    targeting of, 47–48
Afrique Sur Seine (film), 286–287

Aftenposten (Norwegian newspaper),
    324, 327
Aga Khan group (Kenya), 221, 231
agency, discourse as enabler of, 8
agenda setting *see also* framing
    in Kenya, on ethnic myths and
        political candidates,
        206–214
    in Nigeria
        on environmental issues, 119,
            121–123, 130, 132–133
        on political scandals, 144–146
    in Norway, on immigrants and
        crime, 323–328
    theory of, 243
    in Uganda (*see* Uganda, media
        coverage of Anti-
        Homosexuality Bill)
Agya Koo (film), 263, 266
Ahmed, Hauwa Baba, 170
Ajzen, I., 188
Alalade, Bode, 169, *171*
albinos, in Tanzania, 18
'AmaNdiya' (song), 42, 46
ANC (African National Congress)
    Afrikaners' discourse on, 65
    street renaming by, 88–90
Anderson, B., 158
Andrew Zondo Road and Primary
    School (Durban), 85–87

Zimbabwe
  British media discourse on land
    redistribution, 305–311
  colonialism and decolonisation,
    298–301
  emigrants from, and xenophobia,
    43–44
  ethnic identity politics in, 104,
    105–107
  uMthunywa (isiNdebele language
    newspaper)

background to, 102, 103–105
significance of for identity,
  100–102, 108–113
Zimbabwe African National Union:
  Patriotic Front (ZANU PF),
  106, 298–299
Zimbabwe Newspapers Group
  (Zimpapers), 103
Zondo, Andrew, 85–87
Zulus, 88–89
Zuma, Jacob, 18

www.ingramcontent.com/pod-product-compliance
Lightning Source LLC
Chambersburg PA
CBHW071831270326

41929CB00013B/1964